Expanded 2nd Edition

UNDERSTANDING *by* DESIGN

PEARSON

Merrill
Prentice Hall

Upper Saddle River, New Jersey
Columbus, Ohio

Grant Wiggins and Jay McTighe

Association for Supervision and Curriculum Development
1703 N. Beauregard St. • Alexandria, VA 22311-1714 USA
Phone: 800-933-2723 or 703-578-9600 • Fax: 703-575-5400
Web site: www.ascd.org • E-mail: member@ascd.org
Author guidelines: www.ascd.org/write

All Web links in this book are correct as of the publication date below but may have become inactive or otherwise modified since that time. If you notice a deactivated or changed link, please e-mail books@ascd.org with the words "Link Update" in the subject line. In your message, please specify the Web link, the book title, and the page number on which the link appears.

Library of Congress Cataloging-in-Publication Data

Wiggins, Grant P., 1950–
   Understanding by design / Grant Wiggins and Jay McTighe.— Expanded 2nd ed.
     p. cm.
   Includes bibliographical references and index.
   ISBN 1-4166-0035-3 (alk. paper)
   1. Curriculum planning—United States. 2. Curriculum-based assessment—United States. 3. Learning. 4. Comprehension. I. McTighe, Jay. II. Title.

   LB2806.15.W54 2005
   375'.001—dc22

This special edition is published by Merrill/Prentice Hall, by arrangement with the Association for Supervision and Curriculum Development.

Vice President and Executive Publisher: Jeffery W. Johnston
Executive Editor: Kevin M. Davis
Director of Marketing: Ann Castel Davis
Marketing Manager: Autumn Purdy
Marketing Coordinator: Brian Mounts

This book was printed and bound by Banta Book Group. The cover was printed by Phoenix Color Corp.

10 9 8 7 6 5 4 3
ISBN: 0-13-195084-3

Expanded 2nd Edition

Understanding by Design

List of Figures

Preface

To first-time readers of *Understanding by Design* (UbD), we welcome you to a set of ideas and practices that may confirm much of what you believe and do as an educator. In one sense, all we have tried to do is pull together what best practice in the design of learning has always looked like. However, we predict that at least a few of our ideas may cause you to reflect on and perhaps rethink your own habits (or those of colleagues) related to planning, teaching, and assessing. For some readers, the material on the following pages may well "rock your world" and demand a vigorous rethinking of comfortable habits. Regardless of your entry point or degree of comfort as you read, we trust that the ideas of *Understanding by Design* will enhance your capacities in creating more engaging and effective learning, whether the student is a 3rd grader, a college freshman, or a faculty member.

Readers familiar with the first edition of *Understanding by Design* are forgiven for any puzzlement or angst they may feel upon looking over the Table of Contents of this second edition. We have overhauled the text from top to bottom, based on six years of constant research and development by the authors, our staffs, a dozen members of the ASCD-supported Training Cadre, and countless educators around the world. The resulting refinements will come as no surprise to those practitioners who have worked with us closely over the past six years. They always ask (with a mixture of laughter and dread): So, what changes have you made *this* time? The answer, in brief: We have revised the UbD Template, the key terms of UbD, dozens of worksheets, and some of the big ideas—a number of times—based on feedback from users, our own observations, and the deep desire to continuously improve.

We have worked with thousands of K–16 educators in all 50 states and 8 foreign countries since the first edition was written, and each time we work we get a new idea—a peril of the profession, alas, for those readers who crave a little more stability. Indeed, this is who we are. And, more important, this is what the work of teaching for understanding is all about: digging deeper, continually asking the essential questions, rethinking. So, although we apologize for sometimes making it difficult to follow our path, we make no apologies for practicing what we preach: We keep trying to better understand design and understanding.

As for a concrete list and explanation of the key changes in this second edition, here are the highlights:

• The UbD Template for unit design now provides a structural foundation for the revised book. This prominence reflects not only the fact that the template has proven its practical benefit as a tool in design for understanding, but also our belief in its overarching value for cultivating better habits of planning.

• The UbD Template has been revised to be clearer and more user-friendly, we think, in its overall look and feel as well as its integration of form and content. The refinements occurred as a result of continuously reasking the following essential question: Does this proposed element involve what the *final product* should contain or is it only a *process move* leading to a better design? All the changes and refinements in the template stem from an affirmative answer to the first part of that question; the template represents a form for the final design, with elements aligned. (All of the key process moves, whereby designers are helped to think through the elements of design more clearly and carefully, are found as worksheets and design tools in the *Understanding by Design Professional Development Workbook* [McTighe & Wiggins, 2004]).

• We have greatly sharpened the meaning of *understanding* in conceptual, as well as practical, terms—an irony that nicely illustrates just what working for understanding is all about; that is, constantly rethinking the big ideas. We offer more specific guidelines on how to frame desired understandings (i.e., as full-sentence generalizations) and put much greater emphasis on the goal of transfer (because an essential indicator of understanding is the ability to transfer learning to new settings and challenges, as opposed to mere recall).

• We have laid out a much more careful argument about what essential questions are and are not. This turned out to involve more painstaking back-and-forths of drafts of Chapter 5 (Essential Questions: Doorways to Understanding) than were necessary for any other part of the revision. Why? Because we saw an inconsistency between the original account and widespread practice. The argument can be framed by a set of essential questions: Must an essential question be timeless and overarching? Or can there be more specific essential questions for use in achieving unit goals? Does an essential question have to be philosophical and open-ended? Or can it—should it—point toward specific understandings? In short, what do (and what should) we mean by *essential?* Does it mean essential for living and thinking our whole lives, essential to the expert's view of things, or essential to successful teaching? People in the humanities tend to favor the first view; people in the sciences tend to favor the second view; people in elementary schools or teaching basic skill courses tend to favor the third view. Our ultimate answer: yes—all three! So the new chapter tries to bring more tidiness to an inherently untidy matter.

• We created the acronym WHERETO by adding TO to the original acronym WHERE in Stage 3 of the UbD Template. We did this to honor two ideas we knew to be important in instructional planning: differentiation ("**T**ailor" the work, as needed) and sequence ("**O**rganization" of the activities for maximal impact). The addition of the *T* reflects not only common sense about a key challenge of instructional planning—personalizing the work for maximal effectiveness—but also an adjustment that grew out of a two-year research project whereby we asked thousands of educators to identify specific exemplary designs and the characteristics these exemplars all had in common. (The exercises and results are described in Chapter 9.)

We added the *O* for two reasons. This edition introduces a discussion of the big picture of design—curriculum frameworks—expressed in Understanding by Design terms. In the first edition, we discussed organization in a general way in terms of the history of the idea of a "spiral curriculum." We also discussed it in terms of units as stories. But with greater clarity on our part about unit design and how units frame and are framed by courses and programs, it seemed necessary to distinguish unit flow from course and program flow. So the *O* enables us to usefully discuss sequence *within* units while considering separately sequence *across* units. And, if truth be told, the second reason is that we wanted the acronym to end in a letter that made it easier to remember, and *O* seemed just right—the design signifies "Whereto?" in our planning.

• We deleted or minimized sections on teaching for understanding (and the habits of mind required), having decided this topic was outside the scope of the book. Our purpose has always been to discuss the key elements of the goal of understanding and how to design for it. Teaching for understanding (including preparing students, parents, and staff for a shift in emphasis) requires its own separate and thorough treatment. In our view, some of the later chapters in the first edition no longer seemed to fit with that sharpened sense of purpose.

• We have included more examples, across grade levels and subject, to reflect the happy fact that the book has become widely used by elementary school staff and college professors, two groups that were not initially included in the target audience. The original book was written primarily for an audience working from the upper elementary grades through high school (grades 4–12), as the examples and text suggested. (In retrospect, our caution in limiting the audience seems silly. We thought that a focus on "design for understanding" would have great resonance only in the upper grades of the K–12 system, and we had not yet worked enough with college faculty to generate good examples.) Yet, despite the limitations of the original examples, to our delight the arguments seem to have spoken to educators at all levels.

Readers at both ends of the K–16 spectrum will now find that their concerns are better reflected in the materials, with illustrations drawn from many workshops with faculty at all levels of schooling. Alas, it was simply impossible to include grade-specific and subject-specific examples for each idea; the text would be unreadable. So, although we have greatly expanded the examples, we ask readers to be open-minded and imaginative in their reading when the examples seem a bit far afield. Additional grade-specific or subject-specific examples appear on the subscription Web site that supports the work: http://ubdexchange.org.

Acknowledgments

Many individuals, far too numerous to mention, have helped us develop and refine the ideas and materials of *Understanding by Design*. Nonetheless, a few deserve special acknowledgment. First, we owe a debt of gratitude to the members of the UbD Training Cadre—John Brown, Ann Cunningham-Morris, Marcella Emberger, Judith Hilton, Catherine Jones, Everett Kline, Ken O'Connor, Jim Riedl, Elizabeth Rutherford, Janie Smith, Elliott Seif, Michael Short, Joyce Tatum, and Allison Zmuda. Their helpful feedback and guidance, based on extensive experience conducting professional development in Understanding by Design (UbD), has resulted in greater precision of language, clarity of examples, and supportive scaffolding. We especially appreciate the helpful advice provided by Elliott and Allison over the course of countless hours of review and conversation as the book was brought to completion.

Special thanks go to Lynn Erickson, whose work on concept-based education was vital in our own thinking about understanding; Denise Wilbur, Grant's senior colleague at Authentic Education, who was an invaluable codesigner, critic, and editor as the book came together; and Everett Kline, who has been a colleague in this work for almost 20 years and has never failed to bring enthusiastic and helpful questions and criticisms to the authors. We offer heartfelt thanks to the many thousands of other educators who have participated in UbD workshops and conferences. Their helpful feedback, penetrating questions, and design struggles helped us shape and sharpen the materials and the arguments.

There would be no *Understanding by Design* had it not been for the endless support and enthusiasm provided by Sally Chapman at ASCD. Sally was the first to have the vision of a partnership between the authors and the confidence in us to undertake and persist with the journey (even when the book was a year past deadline). We are very grateful. She has had the patience of Job (most of the time).

We are also thankful to ASCD's publishing staff for their ability to fashion an unwieldy manuscript into a well-designed final product and to accept a belated book with good cheer. The manuscript is the better for their flexibility and talents.

Finally, we once again thank our families for tolerating the endless phone calls, the trips back and forth between Maryland and New Jersey, and the hours spent on the road using and refining these materials. We trust that they—again—understand.

Introduction

To begin with the end in mind means to start with a clear understanding
of your destination. It means to know where you're going so that you
better understand where you are now so that the steps you take are
always in the right direction.
—Stephen R. Covey, *The 7 Habits of Highly Effective People,* 1989, p. 98

That's what I find so exciting about this process: it is so much better
for me and the students to be in the middle of a UbD. Everything seems
so relaxed, I'm more confident, and the students are very excited. They
seem to sense something more at the core of what we're doing. I suppose
they sense the goal: the goal is usually not revealed as completely
and clearly. I know what my students know, I know what they don't
know, and I know what I need to do. How liberating.
—A teacher reflecting on using UbD

Consider the following four vignettes and what they suggest about understanding and the design of curriculum and assessments. Two are true. Two are
fictionalized accounts of familiar practice.

1. As part of a workshop on "understanding," a veteran high school English
teacher entered the following reflection in a learning log about her own experience as a high school student:

*I felt then that my brain was a way station for material going in one ear and
(after the test) out the other. I could memorize very easily and so became
valedictorian, but I was embarrassed even then that I understood much less
than some other students who cared less about grades.*

2. For two weeks every fall, all the 3rd grade classes participate in a unit on
apples. The 3rd graders engage in a variety of activities related to the topic. In
language arts, they read about Johnny Appleseed and view an illustrated film-
strip of the story. They each write a creative story involving an apple and then
illustrate their stories using tempera paints. In art, students collect leaves
from nearby crab apple trees and make a giant leaf-print collage that hangs on

the hallway bulletin board adjacent to the 3rd grade classrooms. The music teacher teaches the children songs about apples. In science, they use their senses to carefully observe and describe the characteristics of different types of apples. During mathematics, the teacher demonstrates how to scale up an applesauce recipe to make enough for all the 3rd graders.

A highlight of the unit is the field trip to a local apple orchard, where students watch cider being made and go on a hayride. The culminating unit activity is the 3rd grade apple fest, a celebration in which parents dress in apple costumes and the children rotate through various activities at stations— making applesauce, competing in an apple word-search contest, bobbing for apples, and completing a math skill sheet containing word problems involving apples. The fest concludes with selected students reading their apple stories while the entire group enjoys candy apples prepared by the cafeteria staff.

3. A test item on a National Assessment of Educational Progress (NAEP) mathematics assessment presented the following question to 8th grade students, as an open-ended prompt demanding a written answer: "How many buses does the army need to transport 1,128 soldiers if each bus holds 36 soldiers?" Almost one-third of the 8th graders gave the following answer: "31 remainder 12" (Schoenfeld, 1988, p. 84).

4. It's late April and the panic is beginning to set in. A quick calculation reveals to the world history teacher that he will not finish the textbook unless he covers an average of 40 pages per day until the end of school. He decides, with some regret, to eliminate a short unit on Latin America and several time-consuming activities, such as a mock UN debate and vote and discussions of current international events in relation to the world history topics they've studied. To prepare his students for the departmental final exam, it will be necessary to switch into a fast-forward lecture mode.

Each of these vignettes reveals some troubling aspect of *understanding* and *design*. (By the way, the odd-numbered vignettes are true; the others might as well be, given common practice.)

The reflection of the high school English teacher reveals a familiar truth— even "good" students don't always have deep understanding of what's been taught despite the fact that conventional measures (course grades and cumulative GPA) certify success. In her case, testing focused predominantly on the recall of information from textbooks and class presentations. She reported that she was rarely given assessments that called for her to demonstrate deeper understanding.

The fictitious unit on apples presents a familiar scene—the *activity*-oriented curriculum—in which students participate in a variety of hands-on activities. Such units are often engaging for students. They may be organized, as in this case, around a theme and provide interdisciplinary connections. But questions about the value of the work remain. To what ends is the teaching directed? What are the big ideas and important skills to be developed during the unit? Do the students understand what the learning targets are? To what extent does the *evidence* of learning from the unit (e.g., the leaf-print collage, the creative-writing stories, the completed word searches) reflect worthwhile content standards? What understandings will emerge from all this and endure?

The NAEP mathematics test item reveals another aspect of understanding, or lack thereof. Although the students computed accurately, they had not grasped the meaning of the question, nor had they apparently understood how to use what they knew to reach an answer of 32 buses. Could it be that these students had mastered the out-of-context drill problems in the math book and on worksheets, but had been given little opportunity to apply mathematics in the context of real-world applications? Should we conclude that the students who answered "remainder 12" *really* understand division and its use?

Nearly every teacher can empathize with the world history teacher's struggle, given the pressures to "cover" material. The challenge is exacerbated by the natural increase of knowledge in fields such as science and history, not to mention external testing obligations and additions to the curriculum in recent years (e.g., computer studies and drug education). But at its worst, a *coverage* orientation—marching through the textbook irrespective of priorities, desired results, learner needs and interests, or apt assessment evidence—may defeat its own aims. For what do students remember, much less understand, when there is only *teaching* with no opportunity to really *learn*—to work with, play with, investigate, use—the key ideas and points of connection? Such an approach might correctly be labeled, "Teach, test, and hope for the best."

The twin sins of design

Interestingly enough, we think, both the apples unit and the world history class suffer from the same general problem, though what is taking place in both classrooms clearly looks very different. Though in the elementary classroom the students are doing loads of hands-on activity and in the history classroom a teacher is lecturing to students, both cases reveal no clear intellectual goals. We call the two versions of the problem the "twin sins" of typical instructional design in schools: activity-focused teaching and coverage-focused teaching. Neither case provides an adequate answer to the key questions at the heart of effective *learning*: What is important here? What is the point? How will this experience enable me as a learner to meet my obligations? Put simply, in a phrase to be considered throughout this book, the problem in both cases is that there are no explicit big ideas guiding the teaching and no plan for ensuring the learning.

What this book is about

As the title suggests, this book is about good design—of curriculum, assessment, and instruction—focused on developing and deepening understanding of important ideas. Posed as a question, considered throughout the book and from many perspectives, the essence of this book is this: *How do we make it more likely—by our design—that more students really understand what they are asked to learn?* So often, by contrast, those who "get it" are learners who come to us already able and articulate—understanding by good fortune. What must our planning entail to have an intellectual impact on everyone: the less experienced; the highly able, but unmotivated; the less able; those with varied interests and styles?

To explore such questions we must surely investigate the purpose of the designs—in our case, understanding. So what do we mean when we say that we want students to *understand* as opposed to merely take in and recall? How is it possible for a student to know lots of important things but not understand what they mean—something we have all seen as teachers? And vice versa: How can another student make lots of mistakes about the facts—and not even do all the assigned work—but nonetheless penetrate to the key ideas? Thus, although the book is about the design of curriculum to engage students in exploring big ideas, it is also an attempt to better understand *understanding,* especially for purposes of assessment.

As you shall see, we propose that a helpful way to think about what understanding is, how to design for it, and how to find evidence of it in student work is to realize that understanding has various facets. Everyday language reveals the variety of connotations, hence the need to clarify them. Think about the difference, for example, between saying, "He didn't understand the French speaker" and "She didn't understand what the primary source documents meant." There are different kinds of understanding; we need to be clear about which ones we are after. Understanding, we argue, is *not* a single goal but a family of interrelated abilities—six different facets of transfer—and an education for understanding would more deliberately develop them all.

This dual purpose—clarifying the goal called "student understanding" while exploring the means called "good design"—raises a host of vital questions in the real world of teaching, of course. What is the best way to design for both content mastery and understanding? How can we accomplish the goal of understanding if the textbooks we use dispense volumes of out-of-context knowledge? How realistic is teaching for understanding in a world of content standards and high-stakes tests? Thus, in the book, we do the following in an attempt to answer these and other questions:

• Propose an approach to curriculum and instruction designed to engage students in inquiry, promote transfer of learning, provide a conceptual framework for helping students make sense of discrete facts and skills, and uncover the big ideas of content.

• Examine an array of methods for appropriately assessing the degree of student understanding, knowledge, and skill.

• Consider the role that predictable student misunderstandings should play in the design of curricula, assessments, and instruction.

• Explore common curriculum, assessment, and instruction practices that may interfere with the cultivation of student understanding, and propose a *backward design* approach to planning that helps us meet standards without sacrificing goals related to understanding.

  • Present a theory of *six facets of understanding* and explore its theoretical and practical implications for curriculum, assessment, and teaching.

  • Present a unit template to assist in the design of curricula and assessments that focus on student understanding.

  • Show how such individual units should be nested in a larger, more coherent framework of courses and programs also framed around big ideas, essential questions, and core assessment tasks.

  • Propose a set of design standards for achieving quality control in curriculum and assessment designs.

  • Argue that designers need to work smarter, not harder, by sharing curriculum designs worldwide via a searchable Internet database.

The book's audience

This book is intended for educators, new or veteran, interested in enhancing student understanding and in designing more effective curricula and assessments to achieve that end. The audience includes teachers at all levels (elementary through university), subject matter and assessment specialists, curriculum directors, preservice and inservice trainers, school-based and central office administrators and supervisors. We provide numerous examples, from all levels of schooling, throughout the book, but never enough to suit any one audience at any one time, alas. Further examples from all subjects and levels can be found in the *Understanding by Design Professional Development Workbook* (McTighe & Wiggins, 2004) and on the UbD Web site (http://ubdexchange.org).

Key terms

A few words about terminology are in order. We talk a good deal in the book about *big ideas* that should be the focus of education for understanding. A big idea is a concept, theme, or issue that gives meaning and connection to discrete facts and skills. Here are some examples: adaptation; how form and function are related in systems; the distributive property in mathematics (whereby we can use any number of groupings and subgroupings to yield the "same" numbers); problem solving as the finding of useful models; the challenge of defining *justice;* and the need to focus on audience and purpose as a writer or speaker. In an education for understanding, a vital challenge is to highlight the big ideas, show how they prioritize the learning, and help students understand their value for making sense of all the "stuff" of content.

  Educators involved in reform know that the words *curriculum* and *assessment* have almost as many meanings as there are people using the terms. In this book, *curriculum* refers to the specific blueprint for learning that is derived from *desired results*—that is, content and performance standards (be they state-determined or locally developed). Curriculum takes content (from external standards and local goals) and shapes it into a plan for how to conduct effective and engaging teaching and learning. It is thus more than a list of topics and lists of key facts and skills (the "inputs"). It is a map for how to achieve the "outputs" of desired student performance, in which appropriate learning activities and assessments are suggested to make it more likely that students achieve the desired results.

The etymology of the word suggests this: *Curriculum* is the particular "course to be run," given a desired end point. A curriculum is more than a traditional program guide, therefore; beyond mapping out the topics and materials, it specifies the most appropriate experiences, assignments, and assessments that might be used for achieving goals. The best curricula (and syllabi), in other words, are written from the point of view of the desired learnings, not merely what will be covered. They specify what the learner should have achieved upon leaving, what the learner needs to do to achieve, and what the teacher needs to do to achieve the results sought. In sum, they specify the desired output and means of achieving it, not just a list of content and activities.

By *assessment* we mean the act of determining the extent to which the desired results are on the way to being achieved and to what extent they have been achieved. Assessment is the umbrella term for the deliberate use of *many* methods of gathering evidence of meeting desired results, whether those results are state content standards or local curricular objectives. The collected evidence we seek may well include observations and dialogues, traditional quizzes and tests, performance tasks and projects, as well as students' self-assessments gathered over time. *Assessment* is thus a more learning-focused term than *evaluation*, and the two should not be viewed as synonymous. Assessment is the giving and using of feedback against standards to enable improvement and the meeting of goals. Evaluation, by contrast, is more summative and credential-related. In other words, we need not give a grade—an evaluation—to everything we give feedback to. In fact, a central premise of our argument is that understanding can be developed and evoked only through multiple methods of ongoing assessment, with far greater attention paid to formative (and performance) assessment than is typical.

By *desired results* we mean what has often been termed *intended outcomes, achievement targets,* or *performance standards.* All four terms are meant to shift our focus away from the inputs to the output: what the student should be able to know, do, and understand upon leaving, expressed in performance and product terms. *Desired result* reminds us also that, as "coaches," we will likely have to adjust *our* design and performance en route, if feedback shows that we are in danger of not achieving the successes sought.

The word *understanding* turns out to be a complex and confusing target despite the fact that we aim for it all the time. The word naturally deserves clarification and elaboration, which is the challenge for the rest of the book. For now, though, consider our initial working definition of the term: To *understand* is to make connections and bind together our knowledge into something that makes sense of things (whereas without understanding we might see only unclear, isolated, or unhelpful facts). But the word also implies doing, not just a mental act: A performance ability lies at the heart of understanding, as Bloom (1956) noted in his Taxonomy in discussing application and synthesis. To understand is to be able to wisely and effectively *use*—transfer—what we know, in context; to *apply* knowledge and skill effectively, in realistic tasks and settings. To have understood means that we show evidence of being able to transfer what we know. When we understand, we have a fluent and fluid grasp, not a rigid, formulaic grasp based only on recall and "plugging in."

When we speak of the product of this achievement—*an* understanding, as a noun—we are describing particular (often hard-won) insights. For example, we talk about scientists' current understanding that the universe is expanding or the postmodern understanding of authors as not being privileged commentators on the meaning of their books. The great challenge in teaching is to enable such subtle adult understandings to become student understandings—without reducing the understanding to a mere simplistic statement for recall. If the student gains a genuine understanding, we typically say they "*really* get it." With our help as designers and coaches, they "come to an understanding."

Yet, for years, curriculum guides have argued against framing objectives in terms of understandings. Bloom (1956) argued that the word is too ambiguous to use as a foundation for teaching goals and their assessments; hence, the writing of the Taxonomy. But an important conceptual distinction remains and needs pondering: the difference between *knowing* and *understanding.* Pinning this distinction down in theory and in practice has not been easy. We propose in the book that insufficient attention has been paid to the fact that there are *different kinds* of understandings, that knowledge and skill *do not* automatically lead to understanding, that student *misunderstanding* is a far bigger problem than we may realize, and that assessment of understanding therefore requires evidence that *cannot* be gained from traditional fact-focused testing alone.

What this book *isn't* about

1. *Understanding by Design* is not a prescriptive program. It is a way of thinking more purposefully and carefully about the nature of *any* design that has understanding as the goal. Rather than offering a step-by-step guide to follow—something that is antithetical to good design, whether in education or architecture—the book provides a conceptual framework, many entry points, a design template, various tools and methods, and an accompanying set of design standards. We offer no specific guidance about what the content of curriculum should be—except that its priorities should center on the big ideas and important performance tasks of the chosen topic. What we provide, rather, is a way to design or redesign *any* curriculum to make student understanding (and desired results generally) more likely.

2. *Understanding by Design* is not a philosophy of education, nor does it require a belief in any single pedagogical system or approach. We offer guidance on how to tackle any educational design problem related to the goal of student understanding. Nowhere do we specify which "big ideas" you should embrace. Instead, we help you better focus your design work on how to achieve understanding of the important ideas that you (or established standards) target. (We do offer many examples of big ideas in various disciplines.) The book should not be seen as competing with other programs or approaches, therefore. In fact, the proposed view of understanding and the backward design process are compatible with a full range of prominent educational initiatives, including *Problem-Based Learning Across the Curriculum* (Stepien & Gallagher, 1997), Socratic seminar, *4MAT* (McCarthy, 1981), *Dimensions of Learning* (Marzano & Pickering, 1997), teaching to state content standards, Core Knowledge, the *Skillful Teacher* (Saphier & Gower, 1997), and the materials from the Project Zero team at the Harvard Graduate School of Education entitled *Teaching for Understanding* (Wiske, 1998; Blythe & Associates, 1998). In fact, over the past five years, college professors using the lecture format, Montessori teachers, and educators working in schools using the International Baccalaureate, *Success for All*, the advanced placement program, and the Coalition of Essential Schools philosophy have all used our work to improve their designs.

3. The book presents a robust approach to *planning*. We say little about *teaching* strategies per se, even though we believe that a variety of instructional approaches can develop and deepen student understanding. Regardless of particular techniques, we assume that all purposeful and effective teachers follow a cycle of plan-revise-teach-assess-reflect-adjust many times. This is a noteworthy caution because crucial *redesign* information will necessarily be derived from an analysis of student work and from preassessment. (See Chapter 11 on the design process.)

4. This book is primarily focused on the design of curricular units (as opposed to individual lessons or broader programs). Although we strongly recommend that individual units be grounded in the broader context of programs and courses (as discussed in Chapter 12), we deliberately restrict our attention in this book to the more nitty-gritty and teacher-friendly work of unit design. In working with thousands of teachers over the years, we have found that the unit provides a comfortable and practical entry point for this design process. Although it may seem natural to apply the UbD approach to a system of daily lesson planning, we discourage it. Individual lessons are simply too short to allow for in-depth development of big ideas, exploration of essential questions, and authentic applications. In other words, a single lesson provides too short a time frame for meeting complex goals. Of course, lesson plans should logically flow from unit plans: Lessons are typically more purposeful and connected when informed by larger unit and course designs.

5. Although teaching for in-depth understanding is a vital aim of schooling, it is, of course, only one of many. We are thus not suggesting that *all* teaching

and assessment be geared *at all times* toward deep and sophisticated understanding. There are clearly circumstances when this is neither feasible nor desirable: Learning the alphabet; acquiring certain technical skills, such as keyboarding; or developing the basics in foreign language do not call for in-depth understanding. In some cases, the developmental level of students will determine the extent to which conceptualization is appropriate; at other times the goals of a course or program will make in-depth understanding a lesser or tangential goal. Sometimes "familiarity" is an appropriate and sufficient goal for certain topics at certain points in time. There is neither the time nor the need to go into depth on everything, and it would be counterproductive when the goal is to convey a sense of the larger whole. The book is thus built upon a conditional premise: *If* you wish to develop greater in-depth understanding in your students, *then* the ideas and processes of *Understanding by Design* apply.

A few helpful cautions and comments

We offer three warnings, though, for readers willing and ready to plan and teach for understanding. First, although educators often talk about wanting to get beyond mere coverage to ensure that students really understand what they learn, you may find that what you previously thought was effective teaching for understanding really wasn't. You may also discover that you aren't quite as clear as you might be about what, specifically, your students should leave understanding. In fact, we predict that you will be somewhat disturbed by how hard it is to specify the understandings and what they look like in assessment, and how easy it is to lose sight of goals related to understanding in the midst of planning, teaching, and evaluating student work.

Second, though many courses of study appropriately focus on skills (such as reading, algebra, physical education, and introductory Spanish), teacher-designers may well find after reading this book that there are, indeed, big ideas essential for learning key skills with fluency—namely, understanding how to *use* skills *wisely*—that need greater attention in their plans. For example, a big idea in literacy development is that the meaning of the text is not in the text but between the lines, in the interaction between the active reader and the text. Getting students to understand this is not only difficult but requires a very different design and presents a very different teaching problem than that of focusing only on discrete reading strategies. The challenge is, at its core, to help students overcome the misunderstanding that reading is only decoding, and to help them know what to do when decoding alone does not yield meaning.

Third, though many teachers believe that to design for understanding is incompatible with established content standards and state testing, we think that by the time you have read the entire book, you will consider this to be false. Most state standards identify or at least imply big ideas that are meant to be understood, not merely covered. Consider these examples from Ohio's standards for 11th grade social studies and California's standards for physics:

Trace key Supreme Court decisions related to a provision of the Constitution (e.g., cases related to reapportionment of legislative districts, free speech, or separation of church and state).

Energy cannot be created or destroyed, although in many processes energy is transferred to the environment as heat. As a basis for understanding this concept:

a. Students know heat flow and work are two forms of energy transfer between systems. . . .

▓ MISCONCEPTION ALERT!

1. *Only alternative or progressive methods of teaching and assessing can yield understanding. This is all about process as opposed to content.* Nothing could be further from the truth. You cannot understand without subject matter knowledge. All so-called traditional approaches to learning at the college level, for example, aim at and often succeed in yielding in-depth understanding. The challenge is not to choose this or that tactic to the exclusion of others, but to *expand* and better *target* our teaching repertoire, based on a more careful consideration of what our learning goals imply. In practice, we find that all teachers, regardless of educational philosophy, are typically hemmed in by a too-limited set of design options. A challenge is to make sure that teachers use a greater diversity of appropriate methods of instruction than they typically do now, regardless of their philosophy. (See Chapters 9 and 10.)

2. *We are against traditional testing.* Not so. Here, too, we seek to expand the normal repertoire to make sure that more *appropriate diversity* and validity is found in classroom assessment, based on the diversity of goals typically found in most programs. The challenge is to know which method to use when and why, and to better understand the strengths and weaknesses of *each* form of assessment. (See Chapters 7 and 8.)

3. *We are against letter grades.* Why would we be, *if* the grades correspond to a valid assessment of understanding? Letter grades are here to stay, by and large, and nothing in this book is incompatible with grades, transcripts, report cards, and college admission standards. On the contrary, the book should help teachers (especially those at the secondary and collegiate levels) better articulate and justify their grading system, providing students with more fair assessments, improved feedback, and greater clarity about what the grades stand for.

More generally, once you understand the elements we propose as central to good design, we expect that your approach to *all* your design obligations will change.

We predict that you will experience two quite different feelings as you read. At times you will say to yourself, "Well, of course, this is just common sense! This merely makes explicit what good planners have always done." At other times you will feel that we are proposing provocative and counterintuitive ideas about teaching, learning, assessment, and planning. To help you in the latter case, we will offer sidebars about potential misunderstandings—we call them "Misconception Alerts"—in which we try to anticipate reader confusion in the lines of argument and ideas being proposed.

The presence of these particular sidebars conveys a vital message: Teaching for understanding must successfully predict potential misunderstandings and rough spots in learning if it is to be effective. *Indeed, central to the design approach we propose is that we need to design lessons and assessments that anticipate, evoke, and overcome the most likely student misconceptions.* The first such sidebar appears on this page.

You will also find a few sidebars entitled "Design Tips." These will help you see how to begin to translate the theories of UbD to the practical work of planning, teaching, and assessing. We have also provided a Glossary to help you navigate the language used throughout the book. To give you some sense of how the designer's thought process works, we follow a fictional teacher, Bob James, as he designs (and redesigns) his unit on nutrition. (The companion *UbD Professional Development Workbook* provides an extensive set of design tools, exercises, and examples to assist designers.)

So, reader, brace thyself! We are asking you to explore key ideas and to rethink many time-honored habits about curriculum, assessment, and instruction. Such rethinking practices what we preach. Because, as you will see, teaching for understanding *requires* the learner to rethink what appeared settled or obvious—whether *learner* refers to a young student or a veteran educator. We believe that you will find much food for thought, as well as many practical tips about how to achieve student understanding by design.

Chapter 1

Backward Design

Design, v.,—To have purposes and intentions; to plan and execute
—*Oxford English Dictionary*

The complexity of design work is often underestimated. Many people believe they know a good deal about design. What they do not realize is how much more they need to know to do design well, with distinction, refinement, and grace.
—John McClean, "20 Considerations That Help a Project Run Smoothly," 2003

Teachers are designers. An essential act of our profession is the crafting of curriculum and learning experiences to meet specified purposes. We are also designers of assessments to diagnose student needs to guide our teaching and to enable us, our students, and others (parents and administrators) to determine whether we have achieved our goals.

Like people in other design professions, such as architecture, engineering, or graphic arts, designers in education must be mindful of their audiences. Professionals in these fields are strongly client-centered. The effectiveness of their designs corresponds to whether they have accomplished explicit goals for specific end-users. Clearly, students are our primary clients, given that the effectiveness of curriculum, assessment, and instructional designs is ultimately determined by their achievement of desired learnings. We can think of our designs, then, as software. Our courseware is designed to make learning more effective, just as computer software is intended to make its users more productive.

As in all the design professions, standards inform and shape our work. The software developer works to maximize user-friendliness and to reduce bugs that impede results. The architect is guided by building codes, customer budget, and neighborhood aesthetics. The teacher as designer is similarly constrained. We are not free to teach any topic we choose by any means. Rather, we are guided by national, state, district, or institutional standards that specify what students should know and be able to do. These standards provide a useful framework to help us identify teaching and learning priorities and guide our design of curriculum and assessments. In addition to external standards, we must also factor in the needs of our many and varied students when designing learning experiences. For example, diverse student interests, developmental levels, large classes, and previous achievements must always shape our thinking about the learning activities, assignments, and assessments.

Yet, as the old adage reminds us, in the best designs form follows function. In other words, all the methods and materials we use are shaped by a clear conception of the vision of desired results. That means that we must be able to state with clarity what the student should understand and be able to do as a result of any plan and irrespective of any constraints we face.

You probably know the saying, "If you don't know exactly where you are headed, then any road will get you there." Alas, the point is a serious one in education. We are quick to say what things *we* like to teach, what activities *we* will do, and what kinds of resources *we* will use; but without clarifying the desired results of our teaching, how will we ever know whether our designs are appropriate or arbitrary? How will we distinguish merely interesting learning from *effective* learning? More pointedly, how will we ever meet content standards or arrive at hard-won student understandings unless we think through what those goals imply for the learner's activities and achievements?

Good design, then, is not so much about gaining a few new technical skills as it is about learning to be more thoughtful and specific about our purposes and what they imply.

Why "backward" is best

How do these general design considerations apply to curriculum planning? Deliberate and focused instructional design requires us as teachers and curriculum writers to make an important shift in our thinking about the nature of our job. The shift involves thinking a great deal, first, about the specific learnings sought, and the evidence of such learnings, before thinking about what we, as the teacher, will do or provide in teaching and learning activities. Though considerations about what to teach and how to teach it may dominate our thinking as a matter of habit, the challenge is to focus first on the desired learnings from which appropriate teaching will logically follow.

Our lessons, units, and courses should be logically inferred from the results sought, not derived from the methods, books, and activities with which we are most comfortable. Curriculum should lay out the most effective ways of achieving specific results. It is analogous to travel planning. Our frameworks should provide a set of itineraries deliberately designed to meet cultural goals rather than a purposeless tour of all the major sites in a foreign country. In short, the best designs derive backward from the learnings sought.

The appropriateness of this approach becomes clearer when we consider the educational purpose that is the focus of this book: understanding. We cannot say *how* to teach for understanding or *which* material and activities to use until we are quite clear about which specific understandings we are after and what such understandings look like in practice. We can best decide, as guides, what "sites" to have our student "tourists" visit and what specific "culture" they should experience in their brief time there only if we are clear about the particular understandings about the culture we want them to take home. Only by having specified the desired results can we focus on the content, methods, and activities most likely to achieve those results.

But many teachers begin with and remain focused on textbooks, favored lessons, and time-honored activities—the inputs—rather than deriving those means from what is implied in the desired results—the output. To put it in an odd way, too many teachers focus on the *teaching* and not the *learning*. They spend most of their time thinking, first, about what they will do, what materials they will use, and what they will ask students to do rather than first considering what the learner will need in order to accomplish the learning goals.

Consider a typical episode of what might be called *content*-focused design instead of *results*-focused design. The teacher might base a lesson on a particular topic (e.g., racial prejudice), select a resource (e.g., *To Kill a Mockingbird*), choose specific instructional methods based on the resource and topic (e.g., Socratic seminar to discuss the book and cooperative groups to analyze stereotypical images in films and on television), and hope thereby to cause learning (and meet a few English/language arts standards). Finally, the teacher might think up a few essay questions and quizzes for assessing student understanding of the book.

This approach is so common that we may well be tempted to reply, What could be wrong with such an approach? The short answer lies in the basic questions of purpose: Why are we asking students to read this particular novel—in other words, what *learnings* will we seek from their having read it? Do the students grasp why and how the purpose should influence their studying? What should students be expected to understand and do upon reading the book, related to our goals beyond the book? Unless we begin our design work with a clear insight into larger purposes—whereby the book is properly thought of as a means to an educational end, not an end unto itself—it is unlikely that all students will *understand* the book (and their performance obligations). Without being self-conscious of the specific understandings about prejudice we seek, and how reading and discussing the book will help develop such insights, the goal is far too vague: The approach is more "by hope" than "by design." Such an approach ends up unwittingly being one that could be described like this: Throw some content and activities against the wall and hope some of it sticks.

Answering the "why?" and "so what?" questions that older students always ask (or want to), and doing so in concrete terms as the focus of curriculum

Design Tip

Consider these questions that arise in the minds of all readers, the answers to which will frame the priorities of coached learning: How should I read the book? What am I looking for? What will we discuss? How should I prepare for those discussions? How do I know if my reading and discussions are effective? Toward what performance goals do this reading and these discussions head, so that I might focus and prioritize my studies and note taking? What big ideas, linked to other readings, are in play here? These are the students' proper questions about the learning, not the teaching, and any good educational design answers them from the start and throughout a course of study with the use of tools and strategies such as graphic organizers and written guidelines.

planning, is thus the essence of understanding by design. What is difficult for many teachers to see (but easier for students to feel!) is that, without such explicit and transparent priorities, many students find day-to-day work confusing and frustrating.

The twin sins of traditional design

More generally, weak educational design involves two kinds of purposelessness, visible throughout the educational world from kindergarten through graduate school, as noted in the Introduction. We call these the "twin sins" of traditional design. The error of activity-oriented design might be called "hands-on without being minds-on"—engaging experiences that lead only accidentally, if at all, to insight or achievement. The activities, though fun and interesting, do not lead anywhere intellectually. As typified by the apples vignette in the Introduction, such activity-oriented curricula lack an explicit focus on important ideas and appropriate evidence of learning, especially in the minds of the learners. They think their job is merely to engage; they are led to think the learning *is* the activity instead of seeing that the learning comes from being asked to consider the *meaning* of the activity.

A second form of aimlessness goes by the name of "coverage," an approach in which students march through a textbook, page by page (or teachers through lecture notes) in a valiant attempt to traverse all the factual material within a prescribed time (as in the world history vignette in the Introduction). Coverage is thus like a whirlwind tour of Europe, perfectly summarized by the old movie title *If It's Tuesday, This Must Be Belgium,* which properly suggests that no overarching goals inform the tour.

As a broad generalization, the activity focus is more typical at the elementary and lower middle school levels, whereas coverage is a prevalent secondary school and college problem. Yet, though the apples and world history classrooms look quite different with lots of physical activity and chatter in the former versus lecturing and quiet note taking in the latter, the design result is the same in both cases: No guiding intellectual purpose or clear priorities frame the learning experience. In neither case can students see and answer such questions as these: What's the point? What's the big idea here? What does this help us understand or be able to do? To what does this relate? Why should we learn this? Hence, the students try to engage and follow as best they can, hoping that meaning will emerge.

■ MISCONCEPTION ALERT!

Coverage is not the same as *purposeful survey.* Providing students with an overview of a discipline or a field of study is not inherently wrong. The question has to do with the transparency of purpose. *Coverage* is a negative term (whereas *introduction* or *survey* is not) because when content is "covered" the student is led through unending facts, ideas, and readings with little or no sense of the overarching ideas, issues, and learning goals that might inform study. (See Chapter 10 for more on coverage versus uncoverage.)

Students will be unable to give satisfactory responses when the design does not provide them with clear purposes and explicit performance goals highlighted throughout their work. Similarly, teachers with an activity or coverage orientation are less likely to have acceptable answers to the key design questions: What should students understand as a result of the activities or the content covered? What should the experiences or lectures equip them to do? How, then, should the activities or class discussions be shaped and processed to achieve the desired results? What would be evidence that learners are en route to the desired abilities and insights? How, then, should all activities and resources be chosen and used to ensure that the learning goals are met and the most appropriate evidence produced? How, in other words, will students be helped to see *by design* the purpose of the activity or resource and its helpfulness in meeting specific performance goals?

We are advocating the reverse of common practice, then. We ask designers to start with a much more careful statement of the desired results—the priority *learnings*—and to derive the curriculum from the performances called for or implied in the goals. Then, contrary to much common practice, we ask designers to consider the following questions after framing the goals: What would count as evidence of such achievement? What does it look like to meet these goals? What, then, are the implied *performances* that should make up the assessment, toward which all teaching and learning should point? Only after answering these questions can we logically derive the appropriate teaching and learning experiences so that students might perform successfully to meet the standard. The shift, therefore, is away from starting with such questions as "What book will we read?" or "What activities will we do?" or "What will we discuss?" to "What should they walk out the door able to understand, regardless of what activities or texts we use?" and "What is evidence of such ability?" and, therefore, "What texts, activities, and methods will best enable such a result?" In teaching students for understanding, we must grasp the key idea that *we are coaches of their ability to play the "game" of performing with understanding, not tellers of our understanding to them on the sidelines.*

> **Design Tip**
>
> To test the merits of our claims about purposelessness, we encourage you to sidle up to a student in the middle of any class and ask the following questions:
>
> What are you doing?
>
> Why are you being asked to do it?
>
> What will it help you do?
>
> How does it fit with what you have previously done?
>
> How will you show that you have learned it?

The three stages of backward design

We call this three-stage approach to planning "backward design." Figure 1.1 depicts the three stages in the simplest terms.

Stage 1: Identify desired results

What should students know, understand, and be able to do? What content is worthy of understanding? What *enduring* understandings are desired?

Figure 1.1
UbD: Stages of Backward Design

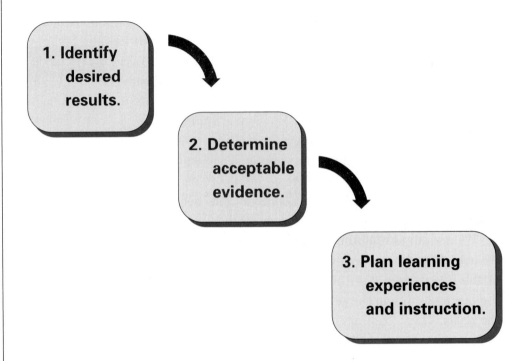

In Stage 1 we consider our goals, examine established content standards (national, state, district), and review curriculum expectations. Because typically we have more content than we can reasonably address within the available time, we must make choices. This first stage in the design process calls for clarity about priorities.

Stage 2: Determine acceptable evidence

How will we know if students have achieved the desired results? What will we accept as evidence of student understanding and proficiency? The backward design orientation suggests that we think about a unit or course in terms of the collected assessment evidence needed to document and validate that the desired learning has been achieved, not simply as content to be covered or as a series of learning activities. This approach encourages teachers and curriculum planners to first "think like an assessor" before designing specific units and lessons, and thus to consider up front how they will determine if students have attained the desired understandings.

Stage 3: Plan learning experiences and instruction

With clearly identified results and appropriate evidence of understanding in mind, it is now the time to fully think through the most appropriate instructional activities. Several key questions must be considered at this stage of backward design: What enabling knowledge (facts, concepts, principles) and skills (processes, procedures, strategies) will students need in order to perform effectively and achieve desired results? What activities will equip students with the needed knowledge and skills? What will need to be taught and coached, and how should it best be taught, in light of performance goals? What materials and resources are best suited to accomplish these goals?

Note that the specifics of instructional planning—choices about teaching methods, sequence of lessons, and resource materials—can be successfully completed only after we identify desired results and assessments and consider what they imply. Teaching is a means to an end. Having a clear goal helps to focus our planning and guide purposeful action toward the intended results.

Backward design may be thought of, in other words, as purposeful task analysis: Given a

■ MISCONCEPTION ALERT!

When we speak of evidence of desired results, we are referring to evidence gathered through a variety of formal and informal assessments during a unit of study or a course. We are not alluding only to end-of-teaching tests or culminating tasks. Rather, the collected evidence we seek may well include traditional quizzes and tests, performance tasks and projects, observations and dialogues, as well as students' self-assessments gathered over time.

worthy task to be accomplished, how do we best get everyone equipped? Or we might think of it as building a wise itinerary, using a map: Given a destination, what's the most effective and efficient route? Or we might think of it as planning for coaching, as suggested earlier: What must learners master if they are to effectively perform? What will count as evidence *on the field,* not merely in drills, that they really get it and are ready to *perform with understanding, knowledge, and skill* on their own? How will the learning be designed so that learners' capacities are developed through use and feedback?

This is all quite logical when you come to understand it, but "backward" from the perspective of much habit and tradition in our field. A major change from common practice occurs as designers must begin to think about assessment *before* deciding what and how they will teach. Rather than creating assessments near the conclusion of a unit of study (or relying on the tests provided by textbook publishers, which may not completely or appropriately assess our standards and goals), backward design calls for us to make our goals or standards specific and concrete, in terms of assessment evidence, as we begin to plan a unit or course.

The logic of backward design applies regardless of the learning goals. For example, when starting from a state content standard, curriculum designers need to determine the appropriate assessment evidence stated or implied in the standard. Likewise, a staff developer should determine what evidence will indicate that the adults have learned the intended knowledge or skill before planning the various workshop activities.

The rubber meets the road with assessment. Three different teachers may all be working toward the same content standards, but if their assessments vary considerably, how are we to know which students have achieved what? Agreement on needed evidence of learning leads to greater curricular coherence and more reliable evaluation by teachers. Equally important is the long-term gain in teacher, student, and parent insight about what does and does not count as evidence of meeting complex standards.

This view of focusing intently on the desired learning is hardly radical or new. Tyler (1949) described the logic of backward design clearly and succinctly more than 50 years ago:

> *Educational objectives become the criteria by which materials are selected, content is outlined, instructional procedures are developed, and tests and examinations are prepared. . . .*

> *The purpose of a statement of objectives is to indicate the kinds of changes in the student to be brought about so that instructional activities can be planned and developed in a way likely to attain these objectives. (pp. 1, 45)*

And in his famous book, *How to Solve It,* originally published in 1945, Polya specifically discusses "thinking backward" as a strategy in problem solving going back to the Greeks:

> *There is a certain psychological difficulty in turning around, in going away from the goal, in working backwards. . . . Yet, it does not take a genius to solve a concrete problem working backwards; anyone can do it with a little common sense. We concentrate on the desired end, we visualize the final position in which we would like to be. From what foregoing position could we get there? (p. 230)*

These remarks are old. What is perhaps new is that we offer herein a helpful process, a template, a set of tools, and design standards to make the plan and resultant student performance more likely to be successful by design than by good fortune. As a 4th grade teacher from Alberta, Canada, put it, "Once I had a way of clearly defining the end in mind, the rest of the unit 'fell into place.'"

The twin sins of activity-based and coverage-based design reflect a failure to think through purpose in this backward-design way. With this in mind, let's revisit the two fictitious vignettes from the Introduction. In the apples vignette, the unit seems to focus on a particular theme (harvest time), through a specific and familiar object (apples). But as the depiction reveals, the unit has no real depth because there is no enduring learning for the students to derive. The work is *hands-on* without being *minds-on,* because students do not need to (and are not really challenged to) extract sophisticated ideas or connections. They don't have to work at understanding; they need only engage in the activity. (Alas, it is common to reward students for mere engagement as opposed to understanding; engagement is necessary, but not sufficient, as an end result.)

Moreover, when you examine the apples unit it becomes clear that it has no overt priorities—the activities appear to be of equal value. The students' role is merely to participate in mostly enjoyable activities, without having to demonstrate that they understand any big ideas at the core of the subject (excuse the pun). All activity-based—as opposed to results-based—teaching shares the weakness of the apples unit: Little in the design asks students to derive intellectual fruit from the unit (sorry!). One might characterize this activity-oriented approach as "faith in learning by osmosis." Is it likely that individual students will learn a few interesting things about apples? Of course. But, in the absence of a learning plan with clear goals, how likely is it that students will develop shared understandings on which future lessons might build? Not very.

In the world history vignette, the teacher covers vast amounts of content during the last quarter of the year. However, in his harried march to get through a textbook, he apparently does not consider what the students will understand and apply from the material. What kind of intellectual scaffolding is provided to guide students through the important ideas? How are students expected to use those ideas to make meaning of the many facts? What performance goals would help students know how to take notes for maximal effective use by the course's end? Coverage-based instruction amounts to the teacher merely talking, checking off topics, and moving on, irrespective of whether students understand or are confused. This approach might be termed "teaching by mentioning it." Coverage-oriented teaching typically relies on a textbook, allowing it to define the content and sequence of instruction. In contrast, we propose that results-oriented teaching employ the textbook as a resource but not the syllabus.

A backward design template

Having described the backward design process, we now put it together in a useful format—a template for teachers to use in the design of units that focus on understanding.

Many educators have observed that backward design is common sense. Yet when they first start to apply it, they discover that it feels unnatural. Working this way may seem a bit awkward and time-consuming until you get the hang of it. But the effort is worth it—just as the learning curve on good software is worth it. We think of Understanding by Design as software, in fact: a set of tools for making you ultimately more productive. Thus, a practical cornerstone of Understanding by Design is a design template that is meant to reinforce the appropriate habits of mind needed to complete designs for student understanding and to avoid the habits that are at the heart of the twin sins of activity-based and coverage-based design.

Figure 1.2 provides a preliminary look at the UbD Template in the form of a one-page version with key planning questions included in the various fields. This format guides the teacher to the various UbD elements while visually conveying the idea of backward design. Later chapters present a more complete account of the template and each of its fields.

Although this one-page version of the template does not allow for great detail, it has several virtues. First, it provides a *gestalt,* an overall view of backward design, without appearing overwhelming. Second, it enables a quick check of alignment—the extent to which the assessments (Stage 2) and learning activities (Stage 3) align with identified goals (Stage 1). Third, the template

Figure 1.2
1-Page Template with Design Questions for Teachers

<table>
<tr><td colspan="2" align="center">Stage 1—Desired Results</td></tr>
<tr><td colspan="2">
Established Goals: (G)

• What relevant goals (e.g., content standards, course or program objectives, learning outcomes) will this design address?
</td></tr>
<tr><td>
Understandings: (U)
Students will understand that . . .

• What are the big ideas?
• What specific understandings about them are desired?
• What misunderstandings are predictable?
</td><td>
Essential Questions: (Q)

• What provocative questions will foster inquiry, understanding, and transfer of learning?
</td></tr>
<tr><td>
Students will know . . .   (K)

• What key knowledge and skills will students acquire as a result of this unit?
• What should they eventually be able to do as a result of such knowledge and skills?
</td><td>
Students will be able to . . .   (S)
</td></tr>
</table>

<table>
<tr><td colspan="2" align="center">Stage 2—Assessment Evidence</td></tr>
<tr><td>
Performance Tasks: (T)

• Through what authentic performance tasks will students demonstrate the desired understandings?
• By what criteria will performances of understanding be judged?
</td><td>
Other Evidence: (OE)

• Through what other evidence (e.g., quizzes, tests, academic prompts, observations, homework, journals) will students demonstrate achievement of the desired results?
• How will students reflect upon and self-assess their learning?
</td></tr>
</table>

<table>
<tr><td align="center">Stage 3—Learning Plan</td></tr>
</table>

Learning Activities: (L)

What learning experiences and instruction will enable students to achieve the desired results? How will the design

W = Help the students know **W**here the unit is going and **W**hat is expected? Help the teacher know **W**here the students are coming from (prior knowledge, interests)?

H = **H**ook all students and **H**old their interest?

E = **E**quip students, help them **E**xperience the key ideas and **E**xplore the issues?

R = Provide opportunities to **R**ethink and **R**evise their understandings and work?

E = Allow students to **E**valuate their work and its implications?

T = Be **T**ailored (personalized) to the different needs, interests, and abilities of learners?

O = Be **O**rganized to maximize initial and sustained engagement as well as effective learning?

can be used to review existing units that teachers or districts have developed. Finally, the one-page template provides an initial design frame. We also have a multipage version that allows for more detailed planning, including, for example, a Performance Task Blueprint and a day-by-day calendar for listing and sequencing key learning events. The *Understanding by Design Professional Development Workbook* (McTighe & Wiggins, 2004, pp. 46–51) includes a six-page template that allows for more detailed planning.

We regularly observe that teachers begin to internalize the backward design process as they work with the UbD Template. Stage 1 asks designers to consider what they want students to understand and then to frame those understandings in terms of questions. In completing the top two sections of the Stage 1 portion of the template, users are prompted to identify the Understandings and Essential Questions to establish a larger context into which a particular unit is nested.

Stage 2 prompts the designer to consider a variety of assessment methods for gathering evidence of the desired Understandings. The two-box graphic organizer then provides spaces for specifying the particular assessments to be used during the unit. Designers need to think in terms of collected evidence, not a single test or performance task.

Stage 3 calls for a listing of the major learning activities and lessons. When it is filled in, the designer (and others) should be able to discern what we call the "WHERETO" elements.

The *form* of the template offers a means to succinctly present the design unit; its *function* is to guide the design process. When completed, the template can be used for self-assessment, peer review, and sharing of the completed unit design with others.

To better understand the template's benefits for the teacher-designer, let's take a look at a completed template. Figure 1.3 shows a completed three-page version of the template for a unit on nutrition.

Notice that the template in Figure 1.3 supports backward design thinking by making the longer-term goals far more explicit than is typical in lesson planning, and we can follow those goals through Stages 2 and 3 to ensure that the design is coherent. The focus on big ideas in Stage 1 is transparent, without sacrificing the more discrete elements of knowledge and skill. Finally, by calling for appropriately different types of assessment, the template reminds us that we typically need varied evidence and assessments grounded in performance to show transfer, if understanding is our aim.

Design standards

Accompanying the UbD Template is a set of Design Standards corresponding to each stage of backward design. The standards offer criteria to use during development and for quality control of completed unit designs. Framed as questions, the UbD Design Standards serve curriculum designers in the same

Figure 1.3
3-Page Nutrition Example

Stage 1—Identify Desired Results

Established Goals:

Standard 6—Students will understand essential concepts about nutrition and diet.
6a—Students will use an understanding of nutrition to plan appropriate diets for themselves and others.
6c—Students will understand their own individual eating patterns and ways in which those patterns may be improved.

What essential questions will be considered?

- What is healthful eating?
- Are you a heathful eater? How would you know?
- How could a healthy diet for one person be unhealthy for another?
- Why are there so many health problems in the United States caused by poor nutrition despite all the available information?

What understandings are desired?

Students will understand that . . .

- A balanced diet contributes to physical and mental health.
- The USDA food pyramid presents *relative* guidelines for nutrition.
- Dietary requirements vary for individuals based on age, activity level, weight, and overall health.
- Healthful living requires an individual to act on available information about good nutrition even if it means breaking comfortable habits.

What key knowledge and skills will students acquire as a result of this unit?

Students will know . . .

- Key terms—protein, fat, calorie, carbohydrate, cholesterol.
- Types of foods in each food group and their nutritional values.
- The USDA food pyramid guidelines.
- Variables influencing nutritional needs.
- General health problems caused by poor nutrition.

Students will be able to . . .

- Read and interpret nutrition information on food labels.
- Analyze diets for nutritional value.
- Plan balanced diets for themselves and others.

Figure 1.3 (continued)
3-Page Nutrition Example

Stage 2—Determine Acceptable Evidence

What evidence will show that students understand?

Performance Tasks:

You Are What You Eat—Students create an illustrated brochure to teach younger children about the importance of good nutrition for healthful living. They offer younger students ideas for breaking bad eating habits.

Chow Down—Students develop a three-day menu for meals and snacks for an upcoming Outdoor Education camp experience. They write a letter to the camp director to explain why their menu should be selected (by showing that it meets the USDA food pyramid recommendations, yet it is tasty enough for the students). They include at least one modification for a specific dietary condition (diabetic or vegetarian) or religious consideration.

What other evidence needs to be collected in light of Stage 1 Desired Results?

Other Evidence:
(e.g., tests, quizzes, prompts, work samples, observations)

Quiz—The food groups and the USDA food pyramid

Prompt—Describe two health problems that could arise as a result of poor nutrition and explain how these could be avoided.

Skill Check—Interpret nutritional information on food labels.

Student Self-Assessment and Reflection:

1. Self-assess the brochure, *You Are What You Eat*.
2. Self-assess the camp menu, *Chow Down*.
3. Reflect on the extent to which you eat healthfully at the end of unit (compared with the beginning).

Figure 1.3 (continued)
3-Page Nutrition Example

Stage 3—Plan Learning Experiences

What sequence of teaching and learning experiences will equip students to engage with, develop, and demonstrate the desired understandings? Use the following sheet to list the key teaching and learning activities in sequence. Code each entry with the appropriate initials of the WHERETO elements.

1. Begin with an entry question (Can the foods you eat cause zits?) to hook students into considering the effects of nutrition on their lives. **H**

2. Introduce the Essential Questions and discuss the culminating unit performance tasks (Chow Down and Eating Action Plan). **W**

3. Note: Key vocabulary terms are introduced as needed by the various learning activities and performance tasks. Students read and discuss relevant selections from the Health textbook to support the learning activities and tasks. As an ongoing activity, students keep a chart of their daily eating and drinking for later review and evaluation. **E**

4. Present concept attainment lesson on the food groups. Then have students practice categorizing pictures of foods accordingly. **E**

5. Introduce the Food Pyramid and identify foods in each group. Students work in groups to develop a poster of the Food Pyramid containing cut-out pictures of foods in each group. Display the posters in the classroom or hallway. **E**

6. Give quiz on the food groups and Food Pyramid (matching format). **E**

7. Review and discuss the nutrition brochure from the USDA. Discussion question: Must everyone follow the same diet to be healthy? **R**

8. Working in cooperative groups, students analyze a hypothetical family's diet (deliberately unbalanced) and make recommendations for improved nutrition. Teacher observes and coaches students as they work. **E-2**

9. Have groups share their diet analyses and discuss as a class. **E, E-2** (Note: Teacher collects and reviews the diet analyses to look for misunderstandings needing instructional attention.)

10. Each student designs an illustrated nutrition brochure to teach younger children about the importance of good nutrition for healthy living and the problems associated with poor eating. This activity is completed outside of class. **E, T**

11. Students exchange brochures with members of their group for a peer assessment based on a criteria list. Allow students to make revisions based on feedback. **R, E-2**

12. Show and discuss the video, "Nutrition and You." Discuss the health problems linked to poor eating. **E**

13. Students listen to, and question, a guest speaker (nutritionist from the local hospital) about health problems caused by poor nutrition. **E**

14. Students respond to written prompt: Describe two health problems that could arise as a result of poor nutrition and explain what changes in eating could help to avoid them. (These are collected and graded by teacher.) **E-2**

15. Teacher models how to read and interpret food label information on nutritional values. Then have students practice using donated boxes, cans, and bottles (empty!). **E**

16. Students work independently to develop the three-day camp menu. Evaluate and give feedback on the camp menu project. Students self- and peer-assess their projects using rubrics. **E-2, T**

17. At the conclusion of the unit, students review their completed daily eating chart and self-assess the healthfulness of their eating. Have they noticed changes? Improvements? Do they notice changes in how they feel and their appearance? **E-2**

18. Students develop a personal "eating action plan" for healthful eating. These are saved and presented at upcoming student-involved parent conferences. **E-2, T**

19. Conclude the unit with student self-evaluation regarding their personal eating habits. Have each student develop a personal action plan for their "healthful eating" goal. **E-2, T**

way that a scoring rubric serves students. When presented to students before they begin their work, the rubric provides them with a performance target by identifying the important qualities toward which they should strive. Similarly, the Design Standards specify the qualities of effective units according to the Understanding by Design framework. Figure 1.4 (p. 28) presents the four UbD Design Standards with accompanying indicators.

The standards contribute to design work in three ways:

• *As a reference point during design*—Teachers can periodically check to see, for example, if the identified understandings are truly big and enduring, or if the assessment evidence is sufficient. Like a rubric, the questions serve as reminders of important design elements to include, such as a focus on Essential Questions.

• *For use in self-assessment and peer reviews of draft designs*—Teachers and peers can use the criteria to examine their draft units to identify needed refinements, such as using the facets to dig deeper into an abstract idea.

• *For quality control of completed designs*—The standards can then be applied by independent reviewers (e.g., curriculum committees) to validate the designs before their distribution to other teachers.

Our profession rarely subjects teacher-designed units and assessments to this level of critical review. Nonetheless, we have found structured peer reviews, guided by design standards, to be enormously beneficial—both to teachers and their designs (Wiggins, 1996, 1997). Participants in peer review sessions regularly comment on the value of sharing and discussing curriculum and assessment designs with colleagues. We believe that such sessions are a powerful approach to professional development, because the conversations focus on the heart of teaching and learning.

We cannot stress enough the importance of using design standards to regularly review curriculum—existing units and courses as well as new ones being developed. It is often difficult for educators, both novice and veteran, to get in the habit of self-assessing their designs against appropriate criteria. A prevailing norm in our profession seems to be, "If I work hard on planning, it must be good." The UbD Design Standards help to break that norm by providing a means for quality control. They help us validate our curriculum's strengths, while revealing aspects that need improvement.

In addition to using the UbD Design Standards for self-assessment, the quality of the curriculum product (unit plan, performance assessment, course design) is invariably enhanced when teachers participate in a structured peer review in which they examine one another's unit designs and share feedback and suggestions for improvement. Such "critical friend" reviews provide feedback to designers, help teachers internalize the qualities of good design, and offer opportunities to see alternate design models. ("Gee, I never thought about beginning a unit with a problem. I think I'll try that in my next unit.")

Figure 1.4
UbD Design Standards

Stage 1—To what extent does the design focus on the big ideas of targeted content?

Consider: Are . . .

○ The targeted understandings enduring, based on transferable, big ideas at the heart of the discipline and in need of uncoverage?

○ The targeted understandings framed by questions that spark meaningful connections, provoke genuine inquiry and deep thought, and encourage transfer?

○ The essential questions provocative, arguable, and likely to generate inquiry around the central ideas (rather than a "pat" answer)?

○ Appropriate goals (e.g., content standards, benchmarks, curriculum objectives) identified?

○ Valid and unit-relevant knowledge and skills identified?

Stage 2—To what extent do the assessments provide fair, valid, reliable, and sufficient measures of the desired results?

Consider: Are . . .

○ Students asked to exhibit their understanding through authentic performance tasks?

○ Appropriate criterion-based scoring tools used to evaluate student products and performances?

○ Various appropriate assessment formats used to provide additional evidence of learning?

○ The assessments used as feedback for students and teachers, as well as for evaluation?

○ Students encouraged to self-assess?

Stage 3—To what extent is the learning plan effective and engaging?

Consider: Will the students . . .

○ Know where they're going (the learning goals), why the material is important (reason for learning the content), and what is required of them (unit goal, performance requirements, and evaluative criteria)?

○ Be hooked—engaged in digging into the big ideas (e.g., through inquiry, research, problem solving, and experimentation)?

○ Have adequate opportunities to explore and experience big ideas and receive instruction to equip them for the required performances?

○ Have sufficient opportunities to rethink, rehearse, revise, and refine their work based upon timely feedback?

○ Have an opportunity to evaluate their work, reflect on their learning, and set goals?

Consider: Is the learning plan . . .

○ Tailored and flexible to address the interests and learning styles of all students?

○ Organized and sequenced to maximize engagement and effectiveness?

Overall Design—To what extent is the entire unit coherent, with the elements of all three stages aligned?

Design tools

In addition to the design standards, we have developed and refined a comprehensive set of design tools to support teachers and curriculum developers. This is hard work! We have found that an array of scaffolds—prompts, organizers, idea sheets, and examples—help educators produce higher-quality designs. A full set of these resources is available in the *UbD Professional Development Workbook*.

We think that a good template serves as an intelligent tool. It provides more than a place to write in ideas. It focuses and guides the designer's thinking throughout the design process to make high-quality work more likely. In practice, curriculum designers work from a copy of the template, supported by specific design tools and numerous filled-in examples of good unit designs. In this way, we practice what we preach with students; models and design standards are provided up front to focus designer performance from the start.[1]

But why do we refer to the template, design standards, and corresponding design tools as "intelligent"? Just as a physical tool (e.g., a telescope, an automobile, or a hearing aid) extends human capabilities, an intelligent tool enhances performance on cognitive tasks, such as the design of learning units. For example, an effective graphic organizer, such as a story map, helps students internalize the elements of a story in ways that enhance their reading and writing of stories. Likewise, by routinely using the template and design tools, users will likely develop a mental template of the key ideas presented in this book: the logic of backward design, thinking like an assessor, the facets of understanding, WHERETO, and design standards.

By embodying the Understanding by Design elements in tangible forms (i.e., the template and design tools), we seek to support educators in learning and applying these ideas. Thus, the design tools are like training wheels, providing a steadying influence during those periods of disequilibrium brought on by new ideas that may challenge established and comfortable habits. Once the key ideas of Understanding by Design are internalized, however, and regularly applied, the explicit use of the tools becomes unnecessary, just as the young bicycle rider sheds the training wheels after achieving balance and confidence.

> ### ▓ MISCONCEPTION ALERT!
>
> Though the three stages present a logic of design, it does not follow that this is a step-by-step process in actuality. As we argue in Chapter 11, don't confuse the logic of the final product with the messy process of design work. It doesn't matter exactly where you start or how you proceed, *as long as you end up with a coherent design* reflecting the logic of the three stages. The final outline of a smoothly flowing college lecture rarely reflects the back-and-forth (iterative) thought process that went into its creation.

Backward design in action with Bob James

Setting: *We are inside the head of Bob James, a 6th grade teacher at Newtown Middle School, as he begins to design a three-week unit on nutrition. His ultimate* *design will be the unit provided above in Figure 1.3. But Bob is new to UbD, so his design will unfold and be revised over time. Throughout the book we'll show his thinking—and rethinking—as he considers the full meaning of the template elements.*

Stage 1: *Identify desired results*

The template asks me to highlight the goals of the unit, and for me that means drawing upon our state standards. In reviewing our standards in health, I found three content standards on nutrition that are benchmarked to this age level:

- Students will understand essential concepts about nutrition.
- Students will understand elements of a balanced diet.
- Students will understand their own eating patterns and ways in which these patterns may be improved.

Using these standards as the starting point, I need to decide what I want my students to take away from the unit. Knowledge and skill are what I have always focused on: knowledge of the food pyramid, the ability to read labels in the store and at home, and so on. Although I've never deliberately thought about *understandings,* per se, I like the concept and think that it will help me focus my teaching and limited class time on the truly important aspects of this unit.

As I think about it, I guess what I'm really after has something to do with an understanding of the elements of good nutrition so students can plan a balanced diet for themselves and others. The big ideas have to do with nutrition and planning meals in a feasible way. Then, the important questions are, So, what is good for you? What isn't? How do you know? What makes it difficult to know and to eat right? (The good taste of junk food makes it difficult!)

This idea is clearly important, because planning nutritious menus is an authentic, lifelong need and a way to apply this knowledge. I'm still a little unclear about what "an understanding" means, though, in this context. I'll need to reflect further on what an understanding is and how it goes beyond specific knowledge and its use. The basic concepts of nutrition are fairly straightforward, after all, as are the skills of menu planning. Does anything in the unit require, then, any in-depth and deliberate *uncoverage*? Are there typical misunderstandings, for example, that I should more deliberately focus on?

Well, as I think about it, I have found that many students harbor the two misconceptions that if food is good for you, it must taste bad; and if it is sold in famous and popular places, it must be okay. One of my goals in this unit is to dispel these myths so that the students won't have an automatic aversion to healthy food and unwittingly eat too much unhealthy stuff. In terms of the potential for engagement—no problem there. Anything having to do with food is a winner with 10- and 11-year-olds. And there are some points to menu planning (such as balancing cost, variety, taste, and dietary needs) that are not at all obvious. This way of thinking about the unit will enable me to better focus on these points.

Stage 2: Determine acceptable evidence

This will be a bit of a stretch for me. Typically in a three- or four-week unit like this one, I give one or two quizzes; have a project, which I grade; and conclude with a unit test (generally multiple choice or matching). Even though this approach to assessment makes grading and justifying the grades fairly easy, I have always felt a bit uneasy that these assessments don't reflect the point of the unit and that the project grade sometimes has less to do with the key ideas and more to do with effort. I think I tend to test what is easy to test instead of assessing for my deeper goals, above and beyond nutritional facts. In fact, one thing that has always disturbed me is that the kids tend to focus on their grades rather than on their learning. Perhaps the way I've used the assessments—more for grading purposes than to help shape and document learning—has contributed somewhat to their attitude.

Now I need to think about what would serve as evidence of the ideas I'm focusing on. After reviewing some examples of performance tasks and discussing "application" ideas with my colleagues, I have decided tentatively on the following task:

> Because we have been learning about nutrition, the camp director at the outdoor education center has asked us to propose a nutritionally balanced menu for our three-day trip to the center later this year. Using the food pyramid guidelines and the nutrition facts on food labels, design a plan for three days, including three meals and three snacks (a.m., p.m., and campfire). Your goal: a tasty and nutritionally balanced menu.

I'm excited about this idea because it asks students to demonstrate what I really want them to take away from the unit. This task also links well with one of our unit projects: to analyze a hypothetical family's diet for a week and propose ways to improve their nutrition. With this task and project in mind, I can now use my quizzes to check students' knowledge of the food groups and food pyramid recommendations, and a lengthier test to check for their understanding of how a nutritionally deficient diet contributes to health problems. Hey! This is one of the better assessment plans I have designed for a unit, and I think that the task will motivate students as well as provide evidence of their understanding.

Stage 3: Plan learning experiences and instruction

This is my favorite part of planning—deciding what activities the students will do during the unit and what resources and materials we'll need for those activities. But according to what I'm learning about backward design, I'll need to think first about what essential knowledge and skills my students will need if they're going to be able to demonstrate in performance the understandings I'm after.

Well, they'll need to know about the different food groups and the types of foods found in each group so that they'll understand the USDA food pyramid recommendations. They'll also need to know about human nutritional needs for carbohydrates, protein, sugar, fat, salt, vitamins, and minerals, and about the various foods that provide them. They'll have to learn about the minimum daily requirements for these nutritional elements and about various health problems that arise from poor nutrition. In terms of skills, they'll have to learn how to read and interpret the nutrition-fact labels on foods and how to scale a recipe up or down, because these skills are necessary for their culminating project—planning healthy menus for camp.

Now for the learning experiences. I'll use resources that I've collected during the past several years—a pamphlet from the USDA on the food groups and the food pyramid recommendations; a wonderful video, "Nutrition for You"; and, of course, our health textbook (which I now plan to use selectively). As I have for the past three years, I'll invite the nutritionist from the local hospital to talk about diet and health and how to plan healthy menus. I've noticed that the kids really pay attention to a real-life user of information they're learning.

My teaching methods will follow my basic pattern—a blend of direct instruction, inductive methods, cooperative-learning group work, and individual activities.

Planning backward to produce this new draft has been helpful. I now can more clearly see and state what knowledge and skills are essential, given my goals for the unit. I'll be able to concentrate on the more important aspects of the topic (and relieve some guilt that I'm not covering everything). It's also interesting to realize that even though some sections of the textbook chapters on nutrition will be especially useful (for instance, the descriptions of health problems arising from poor nutrition), other sections are not as informative as other resources I'll now use (the brochure and the video). In terms of assessment, I now know more clearly what I need to assess using traditional quizzes and tests, and why the performance task and project are needed—to have students demonstrate their understanding. I'm getting a feel for backward design.

Comments on the design process

Notice that the process of developing this draft nutrition unit reveals four key aspects of backward design:

1. The assessments—the performance tasks and related sources of evidence—are thought through prior to the lessons being fully developed. The assessments serve as teaching targets for sharpening the focus of instruction and editing the past lesson plans, because they define in very specific terms what we want students to understand and be able to do. The teaching is then thought of as *enabling* performance. These assessments also guide decisions about what content needs to be emphasized versus that which is not really essential.

2. It is likely that familiar and favorite activities and projects will have to be further modified in light of the evidence needed for assessing targeted standards. For instance, if the apples unit described in the Introduction were planned using this backward design process, we would expect to see revisions in some of the activities to better support the desired results.

3. The teaching methods and resource materials are chosen last, with the teacher keeping in mind the work that students must produce to meet the standards. For example, rather than focusing on cooperative learning because it's a popular strategy, the question from a backward-design perspective becomes, What instructional strategies will be most effective in helping us reach our targets? Cooperative learning may or may not be the best approach, given the particular students and standards.

4. The role of the textbook may shift from being the primary resource to being a support. Indeed, the 6th grade teacher planning the nutrition unit realized the limitations of relying on the text if he is to meet his goals. Given other valuable resources (the USDA materials, the video, and the nutritionist), he no longer felt compelled to cover the book word for word.

This introductory look is intended to present a preliminary sketch of the big picture of a design approach. Bob James will be refining his unit plan (and changing his thinking a few times) as he gains greater insight into understanding, essential questions, valid assessment, and the related learning activities.

A preview

Figure 1.5 presents the key elements of the UbD approach and thus an outline of points to come in the book. In the following chapters we "uncover" this design process, examining its implications for the development and use of assessments, the planning and organization of curriculum, and the selection of powerful methods of teaching. But a few explanatory points about each column in Figure 1.5 are appropriate to prepare you for what is to come throughout the book.

The chart is best read from left to right, one row at a time, to see how the three stages of design might look in practice. An outline of the three-stage design process for each of the three basic elements (the desired results, the assessment evidence, and the learning plan) is highlighted in the column headings. Begin with a key design question; ponder how to narrow the possibilities through intelligent priorities (Design Considerations); self-assess, self-adjust, and finally critique each element of design against appropriate criteria (Filters); and end up with a product that meets appropriate design standards in light of the achievement target (What the Final Design Accomplishes).

In summary, backward design yields greater coherence among desired results, key performances, and teaching and learning experiences, resulting in better student performance—the purpose of design.

Figure 1.5
The UbD Design Matrix

Key Design Questions	Chapters of the Book	Design Considerations	Filters (Design Criteria)	What the Final Design Accomplishes
Stage 1 • What are worthy and appropriate results? • What are the key desired learnings? • What should students come away understanding, knowing, and able to do? • What big ideas can frame all these objectives?	• Chapter 3—Gaining Clarity on Our Goals • Chapter 4—The Six Facets of Understanding • Chapter 5—Essential Questions: Doorways to Understanding • Chapter 6—Crafting Understandings	• National standards • State standards • Local standards • Regional topic opportunities • Teacher expertise and interest	• Focused on big ideas and core challenges	• Unit framed around enduring understandings and essential questions, in relation to clear goals and standards
Stage 2 • What is evidence of the desired results? • In particular, what is appropriate evidence of the desired understanding?	• Chapter 7—Thinking like an Assessor • Chapter 8—Criteria and Validity	• Six facets of understanding • Continuum of assessment types	• Valid • Reliable • Sufficient	• Unit anchored in credible and useful evidence of the desired results
Stage 3 • What learning activities and teaching promote understanding, knowledge, skill, student interest, and excellence?	• Chapter 9—Planning for Learning • Chapter 10—Teaching for Understanding	• Research-based repertoire of learning and teaching strategies • Appropriate and enabling knowledge and skill	Engaging and effective, using the elements of WHERETO: • *Where* is it going? • *Hook* the students • *Explore* and equip • *Rethink* and revise • *Exhibit* and evaluate • *Tailor* to student needs, interests, and styles • *Organize* for maximum engagement and effectiveness	• Coherent learning activities and teaching that will evoke and develop the desired understandings, knowledge, and skill; promote interest; and make excellent performance more likely

Chapter 2

Understanding Understanding

The most characteristic thing about mental life, over and beyond the fact that one apprehends the events of the world around one, is that one constantly goes beyond the information given.
—Jerome Bruner, *Beyond the Information Given*, 1957, p. 218

Education. That which discloses to the wise and disguises from the foolish their lack of understanding.
—Ambrose Bierce, *The Devil's Dictionary*, 1881–1906

This book explores two different but related ideas: design and understanding. In the previous chapter we explored good design in general and what the template specifically calls for. But before we can go into depth about the template, we need to step back and consider the other strand of the book—understanding. Bob James was a bit confused about "understandings." His confusion turns out to be a fairly common problem. When we ask designers in workshops to identify desired understandings and thus to distinguish between desired "knowledge" and "understanding," they are often puzzled. What's the difference? What *is* understanding? And so we pause to consider a question that turns out to be essential: How well do we understand understanding? What is it we are after when we say we want students to understand this or that? Until now, we have written about understanding as if we fully understood what we were after. But as we shall see, the irony is that though we all claim as teachers to seek student understanding of the content, *we* may not adequately understand this goal. This may seem like an odd claim. Teachers knowingly aim for understanding every day, don't they? How can we not know what we are aiming for? Yet plenty of evidence suggests that "to understand" and "to teach for understanding" are ambiguous and slippery terms.

We see some of this conceptual uncertainty in the *Taxonomy of Educational Objectives: Cognitive Domain.* The book was written in 1956 by Benjamin Bloom and his colleagues to classify and clarify the range of possible intellectual objectives, from the cognitively easy to the difficult; it was meant to classify degrees of understanding, in effect. As the authors often note, the writing of the book was driven by persistent problems in testing: Just how should educational objectives or teacher goals be measured in light of the fact that there was (and is) no clear meaning of, or agreement about the meaning of, objectives such as "critical grasp of" and "thorough knowledge of"—phrases that have to be used by test developers?

In the introduction to the Taxonomy, Bloom (1956) and his colleagues refer to *understanding* as a commonly sought but ill-defined objective:

For example, some teachers believe their students should "really understand," others desire their students to "internalize knowledge," still others want their students to "grasp the core or essence." Do they all mean the same thing? Specifically, what does a student do who "really understands" which he does not do when he does not understand? Through reference to the Taxonomy . . . teachers should be able to define such nebulous terms. (p. 1)

Recall that when our health teacher, Bob James, was thinking about his nutrition unit (see Chapter 1), he seemed unsure about what an *understanding* was and how it differed from *knowledge*. In fact, two generations of curriculum writers have been warned to avoid the term *understand* in their frameworks as a result of the cautions in the Taxonomy. For example, in the *Benchmarks for Science Literacy* from the American Association for the Advancement of Science (AAAS), the authors succinctly describe the problem they faced in framing benchmarks for science teaching and assessing:

Benchmarks uses "know" and "know how" to lead into each set of benchmarks. The alternative would have been to use a finely graded series of verbs, including "recognize, be familiar with, appreciate, grasp, know, comprehend, understand," and others, each implying a somewhat greater degree of sophistication and completeness than the one before. The problem with the graded series is that different readers have different opinions of what the proper order is. (1993, p. 312)

Yet the idea of *understanding* is surely distinct from the idea of *knowing* something. We frequently say things like, "Well, he knows a lot of math, but he doesn't really understand its basis," or, "She knows the meaning of the words but doesn't understand the sentence." A further indication is that, 50 years after Bloom, many state standards now specify understandings separate from knowledge. Consider these examples from the California standards in science, which make the distinction explicit, with *knowledge* subsumed under the broader *understanding*:

Newton's laws predict the motion of most objects. As a basis for understanding this concept:

a. Students know how to solve problems that involve constant speed and average speed.

b. Students know that when forces are balanced, no acceleration occurs; thus an object continues to move at a constant speed or stays at rest (Newton's first law).

c. Students know how to apply the law F = ma to solve one-dimensional motion problems that involve constant forces (Newton's second law).

d. Students know that when one object exerts a force on a second object, the second object always exerts a force of equal magnitude and in the opposite direction (Newton's third law). . . .

Scientific progress is made by asking meaningful questions and conducting careful investigations. As a basis for understanding this concept and addressing the content in the other four strands, students should develop their own questions and perform investigations. Students will:

a. Select and use appropriate tools and technology (such as computer-linked probes, spreadsheets, and graphing calculators) to perform tests, collect data, analyze relationships, and display data.

b. Identify and communicate sources of unavoidable experimental error.

c. Identify possible reasons for inconsistent results, such as sources of error or uncontrolled conditions. . . .

Although we might quibble as to whether the statement "Scientific progress is made by asking meaningful questions and conducting careful investigations" is a *concept,* the implication of the standard is clear enough: An understanding is a mental construct, an abstraction made by the human mind to make sense of many distinct pieces of knowledge. The standard further suggests that if students *understand,* then they can provide evidence of that understanding by showing that they know and can do certain specific things.

Understanding as meaningful inferences

But how are understanding and knowledge related? The standard still leaves the relationship murky in the phrase "As a basis for understanding this concept . . ." Is understanding simply a more complex form of knowledge, or is it something separate from but related to content knowledge?

Making matters worse is our tendency to use the terms *know, know how,* and *understand* interchangeably in everyday speech. Many of us would say that we "know" that Newton's Laws predict the motion of objects. And we may say we "know how" to fix our car and "understand" how to fix our car as if the two statements expressed the same idea. Our usage has a developmental aspect, too: What we once struggled to "understand" we say we now "know." The implication is that something that once required a chain of reasoning to grasp hold of no longer does: We just "see it."

Mindful of our tendency to use the words *understand* and *know* interchangeably, what worthy conceptual distinctions should we safeguard in talking about the difference between knowledge and understanding? Figure 2.1 presents some useful distinctions between the terms.

John Dewey (1933) summarized the idea most clearly in *How We Think.* Understanding is the result of facts acquiring meaning for the learner:

Figure 2.1

Knowledge Versus Understanding

Knowledge	Understanding
• The facts	• The meaning of the facts
• A body of coherent facts	• The "theory" that provides coherence and meaning to those facts
• Verifiable claims	• Fallible, in-process theories
• Right or wrong	• A matter of degree or sophistication
• I know something to be true	• I understand why it is, what makes it knowledge
• I respond on cue with what I know	• I judge when to and when not to use what I know

To grasp the meaning of a thing, an event, or a situation is to see it in its relations to other things: to see how it operates or functions, what consequences follow from it, what causes it, what uses it can be put to. In contrast, what we have called the brute thing, the thing without meaning to us, is something whose relations are not grasped. . . . The relation of means-consequence is the center and heart of all understanding. (pp. 137, 146)

Consider an analogy to highlight these similarities and differences: tiling a floor with only black and white tiles. All our factual knowledge is found in the tiles. Each tile has definite traits that can be identified with relative precision and without much argument. Each tile is a fact. An understanding is a pattern visible across many tiles. There are many different patterns, some of them encompassing many or few tiles. Aha! Suddenly we see that small patterns can be grouped into sets of larger patterns—that was not apparent to us at first. And you may see the patterns differently than we do, so we argue about which is the "best" way to describe what we see. The pattern is not really "there" in an important sense, then. We infer it; we project it onto the tiles. The person laying the tiles merely positioned a black one next to a white one; he need not have had any pattern in mind: We may be the first to have seen it.

Let's move the analogy closer to intellectual life. The words on the page are the "facts" of a story. We can look up each word in the dictionary and say we know it. But the meaning of the story remains open for discussion and argument. The "facts" of any story are the agreed-upon details; the understanding of the story is what we mean by the phrase "reading between the lines." (The author may not have "meant" what we can insightfully "infer"—just as in the tiling example; this is one of the debates in modern literary criticism—which view, if any, is privileged.) A well-known example from literacy studies makes the point elegantly:

First you arrange things into groups. Of course one pile may be enough, depending on how much there is to do; but some things definitely need to be separated from the others. A mistake here can be expensive; it is better to do too few things at once than too many. The procedure does not take long; when it is finished, you arrange the things into different groups again, so that they can be put away where they belong. (Bransford & Johnson, 1972, in Chapman, 1993, p. 6)

As a writer referring to this passage notes in a book on critical reading skills,

There is a point which varies depending on the individual reader, at which readers who monitor their own understanding realize that they are not "getting it" even though they know the meanings of all the words, the individual sentences make sense, and there is a coherent sequence of events. . . . At that point, critical readers who want to understand typically slow down, sharpen their attention, and try different reading strategies. (Chapman, 1993, p. 7)

The first passage is a vague account of doing laundry. More generally, the goal in understanding is to take whatever you are given to produce or find something of significance—to use what we have in memory but to go beyond the facts and approaches to use them *mindfully*. By contrast, when we want students to "know" the key events of medieval history, to be effective touch typists, or to be competent players of specific musical pieces, the focus is on a set of facts, skills, and procedures that must be "learned by *heart*"—a revealing phrase!

Understanding thus involves meeting a challenge for thought. We encounter a mental problem, an experience with puzzling or no meaning. We use judgment to draw upon our repertoire of skill and knowledge to solve it. As Bloom (1956) put it, understanding is the ability to marshal skills and facts wisely and appropriately, through effective application, analysis, synthesis, and evaluation. Doing something correctly, therefore, is not, by itself, evidence of understanding. It might have been an accident or done by rote. To understand is to have done it in the right way, often reflected in being able to explain *why* a particular skill, approach, or body of knowledge is or is not appropriate in a particular situation.

Understanding as transferability

It would be impossible to over-estimate the educational importance of arriving at conceptions: that is, meanings that are general because applicable in a great variety of different instances in spite of their difference. . . . They are known points of reference by which we get our bearings when we are plunged into the strange and unknown. . . . Without this conceptualizing, nothing is gained that can be carried over to the better understanding of new experiences.
—John Dewey, *How We Think,* 1933, p. 153

Baking without an understanding of the ingredients and how they work is like baking blindfold[ed] . . . sometimes everything works. But when it doesn't you have to guess at how to change it. . . . It is this understanding which enables me to both creative and successful.
—Rose Levy Berenbaum, *The Cake Bible,* 1988, p. 469

To know *which* fact to use *when* requires more than another fact. It requires understanding—insight into essentials, purpose, audience, strategy, and tactics. Drill and direct instruction can develop discrete skills and facts into automaticity (knowing "by heart"), but they cannot make us truly able.

Understanding is about *transfer,* in other words. To be truly able requires the ability to transfer what we have learned to new and sometimes confusing settings. The ability to transfer our knowledge and skill effectively involves the capacity to take what we know and use it creatively, flexibly, fluently, in different settings or problems, on our own. Transferability is not mere plugging in of previously learned knowledge and skill. In Bruner's famous phrase, understanding is about "going beyond the information given"; we can create new knowledge and arrive at further understandings if we have learned with understanding some key ideas and strategies.

What is transfer, and why does it matter? We are expected to take what we learned in one lesson and be able to apply it to other, related but different situations. Developing the ability to transfer one's learning is key to a good education (see Bransford, Brown, & Cocking, 2000, pp. 51ff). It is an essential ability because teachers can only help students learn a relatively small number of ideas, examples, facts, and skills in the entire field of study; so we need to help them transfer their inherently limited learning to many other settings, issues, and problems.

Consider a simple example from sports. When we grasp the idea that on defense we need to close up available space for the offense, we can use that understanding to adapt to almost *any* move members of the other team make, not just be limited to the one or two positionings we were taught in a three-on-three drill. We can handle entire classes of offensive problems, not just familiar instances. Failure to grasp and apply this idea in context is costly:

> *"When I got the ball in midfield and I started dribbling," said Lavrinenko, the [NCAA men's soccer] championship tournament's outstanding offensive player, "I was looking to pass right away. But my teammates opened up space, and I continued running. When I played the ball to Alexei, 2 players went to him and opened up more space for me."* (New York Times, *December 13, 1999, sec. D, p. 2)*

And because the big idea of "constraining offensive space" *transfers* across sports, it is equally applicable in soccer, basketball, hockey, water polo, football, and lacrosse. The same is true in math or reading: To get beyond mere rote learning and recall, we have to be taught and be assessed on an ability to see patterns, so that we come to see many "new" problems we encounter as variants of problems and techniques we are familiar with. That requires an education in how to problem solve using big ideas and transferable strategies, not merely how to plug in specific facts or formulas.

Big ideas are essential because they provide the basis for the transfer. You must learn that a single strategy underlies all possible combinations of specific moves and settings, for example. The strategy is to get someone on your team open, using various moves and fakes—regardless of what the other team does or whether it looks exactly like what you did in practice. In academics, you must learn to transfer intellectual knowledge and skill:

> *Transfer is affected by the degree to which people learn with understanding rather than merely memorize sets of facts or follow a fixed set of procedures. . . . Attempts to cover too many topics too quickly may hinder learning and subsequent transfer. (Bransford, Brown, & Cocking, 2000, pp. 55, 58)*

This is an old idea, famously framed by Whitehead (1929) almost 100 years ago in his complaint about "inert ideas" in education:

> *In training a child to activity of thought, above all things we must beware of what I will call "inert ideas"—that is to say, ideas that are merely received into the mind without being utilized or tested, or thrown into fresh combinations. . . . Education with inert ideas is not only useless: it is above all things, harmful. . . . Let the main ideas which are introduced be few and important, and let them be thrown into every combination possible. (pp. 1–2)*

In reading, we may not have previously read *this* book by *this* author, but if we understand "reading" and "romantic poetry," we transfer our prior knowledge and skill without much difficulty. If we learned to read by repeated drill and memorization only, and by thinking of reading as only decoding, making sense of a new book can be a monumental challenge. The same is true for advanced readers at the college level, by the way. If we learned to "read" a philosophy text by a literal reading, supplemented by what the professor said about it, and if we have not learned to actively ask and answer questions of meaning as we read, reading the next book will be no easier. (For more on this topic, see Adler and Van Doren, 1940.)

Transfer is the essence of what Bloom and his colleagues meant by application. The challenge is not to "plug in" what was learned, from memory, but modify, adjust, and adapt an (inherently general) idea to the particulars of a situation:

> *Students should not be able to solve the new problems and situations merely by remembering the solution to or the precise method of solving a similar problem in class. It is not a new problem or situation if it is exactly like the others solved in class except that new quantities or symbols are used. . . . It is a new problem or situation if the student has not been given instruction or help on a given problem and must do some of the following. . . . 1. The statement of the problem must be modified in some way before it can be attacked. . . . 2. The statement of the problem must be put in the form of some model before the student can bring the generalizations previously learned to bear on it. . . . 3. The statement of the problem requires the student to search through memory for relevant generalizations. (Bloom, Madaus, & Hastings, 1981, p. 233)*

Knowledge and skill, then, are necessary elements of understanding, but not sufficient in themselves. Understanding requires more: the ability to thoughtfully and actively "do" the work with discernment, as well as the ability to self-assess, justify, and critique such "doings." Transfer involves figuring out which knowledge and skill matters *here* and often adapting what we know to address the challenge at hand.

Here's an amusing transfer task to illustrate the point one more time. See if you can use your knowledge of French pronunciation and English rhymes to "translate" the following song. Say it out loud, at a normal speaking speed:

Oh, Anne, doux
But. Cueilles ma chou.

Trille fort,
Chatte dort.

Faveux Sikhs,
Pie coupe Styx.

Sève nette,
Les dèmes se traitent.

N'a ne d'haine,
Écoute, fée daine.[1]

All of the cases we've discussed here illustrate the importance of confronting students with a real problem for thought if understanding is to be called for and awakened. This is very different from giving students lessons and tests that merely require taking in and recalling from memory, based on highly cued exercises in which learners simply plug in what is unambiguously required. (See Chapters 6 through 8 for further discussions on crafting understandings and meaningful assessments.)

The failure of even our best students to transfer their learning is evident in many areas but is most striking in mathematics. Consider the following examples of test items, all of which are testing the same idea (in each case, approximately *two-thirds* of the tested students did not correctly answer the question):

From the New York State Regents Exam:
To get from his high school to his home, Jamal travels 5.0 miles east and then 4.0 miles north. When Sheila goes to her home from the same high school, she travels 8.0 miles east and 2.0 miles south. What is the measure of the shortest distance, to the nearest tenth of a mile, between Jamal's home and Sheila's home? (The use of the accompanying grid is optional.)

From the NAEP 12th grade mathematics test:
What is the distance between the points (2,10) and (-4, 2) in the xy plane?

☐ 6   ☐ 14
☐ 8   ☐ 18
☐ 10

From a *Boston Globe* article on the Massachusetts MCAS 10th grade math scores:
The hardest question on the math section, which just 33 percent got right, asked students to calculate the distance between two points. It was a cinch—if students knew that they could plot the points and use the Pythagorean

theorem, a well-known formula to calculate the hypotenuse of a right triangle if the lengths of two legs are given. The sixth-hardest math question, which only 41 percent of students got right, also required use of the Pythagorean theorem. "It seems applying the Pythagorean theorem was a weakness for kids," said William Kendall, director of math for the Braintree public schools. "These weren't straightforward Pythagorean theorem questions. They had to do a little bit more." (Vaishnav, 2003)

All three problems require students to transfer their understanding of the Pythagorean theorem to a new situation. It is likely that most students in the United States could not do it, despite the fact that *every* set of state standards identifies a grasp of the Pythagorean theorem as a key desired result.

We can apply *our* understanding to this news without too much difficulty, based on what has been said thus far. We surmise that the $A^2 + B^2 = C^2$ theorem is taught as a fact, a rule for making certain calculations when confronted with a known right triangle and simple tasks. Remove a few blatant cues, however, and students cannot transfer their learning to perform with understanding. Is it any wonder, then, that students do not *understand* what they supposedly *know?* And what few educators seem to realize, therefore, is that drilling students for state tests is a *failing* strategy.

Understanding as a noun

Note again that the word *understand(ing)* has a verb meaning and a noun meaning. *To understand* a topic or subject is to be able to *use* (or "apply," in Bloom's sense) knowledge and skill wisely and effectively. *An understanding* is the successful result of trying to understand—the resultant grasp of an *unobvious* idea, an inference that makes meaning of many discrete (and perhaps seemingly insignificant) elements of knowledge.

A genuine understanding involves another kind of transfer. We go beyond what we see, using big ideas, to make meaning of it, as Dewey noted in the quotation from *How We Think* cited earlier. "Oh, that's just like what we saw when the pioneers headed west!" a student excitedly realizes, when considering 20th-century immigration. That's the kind of transfer we seek! The challenge is to make it more likely *by design* rather than by luck or by natural disposition. With deliberate and explicit instruction in how to transfer (and assessments that constantly demand such transfer), the learner must take what were initially bits of knowledge with no clear structure or power and come to see them as part of a larger, more meaningful, and more useful system. Without lessons designed to bring ideas to life, concepts such as honor, manifest destiny, or the water cycle remain empty phrases to be memorized, depriving learners of the realization that ideas have power.

Here is a link, then, between the discussion in Chapter 1 on priorities in design and the specific goal of student understanding. Designing around big ideas makes learning more effective and efficient. As the authors of *How People Learn* note,

> *Teaching specific topics or skills without making clear their context in the broader fundamental structure of a field of knowledge is uneconomical. . . . An understanding of fundamental principles and ideas appears to be the main road to adequate transfer of training. To understand something as a specific instance of a more general case—which is what understanding a more fundamental structure means—is to have learned not only a specific thing but also a model for understanding other things like it that one may encounter. (Bransford, Brown, & Cocking, 2000, pp. 25, 31)*

Transfer must be the aim of all teaching in school—it is not an option—because when we teach, we can address only a relatively small sample of the entire subject matter. All teachers have said to themselves after a lesson, "Oh, if we only had more time! This is just a drop in the bucket." We can never have enough time. Transfer is our great and difficult mission because we need to put students in a position to learn far more, on their own, than they can ever learn from us.

Paradoxically, transfer heads in the opposite direction from "new" knowledge. An education for understanding asks us to more closely examine prior knowledge and the assumptions by which we claim something to be knowledge. Socrates is the model here. He questioned knowledge claims in order to understand and learn far more. When we are helped to ask certain questions—Why is that so? Why do we think that? What justifies such a view? What's the evidence? What's the argument? What is being assumed?—we learn a different kind of powerful transfer: the ability to grasp what makes knowledge *knowledge* rather than mere belief, hence putting us in a far better position to increase our knowledge and understanding.

The Expert Blind Spot

> Teaching specific topics or skills without making clear their context in the broader fundamental structure of a field of knowledge is uneconomical.
> —Jerome Bruner, *The Process of Education,* 1960, p. 31

Understanding the importance of transfer can help us make sense, then, of those educators, like Bruner, who claim that typical coverage is "uneconomical." How can he say this? It seems so manifestly false: Teaching for understanding is perhaps more *effective,* but how can it possibly be more *efficient?* Can't we address far more content through didactic teaching and textbook coverage than we can by setting up inquiry-based work to help students come to deeper understanding of the material on their own?

But this confuses the *teaching* with the *learning.* Consider Bruner's three reasons for why a traditional coverage approach is uneconomical in the long run:

Such teaching makes it exceedingly difficult for the student to generalize from what he has learned to what he will encounter later. In the second place, [such] learning . . . has little reward in terms of intellectual excitement. . . . Third, knowledge one has acquired without sufficient structure to tie it together is knowledge that is likely to be forgotten. An unconnected set of facts has a pitiably short half-life in memory. (Bruner, 1960, p. 31)

In other words, we as educators fail to understand understanding when we think that coverage works. What we call the Expert Blind Spot is hard at work, causing us to confuse what we (or textbook authors) talk about with the active meaning-making required by the learner to grasp and use meaning. This habitual response by so many of us amounts to saying, "If I cover it clearly, they will 'get it' and be able to call upon it in the future. The more I cover, therefore, the more they will learn, and the better they'll do on the tests."

What we hope you see by the book's end, however, is that this widely held assumption is false; the "yield" from coverage is quite low for most students:

More than 30 years ago, medical educators conducted a study on what first-year medical students remembered of the thousands of new terms that they'd memorized in their first-year gross anatomy course. They were tested and retested over time. The curve that matched most closely to their forgetting of gross anatomy was the same shape as discovered in Ebbinghaus's classic study of memory for nonsense syllables a century ago. *The publication of data like these made a mark in the world of medical education. The teaching of anatomy has since changed radically in schools of medicine. (Shulman, 1999, p. 13 [emphasis added])*

To cover everything is like quickly talking through a connect-the-dots puzzle in which the teacher further confuses students into thinking that understandings are merely more dots to be added to the page, thereby causing the picture to be even less clear and more confusing than it might be. Coverage leaves students with no sense of the whole that seems so obvious to the expert—all but the few most able students will get lost, and perhaps alienated.

Teachers do not optimize performance, even on external tests, by covering everything superficially. Students end up forgetting or misunderstanding *far more than is necessary,* so that reteaching is needed throughout the school experience. (How often have you said to your students, "My goodness, didn't they teach you that in grade X?") So we end up with what we see in so many schools (as verified by NAEP test results): Students in general can do low-level tasks but are universally weak in higher-order work that requires transfer.

The research on learning (considered in greater detail in Chapter 13) merely supports the sobering truth of common sense: If learning is to endure in a flexible, adaptable way for future use, coverage cannot work. It leaves us with only easily confused or easily forgotten facts, definitions, and formulas to plug into rigid questions that look just like the ones covered. Furthermore, we have thereby made it far more difficult for students to learn the "same" things in more sophisticated and fluent ways later. They will be completely puzzled by and often resistant to the need to rethink earlier knowledge. In short, as Lee

Shulman, president of the Carnegie Center for the Advancement of Teaching, put it so well, conventional teaching abets the three "pathologies of mislearning: we forget, we don't understand that we misunderstand, and we are unable to use what we learned. I have dubbed these conditions amnesia, fantasia, and inertia" (Shulman, 1999, p. 12).

Our analysis thus far suggests, then, the need for three types of "uncoverage" in designing and teaching for understanding to avoid forgetfulness, misconception, and lack of transfer:

• Uncovering students' potential misunderstandings (through focused questions, feedback, diagnostic assessment)

• Uncovering the questions, issues, assumptions, and gray areas lurking underneath the black and white of surface accounts

• Uncovering the core ideas at the heart of understanding a subject, ideas that are not obvious—and perhaps are counterintuitive or baffling—to the novice

The evidence of understanding

> What differentiates revolutionary thinkers from non-revolutionary
> ones is almost never a greater knowledge of the facts. Darwin knew
> far less about the various species he collected on the *Beagle* voyage than
> did experts back in England who classified these organisms for him.
> Yet expert after expert missed the revolutionary significance of what Darwin
> had collected. Darwin, who knew less, somehow understood more.
> —Frank J. Sulloway, *Born to Rebel*, 1996, p. 20

If understanding is about making meaning of facts and transferring knowledge to other problems, tasks, and domains, what does such understanding (or lack of it) look like? What should we be seeing if our students are getting better at understanding what they are learning? To pose this question is to shift from talking about our aims to talking about the evidence of whether our aims have been met.

The Sulloway comment about Darwin suggests one line of inquiry. Consider the words we use in describing understanding at the highest levels of research. We often describe understanding as "deep" or "in depth" as opposed to superficial knowledge. You have to "dig" below the "surface" (i.e., the "cover") to "uncover" unobvious "core" insights. Understanding "takes time and practice." Understandings are "hard won," not immediate—maybe even overlooked or unseen by those with lots of knowledge, as Sulloway suggests. The emphasis in all these connotations is on getting below the surface, to the hidden gems of insight. We cannot *cover* concepts and expect them thereby to be understood; we have to *uncover* their value—the fact that concepts are the results of inquiry and argument.

Notice, then, the difference in the two questions at the heart of grappling with goals related to understanding (and all educational goals more generally) via backward design—the questions for the first two of the three stages:

Stage 1: What should students come away understanding?

Stage 2: What will count as evidence of that understanding?

The first question concerns important ideas about content and what should be learned. It asks the designer to be specific about what the student should take away, given the ideas, facts, and skills encountered. (Specifying the understandings we seek is surprisingly difficult, as we discuss in Chapter 6.) The second question is different. It doesn't speak to what should be learned; it concerns acceptable embodiment of those goals: What constitutes appropriate performance and products—output—from students of that learning, determined through assessment.

The second question actually encompasses distinct questions that make up the second stage of backward design:

• Where should we look for evidence? What is the *type* of student work we need to see done well, given the stated standard?

• What should we look for specifically in student performance, regardless of the particular approach, for us to judge the degree to which the student understands?

Loosely speaking, the first question about the evidence involves a design standard for assessment of the work (i.e., what are valid tasks, tests, observations?), and the second question about the evidence concerns the actual evaluation of the work produced, via rubrics or other criteria-related guidelines.

The argument for backward design is predicated on the view that we are not likely to achieve our target of understanding—however we define the term—unless we are clear about what counts as *evidence* of that understanding. And the more we ask that nitty-gritty assessment question, the more many teachers come to

> ### ■ MISCONCEPTION ALERT!
>
> A *standard* is different from a *performance indicator*. A standard represents a goal and belongs in Stage 1. A performance indicator, such as those found often in bulleted lists under state content standards, represents possible assessment evidence. Making matters more confusing, sometimes the standards also refer to learning activities like those we would put in Stage 3. (See *standard* in the Glossary.)

understand that they may not have adequately understood understanding.

Why might we be unsure about what constitutes good evidence of understanding? Because the evidence we tend to focus on or that stands out more readily can easily mislead us if we are not careful. When students provide the answer we seek, it is easy to conflate such recall with understanding. Bloom and his colleagues (1956) remind us of the distinction when they recount a famous story about John Dewey:

Almost everyone has had the experience of being unable to answer a question involving recall when the question is stated in one form, and then having little difficulty . . . when the question is stated in another form. This is well illustrated by John Dewey's story in which he asked a class, "What would you find if you dug a hole in the earth?" Getting no response, he repeated the question; again he obtained nothing but silence. The teacher chided Dr. Dewey, "You're asking the wrong question." Turning to the class, she asked, "What is the state of the center of the earth?" The class replied in unison, "Igneous fusion." (p. 29)

The story beautifully illustrates the need to distinguish the content goal from the evidence, as well as the need to stress transferability in the requirements for evidence. Children cannot be said to understand their own answer, even though it is correct, if they can only answer a question phrased just so. Furthermore, they will not be able to use what they "know" on any test or challenge that frames the same question differently, as apparently happened in the state tests mentioned earlier.

Getting evidence of understanding means crafting assessments to evoke transferability: finding out if students can take their learning and use it wisely, flexibly, creatively. The authors of the Taxonomy note, for example, that "real" knowledge involves using learning in new ways. They call this "intellectual ability" and distinguish it from "knowledge" based on recall and scripted use. Similarly, David Perkins in the book *Teaching for Understanding* defines understanding as "the ability to think and act flexibly with what one knows . . . a flexible performance capability," as opposed to rote recall or "plugging in" of answers (Wiske, 1998, p. 40). A person who has understanding can cope far better than others with ambiguous—that is, real-world—challenges in which what is required does not come packaged as a straightforward cue to stimulate a single response. (Recall the vignette in the Introduction about the class valedictorian who admitted a lack of understanding despite high marks on tests of recall.)

Evidence of understanding that is transferable involves assessing for students' capacity to use their knowledge thoughtfully and to apply it effectively in diverse settings—that is, to *do* the subject. As the authors of *How People Learn* (Bransford, Brown, & Cocking, 2000) write,

Students' abilities to transfer what they have learned to new situations provides an important index of adaptive, flexible learning. . . . Many approaches to instruction look equivalent when the only measure of learning is memory. . . . Instructional differences become more apparent when evaluated from the perspective of how well the learning transfers to new problems and settings. (p. 235)

Students develop flexible understanding of when, where, why, and how to use their knowledge to solve new problems if they learn how to extract underlying principles and themes from their learning exercises. (p. 224 [emphasis added])

The point is nothing new. Bloom and his colleagues (1956) made the same point about "application" in the Taxonomy 50 years ago. An assessment of application had to involve a novel task, requiring transfer; and it ideally involved contextualized and practical use of ideas:

If the situations . . . are to involve application as we are defining it here, then they must either be situations new to the student or situations containing new elements. . . . Ideally we are seeking a problem which will test the extent to which an individual has learned to apply the abstraction in a practical way. (p. 125)

Evidence of understanding requires that we test quite differently, then. We need to see evidence of students' ability to "extract" understandings and apply them in situated problems, in performance—something quite different from merely seeing if they can recall and plug in the underlying principles the teacher or textbook gave them.

This requires us to anchor our assessments in prototypical performances in each area, success at which indicates understanding; for example, the ability to design a science experiment, debug it, and revise it in order to determine the chemical content of a substance; the ability to use the facts and skills learned in history to write a credible narrative about a period in local history. (We refer to these two examples as two of many "core tasks" in a field of study, and we propose that curriculum frameworks and programs be designed around such core tasks, along with the big ideas. For a more detailed discussion of core tasks, see Chapters 7 and 12.) We need to see if students with understandably limited ability can nonetheless transfer—that is, recognize what in their repertoire *might* be useful *here,* in this novel situation, and use it effectively. Thus, we would use far fewer narrow prompts that are intended to elicit the "correct" answer to a familiar question.

The "igneous fusion" example is extreme, but the problem strikes home more than most of us may see or care to admit. We are often too ready to attribute understanding when we see correct and intelligent-sounding answers on our own tests. What may trip us up more than we realize is *apparent* understanding, in other words. And that difficulty is likely exacerbated in a world of high-stakes testing and grading. For as long as education promotes a cat-and-mouse game whereby students have incentive to both please us and *appear* to understand what they are supposed to learn (irrespective of whether they do or not), the challenge of assessing for real understanding becomes greater.

In short, we must be careful: It doesn't matter how we term the difference between knowing and understanding as long as we safeguard the real difference. What we call *understanding* is not a matter of mere semantics. It is a matter of conceptual clarity whereby we distinguish between a borrowed expert opinion and an internalized flexible idea. If our assessments are too superficial and fact-centered, we may miss the distinction in the evidence we collect. It does not matter in the end what we call understanding-related targets, but it matters greatly that we safeguard the distinction between "understand" and "know the right answer when prompted." What matters is that we grasp the challenge of assessing for transfer.

We have to be sharper at specifying what *kinds* of student work and assessment evidence are required if we are to judge a student as really understanding. The authors of the AAAS *Benchmarks for Science Literacy* (1993) cited earlier say that they decided against specifying action verbs or observable behaviors to clarify what kinds of evidence were required to reveal understanding, because "the choice among them is arbitrary" and using particular verbs "would be limiting and might imply a unique performance that was not intended" (pp. 312–313).

Although we concede that there is no unique or inherently perfect assessment task for an understanding target, certain kinds of challenges are more appropriate than others. Knowing what kinds of assessments embody the standards is precisely what many teachers need. Recall that this is why Bloom's Taxonomy was written in the first place. Without specificity concerning what counts as appropriate evidence for meeting the standards, a teacher might well be satisfied by a factual test of knowledge, whereas only a complex piece of inquiry and defense of methods and result will truly do justice to the standard.

If "correct" answers may yield inadequate evidence of understanding, what should we do to make our assessments better distinguish between real and apparent understanding? Before we answer that question, we must deal with another problem first: Sometimes a correct answer hides *misunderstanding*. How is *that* possible? And what are the implications for assessment of understanding? The irony is that we can gain significant insight into designing, assessing, and teaching for understanding by considering the phenomenon of misunderstanding.

Student *mis*understanding and what we can learn from it

Somehow, well-intentioned, able, and attentive students can take away lessons that we never intended. What are we complaining about when we say of students, "They know all the facts, but they put them together all wrong" or, "They just aren't thinking about what they are saying"? *The Catcher in the Rye* is a fixture of high school English courses in the United States, for example, yet many students come away believing the book to be about Holden's "excellent adventure" (to borrow from a recent movie title), the larklike days in the life of a hooky-playing prep school student. Somehow, the fact that Holden is in great emotional pain—and tells the story from his psychiatric hospital bed—is unseen by many students. Similarly, in mathematics, many elementary students struggle mightily with the multiplication of fractions, given the oddity of the answers being smaller than the numbers they started with. Or consider the great challenge of reading: Simple decoding is not so simple. We pronounce "lose" as "loze" and the teacher tells us we are mistaken. But we thought we understood the rule! Why *isn't* the pronunciation of "lose" consistent with the long-vowel rule about words that end in a consonant and *e* (e.g., close, doze, home)?

Misunderstanding is not ignorance, therefore. It is the mapping of a working idea in a plausible but incorrect way in a new situation. Here are some examples:

• One of our children asked: "Dad, are Spanish and English using the same words, but just pronouncing them differently?"

• The same child complained a few years later, "How can 4.28 + 2.72 = 7? Seven isn't a decimal!"

• A high school history student asked her teacher quietly at the end of a unit, "So just what *did* Louisiana purchase?"

• An elementary teacher reported the irritation of one of her 4th grade students at not ever seeing lines of longitude and latitude as she flew cross-country with her family.

• A very bright and learned boy, with advanced placement science courses in his background, thought "error" in science was a function of avoidable mistakes, rather than a principle inherent in the enterprise of induction.

Paradoxically, you have to have knowledge and the ability to transfer in order to misunderstand things.

Thus evidence of misunderstanding is incredibly valuable to teachers, not a mere mistake to be corrected. It signifies an attempted and plausible but unsuccessful transfer. The challenge is to reward the try without reinforcing the mistake or dampening future transfer attempts. In fact, many teachers not only fail to see the value in the feedback of student misunderstanding, they are somewhat threatened or irritated by it. A teacher who loses patience with students who don't "get" the lesson is, ironically, failing to understand—the Expert Blind Spot again. For *attentive* students not to "get" it is to show us that what we thought was clear was really not so. For some teachers, perpetual student misunderstanding is therefore threatening, understandably, because it seems to call into question our methods and implied goals. What the naïve teacher may be overlooking, of course, is that the big ideas are rarely obvious. Indeed, they are often counterintuitive, as we noted in Chapter 1. A word to the wise, then: If you hear yourself saying to a class, "But it's so obvious!" you are most likely falling prey to the Expert Blind Spot! Take time to ponder: Hmmm, what is not obvious to the novices here? What am I taking for granted that is easily misunderstood? Why did they draw the conclusion they did?

Making the matter of greater urgency is the fact that research over the past 20 years confirms the surprising depth and breadth of the phenomenon. Many students, even the best and most advanced, can *seem* to understand their work (as revealed by tests and in-class discussion) only to later reveal significant misunderstanding of what they "learned" when follow-up questions to probe understanding are asked or application of learning is required. Indeed, it is not only our view but also the view of leading cognitive researchers that ferreting out student conceptions and misconceptions and being mindful of them when designing learning is key to better results. (A summary of the research on learning and teaching for understanding is presented in Chapter 13.) Howard Gardner, David Perkins, and their Harvard colleagues at Project Zero have summarized these findings eloquently and thoroughly in the past decade, though the misconception research goes back to work done in science education in the 1970s. As Gardner (1991) explains in summing up the research,

[What] an extensive research literature now documents is that an ordinary degree of understanding is routinely missing in many, perhaps most students. It is reasonable to expect a college student to be able to apply in new context a law of physics, or a proof in geometry, or the concept in history of which she has just demonstrated acceptable mastery in her class. If, when the circumstances of testing are slightly altered, the sought-after competence can no longer be documented, then understanding—in any reasonable sense of the term—has simply not been achieved. (p. 6)

Testing of even a conventional kind can provide evidence of such failures to understand if the tests are designed with misunderstanding in mind. In the Introduction we noted the NAEP math example in which a large minority of students answered "32, remainder 12" buses. Consider this result more generally. Most U.S. teenagers study Algebra I and get passing grades. Yet NAEP (1988) results show that only 5 percent of U.S. adolescents perform well at tasks requiring higher-order use of Algebra I knowledge. The Third International Mathematics and Science Study (TIMSS, 1998) reached a similar conclusion for science in one of the most exhaustive studies to date (*Trenton Times,* 1997). And so did NAEP's recent test, showing "a stark gap between the ability of students in general to learn basic principles, and their ability to apply knowledge or explain what they learned" (*New York Times,* 1997). (The test was a mixture of multiple-choice, constructed response, and performance-task questions.)

For more than a decade in physics, specific tests have been developed and used as assessments targeting key misconceptions. The most widely used test, the Force Concept Inventory, provides a pre- and post-test instrument for measuring progress in overcoming the most common (and surprisingly persistent) misconceptions.

AAAS, in its *Benchmarks* (1993) and *Atlas of Science Literacy* (2001), has provided a rich account of desired understandings in the sciences, coupled with key misunderstandings connected with them:

When a relationship is represented in symbols, numbers can be substituted for all but one of the symbols, and the possible value of the remaining symbol computed. Sometimes the relationship may be satisfied by one value, sometimes more than one, and sometimes not at all.

• Students have difficulty understanding how symbols are used in algebra. They are often unaware of the arbitrariness of the letters chosen. These difficulties persist even after instruction in algebra and into college.

Students of all ages often do not view the equal sign of equations as a symbol of equivalence but rather interpret it as a sign to begin calculating—the right side should show the "answer."

Comparison of data from two groups should involve comparing both their middles and the spreads around them.

The middle of a data distribution may be misleading—when the data are not distributed symmetrically, or when there are extreme high or low values, or when the distribution is not reasonably smooth.

• The concept of the mean is quite difficult for students of all ages to understand even after years of formal instruction. . . . Research suggests that a good notion of "representativeness" may be a prerequisite to grasping the definitions of mean, median and mode. . . . Premature introduction of the algorithm for computing the mean divorced from a meaningful context may block students from understanding what averages are. (AAAS, 2001, pp. 122–123)

To see how easy it is to misunderstand things we think we all know, consider this more basic science question: Why is it colder in winter and warmer in summer? Just about every student in the United States has been taught basic astronomy. We "know" that the Earth travels around the sun, that the orbit is elliptical, and that the Earth tilts at about 20 degrees off its north-south axis. But when graduating Harvard seniors were asked the question (as documented in a video on the misunderstanding phenomenon produced by the Harvard-Smithsonian Center for Astrophysics), few could correctly explain why (Schneps, 1994).[2] They either had no adequate explanation for what they claimed to know or they provided a plausible but erroneous view (such as, the weather changes are due to the earth being closer or farther from the sun).

Similar findings occur when we ask adults to explain the phases of the moon: Many well-educated people describe the phases as lunar eclipses. In a follow-up video series on misconceptions in science entitled *Minds of Their Own*, the Harvard astrophysics group documented how a physics student who can do the same electric circuit problems we give to 4th graders, and describe what is occurring, has a flawed understanding when the question is cast in a novel way (can you light the bulb with only batteries and wires?).

The recognition of inevitable learner misunderstanding in even the best minds, in disciplines as seemingly straightforward and logical as science and mathematics, is actually quite old. Plato's dialogues vividly portray the interplay between the quest for understanding and the habits of mind and misconceptions that may be subconsciously shaping or inhibiting our thinking. Francis Bacon (1620/1960) provided a sobering account of the misunderstandings unwittingly introduced by our own intellectual tendencies operating unawares in the *Organon* 400 years ago. He noted that we project categories, assumptions, rules, priorities, attitudes, and matters of style onto our "reality" and then develop countless ways of "proving" our instinctive ideas to be true: "The human understanding . . . when it has once adopted an opinion draws all things else to support and agree with it" (pp. 45–49). Philosophers and psychologists from Kant and Wittgenstein to Piaget and other modern cognitive researchers have attempted to figure out the puzzle of persistent misunderstanding and the naïve conviction that typically accompanies it—and the self-assessment and self-discipline needed to move beyond both.

Practically speaking, we must begin to design assessments in recognition of the need for conceptual benchmarks, not just performance abilities. We need to design assessments mindful of not only the big ideas but also the *likelihood* that those ideas will be misconceived—and will resist being overcome, as in this biology example cited by Shulman (1999):

> *Biology teachers must wrestle with the durability of student misconceptions of evolution and natural selection. Most students in courses that emphasize evolution and natural selection enter these courses as intuitive Lamarckians. They are convinced that any characteristics acquired by one generation are then transmitted to the next generation. The formal instruction emphasizes the Darwinian refutation of that position. These students may earn A's and B's in the course, demonstrating that they now understand the Darwinian perspective, but quiz them three months later and they're once again dedicated intuitive Lamarckians—as indeed are many of the rest of us. I suspect that forms of fantasia are endemic among students and graduates of higher education, many lying in wait for years before manifesting themselves at critical moments. (p. 12)*

Here are some examples of common misunderstandings for some important ideas, and understandings that reflect the overcoming of them:

• *Impressionism is art in which the painter offers a subjective impression or feeling evoked by the scene.* The opposite is the case: Impressionism was an attempt to paint scenes realistically, not abstractly or by feeling. Impressionism refers to a technical term in philosophy whereby direct sensory impressions are distinguished from the mind's placing of those impressions into ideas.

• *Each month there is a lunar eclipse when the moon is not visible.* The phases of the moon depend on the relative position of the earth, the sun, and the moon, so that we see the part of the moon that is lit by the sun. Ongoing lunar eclipses are *not* the cause of the phases.

• *Science is about finding causes.* Scientists find correlations; talk of "causes" is viewed as too philosophical and unscientific. Modern science, economics, and medicine search for statistical patterns. That's why asking "What caused it?" is not necessarily a question doctors can answer, even as they prescribe effective medicines.

• *When you multiply two numbers, the answer is bigger.* Multiplication is *not* repeated addition. Fractions when multiplied yield a smaller answer, and when divided, a larger answer. How can *that* be? Students often see fractions and decimals as separate number systems; learning to see them as alternate means of representing the "same" quantities is the understanding.

- *History is about the facts, what happened.* A historian is a storyteller, not a mere gatherer and purveyor of facts. Why, then, do so few students realize that there can be and are very different stories of the same important history?

- *You should cup your hands when swimming in order to "catch the water" to move faster.* The greater the surface area, the greater the force. Thus, you should swim with a flat palm to maximize the amount of water being pulled and pushed.

- *Light is light and dark is dark.* Not true. Two light beams intersecting at crest and trough can cancel each other out and cause darkness! Noise-canceling headphones use sound to produce silence. Similarly, mirror-image waves of light or sound cancel each other out.

- *Negative and imaginary numbers are unreal.* Negative and imaginary numbers are no less and no more real than ordinary numbers. They exist to provide the symmetry and continuity needed for essential arithmetic and algebraic laws.

- *Evolution is a controversial idea.* No, the theory of natural selection as the engine of evolution is what is controversial. Theories of evolution predated Darwin by centuries and were not seen as being in conflict with religious doctrine.

- *Our founders were liberals.* The American revolutionaries held that individuals, not governments, had natural rights applied through labor (based on John Locke's views about property). Thus, in one sense, they were "conservatives" (i.e., the right to personal property is fundamental).

- *Irony is coincidence.* Irony is not mere coincidence, though almost every sportscaster misuses the word! Irony is what the wiser person sees that another seemingly wise person does not. The audience sees what Oedipus does not, and the tension between the latter's pride and what we know is the truth is the source of the drama's power.

Given the likelihood of deeply rooted misconceptions and the potential for misunderstanding, a proactive and, for most of us, unfamiliar approach to assessment design is required. To successfully engineer understanding, we have to think backward: What does understanding look like when it is there or not there? We have to be able to describe what it looks like, how it manifests itself, how apparent understanding (or misunderstanding) differs from genuine understanding, which misunderstandings are most likely to arise (thus interfering with our goal), and whether we are making headway in ferreting out and eradicating the key impediments to future understanding. In other words, we have to think through our assessments before we think through our teaching and learning.

Any design depends upon clear purposes, as we have said. Yet the matter is complicated by the mixture of many externally imposed goals (e.g., state content standards) and self-selected goals. How should we prioritize? How do we select wisely from so many obligations to ensure an effective and coherent design? How can we design coherent units while remaining constantly mindful of the many and overlapping course and program goals? We now turn to these questions.

Chapter 3

Gaining Clarity on Our Goals

Alice, speaking to Cheshire Cat:
"Would you tell me, please, which way I ought to go from here?"
"That depends a good deal on where you want to get to," said the Cat.
"I don't much care where," said Alice.
"Then it doesn't matter which way you go," said the Cat.
"—so long as I get somewhere," Alice added as an explanation.
"Oh, you're sure to do that," said the Cat, "if you only walk long enough."
—Lewis Carroll, *Alice's Adventures in Wonderland*, 1865

Life can only be understood backwards; but it must be lived forwards.
—Søren Kierkegaard, *Journals*, 1843

Backward design is goal directed. We aim for specific results and design backward from them accordingly. The desired results of Stage 1 dictate the nature of the assessment evidence needed in Stage 2 and suggest the types of instruction and learning experiences planned in Stage 3. Although it is logical to direct teaching and assessment toward specific purposes, it is important to recognize that all learning targets are not equal. They differ in terms of the nature of the target, the specificity of its description, and the implications for teaching and assessing.

Recall that in Understanding by Design we are tackling two recurring problems in design, the twin sins: aimless coverage of content, and isolated activities that are merely engaging (at best) while disconnected from intellectual goals in the learners' minds. The process of backward design is a deliberate approach to help designers avoid these all-too-common mistakes. To that end, the UbD Template is designed to help educators become more circumspect and analytic about the desired results. Why? Because our goals are often not as clear as they might be, and different kinds of aims are simultaneously in play in any classroom. Thus, the template has distinct places for what we term Established Goals, Understandings, Essential Questions, Knowledge, and Skills (see Figure 3.1). In this chapter we summarize what each of these "desired results" of Stage 1 means and why we think they are necessary.

Figure 3.1
Stage 1—Key Design Elements with Prompts

Stage 1—Identify Desired Results

Established Goals:

In Box **G**, we identify one or more Goals (e.g., content standards, course or program objectives, and learning outcomes) that the design targets. **G**

What understandings are desired?

Students will understand that . . . **U**

In Box **U**, we identify the Enduring Understandings, based on the transferable big ideas that give the content meaning and connect the facts and skills.

What essential questions will be considered?

In Box **Q**, we frame the Essential Questions to guide student inquiry and focus instruction for uncovering the important ideas of the content. **Q**

What key knowledge and skills will students acquire as a result of this unit?

Students will know . . . **K** *Students will be able to . . .* **S**

In this box, under **K** and **S**, we identify the key Knowledge **K** and Skills **S** we want students to know and be able to do. The targeted knowledge and skills **K** **S** can be of three different kinds: (1) they can refer to the building blocks for the desired understandings **U**; (2) they can refer to the knowledge and skills stated or implied in the goals **G**; and (3) they can refer to the "enabling" knowledge and skills needed to perform the complex assessment tasks identified in Stage 2.

By *Established Goals* (reduced to the shorthand word *Goals* on the template), we mean formal, long-term goals, such as state content standards, district program goals, departmental objectives, and exit-level outcomes—the desired results that establish priorities for instruction and assessment. These are inherently abiding aims, providing the rationale for the short-term goals that are lesson- and unit-specific. They typically refer to a complex mixture of academic aims: factual, conceptual, procedural, dispositional, and expert-performance-based. (Thus, habits of mind, such as "tolerance of ambiguity" and "persistence at demanding challenges"; and values and attitudes, such as eagerly reading on one's own and stepping in to mediate a dispute on the playground, are included, along with more academic and topical goals.)

We cannot stress enough the importance of long-term priorities in planning. Justifiable decisions about what to teach, what to leave out, what to emphasize, and what to minimize can be made only if there are agreed-upon priorities related to exit-level objectives. With no long-term goals, there is no perspective—hence no check on the teacher habit of merely teaching to short-term, content-related objectives. Indeed, the greatest defect in teacher lesson plans and syllabi, when looked at en masse, is that the key intellectual priorities—deep understandings of transferable big ideas, and competence at core performance tasks—are falling through the cracks of lessons, units, and courses devoted to developing thousands of discrete elements of knowledge and skill, unprioritized and unconnected. That is why content standards exist (regardless of the quality of specific standards): to prioritize our work, to keep our eyes on the prize, and to avoid the intellectual sterility and incoherence that comes from defining our aims as hundreds of apparently equal, discrete objectives to be "taught" and tested out of context.

In addition to Goals, we ask designers to specify the *Essential Questions* in Stage 1. These are not typical "objectives," to be sure, and some might quibble that posing a question isn't really germane to identifying results for learning. On the contrary, we argue that the Essential Questions highlight the big ideas that are central to the design, ideas that the work will require students to address. Because many of the truly Essential Questions recur and have no final resolution, it is appropriate to say that "seriously pursuing the question" as opposed to "answering" it *is* the desired result. By asking for Essential Questions, we are encouraging designers to avoid coverage and to commit to genuine inquiry—the discussion, reflection, problem solving, research, and debate that are the requisites for developing deep understanding of essential ideas.

Understandings may be thought of as the desired results of any inquiries and reflection on activity we seek to engineer as designers. In other words, Understandings are the constructivist result of attempts by the student to make sense of the work and lessons, using inquiry, performance, and reflection. *Knowledge,* on the other hand, summarizes the relatively straightforward facts and concepts that are to be gained from the learning and teaching activities. Dewey observed that understandings must be "comprehended," but knowledge need only be "apprehended." (Chapters 5 and 6 discuss Essential Questions and Understandings, respectively, at length.)

Skill refers not only to discrete techniques, but also to complex procedures and methods. Here the designer commits to results that require guided practice and coaching, stating what students *will be able to do* by the unit's end, such as "solve problems via long division" or "critique written work against audience and purpose." Skill-related aims focus on techniques and approaches (e.g., perspective drawing, long division, jumping rope) and processes (e.g., reading, research, problem solving), as opposed to performance goals such as "writing powerful essays," which are complex and long-term outcomes, needing many units and courses of study as well as different skills, integrated into performance.

> ### ■ MISCONCEPTION ALERT!
>
> Note that the UbD Design Template frames the work from the perspective of the teacher, not the learner. The learner would not necessarily understand the Goals, Understandings, and Essential Questions as framed on the template, at least initially. The job of Stage 3 is to translate the teacher's desired results in Stage 1 into effective and engaging learning, intelligible to the learner.

As a general rule, we find that many teachers overlook the enabling skills at the heart of long-term successful performance. In workshops with college professors, for example, participants complain most often about student inability to transfer the lessons in the lectures and readings to new issues or cases. When we ask, "To what extent does your syllabus give them practice, coaching, and feedback in how to apply the ideas?" many professors recognize their omission—namely, that merely specifying performance requirements does not prepare students for success.

But the Skill box is meant to include more than just long-term process objectives. The designer is also asked here to *infer* the enabling skills required by the unit performance goals, understandings, and questions (and, therefore, the complex performance tasks identified in Stage 2). It is common for teachers to overlook this analysis. For example, many middle and high school courses call for students to engage in debate or to do a PowerPoint presentation, but learning plans typically pay minimal attention to how those abilities will be developed and supported to ensure fairness in the final results. Far too often it is *assumed* that students will somehow already possess key enabling skills (e.g., study skills, public speaking skills, graphic design skills, group management skills)—with the unfortunate results that cause more educators to complain about the absence of those skills than to target them in their planning. Helping students to "learn how to learn" and "how to perform" is both a vital mission and a commonly overlooked one. Backward design, as embodied in the elements of Stage 1 and the requirement that all three stages be aligned, greatly improves the likelihood that these key capacities will not fall through the cracks.

In short, "content mastery" is not the *aim* of instruction, but a *means*. Content knowledge is most appropriately viewed as the tools and material of intellectual competence, made useful by all the aspects of Stage 1.

Although the various categories of Stage 1 are conceptually distinct, they often overlap in practice. For example, in an art class, students learn the concept of perspective, practice the skill of perspective drawing, and (we hope) begin to demonstrate persistence while attempting to master the skill. Hence the need for a template that reminds us of the distinctions that might get lost in practice.

It is important to recognize that classifying learning goals in this fashion is more than a mere academic exercise. These distinctions have direct and practical implications for better instruction and assessment. Different types of aims require different instructional and assessment approaches. How people develop and deepen their understanding of an abstract concept differs fundamentally from how they become proficient in a skill. Similarly, students do not learn factual information in the same way they acquire habits of mind and control of big ideas over time; understandings have to be inferred from well-designed and well-facilitated experiences, whereas a good deal of knowledge can be learned from readings or lectures. The distinctions in the template remind the designer that different pedagogies are called for as the logical consequences of the aims, not because of some ideological assumptions about "good teaching." (Instructional decisions are discussed more fully in Chapters 9 and 10.)

Consider writing. We can employ mnemonic devices to help students learn and remember rules of grammar (knowledge), and we can offer a guided discussion on what the author has said, but we must use other techniques, such as modeling, guided practice, and feedback, to teach the writing *process* (skill development). For assessment, we can use a multiple-choice format to test grammar knowledge, but we will need performance assessment—actual writing samples—to appropriately judge the overall effectiveness of the process. A student may know the rules of grammar and spelling but be ineffective as a communicator in writing, and vice versa; our assessments need to be sensitive to these distinctions.

The standards movement

When we were writing the first edition of *Understanding by Design,* the standards movement was still so new we hardly mentioned it in the book. Now, of course, nearly every state and province in North America, and most nations beyond, have identified explicit learning goals. Typically known as content standards or learning outcomes, these goals specify what students should know and be able to do in various disciplines.

In theory, clearly written standards provide a focus for curriculum, assessment, and instruction. However, in practice, educators throughout North America have encountered three common problems when attempting to use the standards for educational planning. One may be termed the "overload problem," in which the sheer number of listed content standards frequently outstrips the available time needed to learn them. A quantification of this problem may be seen in the research of Marzano and Kendall (1996). They reviewed 160 national and state-level standards documents in various subject areas, synthesized the material to avoid duplication, and identified 255 content standards and 3,968 discrete benchmarks that delineate what students should know and be able to do. The researchers speculated that if teachers devoted 30 minutes of instructional time to teach each benchmark (and many would require more than one-half hour to learn), we would need an additional 15,465 hours (or 9 more school years) for students to learn them all! This research supports what many teachers have been saying—there is too much content and not enough time, especially if the identified knowledge and skills contained in the standards are viewed as discrete and disconnected.

This is not a new problem. Consider the following remarks:

Each general aim, it seemed, could be analyzed into an almost infinite number of specific aims. The impetus to the procedure led to further and further analysis in an effort to include all desirable specific aims and to make them as definite as possible. Pendleton lists 1,581 social objectives for English. Guiler lists more than 300 aims for arithmetic in grades one to six. Billings found 888 generalizations which were important in the social studies. . . . One course of study for seventh grade social studies lists 135 objectives. A course in another subject contains 85 objectives. One course for junior high school contains 47 . . . pages of objectives.

As a result, the teacher is overwhelmed with aims. The lists are so extensive and complex that no reasonable instructional program can be developed around them. It is found by teachers that they limit work unduly, making it impossible to consider adequately individual pupil needs and interests.

These comments appeared in the most widely used book on curriculum—in 1935 (Caswell & Campbell, 1935, p. 118).[1]

A second common problem is a bit subtler, but no less vexing. We have labeled it the Goldilocks Problem. Like the situation in the fairy tale, some standards are too big. For example, consider the following example in geography: "The student will analyze the regional development of Asia, Africa, the Middle East, Latin America, and the Caribbean, in terms of physical, economic, and cultural characteristics and historical evolution from 1000 A.D. to the present." What exactly does this standard expect us to teach? What should be assessed? One could concentrate an entire academic career on this single goal. It is clearly too global to be helpful to teachers and curriculum writers.

Conversely, some standards are too small, such as this 7th grade history standard: "Compare the early civilizations of the Indus River Valley in Pakistan with the Huang-He of China." Standards and benchmarks such as this fixate on "factlets" that meet someone's sense of what is important but seem a tad esoteric and arbitrary if required of every student in the state. Although standards of this type are specific and easily measurable, they generally miss the big ideas of the discipline and run the risk of sending the message to students (and teachers) that school learning is nothing more than memorizing facts and passing tests of recall and recognition.

A third problem is evident in the following example of a standard in the arts: Students will "recognize how technical, organizational and aesthetic elements contribute to the ideas, emotions and overall impact communicated by works of art." The statement is so nebulous that it practically guarantees that different art teachers will interpret it in different ways, thus defeating one of the intentions of the standards movement—clear, consistent, and coherent educational goals.

Unpacking standards

For years, we have witnessed teacher planners, curriculum developers, and assessment designers struggling with these problems (too many, too big, too small, or too vague) when working with their given content standards. As one means of coping, we suggest that the content standards be "unpacked" to identify the big ideas and core tasks contained within. For example, the world geography standard ("The student will analyze the regional development of Asia, Africa, the Middle East, Latin America, and the Caribbean, in terms of physical, economic, and cultural characteristics and historical evolution from 1000 A.D. to the present") could be reframed around the following larger idea: "The geography, climate, and natural resources of a region influence the lifestyle, culture, and economy of its inhabitants." A companion essential question could be "How does *where* you live influence *how* you live and work?" By unpacking the standard in this fashion, we now have a larger conceptual lens through which we can explore *any* geographic region over time, and compare regions. Coincidentally, we could address the narrow standard ("Compare the early civilizations of the Indus River Valley in Pakistan with the Huang-He of China") using the same big idea and essential question, with the Indus River Valley and the Huang-He of China serving as two particular cases for exploring the same larger, transferable idea.

As for core tasks, most standards documents identify them in tandem with the key skills of which they are a part. In the following examples, key ideas are identified by numbers (1–3), performance indicators are identified by bullets (•), and a sample task is identified by a triangle (△). These examples are from social studies and science, from California and New York, respectively:

Chronological and Spatial Thinking

1. Students compare the present with the past, evaluating the consequences of past events and decisions and determining the lessons that were learned.

2. Students analyze how change happens at different rates at different times; understand that some aspects can change while others remain the same; and understand that change is complicated and affects not only technology and politics but also values and beliefs.

3. Students use a variety of maps and documents to interpret human movement, including major patterns of domestic and international migration, changing environmental preferences and settlement patterns, the frictions

*that develop between population groups, and the diffusion of ideas, techno-
logical innovations, and goods.*

Historical Research, Evidence, and Point of View

*1. Students distinguish valid arguments from fallacious arguments in his-
torical interpretations.*

2. Students identify bias and prejudice in historical interpretations.

*3. Students evaluate major debates among historians concerning alterna-
tive interpretations of the past, including an analysis of authors' use of evidence and the distinctions between sound generalizations and misleading
oversimplifications.*

Science

*1. The central purpose of scientific inquiry is to develop explanations of
natural phenomena in a continuing, creative process.*
Students:

* *formulate questions independently with the aid of references appropriate for guiding the search for explanations of everyday observations.*

* *construct explanations independently for natural phenomena,
especially by proposing preliminary visual models of phenomena.*

* *represent, present, and defend their proposed explanations of
everyday observations so that they can be understood and assessed by
others.*

This is evident, for example, when students:

△ After being shown the disparity between the amount of solid waste
which is recycled and which could be recycled, *students working in small
groups are asked to explain why this disparity exists. They develop a set of
possible explanations and select one for intensive study. After their explanation is critiqued by other groups, it is refined and submitted for assessment.
The explanation is rated on clarity, plausibility, and appropriateness for intensive study using research methods.*

Note that complex processes and mastery of complex performance tasks
are central to these and many other standards, yet educators have been slow
to translate these requirements into more familiar program and course objectives, to the detriment of student performance. And each standard sums up a
big idea at the heart of each discipline—the key concepts underlying successful performance.

Practically speaking, we need only look more carefully at the *key recurring nouns, adjectives, and verbs* in these documents to gain a better sense of
our priorities as teacher-designers. (See Figure 3.2 for an example from math.)
Unpacking content standards in this manner has two virtues. The first is
unapologetically pragmatic. We can manage large amounts of content, especially discrete factual knowledge and basic skills, by clustering the specifics
under two broader conceptual umbrellas containing the big ideas and core
tasks. Teachers can never cover all of the facts and skills on a given topic, given

Figure 3.2
Unpacking Standards

Established Goals:

All students will (connect) mathematics to other learning by understanding the interrelationships of mathematical ideas <u>and the roles</u> that mathematics and (mathematical modeling) play in (other disciplines and in life.)

—New Jersey Mathematics Standard 4.3

Stated or implied Big Ideas in the NOUNS and ADJECTIVES:

- Mathematical modeling in various disciplines and life

Stated or implied real-world performances in the VERBS:

- Give examples of effective mathematical modeling of real-life data or phenomena
- Critically review a mathematical model for its appropriateness to a given real-life situation

Essential Question Ideas:

- What's the pattern?
- How *do* you know if your model is a good one (for a particular situation)?

Understanding Ideas:
Students will understand that . . .

- Mathematical models help us simplify, abstract, and analyze experience using data and so that we might better understand their relationship.
- Mathematical models must be viewed critically so that they do not mislead us.

Performance Task Ideas:

- Have students create a mathematical model for a selected real-world situation (e.g., seasonal temperatures) that has messy data and various plausible models of the relationships.
- Have students critically review a mathematical model for its appropriateness to a given situation (e.g., the Mercator Projection for representing the globe in two dimensions).

time restrictions and content overload. However, they can focus on a smaller set of big ideas and core tasks in the discipline by framing work around essential questions and appropriate performance assessment. The more specific facts, concepts, and skills identified by the content standards (and often assessed on standardized tests) can then be taught in the context of exploring these larger ideas and abilities.

Because big ideas are inherently transferable, they help connect discrete topics and skills. For example, the essential question, "How do effective writers hook and hold their readers?" provides an umbrella for learning a host of important skills and knowledge called for in English or language arts standards (e.g., different author's styles, literary genre, various literary techniques). Similarly in mathematics, the big idea that "All forms of measurement contain errors" can be used to guide learning the basics of measuring with a ruler, as well as more sophisticated concepts in statistics.

> ### ■ MISCONCEPTION ALERT!
>
> In this book, we use the term standards to refer collectively to formally specified learning goals in the subject areas. In some places the *standards* refer only to content, but in others they refer also to "performance indicators" or the equivalent (the New York science example, cited earlier, makes the distinction clearly). Whether they refer only to the "inputs"—content—or to the desired "outputs"—evidence—for our purposes here they are all lumped under the term *standards*. If local designers are trying to map standards into the UbD Template, however, it may be necessary to place so-called indicators, benchmarks, and performance goals in Stage 2 because they speak more to evidence of the standard being met than of the standard per se. In fact, many state and national documents are unclear on this important distinction, so care must be taken in the analysis at the local level.

The second justification for unpacking content standards in this way comes from research on learning from cognitive psychology. Consider the following summaries of findings from the book *How People Learn* (Bransford, Brown, & Cocking, 2000):

> *A key finding in the learning and transfer literature is that organizing information into a conceptual framework allows for greater transfer. (p. 17)*

> *Learning with understanding is more likely to promote transfer than simply memorizing information from a text or a lecture. (p. 236)* [A more detailed discussion of relevant research findings is presented in Chapter 13.]

> *Experts first seek to develop an understanding of problems, and this often involves thinking in terms of core concepts or big ideas. Novices' knowledge is much less likely to be organized around big ideas; novices are more likely to approach problems by searching for correct formulas and pat answers that fit their everyday intuitions. (p. 49)*

What exactly is a *big* idea and a *core* task?

Suppose, then, that we use the backward design process to plan a unit of study. Can we be sure that the unit will cause student understanding? Not necessarily. To be elegant and powerful, the design has to be coherent and focused on clear and worthy intellectual priorities—on what we call "big ideas" and "core tasks." Let us take each of these in turn.

Given that every topic typically encompasses more content than we can reasonably address, we are obliged to make deliberate choices *and set explicit priorities.* Having chosen what to teach (and what not to), we have to help the learners see the priorities within what we ask them to learn. Our designs should clearly signal these priorities so that all learners will be able to answer these questions: What is most important here? How do the pieces connect? What should I pay most attention to? What are the (few) bottom-line priorities?

The big ideas connect the dots for the learner by establishing learning priorities. As a teacher friend of ours observed, they serve as "conceptual Velcro"—they help the facts and skills stick together and stick in our minds! The challenge then is to identify a *few* big ideas and carefully design around them, resisting the temptation to teach everything of possible value for each topic. As Bruner (1960) put it years ago,

> *For any subject taught in primary school, we might ask [is it] worth an adult's knowing, and whether having known it as a child makes a person a better adult. A negative or ambiguous answer means the material is cluttering up the curriculum. (p. 52)*

A big idea may be thought of as a *linchpin.* The linchpin is the device that keeps the wheel in place on an axle. Thus, a linchpin is one that is essential for understanding. Without grasping the idea and using it to "hold together" related content knowledge, we are left with bits and pieces of inert facts that cannot take us anywhere.

For instance, without grasping the distinction between the letter and the spirit of the law, a student cannot be said to understand the U.S. constitutional and legal system—even if that student is highly knowledgeable and articulate about many facts of constitutional history. Without a focus on the big ideas that have lasting value, students are too easily left with forgettable fragments of knowledge. Thus, a student may have memorized all the Amendments to the Constitution and may be able to rattle off the names of key Supreme Court decisions; but if the student is unable to explain how it is possible for laws to change while legal and democratic principles remain the same, then we would judge the understanding as inadequate.

For another example, consider "the five biggest ideas in science," as described in a book by that name (Wynn & Wiggins, 1997). The authors suggest a series of questions that embody five fundamental ideas in science:

> *Question: Do basic building blocks of matter exist? And if so what do they look like?*
>
> *Answer: Big Idea #1—Physics' Model of the Atom*
>
> *Question: What relationships, if any, exist among different kinds of atoms, the basic building blocks of the universe?*
>
> *Answer: Big Idea #2—Chemistry's Periodic Law*

Question: Where did the atoms of the universe come from, and what is their destiny?

Answer: Big Idea #3—Astronomy's Big Bang Theory

Question: How is the matter of the universe arranged in planet earth?

Answer: Big Idea #4—Geology's Plate Tectonics Model

Question: How did life on earth originate and develop?

Answer: Big idea #5—Biology's Theory of Evolution (pp. v–vi)

What makes them the big ideas? According to Wynn & Wiggins (1997), big ideas are "chosen especially for their power to explain phenomena, they provide a comprehensive survey of science" (p. v). Whether you agree with their particular choices, the authors' approach reflects the need to focus on a smaller set of priority ideas and use them to frame teaching and assessment.

Big ideas at the "core" (versus the "basics")

From one perspective, the phrase "big idea" is just right, since we want to signal that some ideas serve as umbrella concepts. But from another point of view, the term "big" can be misleading. A big idea is not necessarily vast in the sense of a vague phrase covering lots of content. Nor is a big idea a "basic" idea. Rather, big ideas are at the "core" of the subject; they need to be uncovered; we have to dig deep until we get to the core. Basic ideas, by contrast, are just what the term implies—the basis for further work; for example, definitions, building-block skills, and rules of thumb. Ideas at the core of the subject, however, are ideas that are the hard-won results of inquiry, ways of thinking and perceiving that are the province of the expert. They are *not* obvious. In fact, most expert big ideas are abstract and *counterintuitive* to the novice, prone to misunderstanding.

Consider some ideas at the core of various fields, contrasted with "basic terms," to see this point more clearly:

Basic Terms	*Core Ideas*
• Ecosystem	• Natural selection
• Graph	• "Best fit" curve of the data
• Four basic operations	• Associativity and transitivity (cannot divide by zero)
• Story	• Meaning as projected onto the story
• Composition of a picture	• Negative space
• Offense and defense	• Spreading the defense, thus opening up space for the offense
• Experiment	• Inherent error and fallibility of experimental methods and results
• Fact versus opinion	• Credible thesis

The big ideas at the core of a subject are arrived at, sometimes surprisingly slowly, via teacher-led inquiries and reflective work by students. (Later in the book we will suggest that "understandings" and "essential questions" should always point beyond the basic knowledge and skill to the core of a subject.)

One of us once watched a group of special education students work to uncover big ideas at the core of *Macbeth*—honor and loyalty. The two teachers shifted deftly between the play (read aloud in chunks to ensure literacy issues didn't get in the way of understanding) and questioning the students' experience with issues of honor. Among the questions they asked were these: What is the difference between things that happen to us and things that we make happen? What is honor? Is there a cost or price for honor? Is it worth it? What is loyalty? Is there tension between loyalty and honor in *Macbeth*? In our own lives?

Students were asked to find answers from the play and their own lives for each question. "Why is defending your honor so hard?" one of the teachers asked, causing a thin, tall fellow to sit bolt upright, show a kind of focus in his eyes that had been absent until then, and answer poignantly about the loss of friends when he stood on principle in defense of another friend. What happened in *Macbeth* suddenly seemed more important but also complex—human. The student had made the transfer, and had an insight: The core of the idea of loyalty involves inescapable dilemmas, because loyalties invariably collide. Learning that does not penetrate to the core of what is vital about an idea yields abstract, alien, and uninteresting lessons. When we say we want students to understand the knowledge they are learning, we are not being redundant or naïve about its value, given the time and obligations we have.

A big idea at the core of mathematics is "unitizing"—the ability of a numeral to represent different numbers. Place value is not understandable unless learners grasp this: "Unitizing requires that children use numbers to count not only objects but also groups—and to count them both simultaneously. The whole is thus seen as a group of a number. . . . For learners, unitizing is a shift of perspective" (Fosnot & Dolk, 2001b, p. 11).

A big idea is therefore both central to coherent connections in a field of study *and* a conceptual anchor for making facts more understandable and useful. Once again we invoke an old notion. Bruner (1960) famously described such conceptions as "structure":

> *Grasping the structure of a subject is understanding it in a way that permits many other things to be related to it meaningfully. To learn structure, in short, is to learn how things are related. . . . To take an example from mathematics, algebra is a way of arranging knowns and unknowns in equations so that the unknowns are made knowable. The three fundamentals involved . . . are commutation, distribution, and association. Once a student grasps the ideas embodied by these three fundamentals, he is in a position to recognize wherein "new" equations to be solved are not new at all. (pp. 7–8)*

Not long after, Phillip Phenix wrote in *Realms of Meaning* (1964) of the importance of designing around "representative ideas," because they enable learning that is both effective and efficient:

Representative ideas are clearly of great importance in economizing learning effort. If there are certain characteristic concepts of a discipline that represent it, then a thorough understanding of these ideas is equivalent to a knowledge of the entire discipline. If knowledge within a discipline is organized according to certain patterns, then a full comprehension of those patterns goes far toward making intelligible the host of particular elements that fit into the design of the subject. (p. 323)

And, he noted, such "big ideas" have an unusual characteristic: They generate new knowledge in the field while also being helpful to novice learners.

Consider a course on educational assessment, in which one big idea is "credible evidence." The more technical and specific concepts (such as validity and reliability) and the more technical skills (such as computing standard deviations) are properly subsumed under this idea, with its transferability to other areas where we might find similar questions (e.g., "How credible are the results? How confident are we in our findings?"). A related big idea is that *all* educational assessment should be like civil law: We need a "preponderance of evidence" in order to "convict" a student of meeting stated goals. Why a preponderance? Because each measure has inherent error (another big idea) and any single test result is inadequate to "convict." Without being able to intelligently discuss error *in general* in this way, students in an assessment course cannot be said to understand "reliability" and its importance even if they can accurately define the term or compute it using coefficients.

Our colleague Lynn Erickson (2001) offers a useful working definition of "big ideas." They are

- Broad and abstract
- Represented by one or two words
- Universal in application
- Timeless—carry through the ages
- Represented by different examples that share common attributes (p. 35)

More generally, then, as we see it, a big idea can be thought of as

- Providing a focusing conceptual "lens" for any study
- Providing breadth of meaning by connecting and organizing many facts, skills, and experiences; serving as the linchpin of understanding
- Pointing to ideas at the heart of expert understanding of the subject
- Requiring "uncoverage" because its meaning or value is rarely obvious to the learner, is counterintuitive or prone to misunderstanding
- Having great transfer value; applying to many other inquiries and issues over time—"horizontally" (across subjects) and "vertically" (through the years in later courses) in the curriculum and out of school

Our last criterion, transfer, turns out to be vital, as suggested by what Bloom (1981) and his colleagues said about the nature and value of big ideas:

In each subject field there are some basic ideas which summarize much of what scholars have learned. . . . These ideas give meaning to much that has been learned, and they provide the basic ideas for dealing with many new problems. . . . We believe that it is a primary obligation of the scholars [and] teachers to search constantly for these abstractions, to find ways of helping students learn them, and especially to help students learn how to use them in a great variety of problem situations. . . . To learn to use such principles is to possess a powerful way of dealing with the world. (p. 235)

In other words, a big idea, is not "big" merely by virtue of its intellectual scope. It has to have pedagogical power: It must enable the learner to make sense of what has come before; and, most notably, be helpful in making new, unfamiliar ideas seem more familiar. Thus, a big idea is not just another fact or a vague abstraction but a conceptual tool for sharpening thinking, connecting discrepant pieces of knowledge, and equipping learners for transferable applications.

In pedagogical practice, a big idea is typically manifest as a helpful

- Concept (e.g., adaptation, function, quantum, perspective)
- Theme (e.g., "good triumphs over evil," "coming of age," "go West")
- Ongoing debate and point of view (e.g., nature versus nurture, conservatives versus liberals, acceptable margin of error)
- Paradox (e.g., freedom must have limits, leave home to find oneself, imaginary numbers)
- Theory (e.g., evolution via natural selection, Manifest Destiny, fractals for explaining apparent randomness)
- Underlying assumption (e.g., texts have meaning, markets are rational, parsimony of explanation in science)
- Recurring question (e.g., "Is that fair?" "How do we know?" "Can we prove it?")
- Understanding or principle (e.g., form follows function, the reader has to question the text to understand it, correlation does not ensure causality)

Note, then, that a big idea can manifest itself in various formats—as a word, a phrase, a sentence, or a question. Put the other way around, a core concept, an essential question, and a formal theory are all about big ideas, expressed in different ways. However, as we explore in later chapters, the way we frame the big ideas is important and not merely a matter of taste or style. Framing the big ideas in terms of what we want the learner to come to understand about them turns out to be critical to good design work.

A prioritizing framework

Because we typically face more content than we can reasonably address, and because it is often presented as if everything were equally important for students, we are obliged to make choices and frame priorities. A useful framework for establishing priorities around big ideas may be graphically depicted using the three nested ovals shown in Figure 3.3. Consider the blank background

Figure 3.3
Clarifying Content Priorities

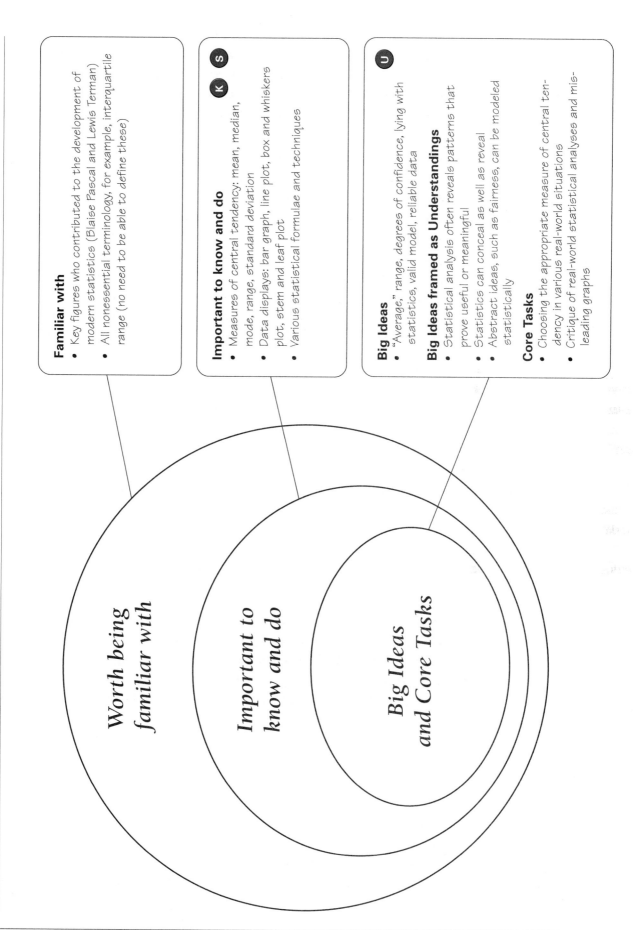

Familiar with
- Key figures who contributed to the development of modern statistics (Blaise Pascal and Lewis Terman)
- All nonessential terminology, for example, interquartile range (no need to be able to define these)

Important to know and do
- Measures of central tendency: mean, median, mode, range, standard deviation
- Data displays: bar graph, line plot, box and whiskers plot, stem and leaf plot
- Various statistical formulae and techniques

Big Ideas
- "Average," range, degrees of confidence, lying with statistics, valid model, reliable data

Big Ideas framed as Understandings
- Statistical analysis often reveals patterns that prove useful or meaningful
- Statistics can conceal as well as reveal
- Abstract ideas, such as fairness, can be modeled statistically

Core Tasks
- Choosing the appropriate measure of central tendency in various real-world situations
- Critique of real-world statistical analyses and misleading graphs

Worth being familiar with

Important to know and do

Big Ideas and Core Tasks

outside the largest circle as representing the field of all possible content (e.g., topics, skills, resources) that might be examined during the unit or course. Clearly, we cannot address it all, so we move within the outer oval to identify knowledge that students *should be familiar with*. During the unit or course, what do we want students to hear, read, view, research, or otherwise encounter? For example, in an introductory unit on statistics, we may want students to become aware of key historical figures, including Blaise Pascal and Lewis Terman, along with the history of the bell curve. Broad-brush knowledge, assessed through traditional quiz or test questions, would be sufficient, given the introductory nature of the unit.

In the middle oval we sharpen and prioritize our choices by specifying important knowledge, skills, and concepts that have connective and transfer power, within this unit and with other units of study on related topics. For instance, we would expect students to come to know measures of central tendency (mean, median, mode, range, quartile, standard deviation), and to develop skill in plotting data on various types of graphic displays.

But, again, there is another way to think about the middle oval: It identifies the prerequisite—that is, *enabling*—knowledge and skill needed by students in order for them to successfully accomplish key complex performances of understanding, that is, transfer tasks. For example, a high school mathematics teacher introduces a statistics unit by presenting his students with the following performance task:

> *Your math teacher will allow you to select the method by which measure of central tendency—mean, median or mode—your quarterly grade will be calculated. Review your grades for quizzes, tests, and homework to decide which measure of central tendency will be best for your situation. Write a note to your teacher explaining why you selected that method, and why you believe it to be the most "fair" and "informative" approach to the grade.*

The performance task requires that students really understand these measures of central tendency (so that they can determine the preferred method of averaging and explain why) in a qualitatively different manner than if they simply had to define the terms. In addition, the task is likely to stimulate the students' interest in *wanting* to understand the distinctions, because it is in their interest to do so. (We say more about framing goals as performance tasks later in this chapter.)

The innermost oval requires finer-grain decisions. This is where we select the Big Ideas that will anchor the unit or course, and also specify the transfer tasks at the heart of this subject. Continuing with the statistics unit example, the inner oval would highlight big ideas (e.g., sampling, margin of error, finding patterns in data, making predictions, degrees of confidence) and key performance challenges (e.g., determining the meaning of "average" for a given set of data, developing a "fair" solution).

The three-ovals graphic organizer has proven to be a useful tool for teachers to use when attempting to prioritize the content for a unit or course. In fact, many users have observed that they were able to eliminate some things that they "always taught" once they realized that these things fell in the outer oval and deserved minimal attention compared with more important ideas and processes. (By the way, the same tool has been used at the macro level for conducting a curriculum audit. In other words, what are the priorities reflected in our current curriculum? Are we properly concentrating on important, transferable ideas, or does our curriculum merely cover lots of information?)

More tips for finding big ideas

In addition to the three-ovals organizer, we recommend that curriculum designers consider the following strategies for identifying big ideas.

1. Look carefully at state standards. Many of them either state or imply big ideas, especially in the descriptive text that precedes the list of standards. For example, look at the explanations in these Ohio standards in economics and physical science (we've added emphasis to highlight various big ideas):

Students use economic reasoning skills *and knowledge of major economic concepts, issues and systems in order to make informed choices as producers, consumers, savers, investors, workers and citizens in an interdependent world.*

By the end of the K–12 program:

A. *Explain how the* scarcity of resources requires people to make choices *to satisfy their wants.*

B. Distinguish between goods and services *and explain how people can be both buyers and sellers of goods and services.*

C. *Explain ways that people may obtain goods and services.*

Students demonstrate an understanding of the composition of physical systems and the concepts and principles that describe and predict physical interactions and events in the natural world. This includes demonstrating an understanding of the structure and properties of matter, *the properties of materials and objects,* chemical reactions *and the* conservation of matter. *In addition, it includes understanding the* nature, transfer and conservation of energy; *motion and the forces affecting motion; and the nature of waves and interactions of matter and energy.*

Or consider these 6th grade social studies standards from California (again, we've added emphasis to highlight big ideas):

1. *Students describe what is known through* archaeological studies *of the* early physical and cultural development of humankind *from the Paleolithic era to the agricultural revolution.*

• *Describe the* hunter-gatherer societies, *including the development of tools and the use of fire.*

• *Identify the locations of human communities that populated the major regions of the world and* describe how humans adapted to a variety of environments.

• *Discuss the climatic changes and human modifications of the physical environment that gave rise to the* domestication of plants and animals *and new sources of clothing and shelter.*

2. Circle the key *recurring nouns* in standards documents to highlight big ideas and the *recurring verbs* to identify core tasks. This simple technique was mentioned earlier (see Figure 3.2).

3. Refer to existing lists of transferable concepts. For example, when searching for big ideas for a given topic, consider these possibilities:[2]

abundance/scarcity	democracy	migration
acceptance/rejection	discovery	mood
adaptation	diversity	order
aging/maturity	environment	patterns
balance	equilibrium	perspective
change/continuity	evolution	production
character	exploration	proof
community(ies)	fairness	repetition
conflict	friendship	rhythm
connections	harmony	survival
cooperation	honor	symbol
correlation	interactions	system
courage	interdependence	technology
creativity	invention	tyranny
culture	justice	variance/variable
cycles	liberty	wealth
defense/protection	loyalty	

4. Ask one or more of the following questions about a topic or content standard:

Why study . . . ? So what?

What makes the study of . . . "universal"?

If the unit on . . . is a story, what's the "moral of the story"?

What's the "big idea" implied in the skill or process of . . . ?

What larger concept, issue, or problem underlies . . . ?

What couldn't we do if we didn't understand . . . ?

How is . . . used and applied in the larger world?

What is a "real-world" insight about . . . ?

What is the value of studying . . . ?

5. Generate big ideas as an outgrowth of related and suggestive pairs. This helpful approach has two virtues: (1) it indicates the kinds of inquiries that must be made (e.g., compare and contrast), and (2) it suggests the kind of *rethinking* that learners will need in order to understand the ideas and find them useful. Here is a list of pairs to consider:

absorb & reflect	harmony & dissonance	meaning & syntax
action & reaction	idiom & language	nation & people
capital & labor	important & urgent	nature & nurture

constant & variable	light & shadow	power & governance
continuity & change	like & unlike	sign & signified
factor & result	literal & figurative	structure & function
fate & freedom	matter & energy	sum & difference

Consider the pair "fate and freedom" and its use across many subjects. A relevant set of essential questions for design might include these: To what extent are we free or fated? To what extent is biology or culture destiny? Is "free will" a romantic and naïve belief or the bedrock of modern thought and action? In what sense was the Revolutionary War, the Holocaust, or recent religious warfare "fated" to happen—or to what extent is such an argument defeatist? In what sense were atomic warfare and global warming the fated results of scientific advance? Is there freedom in mathematics, or are all the results "fated" (though perhaps unknown to us at present)?

The teacher's "new clothes"

If a big idea inherently *seemed* powerful and meaningful, education would be so much easier! Alas, what is big to the teacher or the expert in the field is often abstract, lifeless, confusing, or irrelevant to the child. What may be a vital conception to the expert in the field of study may well seem nonsensical, unintelligible, or of little interest to the novice. Even the lists presented here look fairly inert and uninteresting to anyone without the understandings required to grasp their significance. Indeed, the challenge of teaching for understanding is largely the challenge of making the big ideas in the field become big in the mind of the learner.

This is hard to do—much harder than novice educators typically understand. The Expert Blind Spot dogs teachers at every step. To the *teacher*, the power of the big ideas and the importance of the lessons is so—obvious! "Come, let me introduce you to this interesting notion . . ." From the *student's* perspective, this situation is not unlike the story of the "Emperor's New Clothes." You remember the story: Crooked tailors claim to be crafting clothes out of the finest gold yarn—so fine that you have to be quite sophisticated to see it. The story ends, as we all know, with the king walking naked, with only the naïve child saying what the adults cannot quite bring themselves to see or say: "But he has nothing on!" Often in school, the "fine" ideas seem like the emperor's new clothes: simply not visible to the learner, though teacher, textbook author, and expert researcher keep oohing and aahing about the handiwork.

What we easily forget is that the ideas at the core of modern subject areas are typically abstract, not obvious, and often completely counterintuitive, hence prone to mystery and misunderstanding. Consider the following: The earth does not appear to move to human observers; there are no obvious signs of our being descended from primates; it seems bizarre that our democratic founders kept slaves; the text of *Hamlet* seems to have nothing to do with adolescent angst and depression; and derivatives and integrals make no conceptual sense to the novice calculus student (just as they did not to many expert mathematicians when they were first proposed!).

We struggle to grasp big ideas and see their value, just as great minds before us did, and the situation becomes worse when teachers and textbooks treat them as facts. Yet once we as teachers see the big ideas clearly, we become prone to thinking that they are obvious to learners. The challenge of designing and teaching for understanding is ironically, therefore, dependent upon once again seeing like a child, so that the big ideas and their value is not at all obvious. An example of this challenge is the arithmetic idea of unitizing mentioned earlier: "Unitizing these ten things as one thing—one group—requires almost negating their original idea of number. It is a huge shift in thinking for children, and in fact, was a huge shift in mathematics, taking centuries to develop" (Fosnot & Dolk, 2001b, p. 11).

Big ideas are abstractions, and the design challenge is to bring those abstractions to life and to make them seem vital. To say that we ought to design around big ideas is therefore more challenging than we may have first thought. Attending carefully to likely student *misunderstanding* becomes more central to the design process because the big ideas *cannot* be grasped through telling and reading alone and are likely to be misunderstood when first encountered.

Because scholarly big ideas are essential for understanding yet easily misunderstood, our instructional designs will work best if they require students to constantly consider the big ideas anew and move carefully to the core of the ideas. Big ideas are not like definitions that can be learned and filed away mentally, to be used straightforwardly. They are more like "guiding conjectures" (in Bruner's phrase), subject to refinement and adjustment as we learn more.

Our designs must help learners ask and re-ask questions about big ideas *in action,* not unlike a move learned in athletics. A move may work well for a while (e.g., faking left, going right), but eventually the move has to be rethought when it stops working in games. What once worked comes to be seen as inadequate. In a good education, the same is true of ideas: The idea of "good guy versus bad guy" in history and literature has to be rethought in light of the shades of gray (and the ironies) in adult life and literature. One of our favorite humorous examples of how to do this occurs in an introductory episode in the third Indiana Jones movie, *Indiana Jones and the Last Crusade*. So who *are* the good guys? Within

---

■ MISCONCEPTION ALERT!

"I focus mostly on skills, so there aren't any big ideas in what I teach." This is one of the most common concerns we have heard over the past years. We hear it especially from teachers of physical education, mathematics, beginning world languages, primary grades, and vocational courses. We contend that this belief is based on a misunderstanding about big ideas and their crucial role in *all* learning. The skills teacher may be confusing the purpose of her teaching with the means of achieving her goals.

Of course, it is true that teachers of reading, mathematics, Spanish, and Pascal are trying to reach a skill goal: fluency in a language. That fluency is composed of many skills, used in performance. But fluency is more than skill; it is the wise use of many skills, based on clear ideas about their value, why a skill works or doesn't work, and when to use it. What we are claiming, based on both common sense and the research in cognition, is that no skill can be integrated into a powerful repertoire unless the learner understands the big ideas related to using the skill wisely.

the first 10 minutes, all our unthinking assumptions of movie stereotypes are overthrown in rapid succession: The Boy Scout becomes the thief, the thieves are entitled to their archaeological bounty, the bad guys wear white, the sheriff sides with the bad guys, Dad is no help at all, and the bad guy is a good guy who so admires young Indy that he gives Indy his hat.

That is why converting our goals and content standards into *questions* is so crucial. We signal to the students not only what the big ideas are, but also that their job as lifelong learners is to keep inquiring into their meaning and value forever. Naïve thinking develops into more sophisticated thinking through provocative questions and performance challenges by which *ideas* are tested, confirmed, and refined; and through the use of content as a *means* of inquiry.

The Misconception Alert points out the importance of linking big ideas with the teaching of skills. Consider, for example, persuasive writing as a desired achievement. At first blush, it would appear that we are dealing exclusively with a performance based on a set of straightforward skills to be learned through practice and feedback. But on further reflection, we note a key conceptual element here, something that must be understood apart from the particular writing skills. Students must come to an understanding of *persuasion* and how it works if their writing and speaking are to ever be truly persuasive. They must come to understand *which* techniques of persuasion work and why, and also must learn the subtleties in the roles that audience, topic, and medium play in effective persuasion. In short, to learn to write or speak persuasively, students must understand the *purpose* of the genre, the *criteria* by which we judge effectiveness of persuasion, and the *strategies* most likely to work in persuading specific *audiences*. That requires having a clear idea about what persuasion is and isn't.

Putting it this way makes clear that understanding what persuasion is about may well be developed by means other than writing, and that mere skill in writing certain kinds of formats (e.g., a five-paragraph essay) does not indicate an understanding of persuasion. For example, to better understand persuasion so as to better persuade, one might be asked to read famous speeches, critique TV commercials, and read and discuss such literature as Orwell's essay on language and politics. Thus, the skill goal of persuasive writing contains within it various big ideas needing understanding.

Here are some examples of big ideas from various skill areas:

- In cooking, minimize waste and increase taste by using scraps for stocks
- When swimming, push water directly backward to ensure top speed and efficiency
- When reading to comprehend, practice "reading between the lines" instead of merely decoding
- In life, develop self-sufficiency for various life skills (e.g., budgeting)

Design Tip

In skill-focused courses of study, look for big ideas in

- The value of the skill—what the skill helps you do more effectively or efficiently
- Underlying concepts (e.g., "persuasion" when teaching the skills of persuasive writing or debate)
- Issues of strategy—effective tactics, including *when* to use a particular skill
- Why the skill works—the theories underlying the skill, so that greater transfer can happen

• In team sports (e.g., soccer, basketball, football), create space to spread the defense and to create offensive opportunities

• In science and mathematics, understand the concept of error in observation and measurement

Framing goals in terms of transfer tasks

We noted in Figure 3.3 (p. 71) that priorities can be established not only by building upon the big ideas but also by focusing schoolwork around transfer tasks derived from authentic challenges in the field. By *core task* we mean the most important performance demands in any field. For example, a core task in science is to design and debug a controlled experiment from scratch. In drama, a core task is to act with full and graceful empathy, in role, on stage. Authentic *challenges* involve realistic situations, where the context of the task is as faithful as possible to real-world opportunities and difficulties. A core task in history is to construct a defensible narrative, using all relevant sources. A constant challenge in such a task is that the sources are likely to be incomplete and conflicting. In mathematics, a key task is to model a complex phenomenon quantitatively; the typical challenge is that real-world data is always messy, with many errors and outliers.

These kinds of tasks and challenging situations in which they occur reflect the transfer with big ideas we seek for students to do over the long term. They are not merely interesting assessments. Core tasks with authentic challenges embody our educational aims: The goal of schooling is fluent and effective performance in the world, not mere verbal or physical response to narrow prompts. Transfer, reflective of understanding, involves expertly addressing authentic challenges at core tasks, where content is a means. And, most important, successful transfer means that students can perform well with minimal or no hand-holding, guiding, or cueing by teachers. Here are further examples of such goal-embodying tasks and challenges:

• A challenge in reading a text is to gain a deep understanding of what the text might mean, despite the obstacles of one's assumptions, biases, and limited tools and experience as a reader. (Put differently, a challenge is to avoid confusing one's "response" as a reader with one's "understanding" of the text.)

• A challenge in history is to tell a credible, informative, and supportable "story" using available sources. So various performances would involve tasks in which learners display their achievement in scenarios such as those involving journal or newspaper articles, museum exhibits, or lectures to others.

• A challenge in music is to turn a complex set of instructions into a fluent and moving whole, more than just the sum of the notes. Our performance of a particular piece of music (and critiques of other peoples' performances) will reflect a grasp of the challenge.

• A challenge in science is to isolate the most salient variables from a wealth of possibilities. All key performance tasks center on a particular experiment and a successful design, debugged; or on a rebuttal in a journal of someone else's proposed design. Various performances reflect our achievement—for example, talking about the text intelligently in a group, writing an informative paper, or doing an insightful book review.

• A challenge in studying another language is to successfully translate meaning idiomatically, not just do a one-to-one translation of each word. Many different written and oral tasks get at this challenge, with the difficulty increased by the colloquialisms and idioms used.

• A challenge in mathematics is to model complex phenomena in purely quantitative terms when there are sufficient anomalies and outliers to make us unsure what is pattern and what is noise. (And speaking of noise, a major challenge in public speaking is to inform and delight *this* audience, in *this* setting, despite inevitable "noise," in both the literal and figurative senses.)

To make these examples of transfer more robust, consider the following rubric, which can be used to self-assess and peer review the design of any assessments purporting to involve true application with authentic challenges.

Transfer Demand/Degree of Cue

4 The task looks unfamiliar, even odd or puzzling, and is presented without cues as to how to approach or solve it. Success depends upon a creative inventory or adaptation of one's knowledge, based on understanding both the content and the situation—"far transfer." Carefully thinking through what the task does and does not ask and provide is required; identifying that additional problems, not obvious at first, have to be worked through. As a result, the task may seem undoable to some (even though it is likely doable by all if prior learning were effectively tapped). Not all students may succeed, therefore, and some may give up—even if they appear to have had control over the content previously.

3 The task may look unfamiliar but is presented with clues or cues meant to suggest the approach or content called for (or to narrow the options considerably). Success depends upon realizing what recent learning applies in this somewhat ambiguous or different scenario—"near transfer." The main challenge for the learner is to figure out what kind of problem this is, from the information given. Having realized what the task demands, the learner should be able to follow known procedures to solve it. Some learners who seemed skilled and knowledgeable on past tests may not successfully complete the task.

2 The task is presented with explicit reference to ideas, topics, or tasks previously studied, but no reference is made to the specific rule or formula that applies. Minimal transfer is required. Success requires the student only to recognize and recall which rule applies and use it, based on a familiar problem statement. The only transfer involves dealing with variables, categories, or situational details different from those in the teaching examples; and in realizing which rule applies from a few obvious recent candidates.

1 The task is presented so that the student need only follow directions and use recall and logic to complete it. No transfer is required, only the plugging in of a technique or content related to just-completed learning or examples.

Challenging tasks at the core of a subject can clearly help us prioritize our aims if we think of them as organizing clusters of related knowledge and skill. They would thus be the performance equivalent of Phenix's "representative ideas." What, then, are the *representative challenges* in each field? (UbD Template Stage 2: What are the key tasks signifying the ability to meet the key challenges, with core content?) What does it mean to "do" the subject, to use core content wisely and effectively in "challenging" and realistic circumstances? (This point is pursued further in Chapter 7). Without good answers to these questions, we run the risk of merely listing lots of knowledge and skill as our goals, so that the big ideas and core performance abilities fall through the cracks despite our best intentions.

A core task is thus not quite the same as a specific test. It summarizes a host of related performance demands, in varying situations. It embodies key state standards and local goals and thus properly belongs in our Stage 1 thinking. It specifies the conditions that any proposed assessment of performance in Stage 2 should meet, to ensure that we don't focus on arbitrary projects or tests. Curricula are means to authentic performance. What are the most important tasks and challenges in every field and in adult life? That is a Stage 1 question. What specific assessment tasks and challenges will we put before students to measure student progress toward our goals? That is the specific "evidence" question of Stage 2.

Clarity about complex core tasks makes it far more likely that our goals will be intellectually vital and coherent. When goals are conceived only as lists of facts and skills, design and instruction end up as inert bits and pieces out of context. Transfer is completely bypassed, in other words, as a goal. To avoid that oversight, we must always ask of knowledge and skill goals, "For what kinds of important capacities will this content actually equip us?" instead of merely asking, "What knowledge and skill is (potentially) important?" Overarching performance

■ MISCONCEPTION ALERT!

Some readers may think that we have done an inadequate job of linking our work to the longstanding literature in "task analysis." But, as this account of the elements of Stage 1 suggests, framing goals is profoundly difficult. It might be said, paradoxically, to be the most challenging aspect of instructional design. So although the *idea* of task analysis is conceptually identical with backward design, we cannot just "begin" with specific goals and move swiftly from there. We believe that task analysis has been persistently hobbled by an excessively behavioristic and atomistic view of educational goals, that the procedure varies by context and goal, and that the results of such analysis have thus been confusing, as noted by recent writers on task analysis (Jonassen, Tessmer, & Hannum, 1999).

As we suggest here (and make clear in later chapters on performance), we must design backward from very complex ideas and "messy" performances. Most task analyses assume, by contrast, that any task that puts our goals in terms of measurable behaviors and clear subskills is valid. We believe that the reason for the persistent failure of instructional design to do justice to understanding as an aim is that task analyses have depended on easy-to-manage goals rather than the most valid ones.

goals thus serve as the criteria for deciding what to emphasize and what to omit, just as happens in any performance-based area such as drama, athletics, and carpentry. Furthermore, by considering each academic program area as the "discipline" of thinking and acting in certain ways, of "doing" the subject, we become more properly attentive to ongoing results (the "learning"), as is the case with coaches.

Backward design in action with Bob James

Does anything in the unit require in-depth and deliberate uncoverage? Well, sure. It isn't easy to grasp the idea that nutritional needs vary according to individual characteristics. There is no such thing as a one-size-fits-all diet. Are there typical misunderstandings, for example, that I ought to more deliberately focus on? Well, as I think about it, I *have* found that many students harbor the belief (misconception) that if food is good for you, it must taste bad. One of my goals in this unit is to dispel this myth so that they won't have an automatic aversion to healthy food.

Thinking beyond core tasks for nutrition was *very* useful. It helped me get beyond the factual stuff to consider what people actually do with this information, as professionals and laypersons. Several core tasks come to mind—we use knowledge of nutrition to plan healthful meals and balanced diets, to become more critical of food advertising, and to make lifestyle adjustments. Just thinking this through has helped me to clarify my goals and has given me some ideas for assessment.

Are there typical misunderstandings that my students have about nutrition? Let's see what the Project 2061 *Benchmarks* say: "Lower elementary-school children . . . may believe that energy and strength result from exercise but not nutrition. . . . After instruction, middle-school students are often unable to explain their knowledge in scientific terms." Hmmm. I've heard that first mistake before. I think I'll plan a quiz early in the unit to check for this misconception.

As I think more about misconceptions, I recall that many students harbor the belief that if food is good for you, it must taste bad, and vice versa. One of my goals in the unit is to dispel this myth so that they won't have an automatic aversion to healthy food. I think I'll include some informal checks to see if this year's students harbor this misunderstanding, too.

In summary

Having spoken generally about the need for greater intellectual clarity, cohesion, and validity in our goals, we need to return to what we said earlier about understanding; because it turns out that when we scrutinize the goal we call "understanding," the goal is not one, but many.

Chapter 4

The Six Facets of Understanding

> There are many different ways of understanding, overlapping
> but not reducible to one another and, correspondingly, many different
> ways of teaching to understand.
> —John Passmore, *The Philosophy of Teaching,* 1982, p. 210

> LAUNCE: What a block art thou, that thou canst not! My staff understands me.
> SPEED: What thou sayest?
> LAUNCE: Ay, and what I do too: look thee, I'll but lean,
> and my staff understands me.
> SPEED: It stands under thee, indeed.
> LAUNCE: Why, stand-under and under-stand is all one.
> —William Shakespeare, *The Two Gentlemen of Verona,* c. 1593

Thus far in our analysis of understanding we have treated it as one notion, distinct from something called "knowledge." Yet problems arise when we look more closely at our language, as we work to frame understanding-related goals. The word *understanding* has various meanings, and our usage suggests that understanding is not one achievement but several, and it is revealed through different kinds of evidence.

In terms of synonyms for the noun form of the word, we talk about *insight* and *wisdom*—both clearly different from (yet somehow related to) knowledge. Yet our language also suggests that real understanding is something beyond a mere "academic" understanding. The phrases "egghead" and "pointy-headed intellectual" suggest that mere intellectual prowess can be sham understanding, and that too much learning can sometimes *impede* understanding.

The verbs we use are equally instructive. You only understand it, we say, if you can teach it, use it, prove it, connect it, explain it, defend it, read between the lines, and so on. The argument for performance assessment as a necessity, not a luxury, is thus clearly linked to these usages: Students must *perform effectively with knowledge* to convince us that they really understand what quizzes and short-answer tests only suggest they get. In addition, particular understandings can differ. We talk about seeing things from an interesting perspective, implying that complex ideas generate invariably and legitimately diverse points of view.

But the term has other meanings as well. There is an interpersonal as well as an intellectual meaning—implied in English, but explicit in other languages (the French verbs *savoir* and *connaître,* for example). We try to understand ideas but we also work to understand other people and situations. We talk of "coming to understand" or of "reaching an understanding," in the context of social relations. Revealingly, we sometimes talk of "changing our mind" *and* "having a change of heart" after a great effort to understand complex matters.

The *Oxford English Dictionary* tells us that the verb *understand* means "to apprehend the meaning or import" of an idea. At its most basic, the idea is found in the legal system when we determine competency to stand trial, whether in reference to a child or an adult with impeded faculties, by one's ability to understand the import of one's actions. When we think of meaning or import in the more sophisticated sense, we are referring to ideas like wisdom, the ability to rise above naïve, ill-considered, or inexperienced points of view. We often call this capacity "perspective," the ability to escape the passions, inclinations, and dominant opinions of the moment to do what circumspection and reflection reveal to be best.

Sometimes, though, we need the *opposite* of distance to "really understand." We need to strive for rapport, as in "Boy, do I understand what you're going through . . ." A failure to understand interpersonally typically involves a failure to consider or imagine there *being* different points of view, never mind "walking in their shoes." (Piaget wryly noted years ago that egocentric persons have only one point of view—theirs.) It has become a cliché phrase of gender relations that one side or the other says to the other: "You just don't understand . . ." Deborah Tannen's (1990) highly successful book on gender differences in conversation, entitled *You Just Don't Understand,* suggests how interpersonal understanding requires grasping unstated but very real, differing styles and purposes for conversation. Similarly, a lack of empathic understanding is evident in cross-cultural conflict, as revealed in the following quotes from an article a few years back in the *New York Times* about a flare-up of violence in the Middle East:

> *Both sides were taken aback by the speed and fury with which the ancient hatreds resurfaced, however, and there were some voices predicting that the conflagration would produce a renewed sense that two peoples cannot live in such close quarters without coming to some form of understanding.*

> *"We will come to [the idea of peace] out of fatigue. We will come to this idea out of a very painful understanding that the way to war leads us nowhere."* (MacFarquhar, 1996, p. A1)

Is there a link between an agreement born of mutual respect with wise perspective and "intellectual" insight into the problem? It is certainly plausible to say that the failures in Middle East policy may be more a function of a lack of empathy than any lack of knowledge on everyone's part. Perhaps the same is true in school studies. To really understand a novel, a scientific theory, or a period in history you have to have sufficient respect and empathy for the possibility that the author understands something you don't and might profit from understanding. The same is true in class discussions: Many students sometimes do not "hear" the contributions made by students they disrespect.

In short, sometimes understanding requires detachment; at other times it requires heartfelt solidarity with other people or ideas. Sometimes we think of understanding as highly theoretical, at other times as something revealed in effective real-world application. Sometimes we think of it as dispassionate critical analysis, at other times as empathetic response. Sometimes we think of it as dependent upon direct experience, at other times as something gained through detached reflection.

If nothing else, these observations suggest the need for greater circumspection. Understanding is multidimensional and complicated. There are different types of understanding, different methods of understanding, and conceptual overlap with other intellectual targets.

Because of the complexity of the issue, it makes sense to identify different (though overlapping and ideally integrated) aspects of understanding. We have developed a multifaceted view of what makes up a mature understanding, a six-sided view of the concept. When we truly understand, we

- *Can explain*—via generalizations or principles, providing justified and systematic accounts of phenomena, facts, and data; make insightful connections and provide illuminating examples or illustrations.
- *Can interpret*—tell meaningful stories; offer apt translations; provide a revealing historical or personal dimension to ideas and events; make the object of understanding personal or accessible through images, anecdotes, analogies, and models.
- *Can apply*—effectively use and adapt what we know in diverse and real contexts—we can "do" the subject.
- *Have perspective*—see and hear points of view through critical eyes and ears; see the big picture.
- *Can empathize*—find value in what others might find odd, alien, or implausible; perceive sensitively on the basis of prior direct experience.
- *Have self-knowledge*—show metacognitive awareness; perceive the personal style, prejudices, projections, and habits of mind that both shape and impede our own understanding; are aware of what we do not understand; reflect on the meaning of learning and experience.

These facets are manifestations of transfer ability. We use these different but related facets for judging understanding in the same way that we use varied criteria for judging a single, complex performance. For example, we say that "good essay writing" is composed of prose that is persuasive, organized, and clear. All three criteria need to be met, yet each is different from and somewhat independent of the other two. The writing might be clear but unpersuasive; it might be well organized but unclear and only somewhat persuasive.

Similarly, a student may have a sophisticated explanation of a theory but not be able to apply it; a student may see things from a critical distance but lack empathy. The facets reflect the different connotations of understanding we considered in Chapter 3. From an assessment perspective, the six facets offer various indicators of—windows on—understanding. Thus, they can guide the selection and design of assessments to elicit understanding. From a broader educational perspective, the facets suggest a goal: In teaching for transfer, complete and mature understanding ideally involves the full development of all six kinds of understanding.

We'll now examine the facets in more detail by

• Introducing each facet with a brief definition, followed by one or two apt quotes and questions that might be typical of someone wishing to understand.

• Offering two examples for each facet, one from daily public life and one from the classroom, as well as an example of what a lack of understanding looks like.

• Providing an analysis of the facet, offering a brief look at the instructional and assessment implications to be explored later in this book.

Facet 1: Explanation

Explanation: sophisticated and apt theories and illustrations, which provide knowledgeable and justified accounts of events, actions, and ideas.

> It was never the flavor of desserts alone that beguiled me. It was also my fascination with the variety of textures derived from so few ingredients. When reading through cookbooks I encountered endless variations of cakes and buttercreams. . . . But nowhere was there an explanation of how they compared to each other. . . . It became increasingly apparent to me that there were certain basic formulas from which all these seemingly endless disparate recipes evolved.
> —Rose Levy Berenbaum, *The Cake Bible,* 1988, pp. 15–16

> We see something moving, hear a sound unexpectedly, smell an unusual odor, and we ask: What is it? . . . When we have found out what it signifies, a squirrel running, two persons conversing, an explosion of gunpowder, we say that we understand.
> —John Dewey, *How We Think,* 1933, pp. 137, 146

Why is that so? What explains such events? What accounts for such action? How can we prove it? To what is this connected? What is an illustrative example? How does this work? What is implied?

↙ A cook explains why adding a little mustard to oil and vinegar enables them to mix: The mustard acts as an emulsifier.

↙ A 9th grade physics student provides a well-argued account of why the car on the air track accelerates the way it does when the incline of the roadway is varied.

✘ A 10th grade student knows the formula for the acceleration of bodies due to gravitational force but doesn't know what all the symbols mean in the formula or how to use the formula to compute specific rates of acceleration.

Facet 1 involves the kind of understanding that emerges from and reveals itself in a sound theory, an account that makes sense of puzzling, isolated, or opaque phenomena, data, feelings, or ideas. It is understanding revealed through performances and products that clearly, thoroughly, and instructively explain how things work, what they imply, where they connect, and why they happened.

Knowledge of why and how

Understanding is thus not mere knowledge of facts but inference about why and how, with specific evidence and logic—insightful connections and illustrations. Here are some examples:

• We can state the Pythagorean theorem. But what is the proof, on what axioms does it depend, what follows from the theorem, and why is the theorem so important?

• We may know that different objects fall to the ground with apparent uniformity of acceleration. But how is that so? Why does mass not make a difference in acceleration? To understand in this sense is to connect facts and ideas—often seemingly odd, counterintuitive, or contradictory facts and ideas—into a theory that works.

• We may know how to string a guitar and play songs in tune but not understand the harmonic principles and physics at work.

As Dewey (1933) explained, to understand something in this sense "is to see it in its relations to other things: to note how it operates or functions, what consequences follow from it, what causes it" (p. 137). We go beyond the information given to make inferences, connections, and associations—a theory that works. Powerful and insightful models or illustrations are the results of this understanding. We, on our own, can bind together seemingly disparate facts into a coherent, comprehensive, and illuminating account. We can predict heretofore unsought or unexamined results, and we can illuminate ignored or seemingly unimportant experiences.

What do we mean by a theory that works? Let us first consider a successful adult theory, the example of modern physics. Galileo, Kepler, and finally Newton and Einstein developed a theory capable of explaining the movement of all physical objects, from falling apples to comets. The theory predicts tides, the location of planets and comets, and how to put the nine ball in the corner pocket.

The theory was not obvious or the result of a mere cataloging of facts. The authors had to imagine a frictionless world, with movement on earth a special case. Of course, their critics had a field day with the idea that there was a force—gravity—everywhere on earth, acting at a distance, but by no discernible means and (contrary to the ancient Greek view and common sense) acting in such a way that the weight of an object had no effect on its rate of descent to earth. The theory eventually won over competing theories because, despite its counterintuitive elements, it did a better job than any competing theory of explaining, ordering, and predicting phenomena.

Similarly, a middle school student who can explain why steam, water, and ice, though superficially different, are the same chemical substance has a better understanding of H_2O than someone who cannot. A college student who can explain shoe prices and their fluctuation as a function of market forces has a better understanding of shoe cost than someone who cannot. Learners reveal an understanding of things—perhaps an experience, a lesson by the teacher, a concept, or their own performance—when they can transfer their abstract knowledge into giving good accounts that provide a useful framework, logic, and telling evidence to support claims.

Understandings involve more *systematic* explanations, where a response is subsumed under general and powerful principles:

> *Understanding the distributive property is [a] big idea. Realizing that* 9×5 *can be solved by adding* 5×5 *and* 4×5 *or any combination of groups of five that add up to 9 involves understanding about the structure of the part-whole relationships involved. (Fosnot & Dolk, 2001a, p. 36)*

Facet 1 calls for students to be given assignments and assessments that require them to explain what they know and give good reasons in support of it before we can conclude that they understand what was taught.

Supporting our opinions

Thus, merely giving back on tests the official theory of the textbook or the teacher is not evidence of understanding. We need to explain *why* our answer is correct, why the fact exists, why the formula works; we need to supply support for our opinions. When assessing, we look for good explanations from students, calling upon them to reveal their understanding by using such verbs as *support, justify, generalize, predict, verify, prove,* and *substantiate.*

Regardless of the subject content or the age or sophistication of the students, when the students understand in the sense of Facet 1, they have the ability to "show their work." We are also implying for assessment that the students must be confronted with new facts, phenomena, or problems to see if they can, on their own, subsume the information under the correct principle and explain away apparent counterarguments and counterexamples. Such explaining involves the kind of capacities labeled "analysis" and "synthesis" in Bloom's Taxonomy.

Students with in-depth understanding in this sense have greater control—over data and over robust connections—than those with more limited understanding. They grasp the subtler examples, implications, and assumptions of the current work. Teachers invariably describe such understandings as insightful, thorough, nuanced, or thoughtfully qualified (as opposed to merely superficial, isolated, glib, sweeping, or grandiose theorizing). An explanation or theory lacking such understanding is typically not so much wrong as it is incomplete or naïve. It is not wrong to say that weather depends upon wind, that all triangles are the same, or that cutting out sugar will make you lose weight; rather, these convey naïve or simplistic views (as opposed to qualified and data-supported conceptions).

From a design point of view, Facet 1 calls for building units around questions, issues, and problems that demand student theories and explanations, such as those found in problem-based learning and effective hands-on and minds-on science programs. The implications for assessment are straightforward: Use assessments (e.g., performance tasks, projects, prompts, and tests) that ask students to provide an explanation on their own, not simply recall; to link specific facts with larger ideas and justify the connections; to show their work, not just give an answer; and to support their conclusions.

Facet 2: Interpretation

Interpretation: interpretations, narratives, and translations that provide meaning.

> [Juzo Itami's films] revealed truths to the Japanese they never knew existed—even though they were right there in their daily life. "He could express the inside story about things people think they understand but really don't," said film critic Jun Ishiko.
> —Kevin Sullivan, *Washington Post,* December 22, 1997, p. C1

> Narratives and their interpretations traffic in meanings and meanings are intransigently multiple.
> —Jerome Bruner, *The Culture of Education,* 1996, p. 90

What does it mean? Why does it matter? What of it? What does it illustrate or illuminate in human experience? How does it relate to me? What makes sense?

✔ A grandfather tells stories about the Depression to illustrate the importance of saving for a rainy day.

✔ A college freshman shows how *Gulliver's Travels* can be read as a satire on British intellectual life; it's not just a fairy tale.

✗ A middle school student can translate all the words but does not grasp the meaning of a Spanish sentence.

The object of interpretation is meaning, not merely a plausible account. Interpretation traffics in powerful stories, not abstract theories, for its insights. Understanding of this kind occurs when someone sheds interesting and significant light on current or past experience. Yet interesting interpretations are always contestable and "intransigently multiple," as Bruner noted, and as the following excerpts from two reviews of *The Beginning of Wisdom: Reading Genesis* by Leon Kass make clear:

Mr. Kass's dense book is extraordinary. It soberly works through the text and demands comparable labors from its readers, piercing through two millenniums of commentary. It may not always convince and more historical background would help at times, but its analyses and hypotheses will leave no reader's understanding of Genesis unchanged. (Rothstein, 2003, p. B7)

Yes, at the beginning of the 21st century, Kass presents a laboriously written apologia for patriarchy. In the process he turns Genesis into moral lessons for contemporary people of the covenant. . . . Bringing a bias for patriarchy to what is itself a patriarchal book, Kass finds there what he already believes. . . . Outlandish moralisms pepper this book, making the patriarchy of Genesis look far more pernicious than it is. . . . The Book of Genesis according to Kass is not for this reviewer the beginning of wisdom. To the contrary, it is the beginning of folly—inspired by the zeal of a patriarchal convert to biblical study. (Trible, 2003, sec. 7, p. 28)

Telling stories in order to understand is no mere enrichment of the mind; without them we are, to use Kierkegaard's phrase, reduced to fear and trembling (Kierkegaard, in Bruner, 1996, p. 90).

We value good storytellers with reason. A good story both enlightens and engages; it helps us remember and connect. A clear and compelling narrative can help us find meaning in what may have previously seemed to be abstract or irrelevant:

The features of parables reveal why they make effective teaching devices. Their concreteness, specificity, and narrative organization capture our attention. Their profundity—that they seem to signify more than simply the story itself—engages our intellect. We want to figure out what the story is "trying to tell us." So we start pondering it. Their opaqueness—that they resist easy deciphering—gives us material for reflection. (Finkel, 2000, p. 13)[1]

Stories help us make sense of our lives and the lives around us, whether in history, literature, or art. The deepest, most transcendent meanings are found, of course, in the stories, parables, and myths that anchor all religions. A story is not a diversion; the best stories make our lives more understandable and focused.

Meanings: Transforming understanding

But a "story" is more than a language arts concept. The meanings and patterns we ascribe to *all* events, data, or experiences transform our understanding and perception of particular facts. The student possessing this understanding can show an event's significance, reveal the data's importance, or provide an interpretation that strikes a deep chord of recognition and resonance. Consider how the words and imagery of Martin Luther King Jr.'s memorable March on Washington speech ("I have a dream") crystallized the many complex ideas and feelings behind the civil rights movement. Or think of how the best newspaper editorials make sense of complex political currents and ideas.

Meaning, of course, is in the eye of the beholder. Think of what November 22, 1963 (the day of President John F. Kennedy's assassination), means to those of us who came of age in the 1960s, or September 11, 2001, to all of us today. Or consider how differently a mother, a police officer, or an adolescent in a foster home might perceive the same newspaper account of severe child abuse. Social workers and psychologists might well have an accepted theory of child abuse in the sense of Facet 1. But the meaning of the event, hence an understanding of it, may have little to do with the theory; the theory may be only a scientific account, with no bearing, for example, on the abused person's view of the event and the world.

Making sense—of others' stories or of empirical data—involves translation and interpretation in the broadest sense. Whether we think of a struggling student taking German 1, a 12th grader reading *King Lear,* a 6th grade student pondering the curve implied in a data set, a graduate student poring over the Dead Sea Scrolls, or a police detective making sense of bank records and phone calls, the challenge is the same: understanding the meaning of a "text" when the overall meaning is a puzzle to the reader or the facts tell no self-evident story. In fields like history and archaeology, we must reconstruct the meaning of events and artifacts from clues provided by the historical record. In economics, meaning comes from the ability to determine broad economic trends by interpreting the most salient consumer and business indicators. In mathematics, interpretation is called for in drawing conclusions from limited data. With this type of understanding, teachers ask learners to make sense of, show the significance of, decode, or make a story meaningful.

A challenge: Bringing any "text" to life

In classrooms, this facet—interpretation—most often manifests itself in discussions of the significance of books, works of art, or past and present experiences. The challenge in teaching is to bring any "text" to life by showing how, through study and discussion, it can speak to our concerns. For example, we all struggle in our relationships with our parents, and Shakespeare offers us great insights if only we can make meaning of the challenging language in *King Lear.*

Understanding is not merely about a logically defensible theory (as in Facet 1) but also about the significance of the results. This holds in mathematics, too, as Henri Poincaré (1913/1982), a famous French mathematician, reminds us:

What is it to understand? Has this word the same meaning for all the world? To understand the demonstration of a theorem, is that to examine successively each of the syllogisms composing it and to ascertain its correctness, its conformity to the rules of the game? . . . For some, yes; when they have done this, they will say they understand. For the majority, no. Almost all are more exacting; they wish to know not merely why the syllogisms . . . are correct, but why they link together in this order rather than another. In so far as to them they seem engendered by caprice and not by an intelligence always conscious of the end to be attained, they do not believe they understand. (p. 431)

When interpreting, students move between the text and their own experience to find legitimate but *varying* interpretations, as noted. In the interpretive realm, unlike the realm of scientific explanation, it is not only acceptable but likely that different understandings of the same "text" (book, event, experience) will be proposed. Indeed, modern literary criticism has been enlivened by the idea that not even the author's view is privileged, that regardless of author intent, texts can have unintended meanings and significance. A text or a speaker's words will always have different valid readings. All interpretations are bound by the personal, social, cultural, and historical contexts in which they arise.

On the other hand, not just anything goes. Some understandings of a text, work of art, person, or event are more insightful or defensible than others; a reading, a history, or a psychological case is stronger than another by virtue of its coherence, thoroughness, and documentation. The pinnacle of educational expertise, for example, is a personal dissertation—and its defense.

Explanation and interpretation are thus related but different. Theory is general; interpretations are contextual and specific. The act of interpretation is more fraught with inherent ambiguity than the act of theory building and testing: we may not agree on the right theoretical explanation but we expect there to be only one theory surviving by the end. But there will always be as many meanings as there are thoughtful interpreters. A jury trying to understand a case of child abuse, for example, looks at significance and intent, not agreed-upon general findings from theoretical science. The theorist builds objective and general knowledge about the phenomenon called abuse, but the novelist or journalist may offer as much or more insight into the "why?" We may know the relevant facts and theoretical principles, but we can and must still always ask, What does it all mean? What is its importance—to me, to us? How should we understand this *particular* case?

A theory needs to be true in order to work; a story need only have verisimilitude and provide illumination. The existence of three competing theories for the same physical phenomenon is intellectually unacceptable, but the existence of many different plausible and insightful interpretations of the same human events is not only acceptable but enriching to meaning.

Theories provide various meanings, too—sometimes leading far from the detached conceptions of their founders. Sulloway (1996) underscores the point that the revolutionary aspect of Darwin's work was not in the facts or even in a theory of evolution (because other such theories had been proposed) but in his conception of evolution as occurring through *unpredictable* (i.e., "purposeless") adaptation—an idea that threatens the worldview and religious sensibilities of many people, to this day.

The stories we learn to tell about ourselves and our world point to the true meaning of constructivism. When we say that students must make their own meaning, we mean that it is futile to hand students prepackaged "interpreta-tions" or statements of "significance" without letting them work through the issues. No one can decide for someone else the meaning of Darwinism—even if there is an agreed-upon theoretical construct in science called "evolutionary theory." Didactic teaching of *the* interpretation will mislead students about the truly arguable nature of all interpretation.

Developing interpretations

The inherently ambiguous nature of specific texts, data, and experiences requires an education that makes students—not just teachers and textbook writers—develop interpretations, and that ensures that students' ideas receive the feedback necessary to force continual testing and revision of those accounts. Students must have activities and assessments that ask them to interpret *inherently ambiguous* matters—far different than typical "right answer" testing. Schooling cannot be the learning of what someone else says is the sig-nificance of something, except as a way to model meaning-making or as a pre-lude to testing the interpretation so as to better understand the possibilities.

To be educated for autonomous intellectual performance as adults, stu-dents need to see how disciplinary understandings are built from the inside. Examples include inviting students to fashion an oral history out of disparate interviews, to develop a mathematical conclusion out of messy data, or to cre-ate an artistic interpretation subject to peer review, based on a careful reading. In short, students must have firsthand knowledge of the history of knowledge creation and refinement if they later are to find meaning in knowledge.

Facet 3: Application

Application: ability to use knowledge effectively in new situations and diverse, realistic contexts.

> [By understanding] I mean simply a sufficient grasp of concepts,
> principles, or skills so that one can bring them to bear on new problems
> and situations, deciding in which ways one's present competencies can
> suffice and in which ways one may require new skills or knowledge.
> —Howard Gardner, *The Unschooled Mind,* 1991, p. 18

> Use it or lose it.
> —Anonymous

How and where can we use this knowledge, skill, or process? How should my thinking and action be modified to meet the demands of this particular situation?

✔ A young couple uses their knowledge of economics (e.g., the power of compound interest and the high cost of credit cards) to develop an effective financial plan for saving and investing.

✔ Seventh grade students use their knowledge of statistics to accurately project next year's costs and needs for the student-run candy and supply store.

✘ A physics professor cannot diagnose and fix a broken lamp.

To understand is to be able to use knowledge. This is an old idea in U.S. education—indeed, an old idea in the long tradition of U.S. pragmatism and cultural disdain for ivory-tower, academic thinking. We say to young and old alike, "You need to walk the walk, not just talk the talk." Bloom (1956) and his colleagues saw application as central to understanding and quite different from the kind of endless plugging-in and fill-in-the-blanks pseudoperformance found in so many classrooms:

> Teachers frequently say: "If a student really comprehends something, he can apply it. . . ." Application is different in two ways from knowledge and simple comprehension: The student is not prompted to give specific knowledge, nor is the problem old-hat. (p. 120)

Matching knowledge to a context

Understanding involves matching our ideas, knowledge, and actions to context. In other words, understanding involves tact in the older sense of that term, made famous by William James (1899/1958) when he referred to the tact needed for teaching, namely "knowledge of the concrete situation" (as opposed to theoretical understanding—Facet 1—i.e., academic knowledge of child psychology).

The implications for teaching and assessment are straightforward and at the heart of the performance-based reforms that we have been a part of for the last two decades. We show our understanding of something by using it, adapting it, and customizing it. When we must negotiate different constraints, social contexts, purposes, and audiences, we reveal our understanding as performance know-how, the ability to accomplish tasks successfully, with grace under pressure, and with tact.

Application of understanding is thus a context-dependent skill, requiring the use of new problems and diverse situations in assessment. Bloom (1981) and his colleagues said something quite similar:

> It is evident that the problem or task must be a new one. . . . It also seems likely that students must have a great deal of latitude in defining the problem or task if they are to relate their own ideas . . . or experiences to it. (p. 267)

In fact, Bloom (1981) and his colleagues stress the point we make throughout the book—that an education for performance, based on understanding applied, is of the highest priority:

> Synthesis is what is frequently expected of the mature worker, and the sooner the students are given opportunities to make syntheses on their own, the sooner they will feel that the world of school has something to contribute to them and to the life they will live in the wider society. (p. 266)

Real-world problems

The problems that we develop for students should be as close as possible to the situation in which a scholar, artist, engineer, or other professional attacks such problems. The time allowed and the conditions of work, for example, should be as far away as possible from the typical controlled exam situation. Bloom, Madaus, and Hastings (1981) take this view:

> The adequacy of the final product may be judged in terms of:
> a. the effect it has on the reader, observer, or audience,
> b. the adequacy with which it has accomplished the task, and/or
> c. evidence on the adequacy of the process by which it was developed. (p. 268)

Or as Gardner (1991) argues:

> The test of understanding involves neither repetition of information learned nor performance of practices mastered. Rather it involves the appropriate application of concepts and principles to questions or problems that are newly posed. . . . Whereas short-answer tests and oral responses in classes can provide clues to student understanding, it is generally necessary to look more deeply. . . . For these purposes, new and unfamiliar problems, followed by open-ended clinical interviews or careful observations, provide the best way of establishing the degree of understanding . . . attained. (pp. 117, 145)

Swiss child psychologist Jean Piaget (1973/1977) argued more radically that student understanding reveals itself by student innovation in application. He said that many so-called application problems, especially in mathematics, were not truly novel and hence not indicative of understanding:

> Real comprehension of a notion or a theory implies the reinvention of this theory by the student. Once the child is capable of repeating certain notions and using some applications of these in learning situations he often gives the impression of understanding; however, this does not fulfill the condition of reinvention. True understanding manifests itself by new spontaneous applications. (p. 731)

Thus, the instructional and assessment implications of Facet 3 call for an emphasis on performance-based learning: work that focuses on and culminates in more authentic tasks, supplemented by more conventional tests (see Wiggins, 1998; McTighe, 1996–1997).

If understanding is to blossom, students need to have a clear performance goal and be required to keep that goal in constant view as they work. The case method in law and the problem-based learning method in medicine exemplify this point. By engaging in this kind of effort, students learn they are not "done" with a project or lesson simply because they worked hard, followed directions, and turned in a product. Instruction and the design of core challenges and performance tasks must require students to constantly self-assess their performance and production against standards.

Facet 4: Perspective

Perspective: critical and insightful points of view.

> The profit of education is the ability it gives to make distinctions that penetrate below the surface. . . . One knows that there is a difference between sound and sense, between what is emphatic and what is distinctive, between what is conspicuous and what is important.
> —John Dewey, in A. H. Johnson, *The Wit and Wisdom of John Dewey,* 1949, p. 104

> An important symptom of an emerging understanding is the capacity to represent a problem in a number of different ways and to approach its solution from varied vantage points; a single, rigid representation is unlikely to suffice.
> —Howard Gardner, *The Unschooled Mind,* 1991, p. 13

From whose point of view? From which vantage point? What is assumed or tacit that needs to be made explicit and considered? What is justified or warranted? Is there adequate evidence? Is it reasonable? What are the strengths and weaknesses of the idea? Is it plausible? What are its limits? So what?

✔ A 10-year-old girl recognizes in TV advertising the fallacy of using popular figures to promote products.

✔ A student explains the Israeli and Palestinian arguments for and against new settlements on the Gaza Strip.

✘ A bright but rigid student refuses to consider that there is another way to model the phenomena mathematically. She just "knows" that there is only one way—hers.

To understand in this sense is to see things from a dispassionate and disinterested perspective. This type of understanding is not about any student's particular point of view but about the mature recognition that any answer to a complex question typically involves a point of view; hence, an answer is often one of many possible plausible accounts. A student with perspective is alert to what is taken for granted, assumed, overlooked, or glossed over in an inquiry or theory.

Perspective involves making tacit assumptions and implications explicit. It is often revealed through an ability to ask, What of it? and to see an answer—even a teacher's or a textbook's answer—as a point of view. This type of perspective is a powerful form of insight, because by shifting perspective and casting familiar ideas in a new light, one can create new theories, stories, and applications.

The advantage of perspective

In the critical-thinking sense of the term, students with perspective expose questionable and unexamined assumptions, conclusions, and implications. When students have or can gain perspective, they can gain a critical distance from the habitual or knee-jerk beliefs, feelings, theories, and appeals that characterize less careful and circumspect thinkers.

Perspective involves the discipline of asking, How does it look from another point of view? How, for example, would my critics see things? In his autobiography, Darwin (1958) noted that this critical stance was key to his success in defending his controversial theory:

> I . . . followed a golden rule that whenever a published fact, a new observation or thought came across me, which was opposed to my general results, to make a memorandum of it without fail and at once; for I had found by experience that such facts and thoughts were far more apt to escape from memory than favorable ones. Owing to this habit, very few objections were raised against my views that I had not at least noticed and attempted to answer. (p. 123)

Thus, perspective as an aspect of understanding is a mature achievement, an earned understanding of how ideas look from different vantage points. Novice learners, those just setting out on the road to mastery, may have a revealing point of view, even when they lack a thorough explanation of things. (Consider the child who speaks out in "The Emperor's New Clothes.") But novices, by definition, lack the ability to deliberately take and consider multiple perspectives, as Gardner points out in the epigraph above.

A more subtle perspective involves grasping the points of view behind teacher and textbook pronouncements. What is the point of view of the authors of U.S. history and physics textbooks concerning what is true, verified, and important? Do other authors share those views? Do different experts, teachers, and authors establish different priorities? If so, with what justification and advantages or disadvantages? That this line of questioning seems too esoteric shows how far we are from giving students needed perspective.

Bruner (1996) notes that "understanding something in one way does not preclude understanding it in other ways. Understanding in any one particular way is only 'right' or 'wrong' from the particular perspective in terms of which it is pursued" (pp. 13–14). Consider the following excerpt from a textbook passage on the Revolutionary War era:

> What, then, were the causes of the American Revolution? It used to be argued that the revolution was caused by the tyranny of the British government. This simple explanation is no longer acceptable. Historians now recognize that the British colonies were the freest in the world, and that their people had rights and liberties which were enjoyed in no other empire. . . . The British government was guilty of a failure to understand the American situation. . . .
>
> The great majority of colonists were loyal, even after the Stamp Act. They were proud of the Empire and its liberties. . . . In the years following the Stamp Act a small minority of radicals began to work for independence. They watched for every opportunity to stir up trouble. (U.S. Department of Health, Education, and Welfare, 1976, p. 38)

Sounds decidedly odd, eh? That's because it is from a *Canadian* high school history textbook. We can quickly grasp here that if students in the United States have achieved a real understanding (as opposed to mere accurate recall) of their text, they can smoothly cope with the historical and historiographical issues raised by this other reading of the "same" history. (Perspective involves weighing different plausible explanations and interpretations, in other words.)

Everyone recognizes the problem of conveying perspective in newspaper reporting, so why isn't it addressed in working with accounts from textbooks (or, more typically, from a single textbook)? Everyone knows that authors' views shape choice of content, emphasis, and style, so shouldn't we help students use these language arts skills in understanding textbooks? What questions and assumptions informed the text's authors? For that matter, what were the original thinkers such as Euclid, Newton, Thomas Jefferson, Lavoisier, Adam Smith, Darwin, and others trying to accomplish? Based on what assumptions? With what blind spots? To what extent do textbooks distort these ideas in trying to simplify them or to satisfy numerous audiences?

Thus, an essential perspective on perspective involves making sure that all coursework asks and answers, What of it? What is assumed? What follows? These are not tangential or "extra-credit" questions in an education for understanding; they are essential. Our instructional and assessment strategies need to better highlight the means and ends of a liberal education, namely, greater control over essential questions and ideas so the student can see both intrinsic and extrinsic value in intellectual life. Indeed, in the *Oxford English Dictionary,* one definition of the verb *understand* is "to know the import" of something. By this criterion, how successful are even the best schools and colleges in bringing about understanding? Few students leave school with an understanding of the value of their schoolwork—of the value of the "discipline" required to learn the disciplines.

Facet 4 promotes the idea that instruction should include explicit opportunities for students to confront alternative theories and diverse points of view regarding the big ideas—not just as a function of hearing other student views different from their own, but as a result of the design of the coursework and materials, which show experts offering different perspectives on the same ideas.

In an earlier era, Joseph Schwab (1978) envisioned an education for understanding at the college level based on shifts of perspective. He developed what he called the art of the "eclectic": the deliberate design of coursework that compelled students to see the same important ideas (e.g., free will versus determinism, the development of personality) from very different theoretical perspectives. We build upon Schwab's idea (and the work of Dewey before him and Bruner after him) to propose that every discussion of "content" requires a consideration of the meaning and value of the content from different points of view if understanding is to occur and mere coverage is to be avoided.

Facet 5: Empathy

Empathy: the ability to get inside another person's feelings and worldview.

> To understand is to forgive.
> —French proverb

> When reading the works of an important thinker, look first for the apparent absurdities in the text and ask yourself how a sensible person could have written them. When you find an answer, when those passages make sense, then you may find that more central passages, ones you previously thought you understood, have changed their meaning.
> —Thomas Kuhn, on reading scientific texts, in R. Bernstein,
> *Beyond Objectivism and Relativism,* 1983, pp. 131–132

How does it seem to you? What do they see that I don't? What do I need to experience if I am to understand? What was the writer, artist, or performer feeling, thinking, seeing, and trying to make me feel and see?

✔ An adolescent empathizes with the restrictive lifestyle of his bedridden grandmother.

✔ From a British national exam: "*Romeo and Juliet*, Act 4. Imagine you are Juliet. Write your thoughts and feelings explaining why you have to take this desperate action."

✘ A natural athlete becomes a coach and berates his young players often because he cannot relate to their struggles to learn the game that came easily to him.

Empathy, the ability to walk in another's shoes, to escape one's own responses and reactions so as to grasp another's, is central to the most common colloquial use of the term *understanding.* When we try to understand another person, people, or culture, we strive for empathy. It is not simply an affective response or sympathy over which we have little control, but the disciplined attempt to feel as others feel, to see as others see. This excerpt from an interview with the singer known as Babyface illustrates the point:

> *"Do women ever come up to you and say, 'How did you know that? How did you feel that?'" I ask, and for the first time, he turns and looks at me evenly: "Yeah, that's the normal response," he says in a voice that suddenly isn't so shy. "It's not that I understand women any better than anyone else, but I do understand feelings. . . . All you have to do is imagine what that girl is going through, just turn it around and put yourself in those same shoes. . . . We're all the same people." (Smith, 1997, p. 22)*

Empathy is different from seeing in perspective, which is to see from a critical distance, to detach ourselves in order to see more objectively. With empathy, we see from inside the person's worldview; we walk in their shoes; we fully embrace the insights that come with engagement. Empathy is warm; perspective is cool, analytic detachment.

A German scholar, Theodor Lipps, coined the term *empathy* at the turn of the 20th century to describe what the audience must do to understand a work or performance of art. Empathy is the deliberate act of trying to find what is plausible, sensible, or meaningful in the ideas and actions of others, even if those ideas and actions are puzzling or off-putting. Empathy can lead us not only to rethink a situation but also to have a change of heart as we come to understand what formerly seemed odd or alien.

Empathy as a way to insight

Empathy is a form of insight because it involves the ability to get beyond odd, alien, seemingly weird opinions or people to find what is meaningful in them. As Thomas Kuhn's remark indicates, intellectual empathy is essential if we are to make sense of ideas that we too quickly reject because of our own assumptions. All scholars need empathy. "If we laugh with derision" at the theories of our predecessors, as anthropologist Stephen Jay Gould (1980) says, we will fail "in our understanding of their world" (p. 149). Similarly, students have to learn how to open-mindedly embrace ideas, experiences, and texts that might seem strange, off-putting, or just difficult to access if they are to understand them, their value, and their connection to what is more familiar. They need to see how unusual or "dumb" ideas can seem rich once we overcome habitual responses, and they need to see how habit can block our understanding of another person's understanding.

A simple example of the need for empathy can be found in our own system of government. Few students know that U.S. senators were appointed, not popularly elected, for more than 100 years. Fewer still understand why such a practice seemed like a good idea then. It is easy to imagine that our forefathers were misguided or hypocrites. However, we can think of assignments and assessments that ask students to role-play the writers of the Constitution so that such views seem less bizarre (even if we find them unacceptable now). The challenge would be to make a case to a group of citizens that appointed offices are in the citizens' best interest. As a postscript, we could ask students to write an essay or journal entry on the pros and cons of our current popular-vote system and to consider the value, if any, of the electoral college.

A change of heart

As we noted in our earlier discussion of language, understanding in the interpersonal sense suggests not merely an intellectual change of mind but a significant change of heart. Empathy requires respect for people different from ourselves. Our respect for them causes us to be open-minded, to carefully consider their views when those views are different from ours.

It becomes easier, then, to imagine schoolwork that deliberately confronts students with strange or alien texts, experiences, and ideas to see if they can get beyond what is off-putting about the work. Indeed, the Bradley Commission on the Teaching of History argued that a primary aim of history is to help students escape their ethnocentric and present-centered views in order to develop historical empathy for people living at different places and times

(Gagnon, 1989). This is, in fact, a common activity in foreign language classes that stress cultural issues.

More experiences in learning

This kind of understanding implies an experiential prerequisite that some people find troublesome. If someone were to refer to experiences like poverty, abuse, racism, or high-profile competitive sports and say, "You cannot possibly understand without having been there," the implication would be that insight from experience is necessary for empathic understanding. To ensure greater understanding of abstract ideas, students must have far more direct or simulated experiences of them than most current textbook-driven courses allow. Think of an intellectual Outward Bound: Learning needs to be more geared toward making students directly confront the effects—and the affect—of decisions, ideas, theories, and problems. The absence of such experiences in school may explain why many important ideas are so misunderstood and learnings so fragile, as the literature on misconception reveals. Assessment also must pay greater attention to whether students have overcome egocentrism, ethnocentrism, and present-centeredness in their answers and explanations.

Facet 6: Self-Knowledge

Self-knowledge: the wisdom to know one's ignorance and how one's patterns of thought and action inform as well as prejudice understanding.

> All understanding is ultimately self-understanding. . . . A person who understands, understands himself. . . . Understanding begins when something addresses us. This requires . . . the fundamental suspension of our own prejudices.
> —Hans-Georg Gadamer, *Truth and Method,* 1994, p. 266

> It is the duty of the human understanding to understand that there are things which it cannot understand, and what those things are.
> —Søren Kierkegaard, *Journals,* 1854

How does who I am shape my views? What are the limits of my understanding? What are my blind spots? What am I prone to misunderstand because of prejudice, habit, or style?

   ✔ A mother realizes that her frustration with her daughter's shyness is rooted in issues from her own childhood.

   ✔ Mindful of her learning style, a middle school student deliberately uses graphic organizers to help her study.

   ✘ "When all you have is a hammer, every problem looks like a nail."

Deep understanding is ultimately related to what we mean by *wisdom.* To understand the world we must first understand ourselves. Through self-knowledge we also understand what we do not understand. "Know thyself" is the maxim of those who would really understand, as the Greek philosophers often said. In a sense, Socrates is the patron saint of understanding. He knew he was ignorant, whereas most people did not realize they were.

In daily life, our capacity to accurately self-assess and self-regulate reflects understanding. *Metacognition* refers to self-knowledge about how we think and why, and the relation between our preferred methods of learning and our understanding (or lack of it). The immature mind is thus not merely ignorant or unskilled but unreflective. A naïve student, no matter how bright and learned, lacks self-knowledge to know when an idea is "out there" or a projection; to know when an idea seems objectively true but really only fits the student's beliefs; or to know how templates or frames for perception shape how and what the student understands.

Intellectual rationalization

Our intellectual blind spots predispose us toward intellectual rationalization: the ability to unendingly assimilate experience to beliefs and to categories that seem not merely plausible ideas but objective truths. Too easily, we keep verifying our favored and unexamined models, theories, analogies, and viewpoints.

Thinking in either-or terms is a common example of such a natural habit, one that we see rampant in education reform and one that Dewey viewed as the curse of immature thought. Students often think in dichotomies without seeing those categories as narrow projections. She's cool. He's a jerk. They're in the jock crowd, not the nerd crowd. That teacher likes me and hates you. Math isn't for girls. Football is for animals. This is a fact. That's wrong.

Salinger (1951) made brilliant use of this propensity in *The Catcher in the Rye*. Holden, the main character, is prone to viewing other adolescent boys and adults as "phonies," and his prejudice conceals more than it reveals. We learn a good deal about Holden's alienation, in fact, when by his own admission his categorization of people as either phony or not breaks down as he considers such interesting and competent adults as the Lunts, the blues piano player, and his teacher. Maturity is evident when we look beyond simplistic categories to see shades of perhaps unexpected differences, idiosyncrasies, or surprises in people and ideas.

We educators, too, are often unthinkingly reliant on and satisfied by neat categories and striking metaphors, seeing their limits and subjectivity only long after the fact. Is the brain really like a computer? Are children really like natural objects or phenomena to be treated as equal variables and "isolated," so that a standardized test can be modeled on the procedures of scientific experiments? To talk of education as "delivery of instructional services" (an economic metaphor and a more modern variant of the older factory model) or as entailing "behavioral objectives" (language rooted in Skinnerian animal training) is to use metaphors, and not necessarily helpful ones.

The fundamental fact is that we lay down rules, . . . and then when we follow the rules, things do not turn out as we assumed. That we are therefore, as it were, entangled in our own rules. This entanglement in our rules is what we want to understand (Aphorism 125). (Wittgenstein, 1953, p. 50)

Nearly 300 years ago, Francis Bacon (1620/1960) provided a thorough account of the misunderstandings introduced by our own habits of thought and the cultural context in which we find ourselves:

The human understanding is of its own nature prone to suppose the existence of more order and regularity in the world than it finds . . . [and] when it has once adopted an opinion draws all things else to support and agree with it. . . . It is the peculiar and perpetual error of the intellect to be more moved and excited by affirmatives than by negatives. . . . Numberless, in short, are the ways, and sometimes imperceptible, in which the affections color and infect the understanding. (Book I, Nos. 45–49, pp. 50–52)

Yet seeing prejudice as always wrong or harmful is also prejudice. Gadamer (1994) and Heidegger (1968), for example, argue that human prejudice is inseparable from human understanding. As Virginia Woolf (1929) noted, a self-conscious exposure of our prejudices may be the key to insight:

Perhaps if I lay bare the ideas, the prejudices that lie behind this statement ["A woman must have money and a room of her own to write fiction"], you will find that they have some bearing upon women and fiction. At any rate, when a subject is highly controversial—and any question about sex is that— one cannot hope to tell the truth. One can only show how one came to hold whatever opinion one does hold. One can only give one's audience the chance of drawing their own conclusions as they observe the limitations, the prejudices, the idiosyncrasies of the speaker. Fiction here is likely to contain more truth than fact. (p. 4)

What self-knowledge demands

Self-knowledge is a key facet of understanding because it demands that we self-consciously question our ways of seeing the world if we are to become more understanding—better able to see beyond our selves. It asks us to have the discipline to seek and find the inevitable blind spots or oversights in our thinking and to have the courage to face the uncertainty and inconsistencies lurking underneath effective habits, naïve confidence, strong beliefs, and worldviews that only seem complete and final. When we talk of subject matter "disciplines," note the root meaning: There is a "discipline" involved that requires courage and persistence because rational understanding makes us question and sometimes undo our strong beliefs.

Practically speaking, a greater attention to self-knowledge means that we must do a better job of teaching and assessing self-reflection in the broadest sense. We do that quite well in some areas of schooling; many programs and strategies help learning-disabled students develop greater metacognition and awareness of their own learning style. The best writing and performing arts classes stress constant self-reflection. But greater attention is needed to the ongoing self-assessment of intellectual performance as well as better understanding of the philosophical abilities that fall under the heading "epistemology"—the branch of philosophy that addresses what it means to know and understand knowledge and understanding, and how knowledge differs from belief and opinion.

Key implications of the facets for teaching and learning

The six facets should permeate our thinking about all three stages of backward design. They can help us clarify the desired understandings, the necessary assessment tasks, and the learning activities that will most likely advance student understanding. They should remind us that understandings are not facts, and that certain learning actions and performance assessments are required to bring about the needed meaning-making by the learner.

In other words, the facets help us avoid the Expert Blind Spot at work when we fall victim to the thinking that says, "Because I understand it, I will tell you my understanding and render teaching and learning more efficient." Ah, if only it were so easy! Alas, in reducing understandings to information (hence, assessments to tests of recall or "plug in"), we perpetuate a misunderstanding about learning: Students come to believe that their job is to memorize the understandings for later recall, as if they were mere facts. Put differently, if understanding is the goal of our teaching, we have to aggressively root out this misunderstanding about learning and help students see that they will often be expected to do more than take in knowledge—namely, make meaning out of something problematic and not obvious.

Good design will establish the idea that there will be a clear need for the learner to make sense of what the teacher teaches. If understanding is the aim, in other words, the design must make the meaning of certain facts and skills a problem, not a glib solution. This happens when an idea, fact, argument, or experience is designed to simultaneously illuminate things and raise questions.

Consider these simple examples of making "the need to understand" clearer. We must read a text in which we know all the words but cannot easily derive a meaning that makes any sense (a common problem when reading philosophy or poetry, for example). We are guided through a lab, only to be puzzled by an unexpected result from the experiment. We are presented with a data set that does not appear sensible, given all the formulas we have learned in math thus far. We encounter two history texts that disagree on the causes and effects of the same events. The soccer coach tells us that even defensive players need to play aggressively on offense.

What any curriculum designed for understanding must do, then, is help students realize that their job is not merely to take in what is "covered" but to actively "uncover" what lies below the surface of the facts and to ponder their meaning. This is, of course, what *constructivism* means: Meaning cannot be taught; it must be fashioned by the learner via artful design and effective coaching by the teacher. Thus, part of what a curriculum designed to develop student understanding will do is "teach" students that their job is not merely to learn facts and skills but also to question them for their meaning. The term *uncoverage* summarizes the design philosophy of guided inquiry into big ideas, whereby knowledge is made more connected, meaningful, and useful.

Although in the abstract it sounds perfectly sensible to ensure that design work is more focused on results, big ideas, and the six facets of understanding, it is likely not yet clear to many readers what this implies for design work in the concrete. If understanding is composed of the six facets, what do they look like in practice? How can we more accurately distinguish between those students with and without understanding? In our consideration of backward design for understanding, we are now ready to look more closely at framing big ideas for instruction in Stage 1; and, later, at framing our assessments to better evoke understanding (as well as to distinguish understanding from non-understanding or misunderstanding) in Stage 2.

We turn first to the element of the UbD Template that cuts across both stages and most easily illustrates how to frame work by big ideas: Essential Questions.

Chapter 5

Essential Questions: Doorways to Understanding

> Given particular subject matter or a particular concept, it is easy
> to ask trivial questions. . . . It is also easy to ask impossibly
> difficult questions. The trick is to find the medium questions
> that can be answered and that take you somewhere.
> —Jerome Bruner, *The Process of Education,* 1960, p. 40

> To question means to lay open, to place in the open. Only a person
> who has questions can have [real understanding].
> —Hans-Georg Gadamer, *Truth and Method,* 1994, p. 365

Any complex unit or course of study will naturally involve many educational targets simultaneously: knowledge, skills, attitudes, habits of mind, and understanding. But, as we have said, if the goal is to help students make good sense and use of what they learn, then the design (and resultant teaching) must explicitly focus on the big ideas that connect and bring meaning to all the discrete facts and skills.

How do we more deliberately stay focused on big ideas? How can we take a mass of content knowledge and shape it into engaging, thought-provoking, and effective work? How can we avoid the twin sins of activity-based and coverage-based design? In UbD, that focus is accomplished in part by framing goals in terms of what we call Essential Questions. (The other approaches, discussed in later chapters, are to specify the desired understandings and key performance tasks.)

What kinds of questions are we referring to? Not just any question will do. Consider the following examples of questions and notice how they differ from ones often posed in daily lessons and textbooks:

- What is a true friend?
- How precise must we be?
- To what extent does art reflect culture or shape it?
- Must a story have a beginning, a middle, and an end?
- Is everything quantifiable?

- Is the subjunctive necessary?
- To what extent is DNA destiny?
- In what ways is algebra real and in what ways is it unreal?
- To what extent is U.S. history a history of progress?
- What is the difference between a scientific fact, a scientific theory, and a strong opinion?
- Must heroes be flawless?
- What should we fear?
- Who is entitled to own what?
- What makes writing worth reading?

These are questions that are not answerable with finality in a brief sentence—and that's the point. Their aim is to stimulate thought, to provoke inquiry, and to spark more questions—including thoughtful student questions—not just pat answers. They are broad, full of transfer possibilities. The exploration of such questions enables us to *uncover* the real riches of a topic otherwise obscured by glib pronouncements in texts or routine teacher-talk. We need to go beyond questions answerable by unit facts to questions that burst through the boundaries of the topic. Deep and transferable understandings depend upon framing work around such questions.

Return to the apples vignette in the Introduction to see the benefit of anchoring curricula in thought-provoking questions that suggest fruitful (sorry!) avenues of inquiry. If the proposed string of "fun" activities suffers from a lack of intellectual focus, notice how we can provide better perspective and the impetus to go into depth by framing the unit with a set of provocative questions such as these: How have planting, growing, and harvest seasons affected life in the United States? How have children's roles at harvest changed over time? Compared to other foods, how good for you are apples? Can today's apple farmers survive economically?

These questions implicitly demand more than just a smorgasbord of activities and bits of knowledge in isolated units. They are asked and made central to the unit to engender probing inquiry and eventual transfer. They suggest that uncoverage is a priority, not a frill or an option if time is left over after learning other "stuff." Such questions, when properly used, thus send all the right signals about understanding as a goal.

Questions: Signposts to big ideas

The best questions point to and highlight the big ideas. They serve as doorways through which learners explore the key concepts, themes, theories, issues, and problems that reside within the content, perhaps as yet unseen: it is through the process of actively "interrogating" the content through provocative questions that students deepen their understanding. For instance, the question "How are stories from different places and times about me?" can lead students to the big ideas that great literature explores universal themes of the human condition and helps us gain insight into our own experiences. Similarly, the question "To what extent can people accurately predict the future?" serves as a launch pad for examining big ideas in statistics (e.g., sampling variables, predictive validity, degrees of confidence, correlation versus causality).

As Bruner (1996) put it, good questions "are ones that pose dilemmas, subvert obvious or canonical 'truths' or force incongruities upon our attention" (p. 127). Good questions elicit interesting and alternative views and suggest the need to focus on the reasoning we use in arriving at and defending an answer, not just whether our answer is "right" or "wrong." Good questions spark meaningful connections with what we bring to the classroom from prior classes and our own life experience. They can and do recur with profit. They cause us to rethink what we thought we understood and to transfer an idea from one setting to others.

In addition to stimulating thought and inquiry, questions can be used to effectively frame our content goals. For example, if a content standard calls for students to learn about the three branches of government, then a question such as "How might a government guard against abuses of power?" helps stimulate student thinking about *why* we need checks and balances, what the framers of the Constitution were trying to achieve, and other governmental approaches to balancing power.

Try it yourself. Instead of thinking of content as stuff to be covered, consider knowledge and skill as the means of addressing questions central to understanding key issues in your subject. This conceptual move offers teachers and curriculum committees a practical strategy for identifying important content ideas while engaging students in the very kind of constructivist thinking that understanding requires.

In short, the best questions serve not only to promote understanding of the content of a unit on a particular topic; they also spark connections and promote transfer of ideas from one setting to others. We call such questions "essential."

What makes a question essential?

In what senses should a question be deemed "essential"? The best questions push us to the heart of things—the essence. *What is democracy? How does this work? What does the author mean? Can we prove it? What should we do? What is its value?* Honest pursuit of such questions leads not only to deeper understandings, but also to more questions.

But essential questions need not be so global. They can go to the heart of a particular topic, problem, or field of study. Thus we can say that each academic field can be *defined* by its essential questions. Consider these examples:

• When error is unavoidable in measurement, what margins of error are tolerable?

• In what ways should government regulate the market system?

- How can we know if the author was serious?
- What are the strengths and limits of the big bang theory?
- Who is a "winner" in athletics?
- What is the relationship between popularity and greatness in literature?
- To what extent is "musical" a culture-bound aesthetic judgment?
- What makes a mathematical argument convincing?
- What is the connection between a country's form of government and the prosperity of its citizens?
- When is it wise in cooking to deviate from the recipe?
- What do "care" and "First, do no harm" mean in the health professions?
- How important is it to listen to our ancestors?

The best such questions are not merely emblematic of their fields but really *alive*. People ask and argue about them outside of school! The most vital discipline-bound questions open up thinking and possibilities for everyone—novices and experts alike. They signal that inquiry and open-mindedness are central to expertise, that we must always be learners. In the more practical sense, a question is alive in a subject if students really engage with it, if it seems genuine and relevant to them, and if it helps them gain a more systematic and deep understanding of what they are learning.

Questions like "What margins of error are tolerable?" are essential in yet another sense. They offer transferability across disciplines—linking not only units and courses in measurement and statistics, but also subjects as diverse as engineering, pottery, and music. Questions essential in this sense are those that encourage, hint at, even *demand* transfer beyond the particular topic in which we first encounter them. They should therefore recur over the years to promote conceptual connections and curriculum coherence.

Four connotations

Just as the six facets described in Chapter 4 represent different ways of characterizing understanding, there are four different but overlapping meanings for the term *essential* when used to characterize questions. One meaning involves *important questions that recur throughout all our lives.* Such questions are broad in scope and timeless by nature. They are perpetually arguable: What is justice? Is art a matter of taste or principles? How far should we tamper with our own biology and chemistry? Is science compatible with religion? Is an author's view privileged in determining the meaning of a text? We may arrive at or be helped to grasp understandings for these questions, but we soon learn that answers to them are invariably provisional. In other words, we are likely to change our minds in response to reflection and experience concerning such questions as we go through life, and changes of mind are not only expected but beneficial. A good education is grounded in such lifelong questions, even if we sometimes lose sight of them while focusing on content mastery. The big-idea questions signal that education is not just about learning "the answer" but about learning how to learn.

A second connotation for *essential* refers to *core ideas and inquiries within a discipline.* Essential questions in this sense are those that point to the core of big ideas in a subject and to the frontiers of technical knowledge. They are historically important and very much alive in the field. "What is healthful eating?" engenders lively debate today among nutritionists, physicians, diet promoters, and the general public (despite the fact that much is known and understood about nutrition). "Is any history capable of escaping the social and personal history of its writers?" has been widely and heatedly debated among scholars for the past 50 years and compels novices and experts alike to ponder potential bias in any historical narrative.

A third important connotation for the term *essential* refers to what is needed for learning core content. In this sense, we can consider a question essential if it *helps students effectively inquire and make sense* of important but complicated ideas, knowledge, and know-how—a bridge to findings that experts may believe are settled but learners do not yet grasp or see as valuable. In what ways does light act like a wave? How do the best writers hook and hold their readers? What models best describe a business cycle? Actively exploring such questions helps the learner to arrive at important understandings as well as greater coherence in content knowledge and skill. For example, as noted earlier, in soccer the players must come to understand the importance of repeatedly asking, "How can we create more open space on offense?" (i.e., spread the defense and exploit open space to enhance scoring opportunities) in order to address the more obvious question, "How might we win more games?"

A fourth meaning for the term *essential* refers to questions that *will most engage a specific and diverse set of learners.* Some adult questions may be important in the grand scheme of things (as judged by both specialists and teachers) but of no apparent relevance, meaning, interest, or importance to particular students. In this sense, questions are essential if they hook and hold the attention of *your* students.

To call a question "essential" is thus ambiguous. On the one hand, a question can be essential even if students do not grasp its power upon hearing it for the first time. As we have noted, big ideas are abstract, not obvious—in some cases, counterintuitive. On the other hand, if the question does not soon speak to the learner by signaling interesting or useful inquiries and insights, then a narrow focus on that question may be counterproductive. Yet caution is also needed: A punchy question might provoke lively discussion among your students but not point to big ideas and the goals of the unit. The challenge in design and instruction is to make essential questions (in the first two "objective" senses) accessible, thought-provoking, challenging, and a priority—sooner rather than later. The challenge can be met in various ways: through provocative experiences that "naturally" give rise to the essential questions, or through concrete entry questions, the discussion of which points toward the core of big ideas and issues. In practice, then, this is a Stage 3 problem—the challenge of translating the desired results of Stage 1 into "kid-friendly" terms for teaching. (We provide tips for doing this in Chapter 9.)

These various connotations of *essential* have implications for finer-grained distinctions in question types that we examine later in the chapter. For now, let's consider the common characteristics—the "essential" aspects—of the various kinds of essential questions. We propose that a question is essential if it is meant to

1. Cause genuine and relevant inquiry into the big ideas and core content.

2. Provoke deep thought, lively discussion, sustained inquiry, and new understanding as well as more questions.

3. Require students to consider alternatives, weigh evidence, support their ideas, and justify their answers.

4. Stimulate vital, ongoing rethinking of big ideas, assumptions, prior lessons.

5. Spark meaningful connections with prior learning and personal experiences.

6. Naturally recur, creating opportunities for transfer to other situations and subjects.

The importance of intent

Using these criteria requires great care. Note that they refer not to any innate characteristic of a question itself but to its powers in context. No question is *inherently* essential (or trivial, complex, or important). It all comes down to purpose, audience, and impact: What do you as a teacher-designer intend to have students do with the question? Is the goal lively inquiry or the recall of a single right answer? The six criteria make clear what the aim must be for the question to be deemed essential: The goal must be robust and revealing inquiry, leading to deeper understandings and new questions.

When we pose a so-called essential question, we do so to signal the understanding-related goals and the inquiries they imply for the unit, as the italicized stem statement preceding the six criteria suggests: *To what extent is the question meant to . . . ?* The essentialness of the question depends upon *why* we pose it, *how* we intend students to tackle it, and *what* we expect for learning activities and assessments as a result. Do we envision an open exploration, including debate, around "open" issues, or do we plan to simply lead the students to a prescribed answer? Do we hope that our questions will spark students to raise their own questions about the text, or do we expect a conventional interpretation? Do we intend that students confront a common misconception and try to "unpack" the fallacies? Is our question meant to stay alive after the unit is over and to recur, or do we expect the question to be settled by unit's end?

Thus, if we look only at the wording of a question, out of context, we cannot tell whether the question is or is not essential. Consider, for example, the question "What is a story?" It seems to seek a specific and familiar answer. But we cannot say without looking at the whole design—especially the assessments—whether this question is essential or not. Clearly, if we ask the question with the intent of having students chime back with "plot, characters, setting, theme," then the question (as pursued) is not essential in terms of the six criteria. However, if the question is being asked to first elicit well-known story elements but then overturn that conventional definition through a study of postmodern novels, then the question *is* essential. It's almost as if the emphasis of the question has changed: "So what *is* a story?"

More generally, questions such as "What is *x*?" may seek complex and probing inquiry, or they may be fishing for a simple definition. Questions like "Why did *y* happen?" may seek high-level investigations, or they may require only recalling what the text said. In the absence of well-designed and deliberate inquiry as a follow-up to our asking the question, even essential-sounding questions end up merely rhetorical. Conversely, questions that sound rather mundane in isolation might become increasingly provocative as the answers become increasingly paradoxical, and the design makes clear that digging deeper is mandatory.

More than format

Thus, we cannot say a question is or is not essential based only on the language used in its phrasing. Yet many educators were taught that a question should be phrased in a certain way to signal an intent to instigate inquiry, discussion, or argument rather than the recall of learned facts. So it is common for new teachers to be advised to avoid yes/no or who/what/when formulations of a question if the goal is critical thinking or inquiry. Although we appreciate the concern that teachers need to clearly signal their intentions to learners, we don't think a hard-and-fast rule about wording is the key issue. Rather, what is at stake is the whole design: Is it clear to students that their job is inquiry?

For example, a teacher might be encouraged to revise the question "Is light a particle or a wave?" because the phrasing suggests that a factual and final answer is sought. Although the advice makes some sense, the reality is different when the question is followed by experiments designed to have deliberately ambiguous results. Thus the deeper intent of the question is soon revealed by the paradoxical lab results in which light exhibits both wave-like and particle-like behavior.

In fact, many yes/no, either/or, and who/what/when questions offer the potential to spark impressive curiosity, thought, and reflection in students, depending upon how they are posed and the nature of the follow-ups. Consider the following examples and imagine the lively discussion, sustained thinking, and insights they might evoke:

- Is the universe expanding?
- Does Euclidean geometry offer the best map for the spaces we live in?
- Who should lead?
- Is *The Catcher in the Rye* a comedy or a tragedy?
- Is a democracy that suspends freedoms a contradiction in terms?

- What is the "third" world? Is there a "fourth"?
- When is victory assured?
- Is punctuation necessary?
- Are numbers real?

We can turn the point around: We accomplish little if the questions seem to invite exploration and argument but the discussion and follow-up work inhibit them. Teachers sometimes ask intriguing questions as a setup for very specific and bland teaching, as if a momentarily engaging conversation will build enough momentum toward the mastery of a pat lesson. We all understand that such questions as "How many degrees are there in a triangle?" and "What were the Intolerable Acts?" are leading toward specific factual answers. But questions such as "What would life in the United States be like without the Bill of Rights?" and "Is this water clean?" which *seem* open and might indeed cause lively conversation, may simply be intended as a warm-up before a lecture on the Bill of Rights or a canned hands-on science demonstration that acts as if the discussion never occurred. Similarly, teacher questions that sound like they anticipate a wide variety of responses—"To what extent . . . ?" "In what ways . . . ?"—may end up having only one "right" answer, to be gleaned from the textbook. If questions elicit thoughtful and varied student responses that will ultimately have no effect on the direction of the class or the design of the work, they are merely rhetorical questions, despite their seemingly open-ended form.

Ultimately, then, looking at the questions alone and even the teacher's stated intent in Stage 1 is not what matters. We must look at the whole design and consider this: How serious is the designer about the question being pursued? This is one of many aspects of *alignment* considered in the fourth UbD Design Standard. We need always to consider the larger context—the assignments, assessments, and follow-up questions we envision—to determine whether the question *ends up* being essential.

Essential questions in skill areas

Some teachers have argued that essential questions may work fine in certain subjects like history, English, or philosophy but not in skill-focused areas such as mathematics, chemistry, reading, physical education, and world languages. Some have even said matter-of-factly that there simply can't be any essential questions in skill areas. A teacher once said to us in a workshop that there were no big ideas or essential questions in her course, by its very nature. What was the course, we asked? Life Skills, she replied, without any hint of irony. That teacher has lost sight of her purpose, we think. Her job is not merely to teach a set of simple skills. Her job is to teach certain skills in order to develop *self-sufficiency*—a big idea from which many vital questions flow; for example, "What few skills do I most need to develop to be self-sufficient?" "What must I learn to do (versus have others do for me) to maximize my self-sufficiency?"

In fact, big ideas—hence important questions—underlie all skill mastery, and considering such questions is key to fluent and flexible performance. We have found that essential questions can be fruitfully framed around four categories of big ideas relevant to effective skill learning: (1) key concepts, (2) purpose and value, (3) strategy and tactics, and (4) context of use. Let's consider an example from physical education. For any sports that involve the skill of swinging with long-handled objects, such as baseball, golf, and tennis, *key concepts* include power, torque, and control. Thus, we might frame a question for exploring these ideas, such as "How does torque affect power?" We could pose the question "How can you hit with greatest power without losing control?" to help learners develop effective *strategies* for their swings (e.g., keeping eyes on the ball and follow-through). A third question relates to *context:* "When should we swing softly?"

The same categories are useful in academic skill areas, such as reading: "How do you know that you comprehend what you are reading?" (key concept); "Why should readers regularly monitor their comprehension?" (purpose and value); "What do good readers do when they don't understand the text?" (strategy); and "When should we use 'fix-up' strategies?" (context of use).

We have noted that when judging the essentialness of questions, intent is everything, as reflected in the entire design of work and evidence. Similarly, questions in skill areas are essential only when asked in a context of genuine performance challenges, where ongoing judgments are required. Skills are means, not ends; the aim is fluent, flexible, and effective performance. That requires the ability to make wise choices from our repertoire, in context: understanding *which* skill to use *when, how,* and *why,* when confronted with complex performance challenges. For example, the question "What is the pattern and how do you know?" is central to all mathematical thought and problem solving. But if the assessments call only for a single response, on cue, in simple prompted exercises, with simplified data, out of context, then they have bypassed the important issues central to genuine performance. Thus, it only *seems* that skill areas have no essential questions because the mostly commonly used assessments unfortunately require no transfer, no judgment.

Topical versus overarching essential questions

Making matters more complicated is the fact that essential questions differ in scope. For example, teachers typically ask, "What lessons should we learn from the Vietnam War?" and "How do the best mystery writers hook and hold their readers?" to help students come to particular understandings in a unit. They refer specifically to the topic (e.g., Vietnam War, mysteries) and they are meant to be settled—if only provisionally, in the teacher's mind—by unit's end.

The more general essential questions, however, take us beyond any particular topic or skill; they point toward the more general, transferable understandings. They do not refer to the topic content but to the big ideas that cut across units and courses. For example, "What lessons have we learned or not learned from U.S. military involvement in foreign regional conflicts?" is a more general essential question, linked to the question about the Vietnam War. "How do the best writers and speakers hold their audience?" is the broader question linked to the one on mystery writing.

We refer to the more specific essential questions as "topical" and the more general questions as "overarching." We believe that the best units are built upon *related sets* of such questions. Figure 5.1 presents matched examples of these two types of essential questions in various subject areas.

The questions in the second column, when pursued, lead to specific topical understandings within a unit. The questions in the first column, however, are different. They make no mention of the specific content of the unit. They point beyond the topic content toward broader, transferable understandings that cut across the unit or units alluded to in the second column. Note, too, that the last three rows of related questions signal that a number of topical inquiries may be needed before we can fully and effectively tackle an overarching question of some scope.

Overarching questions are therefore valuable for framing courses and programs of study (e.g., the K–12 health curriculum) around the truly big ideas. Their use as conceptual pillars strengthens a multiyear curriculum, making it more coherent and connected. (The design of courses and programs around broad, recurring essential questions with great transferability is pursued more thoroughly in Chapter 12.)

It may seem as if the topical essential questions are not really essential because they often seem to seek a "right" answer. But, again, we must beware judging the matter by the language only. If our intent is true inquiry, it will be reflected in what we actually ask students to do (or not do) with the questions in Stages 2 and 3. Will the learning activities make clear that no simple answer is forthcoming? Will the assessments require explanation and justification, not simply a right or wrong answer? As the saying goes, "The proof is in the pudding." Are all "good" topical questions essential? No, for the same reason: Any question that is meant to culminate quickly in a fact or a completely settled conclusion is not essential, because no sustained inquiry and argument is intended or warranted. We sometimes call such questions "leading" because the intent is not so much to foster thinking and inquiry as to underscore an important point we want students to note.

To call a question "leading" is not to condemn it! Leading questions have their place in assessing and teaching, as Socrates demonstrated many times in the Dialogues. (Leading questions belong in Stages 2 and 3, in other words). We ask different types of questions to serve different educational goals. Our point is that leading questions—the kinds of questions students now most often encounter, alas—cannot be the foundation of a design for understanding because they fixate on facts and demand only recall, not the thoughtful use of big ideas.

Figure 5.1
Overarching and Topical Essential Questions

Overarching	Topical
• In what ways does art reflect, as well as shape, culture?	• What do ceremonial masks reveal about the Inca culture?
• From whose perspective is this, and what difference does it make?	• How did Native Americans view the "settlement" of the West?
• How do our various body systems interact?	• How does food turn into energy?
• To what extent do we need checks and balances on government power?	• To what extent does separation of powers (e.g., three branches of government, two houses of Congress) cause deadlock in U.S. government?
• Are there useful ways for distinguishing inherent error from avoidable error in the sciences?	• What are possible sources of measurement error in this experiment? • Is there a greater margin of error in this experiment than the last one?
• What are common factors in the rise and fall of powerful nations?	• Why did the Roman Empire collapse? • Why did the British Empire end? • What explains the United States' rise to world prominence?
• How do authors use different story elements to establish mood?	• How does John Updike use setting to establish a mood? • How does Ernest Hemingway use language to establish a mood? • How does Toni Morrison use images and symbols to establish mood?

A finer-grained look at essential questions

A useful framework for categorizing different types of essential questions is thus formed by the intersection of the two previously discussed elements: intent and scope. The chart in Figure 5.2 suggests four types of essential questions; it functions as a design tool for generating a mix of essential questions for units and courses.

An examination of the four categories of questions in the chart yields several important insights:

1. Framing a unit *with only topical questions* that focus on particular ideas and processes does not ensure transfer, regardless of how provocative or

Figure 5.2

An Essential Question Chart

Intent	Scope	
	Overarching	**Topical**
Open: To challenge students to think more deeply and creatively about important recurring and unsettled issues. Teachers pose these arguable questions as a means of engaging students in thinking like experts in the field. No definitive answer is expected.	These are broad and deep questions that remain open and alive in the discipline—perhaps forever. They cut across unit, course, and (sometimes) subject boundaries. • To what extent is U.S. history a history of progress? What is "progress"? • To what extent is DNA destiny? • Who is a true friend?	These questions stimulate inquiry and deepen understanding of important ideas within the unit. It is not expected that they will be answered by unit's end. • How might Congress have better protected minority rights in the 1950s and 1960s? • Should we require DNA samples from every convicted criminal? • Should Frog have lied to Toad?
Guiding: To guide student inquiry toward a deeper understanding of a big idea. Teachers pose these questions as a means of uncovering desired understandings. Students construct meaning as they wrestle with the question.	These are general questions that cut across unit, course, and subject boundaries but that yield one or more desired understandings. • How much progress in civil rights has the United States made since the founding of the country? • How do recent developments in genetics affect the nature/nurture argument? • What are the signs of a "fair weather" friend?	These are unit-specific questions that converge toward one or a few settled understandings of important ideas. • What were the defining moments of the civil rights movement? • How is reliability ensured in DNA testing? • In what ways was Frog acting like a friend in the story?

related to core content the questions may be. Topical questions are *necessary* for focusing on desired unit priorities but not *sufficient* to yield the broader understandings that students need in order to make connections *across* units. Thus, given their topical nature, such questions alone are unlikely to elicit the kind of broad connections and rethinking we seek.

2. Framing the unit *with only overarching and open questions* may cause a drift into aimless discussion without ever touching down on the particular understandings related to content standards and core content. The unanswerable nature of these questions will likely frustrate some students (and their parents)—all the more so if the discussion is unconnected with content mastery. A diet of only the most open, overarching questions will not typically

meet the first criterion (linking to core content) and will thus be difficult to justify in a results-focused design.

3. Framing units *with only guiding questions* makes it unlikely that students will have the intellectual freedom and invitation to ask questions needed in a curriculum dedicated to understanding. The idea that uncoverage is vital will be lost.

4. The best topical questions depend for their essentialness on being explicitly matched with related overarching questions. This signals to the learner that the learning process has stages and rhythms whereby answers lead to other questions and new inquiries suggest the need to revisit earlier answers. Topical questions that lead to final or unassailable answers, unconnected to bigger ideas and questions, are more appropriately placed in Stage 3 as part of the teaching.

■ MISCONCEPTION ALERT!

Some readers may wonder whether a topical question can *ever* be essential, given our six criteria (especially the criteria that refer to questions that recur and focus on big ideas). They may prefer to define an essential question as one that must be overarching and open, in other words. Although this is a reasonable stance, we have chosen to call the best topical questions "essential," mindful of the third broad meaning of *essential* offered earlier: Some topical questions are essential for student understanding of core content, and they point to or imply big ideas.

Or readers might object by saying that all topical guiding questions are leading, because they often point toward a specific answer. But though a leading question and a topical essential question may sound the same, their purposes are quite different. A leading question points to factual knowledge and a definitive answer, whereas a focused essential question seeks to prompt genuine inquiry leading to eventual understandings—inferences drawn from facts that are certainly provisional but not meant to be final. A leading question is answerable by just remembering what was said or read, or knowing where to find it in the book. A topical essential question demands analysis, interpretation, construction of arguments—in other words, real thought.

Essential questions: Emphasis on the plural

As this discussion suggests, a single question cannot accomplish everything. Given the different meanings of *essential* and the different goals we have as designers, the most useful way to think about essential questions is in terms of *sets* of interrelated questions. The best units are built around essential questions that, in their *variety* and *balance,* are most effective. Consider a few examples:

Topical Essential Questions: What do we learn from Helen Keller's My Life *and* The Diary of Anne Frank? *How would you compare and contrast their lives? What did each writer "see" and "not see"?*

Overarching Essential Questions: What "fictions" find their way into nonfiction? What can't the writer of an autobiography see? What can the writer see that others cannot?

Topical Essential Question: What is the value of place value?

Overarching Essential Questions: What are the strengths and weaknesses of mathematical language? What are the limits of mathematical representation? Can everything be quantified?

Topical Essential Questions: What is magnetism? What is electricity? What is gravity?

Overarching Essential Questions: If a force can't be directly seen, how do we know it is there? What makes a theory "scientific" as opposed to merely speculative? In what ways are forces in physics similar to intangible "forces" in human conduct? Is psychology more like physics or history?

Such sets don't just offer a balance between topical, overarching, guiding, and open inquiries. A *family* of questions signals lively and iterative movement between narrow and broad inquiries, and between tentative and deeper understandings and further needed inquiries. The art of teaching for understanding requires a delicate mix of open and guiding as well as topical and overarching inquiries. By striking the right balance, we show that intellectual freedom and creativity are valued alongside the most powerful insights of experts.

Tips for generating essential questions

How might we come up with the best family of questions for framing our units? We might begin to identify useful topical questions by using the format of the quiz show *Jeopardy.* Given the content found in a textbook—the "answers" to be learned—what is an important question about a big idea (and the related research it suggests) for which the textbook provides a good summary answer? Don't get bogged down in all the distinctions about types of questions made earlier—just brainstorm a list of good questions in which to anchor the unit.

Let's return to the "three branches of government" example. If that phrase is an "answer," then what is a good question that would help students come to understand the underlying idea and its value? How about, "Why do we need a balance of powers? What's the alternative?" Or we could frame the challenge this way: "What were some of the questions our Founders were asking *themselves* that led to their proposal?" A more specific question for the unit might be this: "Why did the Federalists advocate for a balance of powers, and what were the arguments on the other side?"

Once we have identified one or more topical questions, we need to consider broader questions that will take us beyond the specific content in a provocative and transfer-rich way. Consider this: "What structure of government best suits the fact, to quote the *Federalist Papers,* that 'all men are not angels'? What follows about government if you reject this premise about human nature?" Let's go even broader and more arguable: "When is it wise to share power? When do we gain (and when might we lose) power by sharing it?" All of these more overarching questions are thought provoking, have transfer value, link to prior knowledge, and require core content—in other words, they meet our criteria.

Another practical approach is to derive essential questions from national or state content standards. Review a set of standards and identify the key nouns that recur (i.e., the important concepts) and make them the basis of a question. In the following examples, notice how interrogatives have been fashioned from declarative statements.

Life Science: *All students will apply an understanding of cells to the functioning of multi-cellular organisms, including how cells grow, develop, and reproduce. (From Michigan Science Standards)*

Topical Essential Questions: How can we prove that cells make up living things? If we're all made of cells, why don't we look alike?

Overarching Essential Question: How do scientists prove things?

Dance: *Understanding dance as a way to create and communicate meaning. (From National Standards for Arts Education)*

Topical Essential Questions: What ideas can we express through dance? How can motion convey emotion?

Overarching Essential Questions: In what ways do artists express what they think and feel? In what ways does the medium influence the message? What can the artist do that the nonartist cannot?

Physical Education *(6th grade): Applies movement concepts and principles to the learning and development of motor skills. (From National Association for Sport and Physical Education)*

Topical Essential Questions: How do we hit with greatest power without losing control? How important is follow-through for distance and speed?

Overarching Essential Questions: What kind of practice "makes perfect"? What feedback will enhance or improve performance most?

A related process is to derive essential questions from the enduring understandings identified in Stage 1. For example, the understanding that "living things adapt in order to survive harsh or changing environments" naturally suggests a companion question: "In what ways do living things adapt to survive?"

In addition to their function as indicators of understanding in Stage 2, the six facets are also a useful framework for generating provocative questions. Figure 5.3 presents a list of question starters for each facet.

Clearly the learning plan will require curriculum designers to map out a sensible progression for moving from the accessible to the obscure, but the challenge in Stage 1 is related to backward design: What are the questions we want students to be *eventually* able to address well, irrespective of whether we think they can handle such questions at this moment? That, after all, is why Essential Questions are in Stage 1: the ability to ask and thoughtfully consider such questions is a desired result, not just a teaching ploy.

> ### Design Tip
>
> Teachers in UbD workshops frequently ask how many essential questions they should have for a unit. We recommend a variation on the Marine Corps recruiting slogan: We're looking for a few good questions. If they are truly essential, they can (and should) establish priorities and help uncover all key ideas. Do not state questions that you do not intend to actively investigate through discussion, research, problem solving, and other means.

Figure 5.3
Question Starters Based on the Six Facets of Understanding

Explanation

Who _____? What _____? When _____? How _____? Why _____?

What is the key concept/idea in _____?

What are examples of _____?

What are the characteristics/parts of _____?
   Why is this so?

How might we prove/confirm/justify _____?

How is _____ connected to _____?

What might happen if _____?

What are common misconceptions about _____?

Interpretation

What is the meaning of _____?

What does _____ reveal about _____?

How is _____ like _____ (analogy/metaphor)?

How does _____ relate to me/us?

So what? Why does it matter?

Application

How and when can we use this (knowledge/process) _____?

How is _____ applied in the larger world?

How could we use _____ to overcome _____
   (obstacle, constraint, challenge)?

Perspective

What are different points of view about _____?

How might this look from _____'s perspective?

How is _____ similar to/different from _____?

What are other possible reactions to _____?

What are the strengths and weaknesses of _____?

What are the limits of _____?

What is the evidence for _____?

Is the evidence reliable? Sufficient?

Empathy

What would it be like to walk in _____'s shoes?

How might _____ feel about _____?

How might we reach an understanding about _____?

What was _____ trying to make us feel/see?

Self-Knowledge

How do I know _____?

What are the limits of my knowledge about _____?

What are my "blind spots" about _____?

How can I best show _____?

How are my views about _____ shaped by _____
   (experiences, assumptions, habits, prejudices, style)?

What are my strengths and weaknesses in _____?

Tips for using essential questions

The following practical suggestions can help you apply essential questions in your classroom, school, or district:

• Organize programs, courses, units of study, and lessons around the questions. Make the "content" answers to questions.

• Select or design assessment tasks (up front) that are explicitly linked to the questions. The tasks and performance standards should clarify what acceptable pursuit of, and answers to, the questions actually looks like.

• Use a reasonable number of questions (two to five) per unit. Make less be more. Prioritize content for students to make the work clearly focus on a few key questions.

• Frame the questions in "kid language" as needed to make them more accessible. Edit the questions to make them as engaging and provocative as possible for the age group.

• Ensure that every child understands the questions and sees their value. Conduct a survey or informal check, as necessary, to verify this.

• Derive and design specific concrete exploratory activities and inquiries for each question.

• Sequence the questions so they naturally lead from one to another.

• Post the essential questions in the classrooms, and encourage students to organize notebooks around them to make clear their importance for study and note taking.

• Help students to personalize the questions. Have them share examples, personal stories, and hunches. Encourage them to bring in clippings and artifacts to help make the questions come alive.

• Allot sufficient time for "unpacking" the questions—examining subquestions and probing implications—while being mindful of student age, experience, and other instructional obligations. Use question and concept maps to show relatedness of questions.

• Share your questions with other faculty to make planning and teaching for coherence across subjects more likely. To promote overarching questions schoolwide, ask teachers to post their questions in the faculty room or in department meeting and planning areas; type and circulate questions in the faculty bulletin; present and discuss them at faculty and PTSA meetings.

The importance of framing work around open questions

> Let me suggest one answer [to the problem of going into depth
> and avoiding excessive coverage] that grew from what we have done.
> It is the use of the organizing conjecture . . . [which serves] two functions,
> one of them obvious: putting perspective back into the particulars.
> The second is less obvious and more surprising. The questions often
> seemed to serve as criteria for determining where [students] were getting
> and how well they were understanding.
>
> —Jerome Bruner, *Beyond the Information Given*, 1957, pp. 449–450

The point of education is not simply to learn the least controversial findings. Students need to see how penetrating questions and arguments produce knowledge and understanding. If transfer is the key to teaching for understanding, our designs must make clear that questions are not only the cause of greater understanding in the student, but also the *means* by which all content accrues.

In other words, schooling must enable students to be on the inside of how understandings are born, tested, and solidified through inquiry, criticism, and verification. Our students need a curriculum that treats them more like potential performers than sideline observers. They need to experience how their own inquiries and discussions are "essentially" parallel to those of experts, and how even key agreed-upon understandings can change over time as a result of ongoing inquiry. In this way, they come to more deeply understand knowledge as the *result* of inquiries as opposed to disembodied "truths" that are just "out there" to be learned from teachers and texts.

The learners' own questions often do not seem important to them. "I know this sounds stupid . . ." is often the preface to a *wonderful* question. Why the self-deprecation? It is not merely developmental or a function of shyness. An unending dose of straightforward coverage and the sense that school is about "right answers" can easily make it seem as if the experts do not have questions, only the foolish and ignorant do.

A terrible price is paid when genuine intellectual questions get only lip service, perpetually postponed by teachers who claim that they have to cover the content. An unending stream of leading questions will reduce most student questions to these familiar few: Is this going to be on the test? Is this what you want? How long does the paper have to be?

When learning *the* answers is the only goal for students, instruction "covers up" the great and vital questions that *naturally arise* in the unfolding work—resulting in diminished engagement and less understanding. Unending coverage of only what is currently believed will eventually stifle thoughtful inquiry, as the philosopher Hans-Georg Gadamer (1994) suggests:

> *As against the fixity of opinions, questioning makes the object and its possibilities fluid. A person skilled in the "art" of questioning is a person who can prevent questions from being suppressed by the dominant opinion. . . . It is opinion that suppresses questions. (pp. 364–365)*

For its 25th anniversary in 2003, the *New York Times* "Science Times" section highlighted 25 of the most important current questions in science. Consider a few examples:

> *How much of the body is replaceable?*
> *What should we eat?*
> *Are men necessary? Are women necessary?*
> *Can robots become conscious?*
> *When will the next Ice Age begin? (sec. D, p. 1)*

Notice how these questions are qualitatively different from the lifeless questions that permeate a typical science textbook. All of the above questions are "alive" yet can be considered at some level in a K–16 science education—and *should* be considered if school is to be relevant and empowering. To constantly put before learners a curriculum framed by essential questions is to leave a lasting impression about not only the nature of knowledge but also the importance and power of their intellectual freedom.

Uncoverage is thus not merely a nice strategy or philosophy of education; using questions to frame the curriculum is not merely an aesthetic or ideological request on our part. One might say that not exploring key ideas in the content through genuine questioning and sustained inquiry is like leaving all courtroom claims and evidence unexamined, to be taken on faith. Such teaching leads to a hodgepodge of unprioritized ideas and facts that end up feeling like so many random opinions. There must be a deliberate interrogation of the content so that students can see the key understandings as the *result* of connections and inferences (as opposed to authoritative textbook or teacher claims to be taken on faith—as "facts" for memorization).

Although this phrasing may sound odd, it points to an important truth about how all of us, novice and expert, come to understand. We must give students work that enables them to have an "Aha!" equivalent to that felt by the scholar who first came to the understanding. That is, after all, how the pioneer came to understand the unknown: asking questions and testing ideas, like the learner.[1] That's why Piaget so wisely said that "to understand is to invent":

> *Once the child is capable of repeating certain notions and using some applications of these in learning situations he often gives the impression of understanding; however . . . true understanding manifests itself by new spontaneous applications. . . . The real comprehension of a notion or a theory implies the reinvention of this theory by the [student]. (Piaget, in Gruber & Voneche, 1977, p. 731)*

Many content standards documents and local curricula, by contrast, make the mistake of framing content goals as factlike sentences to be "learned" through direct instruction, and they thus run the risk of promoting "coverage" in the worst sense.[2] Coverage then hides from teachers as well as students two crucial understandings about learning and meeting the standards: (1) understanding derives from questions and inquiries, and (2) the meeting of intellectual standards requires not just taking in expert opinions but exploring, even questioning them.

So, what *were* the competing notions, theories, and points of view encountered on the way to adult understanding of the subject? What questions and *arguments* did the various textbook writers have *before* reaching a consensus? Some of this history of ideas is essential if students are to grasp the difference between *understandings* as hard-earned constructions versus ready-to-grasp *knowledge*—if they are to learn to see understandings as judgments or inferences, based on evidence and argument, not unproblematic facts to be covered and learned for recall.

In sum, as the quote from Bruner suggests, the best essential questions have a surprising benefit beyond their ability to provide greater insight and perspective—if we commit to basing our designs upon them. They can serve as *criteria* against which to judge progress in our learning. They keep us focused on inquiry as opposed to just answers.

An essential question is not merely a ploy or a Stage 3 tactic in teaching "stuff," therefore. The essential questions frame the goals. Asking and pursuing them is the obligation of teacher and learner—that's why they belong in Stage 1 (whereas more "teacherly" questions belong in Stage 3). The pursuit of questions thus enables us as teachers and learners to *test* the educative power of the activities and assignments, to ensure that learning is more than merely engaging activity or indiscriminate coverage. Are we making headway in this lesson and unit in answering the question? (If not, students *and* teacher need to adjust. Just as effective coaches and athletes make adjustments based on performance results, effective designers must be open to revising their plan en route.)

Regardless of which specific slant the teacher (or class) chooses as a focus for the work—not every good question can be feasibly explored, after all— what should be clear is that a mix of topical and overarching essential questions renders the design more focused and makes the student's role more appropriately intellectual and active. Without such a focus, the student is left with a mass of unconnected activities and undeveloped ideas—no *perspective* and no clear intellectual *agenda*. With no need to pursue questions, no use of content in the service of inquiry as the essence of the design, the student will be made unwittingly passive. "Listen and read, recall or plug in what is taught" will be the clear message. Without committing ourselves to curriculum designed around essential questions, the twin sins of aimless coverage and activity lurk in waiting, no matter how interesting the teacher or how lively the individual lessons.

Backward design in action with Bob James

Bob James rethinks his original plan, in light of a further consideration of essential questions.

I like this idea of an essential question hovering over all the work and serving as a guide toward deeper inquiry, while also using very precise probing or follow-up questions to sharpen understanding. Ever since I began teaching, I have tried to get my students to stretch their thinking by asking idea-sharpening questions, such as, Can you give another example of . . . ? How does this relate to that? What might happen if . . . ? Do you agree with . . . ? Why? Although I think I'm pretty good at posing these day-to-day questions, I realize that for the nutrition unit I'll have to give more thought to the kinds of broader questions described here.

Well, my unit question—What is healthy eating?—clearly links to the overarching questions—What is healthy living? or What is wellness? Either could focus inquiry and discussion in our entire health education program. And we could just keep asking it in each course and pursue it over time through recurring assessments.

This idea of using unit questions to frame the curriculum has really gotten me thinking. I'm especially intrigued by this notion: If the textbook contains the answers, then what are the questions? As I reflect on my own education, I can't recall ever being in a course in which the content was explicitly framed around important, thought-provoking questions. Some of my teachers and professors asked thought-provoking questions during class, but these unit (and essential) questions are different. I see how they might provide a focus for all the work and knowledge mastery, if done right. I now feel a bit cheated because I'm beginning to realize the power of these overarching questions for pointing to the bigger ideas within a subject or topic.

To see if I was on the right track, I brought up my ideas over lunch with a few of the teachers in the faculty room, and they really got into it! We had a very interesting discussion about my question, which led to others: If left on their own, will children eat what they need nutritionally? Do tastes change as we grow up—in the direction of healthier eating? If so, why? What about others in the animal kingdom, then? Do young animals naturally eat what is good for them? What role does junk-food advertising play in influencing the eating patterns of children and adults? Unfortunately, we were really "cooking" when the 20-minute lunch period ended and I had to leave for recess duty. I think I'll stew on this awhile.

Looking Ahead

If questions both frame units around big ideas and point beyond them to overarching ideas, toward what resolution can we aim? What understandings are we after, in light of the questions framing the work? What do we mean by achieving "understanding" and how does it differ from achieving "knowledge" and "skill"? We now turn to those questions.

Chapter 6

Crafting Understandings

> If the hypothesis . . . introduced is true—that any subject can be taught
> to any child in some honest form—then it should follow that a curriculum
> ought to be built around the great issues, principles, and values that
> a society deems worthy of the continual concern of its members.
> —Jerome Bruner, *The Process of Education,* 1960, p. 52

> Content should be chosen so as to exemplify the representative ideas
> of the disciplines. Representative ideas are concepts that afford an
> understanding of the main features of the discipline. They are not minor
> or subordinate ideas; they disclose the essence of the discipline.
> They are elements of the subject that stand for the whole of important
> aspects of it . . . they are epitomes of the subject.
> —Phillip Phenix, *Realms of Meaning,* 1964, pp. 322–323

In Chapter 2, we summarized what we mean by "understand," stressing that it involves the grasp of big ideas, as reflected in thoughtful and effective transfer. That transfer is typically manifested through performances involving one or more of the six facets of understanding discussed in Chapter 4. Now we take a closer look at the nature of desired understandings. What specifically do we aim to have students understand by unit's end? What exactly are we trying to get students to realize that is not obvious but important? How should we frame these desired understandings in Stage 1?

Rather than provide an immediate answer, we'll practice what we preach and ask readers to do some constructivist work around these questions. Our approach employs a teaching-for-understanding technique known as "concept attainment." Your job is to try to figure out what an understanding is by comparing a set of examples and nonexamples presented in Figure 6.1. In other words, how are the examples in the first column alike? What distinguishes them from the nonexamples in the second column?

Figure 6.1
Understandings: Examples and Nonexamples

Examples of Understandings	Nonexamples of Understandings
• An effective story engages the reader by setting up tensions—through questions, mysteries, dilemmas, uncertainties—about what will happen next.	• Audience and purpose.
• When liquid water disappears, it turns into water vapor and can reappear as liquid if the air is cooled.	• Water covers three-fourths of the earth's surface.
• Correlation does not ensure causality.	• Things are always changing.
• Decoding is necessary but not sufficient in reading for meaning.	• Sounding out, looking at pictures.

Distinguishing characteristics of understandings

Looking at Figure 6.1, what can we generalize about the examples of understandings compared with the nonexamples? A first observation is that all the examples are framed as complete sentences that offer a particular proposition of general significance—that is, they all specify something to be understood. Secondly, the examples focus on big ideas—abstract and transferable. They are like useful maxims, helpful in navigating a complex field. A third characteristic of the understandings has to do with their acquisition. It is unlikely that learners will immediately and completely understand the meaning of the statement simply by hearing or reading it. They will need to inquire, to think about and work with it. In other words, the understanding will need to be uncovered, because it is abstract and not immediately obvious.

Now let's consider the nonexamples to further highlight important distinctions and sharpen our emerging understanding of understandings. The first nonexample ("Audience and purpose") is a phrase, not a sentence. It *refers* to a big idea but offers no specific claims about it. Because it is stated as a phrase, we do not yet know what particular understanding about audience and purpose the designer seeks. The second nonexample ("Water covers three-fourths of the earth's surface") is indeed a sentence, but it does not propose an abstract or transferable idea. Rather, it simply states a straightforward fact. No inquiry is required for understanding the claim. The third nonexample ("Things are always changing") is a truism. It fails to specify what exactly we want the learner to come to understand about the nature of the change process. Such global pronouncements offer no new insight or meaning as stated. The fourth nonexample ("Sounding out, looking at pictures") refers to a set of skills but does not offer any useful, transferable principles or strategies about them. In other words, it provides nothing specific and conceptual to understand.

With these distinctions between examples and nonexamples in mind, let's consider additional examples from various subjects and levels. Notice that the examples meet the characteristics cited above while avoiding the problems represented in the nonexamples.

- No marketer can successfully satisfy all consumers with the same product—given differences in background characteristics and consumption preferences—so they must choose which consumers they can satisfy. *(From a college business course)*
- Living things are designed to survive as individuals and as a species, yet survival of an individual or community often requires the death of another living thing. *(From a 2nd grade unit on "Basic Needs of Living Things")*
- Writing from another person's point of view can help us better understand the world, ourselves, and others. *(From a 9th grade unit on "Insights from the Field," curriculum materials developed by the Peace Corps)*
- Sometimes a correct mathematical answer is not the best solution to messy, "real-world" problems. *(From a high school mathematics course)*
- Invisible diversity makes all classrooms heterogeneous. *(From an undergraduate education methods course)*
- Photographs reflect a point of view, and can mislead as well as reveal. *(From a 4th grade interdisciplinary unit on "History Revealed Through Photographs")*

As these examples suggest, an understanding summarizes a sought-after lesson based on facts and experiences. It summarizes a transferable idea that we want students to grasp *eventually*. It draws conclusions from various facts that make up the content.

Understanding defined

Let us summarize by highlighting several distinguishing features of understandings.

1. An understanding is an important inference, drawn from the experience of experts, stated as a specific and useful generalization.

2. An understanding refers to transferable, big ideas having enduring value beyond a specific topic.

Enduring understandings use discrete facts or skills to focus on larger concepts, principles, or processes. They derive from and enable transfer: They are applicable to new situations within or beyond the subject. For example, we study the enactment of the Magna Carta as a specific historical event because of its significance to a larger idea, the rule of law, whereby written laws specify the limits of a government's power and the rights of individuals, such as due process. This big idea has transcended its roots in 13th-century England to become a cornerstone of modern democratic societies. Students can use this understanding in new situations, such as when studying emerging democracies in the underdeveloped world.

3. An understanding involves abstract, counterintuitive, and easily misunderstood ideas.

4. An understanding is best acquired by "uncovering" (i.e., it must be developed inductively, coconstructed by learners) and "doing" the subject (i.e., using the ideas in realistic settings and with real-world problems).

The design's purpose is to help students draw the inference. Understanding requires that students emulate what practitioners do when they generate new understandings; namely, they consider, propose, test, question, criticize, and verify. An understanding is not accepted on faith but is investigated and substantiated.

The best candidates for "uncoverage" are those concepts and principles that are most prone to misunderstanding. These are typically not obvious and may be counterintuitive. For example, in physics, students often struggle with ideas concerning gravity, mass, force, and motion. When asked to predict which object, a marble or a bowling ball, will strike the ground first when dropped together, many students reveal a common misconception by incorrectly selecting the bowling ball. What important concepts or processes do students have difficulty grasping or frequently misunderstand? What do they typically struggle with? Which big ideas are they likely to harbor a misconception about? These are fruitful topics to select and uncover—to teach for understanding.

5. An understanding summarizes important strategic principles in skill areas.

Many skills are successfully mastered only when they become part of a fluent and flexible repertoire, wisely used in performance. That requires not just drill but insight—the ability to judge which skill to use, when; that is, coming to understand the relevant tactical and strategic principles that apply. For example, to read stories with understanding requires actively applying the idea that authors do not always state what the story is about—that meaning is *between* the lines, not *in* the lines. This understanding sets the context for the use of specific comprehension strategies, such as summarizing, questioning the text, predicting, and using context cues to make meaning.

We must note here the fine work of Lynn Erickson on understandings. Our discussions and correspondence with Lynn, and the careful reading of her work after the publication of the first edition of this book, made us see the need to sharpen our own understanding of understanding! We found, somewhat to our embarrassment, that our treatment of what an understanding is wasn't consistent in the first edition of the book, especially in the examples. It was through Lynn's work on generalizations (mentioned in Chapter 3) that we were able to develop a more coherent and thorough account of what understandings are

> *A generalization is defined formally as . . . concepts stated in a relationship. Universal generalizations have the same characteristics as a concept:*
>
> - *Broad and abstract*
> - *Universal in application*
> - *Generally timeless—carry through the ages*
> - *Represented by different examples (Erickson, 2001, p. 35)*

And Erickson, in turn, reflected our thinking in the revised edition of her book:

> *Generalizations are the enduring understandings, the "big ideas," the answer to the "so what?" of study. (Erickson, 2001, p. 33)*

Topical and overarching understandings

In Chapter 5 we discussed differences in the scope of essential questions, including the difference between questions that are *overarching* and those that are *topical*. Similar distinctions apply to desired understandings: Some are comprehensive and others are more specific. And so here, too, we distinguish between *overarching* and *topical*. Consider the sets of matched examples in Figure 6.2.

As the sets indicate, understandings can be nested, based on different degrees of abstraction or generalization. The understandings in the first column are more general than their partners in the second. They point beyond the particulars of the topic or unit of study toward more transferable knowledge. These targets can thus be described as *overarching understandings* because they provide a link to the big ideas. Delineating the overarching understandings helps address the common student question about work that seems to have no larger purpose: "So what?" The examples in the second column are topic-specific insights; we refer to them as *topical understandings*. They identify the particular understandings we hope to cultivate about specific topics.

We encourage you to specify both topical and overarching understandings in framing your learning goals.[1] (As we make clear in Chapter 12, where we discuss program design, we encourage departments and program-area teams to frame curricula around overarching understandings and essential questions as a way of establishing clear learning priorities for unit design by individual teachers.)

As with topical and overarching essential questions, no hard and fast rule distinguishes topical and overarching understandings. The scope of the course

Figure 6.2

Examples of Overarching and Topical Understandings

Overarching Understandings	Topical Understandings
• A president is not above the law.	• Watergate was a major constitutional crisis, not a "third-rate burglary" (as a Nixon staffer put it) or mere election shenanigans between political parties.
• Democracy requires a courageous, not just a free, press.	
• The modern novel overturns many traditional story elements and norms to tell a more authentic and engaging narrative.	• Holden Caulfield is an alienated antihero, not an average kid on an "excellent adventure."
• Gravity is not a physical thing but a term describing the constant rate of acceleration of all falling objects, as found through experiment.	• Vertical height, not the angle and distance of descent, determines the eventual "splashdown" speed of a falling spacecraft.
• Postulates are *logically* prior in any axiomatic system but developed after the fact to justify key theorems. They are neither true nor self-evident, yet they are not arbitrary.	• The parallel postulate is a crucial foundation to Euclidean geometry, despite its awkwardness and theoremlike nature.
• In a free market economy, price is a function of demand versus supply.	• A baseball card's worth depends on who wants it, not just its condition or the number of similar ones available.
	• Sales figures from eBay reveal that one person's junk is another person's treasure.
• Increased scoring opportunities in certain sports result from creating space on offense in order to spread the defense and get players "open."	• Creating space and exploiting its creation is the key to winning soccer.
	• The defense in soccer needs to prevent the offensive players from getting open in the middle of the field.

content, subject matter priorities, age of students, time allotted to the unit, and other factors will influence the breadth and depth of the targeted understandings. Rather than thinking of the difference as one of absolute size or scope, it is best to think of the overarching understandings as representing the transferable insights eventually sought. In other words, given the specific unit understandings you desire, to what extent can those insights be generalized, to serve the student with connective powers in other work? Put the other way around, what recurring ideas—as embodied in this unit by this topical understanding—should be framing your coursework?

Understandings versus factual knowledge

An understanding makes a claim using facts. It is someone's conclusion, based on evidence and logic. Facts are the grist for understandings; they are data. Understandings offer a theory based on data or interpretation. Thus, as noted earlier, Dewey (1933) argued that a fact requires apprehension, whereas an understanding requires comprehension. To "get" a fact requires only that we grasp the meaning of the words or see the data. To "get" an understanding requires more: Even after the meanings of all the words or data are clear, we may not get their significance. We have to ask questions of the facts, connect them to other facts, and try to apply them in various situations. An understanding has to be worked through and validated as an appropriate and helpful conclusion, not merely accepted as a statement of fact.

Any subtle cartoon or challenging crossword puzzle illustrates this point. Factual knowledge is necessary but insufficient to "get" a joke or clue. One must go beyond the literal meaning and make connections, consider different possibilities, test theories, reason. The same process is required in coming to understand abstract ideas in any domain.

An understanding, then, is an inference drawn from facts. Although we may have clarified this conceptual distinction earlier, in practice the distinction is easy to lose—especially for students. Consider the following two statements: (1) A triangle has three sides and three angles (a fact). (2) A triangle with three equal sides has three equal angles (an understanding). Both look and sound almost the same as sentences. Yet notice that the second sentence, though similar to the first (a fact) in terms of syntax is quite different in terms of what it demands of teacher and learner. The second sentence (an understanding) presents an *inference,* made valid through proof, whereas the first statement is true on inspection, by definition.

Therefore, an understanding is not a straightforward given, but a conclusion inferred *using* givens. This is why "uncoverage" is necessary: What might seem like something the learner can simply accept actually demands analysis (breaking it up into bits) and synthesis (putting it back together in the learner's own words or representations) before true understanding can occur. When our teaching merely covers content without subjecting it to inquiry, we may well be perpetrating the very misunderstanding and amnesia we decry.

Understandings about skills

As already noted, some teachers believe that UbD is not applicable to the teaching of skills. They believe that learning skills is merely a matter of practice and refinement; that is, that there is really nothing to understand. We strongly dispute this contention. Consider the following examples of understandings from subjects that are normally identified as skill areas:

- A muscle that contracts through its full range of motion will generate more force. *(From a unit on golf in a physical education course)*
- The more words I know, the better I can share my ideas and understand others' ideas. *(From a 2nd grade language arts unit on poetry)*
- Body language can change statements to questions, affirmations to negations—and impacts the intensity of a statement. *(From a world language curriculum guide)*
- Scraps and trimmings that most people throw away in cooking can be used to make stocks to enhance flavor while saving money. *(From a unit on soup stocks in a high school cooking course)*

These examples reinforce a point made earlier about teaching for understanding and essential questions: Units and courses that focus on skill development *need to explicitly include* desired understandings. In other words, the learner should come to understand the skill's *underlying concepts*, *why* the skill is important and what it helps accomplish, what *strategies and techniques* maximize its effectiveness, and *when* to use them. As research and practice confirm, understanding-based teaching of skills develops more fluent, effective, and autonomous proficiency than does instruction relying on rote learning and drill-and-practice methods alone. (See Chapter 13 for summaries of research findings regarding the need for understanding-based teaching of skills.)

■ MISCONCEPTION ALERT!

A common phrase used in content standards or lesson framing is that "students will understand how to . . ." do something. This phrasing presents a potential source of confusion in UbD.

Often the phrase is loosely used as a synonym for "learn how to . . ." when, in fact, the desired achievement is actually a discrete skill (e.g., write in cursive, create PowerPoint slides), not an understanding. Such discrete knowledge and skill objectives are placed in fields K and S on the Template.

However, when "understand how to . . ." refers to an array of skills that also require thoughtful attention to underlying concepts and principles, then we *are* dealing with understandings (as well as skills). In such cases, the tips described earlier will apply.

Content standards and understandings

The expectations to teach to identified content standards leave many educators wondering about how their standards connect to UbD. Ideally, all state and provincial standards would be framed as "big idea" understandings, and, in fact, a few state standards have done so. For example, consider these two examples of state standards that clearly reflect big ideas:

- All living things have basic needs in order to survive (i.e., water, air, nutrients, light); plants and animals have different structures for different functions in growth, survival, and reproduction; behavior is influenced by internal cues (e.g., hunger) and external cues (e.g., a change in the environment).
- The migration of groups of people in the United States, Canada, and Latin America has led to cultural diffusion because people carry their ideas and ways of life with them when they move from place to place.

In the main, however, the manner in which standards are presented varies widely across states and, often, across subject areas within the same state. Some standards are presented as lists of discrete objectives, while others are stated broadly. Some so-called understandings turn out to be relatively straightforward facts or skills, as in the following from the Virginia Standards of Learning:

- The earth is one of several planets that orbit the sun, and the moon orbits the earth.
- The student will develop map skills by locating China and Egypt on world maps.

And some standards are just too vague to be helpful to anyone, as in these examples, also from Virginia:

- Important historical figures and groups have made significant contributions to the development of Canada, Latin America, and the United States.
- There are factors that influence consumer demand.

These problems have come to the surface as educators have attempted to build curriculum, assessments, and instruction around their designated standards. To address these concerns, several states have developed supplementary resource guides to assist educators in working with the standards. And a few states have actually reframed their content standards in terms of understandings and essential questions à la UbD.[2] Here are examples from Virginia (History/Social Science) and Michigan (Science):

- *The student will explain how producers use natural resources (water, soil, wood, and coal), human resources (people at work), and capital resources (machines, tools, and buildings) to produce goods and services for consumers.*

Understanding: Producers of goods and services are influenced by natural, human, and capital resources.

Essential question: How do producers use natural, human, and capital resources to produce goods and services? (From Virginia Curriculum Framework—Teacher Resource Guide)

- *All students will apply an understanding of cells to the functioning of multicellular organisms, including how cells grow, develop, and reproduce.*

Essential questions: How can we prove cells make up living things? If we are all made of cells, how come we don't all look alike? (From Michigan Science Benchmark Clarification [MICLIMB Science])

Regardless of how national, state, or local content standards are stated, most educators are obligated to focus on them. The following section offers practical suggestions for using the standards to identify enduring understandings.

Tips for identifying and framing understandings

We noted in the first sets of examples that understandings are framed as full-sentence generalizations or propositions. Given the content topic, what realizations based on inference should the student *come away* understanding?

Sounds easy enough, but it is surprisingly difficult to do. A common problem in framing understandings is to unwittingly restate the topic. "I want students to understand the Civil War" or "I want students to really understand friendship" are indeed sentences about those topics, but they are not propositions regarding the desired understandings. In other words, these statements do not specify what the learner should come away understanding about the Civil War or friendship.

That advice seems clear enough, doesn't it? Yet some teachers respond by merely narrowing the focus of the content, saying, for example, "I want students to understand the causes of the Civil War." Same problem: This simply states the content goal in a more detailed manner, without articulating the learnings that students should take away about the causes. What do you want students to come to understand about those causes and why they matter?

"Ah, now I get it. I want them to understand that there were several significant and interrelated causes of the Civil War—the morality of slavery, fundamentally different views about the role of the federal government, dissimilarities of regional economies, and a clash of cultures." Yes! Now *that* is an example of an understanding that specifically summarizes the insights of experts.

As the example shows, a practical way to frame the challenge is to state the understanding as a proposition or a maxim. Because an understanding is not a fact but an inference, you must consider what generalization sums up the overall conclusions that you (or the textbook authors) have drawn from lots of facts *and* reasoning.

A simple prompt that has proven particularly helpful is to ask designers to finish the sentence *"Students should understand **that** . . ."* Such phrasing ensures a full-sentence answer and prevents the designer from falling back into stating only the topic (e.g., Civil War) or a concept (e.g., friendship). (That is why we have included this prompt in Box U on the Design Template.)

Framing desired understandings as full-sentence propositions is necessary but not sufficient. Not all propositions involve *enduring* understandings, of course. "Students should understand that ice cream plays a surprisingly large role in American life" would not warrant a three-week unit. Nor is it adequate to propose that we want students to understand that "weird stuff happens in history." Although the statement certainly suggests some interesting possibilities, it is hopelessly vague and unhelpful for framing the design of a unit or course. On the other hand, the statement that "Students should understand that great changes have historically occurred more by accident than by design in our history" is a thought-provoking proposition, capable of serving the study of history.

To be a worthy understanding, then, the proposition must be *enduring*. We propose two different connotations for the term:

• The understanding has endured over time and across cultures because it has proven so important and useful.

• The understanding should endure in the mind of the student because it will help the student make sense of the content *and* it will enable transfer of the key ideas. Thus, it should be learned in such a way that it does not fly away from memory once the unit is over or the test is completed.

A practical strategy for determining the worthiness of a proposed understanding and to frame it as a full-blown generalization is to run it though a "filter" of questions such as those in Figure 6.3.

Understandings and developmental issues

Thus far, we have presented a straightforward conception of *understanding*. However, some readers have surely recognized that the matter is not so matter-of-fact! Indeed, an apparent paradox confronts us. For a 1st grader or a novice in the field, many so-called facts are not at all obvious. Whether considering the inexperience of young learners or the history of human thought, we have to face a developmental reality that muddies the distinction between facts and understandings: What is initially a difficult inference can become, over time, an accepted and "obvious" fact. Thus, as with essential questions, no statement is *inherently* a fact or an understanding. It depends upon who the learners are and what their prior experience has been.

Our work as designers is made more challenging by the reality that many things we think of as facts are really hard-won understandings. Consider, for instance, the shape and movement of the planet Earth. These "facts" were once contentiously debated before they became "understood" and accepted. (Incidentally, both of these matters required some fairly esoteric experience to verify—e.g., parallax in observations of stars, simultaneous timings of sunrise at different latitudes.) Many of the things *we* say we know as facts have never been personally verified. We accept them as "givens," even when we do not fully understand them. Worse, many of the big ideas we have to teach may have been taught to us as if they were facts for later recall.

Here is a practical test to show how tricky the distinction between understandings and facts can sometimes be, and why prior experience matters. How would you categorize the following—fact or understanding?

• Color creates mood.
• In non-Euclidean geometries, there are no similar figures, only congruent figures.

Figure 6.3
Identifying Essential Questions and Understandings

Design Tool with Prompts

Use one or more of the following questions to filter topics or big ideas to identify possible essential questions and desired understandings.

Topics and Big Ideas:

What essential questions are raised by this idea or topic? What, *specifically*, about the idea or topic do you want students to come to understand?

Why study _____? So what?

What makes the study of _____ universal?

If the unit on _____ is a story, what's the moral of the story?

What's the Big Idea implied in the skill or process of _____?

What larger concept, issue, or problem underlies _____?

What couldn't we do if we didn't understand _____?

How is _____ used and applied in the larger world?

What is a real-world insight about _____?

What is the value of studying _____?

Essential Questions: Q

Understandings: U

- Communication involves the negotiation of meaning between people.
- The same letter combinations can produce different sounds, words, and meanings.
- Translation is not communication.

Some of these statements may seem like truisms; others may seem esoteric or novel. If you are a language teacher, your answers may differ from those of a math teacher; if you work with young children, your answers may differ from those who teach adults. What we must do, therefore, is carefully consider who our learners are and whether what we call a fact or an understanding really is so to them. (That is why pretesting and ongoing checks for misconceptions are so important, as we discuss in later chapters.)

We noted in Chapter 5 that no question is inherently essential or inessential—it depends upon intent. Similarly, no sentence, on inspection, can be declared to be a fact or an understanding out of context. It depends upon the designer's view as to whether it can be grasped by apprehension or realized only by active learner comprehension, through good design and coaching. The more the claim requires inferences and "uncoverage" to be grasped, and common misconceptions to be overcome, the more it is an understanding. The more we think the learner can get it just by hearing it, reading about it, or encountering it, the more we should consider it a fact and (if it is important) place it in the Knowledge box on the UbD Template.

Once we have settled on appropriate understandings, the goal of cultivating understanding in the learner depends upon the teacher's vigorous resistance of a deep-seated instinct: teaching an understanding as a fact. Indeed, merely *stating* understandings (by either the teacher or the textbook) is the cardinal mistake of "coverage" in the bad sense of the term: treating complex inferences as words to be simply taken in, instead of treating the understanding as a problem to be solved by good design of learning activities.

Here is a case in which elementary teachers often have an advantage over teachers at other levels. Elementary teachers are typically well aware that much of what adults "know" is not at all obvious or sensible to kids. The best elementary teachers understand that teaching constantly requires "uncovering" adult knowledge, not merely "teaching" it. The older students become, the more we assume they will be able to see what experts know as self-evident once they are presented with it. Alas, the research literature on student misunderstandings reveals the naïveté of such an assumption.

We call this problem the Expert Blind Spot throughout the book—the failure to grasp that key lessons involve understandings that have to be engineered, not facts to be transmitted. When the Expert Blind Spot is at work, we have lost sight of this understanding about understanding. What is obvious to us is rarely obvious to a novice—and was once not obvious to us either, but we have forgotten our former views and struggles. (Researchers including Piaget and Duckworth have documented this phenomenon in children: The child not only forgets what he once claimed, but actually denies ever having claimed it—even when confronted with tape recordings of his own voice!)[3] Teachers at the high school and college levels easily forget that many of the things we now call knowledge were once counterintuitive ideas that had to be explored, tested, and put back together for a genuine understanding.

Expressed in the language of the six facets, experts frequently find it difficult to have empathy for the novice, even when they try. That's why teaching is hard, especially for the expert in the field who is a novice teacher. Expressed positively, we must strive unendingly as educators to be empathetic with the learner's conceptual struggles if we are to succeed.

A familiar example of the Expert Blind Spot in action is the assumption that the novice needs to learn all the technical vocabulary that the expert uses—in the absence of any experience that would give the vocabulary meaning:

Knowledge which is mainly second-hand . . . tends to become merely verbal. It is no objection to information that it is clothed in words; communication necessarily takes place through words. But in the degree in which what is communicated cannot be organized into the existing experience of the learner, it becomes mere words: that is . . . lacking in meaning. Then it operates to call out mechanical reactions. . . .

The pupil learns symbols without the key to their meaning. He acquires a technical body of information without ability to trace its connections with the objects and operations with which he is familiar—often he acquires simply a peculiar vocabulary. . . . Knowing [only] the definitions, rules, formulae, etc. is like knowing the names of parts of a machine without knowing what they do. (Dewey, 1916, pp. 187–188, 220, 223)

From the perspective of the expert, jargon and shorthand phrases permit easy and efficient communication; to the novice they are often off-putting barriers to understanding. The challenge in teaching for understanding is to introduce vocabulary when it will most help clarify experience and ideas that arise as a result of the teacher's design.

A simple example from this book can help make the point. Would you have understood *understandings* if we had begun the chapter by just defining them and moving on to other aspects of the design? We led up to the definition by using simple ideas, raising predictable concerns, and considering examples and nonexamples before offering the criteria. To present the criteria up front without explaining why the criteria are needed and how they make sense would have been confusing for many readers. You would have understood *understanding* as a definition but not have been able to use that definition to craft, and evaluate, understandings. (The fact that you *still* may not be ready to craft good understandings is another example of why understanding is learned through, and reflected in, performance.)

A return to the Pythagorean theorem

We discussed in Chapter 2 the common failure of transfer in learning the Pythagorean theorem, so let us revisit that big idea in greater depth. What does it mean to say that "$A^2 + B^2 = C^2$ is true in any right triangle" is an understanding? Why not call it a fact? What does calling it an understanding imply for what we should do (and *not* do) "by design"?

This theorem has profound applicability (e.g., calculating distances and slope in graphing functions or drawing anything accurately to scale), although these implications are not obvious before studying geometry. Yet, despite its familiarity, it is not a straightforward fact, nor obviously true upon inspection. Indeed, it doesn't seem correct at all if you merely look at drawings of right triangles; it is a claim that *needs* proof. The formula amounts to saying, "If you draw a square on each side of the triangle, the areas of the squares on the two smaller sides add up to the area of the square on the largest side—always; *regardless* of the shape of the right triangle." That's not obvious, and neither are its practical uses! (If the theorem were obvious, it would need no proof—it would be an axiom.)

That being the case, it surely makes little sense to treat this claim as a fact to be covered and put away for later recall, even if the sentence sounds familiar. Treating unobvious, big-idea understandings as facts makes it far more likely that we will get the kind of amnesia, inertia, and fantasia that we quoted Shulman as describing in Chapter 2. Anyone can state the theorem as a fact, without the least understanding of its import. Knowing only what the symbols in the sentence mean—how to translate the sentence into words—does *not* equate to understanding it.

What, then, *is* the understanding we want students to obtain? And what misunderstandings must be overcome to get there? Here is an atypically explicit account of many of the interconnected ideas, and facts implied, but rarely stated in textbooks or classrooms that are required to grasp this understanding and its implications:

- The theorem holds true for a right triangle of *any* size or shape.
- The claim is true for *all possible cases,* in fact.
- Because we can prove it for all possible cases, all of trigonometry becomes possible, as does the ability to compare seemingly incomparable shapes and their areas.
- We do not ever rely on a graphic image to make a claim that a theorem is true. The image misleads us, in fact, by making it seem as if the claim were true by inspection of the drawings when the claim is true by logical argument only.
- The proof is deductive, not inductive, in other words. There is no doubt or uncertainty to the conclusion: It follows from our axioms, logic, and prior theorems.

None of these claims is obvious. We can come to an understanding of $A^2 + B^2 = C^2$ only through attempts at proof, satisfying *ourselves* that the conclusion is defensible as a conclusion and important as an idea. It is in that sense that Piaget meant that to *understand* is to *invent:* In some sense, the learner "discovers" the proof as a proof.

Understandings as goals

Stage 1 asks designers to specify one or more desired understandings as a result of a unit or course. It is important to note again that Stage 1 is for the designer, not the learner. The understandings, as written, may not be understandable in that form to the student. As with essential questions, we should not confuse our thinking about desired results (Stage 1) with a learning plan for causing those results (Stage 3). The point is not to make the student recite the understanding in the words in which we wrote it. The point is to clearly frame our goals for ourselves (and colleagues). Think of the understanding as written by the "designer" to the "contractor." It is a blueprint for the building of a learning plan, not the materials for the completed design. Realizing the blueprint— that is, developing the desired understandings—is the aim of the design. The learners' eventual understandings are best revealed in Stage 2 in their own words, or nonverbally, or through various performances, and are caused in Stage 3 by instruction, experiential activities, discussions, and reflections.

Consider the following understandings proposed in Stage 1 for a unit design:

• Total force equals the sum of force each body segment produces if the forces are applied in a single direction with proper sequence and correct timing.

• When all forces are applied sequentially in the same direction with proper timing, maximum acceleration and maximum force is achieved.

• Internal forces or muscular contractions can create, resist, and stop force.

• Internal force production depends on the number of muscles involved, the size of the muscles involved, stretch reflex, the distance through which the muscle contracts, and the speed of the movement. The entire body needs to be involved in movements requiring a great deal of force.

• A muscle that contracts through its full range of motion will generate more force.

• Follow-through allows for deceleration of body parts and results in greater momentum on release or impact, thereby increasing the likelihood of achieving maximum force production.

Sounds like college physics or bioengineering, doesn't it? But these are the desired understandings from the physical education unit on golf cited earlier! Novice golfers are not expected to restate these ideas in these words but to grasp their truth as transferable understandings, reflected in their actions and self-assessments on the golf course, the driving range, and the putting green.

We caution readers, then, to avoid the common misconception that goals for understanding represent statements that learners must "give back" by the time the lessons are over or that the understandings must be simplistic for younger learners or novices in a subject. On the contrary: The understanding of powerful ideas in use remains our worthy target.

Does this mean that you should never utter the stated understanding or turn it into kid-friendly language? We are not saying that. Indeed, in Stage 3 you will plan for bridging the gap between expert and novice understanding. We only caution that verbal knowledge is not the point. Evidence of understanding does not require that students state the understanding in words primarily.

Awareness of predictable misunderstandings

Learners are not blank slates. They come to the learning situation with prior knowledge, experience, and, quite possibly, some misconceptions. Such misunderstandings, as opposed to confusion or inattention, typically flow from prior experience and a plausible inference based on that experience. As a result, a challenge in developing understanding is to help learners become more open-minded and circumspect. Why? Because existing misconceptions get in the way of understanding, and they have to be recognized and rooted out. For new and improved ways of thinking to take hold, old "facts" and habits of thought and action have to be questioned and sometimes unlearned.

Coming to understand is thus more like developing a new golf swing or speaking accent. We may be surprised to find that many of our more able and successful students resist new understandings because they are comfortable with old ones. Without work designed to aggressively ferret and root out the most predictable but unhelpful ways of thinking, students' preconceptions can remain untouched by instruction.

As a practical point, we encourage designers to mentally review predictable misconceptions or possible misunderstandings about a forthcoming topic or skill. Consider these questions: What misinformation do learners harbor about the topic? What are the typical "rough spots" that always seem to crop up, despite best efforts, when teaching the topic?

Ironically, identifying potential misconceptions can help us better understand the understandings we are after and appreciate unavoidable impediments. For example, a predictable misunderstanding about swimming (sometimes implanted by parents) is that you should "cup" your hands and "grab" the water. Although this may make intuitive sense, it violates a basic principle of the physics of movement; namely, we can generate greater force by increasing the surface area in contact with the water. Thus, we want beginning swimmers to understand that they should maintain a flat, rather than a cupped, hand position when pulling their arms through the water.

Understanding that there may not be a single understanding

A call for *enduring* understandings may have caused some readers to wonder if we are being inconsistent when we also call for open essential questions and the need for rethinking. "But what if the desired understanding *is* that there is no official, single, agreed-upon understanding?" Then, *that* is the understanding you wish students to leave with. You might even go further and be more specific about that lack of final understanding, saying, for example, "Historians disagree as to the main causes of the Civil War. Some focus on the evils of slavery while others focus on issues of states rights." In his teaching, Grant (1979) was fond of using the following aphorism as an understanding related to interpretive reading and discussion of great literature:

> There is no right answer to what the text is about. But that doesn't mean that all answers are equal. There may be no right answers, but some answers are better than others, and figuring out what that means and how it can be so is one of your major challenges.

Indeed, a key shift in thinking that must occur if a curriculum for understanding is to achieve its goal is that the learner must be helped to realize that learning is an unending quest for understandings, not the search for "final facts" handed down by the "authorities."

The fallibility and plurality of understandings

Think about what we mean when we say, "Well, it is *my* understanding that . . ." The beauty of the phrase, we think, is that it appropriately implies insight *and* fallibility. Every understanding is always somebody's; and people, even experts, are both fallible and working with incomplete knowledge. It is *your* or *her* or *his* understanding; it is never *the* understanding in a modern democratic world. Understandings can differ—indeed, in the 21st century, they always do, in all fields. The university, in fact, is by definition a "universe" of pluralistic discourse, a space where we agree to disagree as well as to agree and where we are free to make up our mind as well as to change it, based on new argument and evidence. Because an understanding is an inference based on inherently limited evidence, each of us may well come to different conclusions about every important issue.

This notion can understandably bother some folks. They may argue, like Sergeant Friday in the old TV show *Dragnet*—"Just the facts, ma'am." Indeed, the endless political battles over topics like evolution and *Harry Potter* can be viewed as nostalgia—a sentimental attempt to return to that mythical time of Truth, sanitized of all this "relativistic" and "politically correct" wishywashiness about what is Known; to which we respond: it has *never* been that way in the modern world. All expert claims remain human understandings, achieved by real people who reached a considered conclusion. No theory is a fact; it is an understanding, including those of Newton, dieticians of the previous generation, and the current Supreme Court. Think of the new understandings and the old understandings overturned in our lifetime in the "hard" sciences alone: black holes, string theory, fractals, fuzzy logic, dozens of new subatomic particles, dark matter, the genetic basis of disease. Or consider more mundane understandings. Ulcers caused by stress? No, by bacteria. The USDA food pyramid? Which version? And what about the Mediterranean diet?

It is a noble effort to rationalize education by establishing content standards to specify worthy knowledge and skill. But that should not be confused with the mythic existence of a timeless and official set of unchanging "understandings." Such a view is anti-intellectual and doomed to fail in a democratic world peopled with free thinkers in the professions. We do not want understandings to endure in the horrible fascist sense of indifference to feedback and resistance to change.

The best that any of us can do—whether we are a lone teacher, a school or district committee, or a state standards group—is to recall how all our research as students unfolded. The challenge is to come to *reasonable* understandings, based on a consideration of the appropriate and available resources and our goals. We consider the matter carefully, mindful of what experts say, we reach our own understanding, and we submit that understanding to review—for example, the dissertation and its *defense*. Then we hold to that view while always open to reconsideration of the matter, standing ready to change our minds if and when new compelling arguments and evidence come our way.

Yes, the best understandings endure. And it is our job to share with students what experts understand and have understood, and what we have come to understand as their teachers. But it is also our job to treat students with intellectual respect. We must give them practice in reaching, verifying, and, yes, criticizing understandings. That's how modern disciplinary understanding works—we test claims to strengthen or overturn them. We thus help learners to live in a world in which expertise exists but experts also argue and change their minds, in a place and a time where free thinking is their birthright.

Backward design in action with Bob James

In light of the ideas discussed here, our mythical teacher, Bob James, rethinks his original approach to "understanding." (Compare this with his original thoughts at the end of Chapter 1.)

I guess I have always used the words *know* and *understand* interchangeably. But now that I think about it, there have often been times when kids were able to correctly answer the knowledge-recall questions on my tests, and yet I know they didn't really understand the material. I also see that having lots of knowledge doesn't mean you can use what you know. I recall last year when two of my better students, who aced all my quizzes and tests in the nutrition unit, could not analyze their family's menu planning and shopping to come up with a more nutritious plan. (I also noticed that they ate mostly junk food at lunch.) So I guess there is a difference between *know, know how,* and *understanding.*

More important, I'm beginning to realize that my original understanding goals for the unit are not adequate. I merely identified an area of concern— good nutrition—and thought that the state standards sufficiently explained what I was after. But the content standards for nutrition do not specify the particular understandings that my students are supposed to acquire. They merely state that they should understand the elements of good nutrition. So I need to be more specific: What ideas about nutrition should they come to understand and take away from the unit? As I've worked through the issues and the UbD exercises, I'm now much clearer about how to frame my unit goals in terms of specific propositions. I will now focus on three main understandings: (1) a balanced diet contributes to physical and mental health; (2) the USDA food pyramid provides *relative* guidelines for nutrition; and (3) dietary requirements vary for individuals based on age, activity level, weight, and overall health.

Boy, this is difficult, but I already see the benefits of getting sharper on what, specifically, my students need to come away understanding. It will make it easier for me to finish designing the assessments and lessons to produce those understandings.

In summary

The following four rules of thumb can help designers as they craft, select, and edit proposed understandings:

1. A desired understanding is a priority. A unit should focus on a small number of transferable big ideas about which understandings are stated— otherwise there really *are no* priorities.

2. Desired understandings are best stated in propositional form: "Students will understand *that* . . ." [4]

3. Although pertaining to general or abstract ideas, the desired understandings must be stated in clear, unambiguous terms—as *specific and insightful* generalizations.

4. Understandings are of two kinds, topical and overarching. Topical understandings are unit-specific, and overarching understandings are broader and (as the name implies) offer a possible bridge to other units and courses.

Chapter 7

Thinking like an Assessor

> We recognize understanding through a flexible performance. . . .
> Understanding shows its face when people can think and act flexibly around
> what they know. In contrast, when a learner cannot go beyond rote and
> routine thought and action, this signals lack of understanding. . . . To
> understand means to be able to perform flexibly.
> —David Perkins, "What Is Understanding?" in Martha Stone Wiske, Ed.,
> *Teaching for Understanding,* 1998, p. 42

> The most important method of education . . . always has consisted
> of that in which the pupil was urged to actual performance.
> —Albert Einstein, *Ideas and Opinions,* 1954/1982, p. 60

Having clarified how to frame desired results in Stage 1, we now move to the second stage of backward design. Here we consider the assessment implications of our emerging design by asking (and reasking) the assessor's questions:

• What evidence can show that students have achieved the desired results (Stage 1)?

• What assessment tasks and other evidence will anchor our curricular units and thus guide our instruction?

• What should we look for, to determine the extent of student understanding?

Figure 7.1 lists the three stages of backward design and presents the considerations and design standards that apply. Stage 2 summarizes the elements to consider when planning for the collection of evidence from assessments.

Nowhere does the backward design process depart more from conventional practice than at this stage. Instead of moving from target to teaching, we ask, What would count as evidence of successful learning? Before we plan the activities, our question must first be, What assessment of the desired results logically follows Stage 1? And, specifically, what counts as evidence of the understanding sought?

Figure 7.1
The UbD Matrix: Focus on Stage 2

Key Design Questions	Chapters of the Book	Design Considerations	Filters (Design Criteria)	What the Final Design Accomplishes
Stage 1 • What are worthy and appropriate results? • What are the key desired learnings? • What should students come away understanding, knowing, and able to do? • What big ideas can frame all these objectives?	• Chapter 3—Gaining Clarity on Our Goals • Chapter 4—The Six Facets of Understanding • Chapter 5—Essential Questions: Doorways to Understanding • Chapter 6—Crafting Understandings	• National standards • State standards • Local standards • Regional topic opportunities • Teacher expertise and interest	• Focused on big ideas and core challenges	• Unit framed around enduring understandings and essential questions, in relation to clear goals and standards
Stage 2 • **What is evidence of the desired results?** • **In particular, what is appropriate evidence of the desired understanding?**	• Chapter 7—Thinking like an Assessor • Chapter 8—Criteria and Validity	• Six facets of understanding • Continuum of assessment types	• Valid • Reliable • Sufficient	• Unit anchored in credible and useful evidence of the desired results
Stage 3 • What learning activities and teaching promote understanding, knowledge, skill, student interest, and excellence?	• Chapter 9—Planning for Learning • Chapter 10—Teaching for Understanding	• Research-based repertoire of learning and teaching strategies • Appropriate and enabling knowledge and skill	Engaging and effective, using the elements of WHERETO: • Where is it going? • Hook the students • Explore and equip • Rethink and revise • Exhibit and evaluate • Tailor to student needs, interests, and styles • Organize for maximum engagement and effectiveness	• Coherent learning activities and teaching that will evoke and develop the desired understandings, knowledge, and skill; promote interest; and make excellent performance more likely

The mantra of this and the next chapter is to think like an assessor, not a teacher. Recall the logic of backward design, as shown in Figure 7.2. The text linking the first and second column shows what thinking like an assessor means.

As the logic of backward design reminds us, we are obligated to consider the assessment evidence implied by the outcomes sought, rather than thinking about assessment primarily as a means for generating grades. Given the goals, what performance evidence signifies that they have been met? Given the essential questions, what evidence would show that the learner had deeply considered them? Given the understandings, what would show that the learner "got it"? We urge teachers to consider a judicial analogy as they plan assessment. Think of students as juries think of the accused: innocent (of understanding, skill, and so on) until proven guilty by a preponderance of evidence that is more than circumstantial. In a world of standards-based accountability, such an approach is vital.

The following true stories illustrate the problem of failing to carefully consider the evidence needed.

• A kindergarten teacher has each student bring in a poster with 100 items for the hundredth day of school. But when asked to justify the assessment, the teacher refers to the state standard that references the "idea" of number and place value. But the learner had only to glue 100 items onto the poster. The students were not required to use or to explain rows, columns, or patterns. So we really only have evidence that the learner can count to 100, which is not the same as understanding "hundredness" as a concept linked to the base-10 system and the idea of place value, as the standard expects. In fact, because the poster was prepared at home, we do not have adequate evidence that the students did the counting on their own, without parental input.

• A 7th grade general science teacher captures the energy and imagination of his students by announcing that they will have to eat the results of their next science experiment. But what is engaging is not always what is most effective or appropriate, given the time available. In this instance, making peanut brittle offers little in the way of big ideas and enduring understanding for the week of experimentation allotted.

• A college history professor prepares a final exam consisting exclusively of 100 multiple-choice and short-answer questions for a syllabus in which "doing" history with primary sources is stressed as an important goal.

All of these assessments may have some merit when viewed through the lens of the individual lessons, but each needs to align better with curriculum goals. A more rigorous backward design—from the goals, generally (and key ideas to be understood, specifically), to the related assessments they imply—would have provided that link. These mistakes are common and not isolated. In fact, over the last decade we have observed that few educators have an adequate understanding of validity, and many harbor misunderstandings about assessment more generally, as reflected in both their comments and design work.

Figure 7.2
The Logic of Backward Design

Stage 1	Stage 2
If the desired result is for learners to . . .	**Then you need evidence of the student's ability to . . .**
(G) Meet the standards . . .	
Standard 6—Students will understand essential concepts about nutrition and diet.	• Plan a diet for different kinds of people in different kinds of settings.
6a—Students will use an understanding of nutrition to plan appropriate diets for themselves and others.	• Reveal an understanding that the USDA guidelines are not absolute, but "guides"—and that there are other guides (as well as contextual variables).
6c—Students will understand their own eating patterns and ways in which those patterns may be improved.	• Carefully note and analyze the habits of others as well as oneself, and make supported inferences about why people eat the way they do.
(U) Understand that . . .	
• A balanced diet contributes to physical and mental health.	
• The USDA food pyramid presents relative guidelines for nutrition.	
• Dietary requirements vary for individuals based on age, activity level, weight, and overall health.	
• Healthful living requires an individual to act on available information about good nutrition even if it means breaking comfortable habits.	**That suggests the need for specific tasks or tests like . . .**
(Q) Thoughtfully consider the questions . . .	**(T)**
• What is healthful eating?	• Planning meals for diverse groups.
• Are you a healthful eater? How would you know?	• Reacting to excessively rigid or loose dietary plans made by others.
• How could a healthy diet for one person be unhealthy for another?	• Making a good survey of what people actually eat and why.
• Why are there so many health problems in the United States caused by poor eating despite all the available information?	**(OE)**
(K) (S) Know and be able to . . .	Quizzes: On the food groups and the USDA food pyramid
• Use key terms—protein, fat, calorie, carbohydrate, cholesterol.	Prompts: Describe health problems that could arise as a result of poor nutrition and explain how these could be avoided; reflections on one's own eating habits and those of others.
• Identify types of foods in each food group and their nutritional values.	
• Be conversant with the USDA food pyramid guidelines.	
• Discuss variables influencing nutritional needs.	
• Identify specific health problems caused by poor nutrition.	

More to the point of our focus on understanding, many teacher tests tend to focus on the accuracy of knowledge and skill rather than on evidence of *transferability*, based on big ideas in how to use knowledge and skill effectively. Our earlier discussion of the six facets and the need for transferability properly alerted designers to the importance of obtaining evidence of understanding through performance assessments. But the richness and complexity of all the desired results also demand variety in the evidence we collect.

Three basic questions

Thinking like an assessor boils down to a few basic questions. The first question is *What kinds of evidence do we need* to find hallmarks of our goals, including that of understanding? Before we design a particular test or task, it's important to consider the general types of performances that are implied. For example, regardless of content, understanding is often revealed through the exercises of comparing and contrasting or summarizing key ideas. After mapping a general approach to assessment, we then develop the assessment particulars.

The second question assumes that some particular task has been developed, about which we then ask, *What specific characteristics in student responses, products, or performances should we examine* to determine the extent to which the desired results were achieved? This is where criteria, rubrics, and exemplars come into play.

The third question has to do with a test for validity and reliability of the assessment: *Does the proposed evidence enable us to infer a student's knowledge, skill, or understanding?* In other words, does the evidence (Stage 2) align with our goals (Stage 1), and are the results sufficiently unambiguous? Few teachers are in the habit of testing their designs once the assessments have been fleshed out, but such self-testing is key to better results and to fairness.

In this chapter, we consider the first of the three aspects of thinking like an assessor: considering, in general terms, the kind of evidence needed to assess a variety of learning goals generally and understanding specifically. In the following chapter, we address the other two questions, related to criteria and the issues of validity and reliability.

An unnatural process

To think like an assessor prior to designing lessons does not come naturally or easily to many teachers. We are far more used to thinking like an activity designer or teacher once we have a target. That is, we easily and unconsciously jump to Stage 3—the design of lessons, activities, and assignments—without first asking ourselves what performances and products we need to teach toward.

Backward design demands that we overcome this natural instinct and comfortable habit. Otherwise our design is likely to be less coherent and focused

Figure 7.3
Two Approaches to Thinking About Assessment

When thinking like an assessor, we ask—	When thinking like an activity designer (only), we ask—
• What would be sufficient and revealing evidence of understanding?	• What would be fun and interesting activities on this topic?
• Given the goals, what performance tasks must anchor the unit and focus the instructional work?	• What projects might students wish to do on this topic?
• What are the different types of evidence required by Stage 1 desired results?	• What tests should I give, based on the content I taught?
• Against what criteria will we appropriately consider work and assess levels of quality?	• How will I give students a grade (and justify it to their parents)?
• Did the assessments reveal and distinguish those who really understood from those who only seemed to? Am I clear on the reasons behind learner mistakes?	• How well did the activities work? • How did students do on the test?

on the desired results—and more the result of chance and the ability of students. In fact, a chief value of the UbD Template, and the backward design process more generally, is to provide tools and processes for short-circuiting this mental habit of overlooking the soundness of our assessments. Figure 7.3 summarizes how the two approaches—thinking like an assessor and thinking like an activity designer—differ.

The questions in the first column derive from the desired results and are likely to make the eventual activities and instructional strategies point toward the most appropriate assessments. The second column of questions, though sensible from the perspective of teaching and activity design, makes it far less likely that the assessments used will be appropriate. In effect, when we only think like an activity designer, we may well end up with something like the apples unit described in the Introduction. Although some students *may* develop important understandings and meet some standards as a result, it will be more by luck and happenstance than design. (See Chapter 8 for additional considerations regarding validity.)

Attention to the quality of local assessment could not be more important than it is now, when formal accountability demands assessments aligned with standards. Unless we use backward design frequently and carefully it is unlikely that the local assessment will provide the targeted feedback needed

Figure 7.4

A Continuum of Assessments

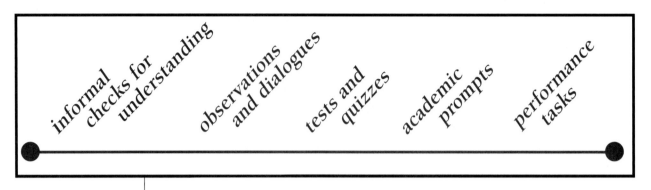

to inform teaching and enhance learning. Greater attention to self-assessment and peer review against design standards can greatly improve school-based assessments.

From snapshot to scrapbook

Effective assessment is more like a scrapbook of mementos and pictures than a single snapshot. Rather than using a single test, of one type, at the end of teaching, effective teacher-assessors gather lots of evidence along the way, using a variety of methods and formats. Thus, when planning to collect evidence of understanding, consider a range of assessment methods such as those shown in Figure 7.4.

This continuum of assessments includes checks of understanding (such as oral questions, observations, dialogues); traditional quizzes, tests, and open-ended prompts; and performance tasks and projects. They vary in terms of scope (from simple to complex), time frame (from short- to long-term), setting (from decontextualized to authentic contexts), and structure (from highly directive to unstructured). Because understanding develops as a result of ongoing inquiry and rethinking, the assessment of understanding should be thought of in terms of a collection of evidence over time instead of an "event"—a single moment-in-time test at the end of instruction—as so often happens in practice.

Given a focus on understanding, a unit or course will naturally be anchored by performance tasks or projects, because these provide evidence that students are able to use their knowledge in context. Our theory of understanding contends that contextualized application is the appropriate means of evoking and assessing *enduring* understandings. More traditional assessments (quizzes, tests, academic prompts, problem sets) round out the picture by assessing essential knowledge and skills that contribute to the culminating performances. The various types of evidence are summarized in Figure 7.5.

Figure 7.5
Types of Evidence

Performance Tasks

Complex challenges that mirror the issues and problems faced by adults. Ranging in length from short-term tasks to long-term, multistaged projects, they yield one or more tangible products and performances. They differ from academic prompts in the following ways:

- Involve a real or simulated setting and the kind of constraints, background "noise," incentives, and opportunities an adult would find in a similar situation (i.e., they are authentic)
- Typically require the student to address an identified audience (real or simulated)
- Are based on a specific purpose that relates to the audience
- Allow students greater opportunity to personalize the task
- Are not secure: The task, evaluative criteria, and performance standards are known in advance and guide student work

Academic Prompts

Open-ended questions or problems that require the student to think critically, not just recall knowledge, and to prepare a specific academic response, product, or performance. Such questions or problems

- Require constructed responses to specific prompts under school and exam conditions
- Are "open," with no single best answer or strategy expected for solving them
- Are often "ill structured," requiring the development of a strategy
- Involve analysis, synthesis, and evaluation
- Typically require an explanation or defense of the answer given and methods used
- Require judgment-based scoring based on criteria and performance standards
- May or may not be secure
- Involve questions typically only asked of students in school

Quiz and Test Items

Familiar assessment formats consisting of simple, content-focused items that

- Assess for factual information, concepts, and discrete skill
- Use selected-response (e.g., multiple-choice, true-false, matching) or short-answer formats
- Are convergent, typically having a single, best answer
- May be easily scored using an answer key or machine
- Are typically secure (i.e., items are not known in advance)

Informal Checks for Understanding

Ongoing assessments used as part of the instructional process. Examples include teacher questioning, observations, examining student work, and think-alouds. These assessments provide feedback to the teacher and the student. They are not typically scored or graded.

Authentic performance—a necessity, not a frill

Understanding is revealed in performance. Understanding is revealed as transferability of core ideas, knowledge, and skill, on challenging tasks in a variety of contexts. Thus, assessment for understanding must be grounded in authentic performance-based tasks.

What do we mean by authentic tasks? An assessment task, problem, or project is authentic if it

• *Is realistically contextualized.* The task is set in a scenario that replicates or simulates the ways in which a person's knowledge and abilities are tested in real-world situations.

• *Requires judgment and innovation.* The student has to use knowledge and skills wisely and effectively to address challenges or solve problems that are relatively unstructured. Rather than a specific prompt or cue that tests a discrete piece of knowledge, realistic challenges require the learner to figure out the nature of the problem. What kind of knowledge and skill is being tapped here? How should I tackle it? Even when the goal may be quite clear, the student has to develop a plan and a procedure for solving the problem or addressing the issue.

• *Asks the student to "do" the subject.* Instead of reciting, restating, or replicating through demonstration what he was taught or already knows, the student has to carry out exploration and work in the discipline of science, history, or any other subject. The student's efforts resemble or simulate the kind of work done by people in the field.

• *Replicates key* challenging *situations in which adults are truly "tested" in the workplace, in civic life, and in personal life.* Real challenges involve specific situations with "messiness" and meaningful goals: important constraints, "noise," purposes, and audiences at work. In contrast, almost all school tests are without context (even when a writing prompt tries to suggest a sense of purpose and audience). In the real world—unlike schools—there is little if any secrecy about the goals or the criteria for success. Moreover, it is advantageous for the performer to ask questions of the "examiner" or boss, and ongoing feedback is typically available from colleagues. Students need to experience what it is like to perform tasks like those in the workplace and other real-life contexts, which tend to be complex and messy.

• *Assesses the student's ability to efficiently and effectively use a repertoire of knowledge and skill to negotiate a complex and multistage task.* Most conventional test items involve isolated bits of knowledge or elements of performance, similar to sideline drills in athletics, which differ from the integrated use of knowledge, skill, and feedback that a game requires. Although drills and tests are appropriate at times, performance is always more than the sum of the drills.

• *Allows appropriate opportunities to rehearse, practice, consult resources, and get feedback on and refine performances and products.* Although there is a role for the "secure" test that keeps questions secret and withholds resource materials from students, that type of testing must coexist with more transparent assessments of students if we are to focus their learning and improve their performance. As the apprenticeship model in the trades has proven, learning is maximized when cycles of *perform-feedback-revise-perform* guide the production of known high-quality products, judged against public performance standards. There is no room for "mystery testing" if we want students to demonstrate their understanding by using information, skills, and relevant resources to perform in context.

A call for greater authenticity in tests is not really new or inappropriate for a world of standards. Bloom and his colleagues signaled the importance of such assessments 40 years ago in the their description of *application* and in their account of synthesis: "a type of divergent thinking [in which] it is unlikely that the right solution to a problem can be set in advance" (Bloom, Madaus, & Hastings, 1981, p. 265).

An assessment approach grounded in authentic work calls for students (and teachers) to come to two important understandings: first, learning how adults in the larger world beyond the school *really* use or don't use the knowledge and skills that are taught in school; and second, how discrete lessons are meaningful, that is, how they lead to higher-quality performance or mastery of more important tasks. Just as the basketball player endures the drudgery of shooting endless foul shots and the flutist endures the monotony of playing scales—both with dreams of authentic achievement—so too must students experience that drills and quizzes have a pay-off in better performances on worthy endeavors.

Designing around problems not just exercises

Designers often find it helpful to consider the more general question implied in the basketball and flute examples to sharpen their assessments: Does the test amount to just simplified "drill" out of context? Or does the assessment require students to really "perform" wisely with knowledge and skill, in a problematic context of real issues, needs, constraints, and opportunities? To get evidence of true understanding requires that we elicit learner judgments made during genuine performance, not just seeing how they respond to easily followed cues that require mere recall and plugging in.

Put in different words, in authentic assessment we have to be sure that we have presented the learner with an *authentic problem*, to invoke an apt distinction made by Dewey almost a hundred years ago:

> *The most significant question which can be asked about any situation or experience proposed to induce [and reveal] learning is what quality of problem it involves . . . but it is indispensable to distinguish between genuine . . . or mock problems. The following questions may aid in making such a discrimination. . . . Does the question naturally suggest itself within some situation or personal experience? Or is it an aloof thing . . . ? Is it the sort of trying that would arouse observation and engage experimentation out side of school? [Or, is it] made a problem for the pupil only because he cannot get the required mark or be promoted or win the teacher's approval, unless he deals with it? (1916, p. 155)*

A variant of Dewey's distinction can be found in all the performance areas, whereby we distinguish exercises from the problems of performance. An exercise involves a straightforward execution of a "move" out of context. A problem is a demand within performance, requiring thought of the many choices and challenges that confront a performer in context. Lay-up drills in basketball are exercises: Players form two lines, one for passers, the other for shooters, and they exchange free shots at the basket. Using that skill (shooting at or making a basket) in a game, however, requires the shooters to also work around the other team's defense.

A similar situation occurs in science. A typical science lab presents an exercise, not a problem: There is a right approach, a right answer, and thus no inherent puzzles or challenges to our understanding. By contrast, having to design and debug an effective, feasible, and cost-sensitive experiment to make sense of a puzzling phenomenon reflects true problem solving. All "doing" of a subject involves problem solving, so our assessments of understanding must be based on real problems, not just exercises requiring discrete facts and skills used in isolation.

Mathematics and history may well be the program areas in most need of thinking through this distinction. Almost every mathematics and history test in K–12 education is a set of exercises, not problems in the sense discussed: One need only respond on cue with the correct move. It doesn't matter whether the topic is adding fractions or understanding the civil rights era, the learner is invariably tested by unambiguous exercises having right answers. An authentic problem related to fractions or history must be like playing a basketball game—just shooting at the basket unhindered or just plugging in the obvious approach or facts isn't enough. The authentic problem solving requires deciding when to use which approach and which facts. Is this problem best solved by using fractions or decimals? Is the civil rights era best understood as a religious or secular movement?

To build math and history assessments out of only exercises (as we so often do) misses the essence of authentic performance in those fields. As we have said, real performance always involves transfer—that is, the flexible use of knowledge and skill in light of particular challenges. It requires puzzling out and making sense of what a situation demands, which is very different from merely responding to a highly structured exercise looking for the right response. Transferability is understanding revealed: The performers must figure out *which* knowledge and skill is needed on their own, without simplifying teacher prompts or cues, to solve the real problems of performance.

Figure 7.6 helps clarify the difference between a problem and an exercise. Note that exercises are necessary but not sufficient in developing competent performance; nor are exercises always reliable indicators of the ability to perform.

■ MISCONCEPTION ALERT!

Our goal in Stage 2 is appropriate evidence, not interesting projects or tasks. Although our aim should always be to make assessments interesting and thought-provoking (because we thereby evoke the best and most thorough work), that is not the main point in Stage 2. Many projects are fun and educational, but they may not provide enough evidence about the understandings sought in Stage 1—particularly if the work involves collaboration and freedom of choice in approach, content, and presentation. Many exercises are less engaging than complex performance tasks, but sometimes they yield more conclusive evidence about a specific understanding or skill. We must ensure that the project is designed backward from the evidence we need, not designed primarily with the learner's interests in mind. Beware of confusing interesting performance tasks or projects with valid evidence. This point is taken up in more detail in Chapter 8.

Figure 7.6
Problems Versus Exercises

	Problem	Exercise
The Framing of the Task	The problem statement is clear, but few if any cues or prompts are offered about how to best frame or solve the problem.	The task is either simple or made simple by specific cues or prompts as to the nature of the challenge or how to proceed in meeting it.
The Approach	Various approaches are possible. Figuring out what kind of problem this is and isn't is a key aspect of the challenge; that is, a strategy is needed. Some combination of logical method with trial and error will likely be required.	There is one best approach (though it might not be stated), and it is suggested by how the exercise is framed. The learner's ability to recognize and use the "right" tactic is a key goal of the exercise.
The Setting	Realistically "noisy" and complicated, typically involving different—sometimes competing—variables related to audience, purpose, criteria for judging work, and more.	Simplified to ensure that the only "variable" is the targeted skill or knowledge. (Similar to sideline drills in athletics or fingering exercises in music.)
The Solution	The goal is an appropriate solution, mindful of various requirements and perhaps competing variables and cost/benefit considerations. There may be a right answer, but it follows from sound reasoning and a supported argument or approach.	The goal is the right *answer*. The exercise is built to ensure that there is only one right answer, by *design*. Though it may be a puzzling challenge, there is a definite right answer that can be found via recall and plugging in of prior knowledge, with little or no modification.
Evidence of Success	The focus shifts from the answer to the justification of the approach and solution.	The accuracy of the answer and the choice of the "correct" approach.

Framing performance tasks using GRASPS

Authentic performance tasks are distinguished from other types of assessments by their particular features. Performance tasks typically present students with a problem: a real-world goal, set within a realistic context of challenges and possibilities. Students develop a tangible product or performance for an identified audience (sometimes real, sometimes simulated). And the evaluative criteria and performance standards are appropriate to the task—and known by the student in advance.

   Because these elements characterize authentic assessments, we can use them during task design. We have created a design tool using the acronym GRASPS to assist in the creation of performance tasks. Each letter corresponds with a task element—Goal, Role, Audience, Situation, Performance, Standards.

Figure 7.7 presents each element with corresponding prompts to help designers construct performance tasks. Often, teachers transform existing assessments or engaging learning activities using GRASPS.

Here is an example of a performance task in science, constructed using GRASPS, for assessing understanding of multivariable experimental design:

• Goal and Role: As a scientist with a consumer research group, your task is to design an experiment to determine which of four brands of detergent will most effectively remove three different types of stains on cotton fabric.

• Audience: Your target audience is the testing department for *Consumer Research* magazine.

• Situation: You have a two-part challenge: (1) to develop an experimental design for isolating the key variables, and (2) to clearly communicate the procedure so that the staff of the testing department can conduct the experiment to determine which cleaner is most effective for each type of stain.

• Product: You need to develop a written experimental procedure (following the given format) outlining the steps in sequence. You may include an outline or graphic format to accompany the written description.

• Standards: Your experimental design needs to follow the criteria for good design accurately and completely; appropriately isolate the key variables; include a clear and accurate written description of the procedure (an outline or graphic to assist the testers is optional); and enable the testing department staff to determine which cleaner is most effective for each type of stain.

Not every performance assessment needs to be framed by GRASPS. However, we propose that at least one core performance task for assessing understanding in a major unit or course be developed in this fashion. Many teachers have observed that tasks framed this way provide students with clear performance targets as well as real-world meaningfulness not found in decontextualized test items or academic prompts.

Performance task vignettes

The following vignettes offer brief descriptions of performance tasks for possible use in assessing student understanding. Notice how they reflect the GRASPS elements.

• From the mountains to the seashore (history, geography; grades 6–8). A group of nine foreign students is visiting your school for one month as part of an international exchange program. (Don't worry, they speak English!) The principal has asked your class to plan and budget a four-day tour of Virginia to help the visitors understand the state's impact on the history and development of our nation. Plan your tour so that the visitors are shown sites that best capture the ways that Virginia has influenced our nation's development. Your task is to prepare a written tour itinerary, including an explanation of why each

Figure 7.7
GRASPS Task Design Prompts

Goal
- Your task is _____ .
- The goal is to _____ .
- The problem or challenge is _____ .
- The obstacles to overcome are _____ .

Role
- You are _____ .
- You have been asked to _____ .
- Your job is _____ .

Audience
- Your clients are _____ .
- The target audience is _____ .
- You need to convince _____ .

Situation
- The context you find yourself in is _____ .
- The challenge involves dealing with _____ .

Product, Performance, and Purpose
- You will create a _____
  in order to _____ .
- You need to develop _____
  so that _____ .

Standards and Criteria for Success
- Your performance needs to _____ .
- Your work will be judged by _____ .
- Your product must meet the following standards _____ .

site was selected. Include a map tracing the route for the four-day tour and a budget for the trip.

• Garden design (mathematics, grades 6–8). You've been asked to plan a flower garden for a company with a logo that has side-by-side circular, rectangular, and triangular shapes. Your final product should be a labeled scale drawing and a list of how many plants of each type and color you need to execute the plan.

• Literary Hall of Fame (English, grades 10–12). The Council of Arts and Letters has announced the establishment of a Hall of Fame to honor the works of notable U.S. authors and artists. Since your class is finishing a course on U.S. literature, you have been asked to submit a nomination for an author to be admitted to the Hall of Fame. Complete the nomination form for an author whom you believe is worthy of induction. Your essay should include your analysis of the author's contribution to U.S. literature and your rationale for recommending the author for inclusion in the Hall of Fame.

• Mail-order friend (language arts, grades K–2). Imagine that you have an opportunity to order a friend by telephone from a mail-order catalog. Think about the qualities that you want in a friend. Before you order your friend over the telephone, practice asking for three characteristics that you want in a friend and give an example of each characteristic. Remember to speak clearly and loudly enough so that the sales person will know exactly what you're looking for. Your request will be taped and assessed against a rubric for clarity as well as how much thought you put into your request.

• Moving Van Go (mathematics and writing, grades 6–9). You are working for a moving company that plans to submit a bid for moving the contents of an office building to a new location. You are responsible for determining the minimum volume of furniture and equipment that must be moved. The exemplary product will take into account (a) the stackability of the items, (b) the interlocking nature of noncubical pieces, (c) the padding to protect the furniture, and (d) the number and size of the boxes needed to pack the small items. You will prepare a written report setting out the volume of items to be moved and a rationale for the findings, and a chart showing how the items will be placed to minimize the volume needed.

• Drywalling a home (mathematics, grades 8–10). When contractors give an estimate on home repairs, how can we know if the cost is reasonable? In this task, you will determine whether a drywalling contractor is giving accurate information, or trying to overcharge an uninformed customer. You will be given room dimensions and cost figures for materials and labor.

• The Cheyenne Indians—what really happened (history, college juniors and seniors). You will research a possible massacre during the Civil War about which no detailed narratives have been written. You will read Senate transcripts and various conflicting first-hand accounts, leading to your own narrative for inclusion in a history book. Your work will be reviewed by your peers and judged by professors serving as textbook editors.

• Fitness plan (physical education and health, secondary level). Playing the role of a trainer at a health club, you will develop a fitness program, consisting of aerobic, anaerobic, and flexibility exercises, for a new client. The fitness plan needs to take into account the client's lifestyle, age, activity level, and personal fitness goals. You will be given detailed descriptions of various clients.

Using the six facets as assessment blueprints

A basic requirement of assessing for understanding is that we need to know the learners' thought processes along with their "answers" or solutions. Their explanation of *why* they did what they did, their *support* for the approach or response, and their *reflection* on the result that we may gain fuller insight into their degree of understanding. Answers without reasons and support are typically insufficient to "convict" the learner of understanding. This is why we require both a dissertation and its defense for a doctorate. Assessment of understanding is enhanced when we make greater use of oral assessments, concept webs, portfolios, and constructed response items of all types to allow students to show their work and reveal their thinking. Selected response formats—multiple choice, matching pairs, true or false—in general provide insufficient (and sometimes misleading) evidence about understanding or its absence.

The six facets of understanding signal the types of performances we need as valid measures of understanding. They map out, in general terms, the kinds of performance evidence we need to successfully distinguish factual knowledge from an understanding of the facts. The value of the facets becomes clearer when we add them to our earlier backward design graphic, as shown in Figure 7.8.

The six facets provide a helpful scaffold for the second column by reminding us, in general, what understanding looks like. We can use the various abilities central to each facet to guide the design process in Stage 2. For example, Facet 1 involves the ability to explain, verify, or justify a position in one's own words. Starting with the stem, "A student who *really* understands . . ." and adding the key words from each facet produces suggestions for the kinds of assessment task we need, as illustrated in Figure 7.9.

This emerging list provides a useful start to a blueprint for assessing understanding. Regardless of our topic or the age of the students we teach, the verbs on this list suggest the kinds of assessments needed to determine the extent to which students understand. Then, in the third column in Figure 7.8, we can get more specific by asking, What kinds of tasks are suitable for the specific desired results of Stage 1 and the students we teach? Which facet (or facets) will most appropriately guide the design of a particular task, with specific performance, process, or product requirements?

Here are some starter ideas for performance tasks built around the six facets of understanding.

Facet 1: Explanation

Explanation asks students to tell the "big idea" in their own words, make connections, show their work, explain their reasoning, and induce a theory from data.

Figure 7.8
The Logic of Backward Design with the Six Facets

Stage 1	Stage 2	
If the desired result is for learners to . . .	***Then you need evidence of the student's ability to . . .***	***So the assessments need to require something like . . .***
understand that • A balanced diet contributes to physical and mental heath. • The USDA food pyramid presents relative guidelines for nutrition. • Dietary requirements vary for individuals based on age, activity level, weight, and overall health. • Healthful living requires an individual to act on available information about good nutrition even if it means breaking comfortable habits. *and thoughtfully consider the questions . . .* • What is healthful eating? • Are you a healthful eater? How would you know? • How could a healthy diet for one person be unhealthy for another? • Why are there so many health problems in the United States caused by poor eating despite all the available information?	*explain* • A balanced diet • The consequences of poor nutrition • Why we eat poorly, despite the information available *interpret* • Food nutrition labels • Data on the impact of fast foods on eating patterns *apply, by* • Planning healthy menus • Evaluating various plans and diets *see from the points of view of* • People of other cultures and regions in terms of their dietary beliefs and habits *empathize with* • A person living with significant dietary restrictions due to a medical condition *reflect on* • Personal eating habits • Whether foods that are good for you always taste bad	• Develop a brochure to help younger students understand what is meant by a balanced diet and the heath problems resulting from poor eating. • Discuss the popularity of fast foods and the challenges of eating a healthful diet in today's fast-paced world. • Plan a menu for a class party consisting of healthy, yet tasty, snacks. • Conduct and present research on the impact of diverse diets (i.e., Antarctica, Asia, the Middle East) on health and longevity. • Describe how your life would be affected (and how it might feel) to live with dietary restrictions due to a medical condition (such as diabetes). • Reflect: To what extent are you a healthy eater? How might you become a healthier eater?

Figure 7.9

Using the Six Facets to Build Assessments for Understanding

A student who *really* understands . . .

Facet 1. Can explain—*Demonstrates sophisticated explanatory power and insight.* Is able to . . .

a. Provide complex, insightful, and credible reasons—theories and principles, based on good evidence and argument—to explain or illuminate an event, fact, text, or idea; show meaningful connections; provide a systematic account, using helpful and vivid mental models.
  - Make fine, subtle distinctions; aptly qualify her opinions.
  - See and argue for what is central—the big ideas, pivotal moments, decisive evidence, key questions, and so on.
  - Make good predictions.

b. Avoid or overcome common misunderstandings and superficial or simplistic views—shown, for example, by avoiding overly simplistic, hackneyed, or imprecise theories or explanations.

c. Reveal a personalized, thoughtful, and coherent grasp of a subject—indicated, for example, by developing a reflective and systematic integration of what she knows. This integration would therefore be based in part upon significant and apt direct or simulated experience of specific ideas or feelings.

d. Substantiate or justify her views with sound argument and evidence.

Facet 2. Can interpret—*Offers powerful, meaningful interpretations, translations, narratives.* Is able to . . .

a. Effectively and sensitively interpret texts, data, and situations—shown, for example, by the ability to read between the lines and offer plausible accounts of the many possible purposes and meanings of any "text" (book, situation, human behavior, and so on).

b. Offer a meaningful and illuminating account of complex situations and people—shown, for example, by the ability to provide historical and biographical background to help make ideas more accessible and relevant.

Facet 3. Can apply—*Uses knowledge in context; has know-how.* Is able to . . .

a. Employ her knowledge effectively in diverse, authentic, and realistically messy contexts.

b. Extend or apply what she knows in a novel and effective way (invent in the sense of innovate, as Piaget discusses in *To Understand Is to Invent*[1]).

c. Effectively self-adjust as she performs.

Facet 4. Sees in perspective—Is able to . . .

a. Critique and justify a position, that is, see it as a point of view; to use skills and dispositions that embody disciplined skepticism and the testing of theories.

b. Place facts and theories in context; know the questions or problem to which the knowledge or theory is an answer or solution.

c. Infer the assumptions upon which an idea or theory is based.

d. Know the limits as well as the power of an idea.

e. See through argument or language that is biased, partisan, or ideological.

(continued on next page)

Figure 7.9 (continued)

---

f. See and explain the importance or worth of an idea.

g. Take a critical stance; wisely employ *both criticism and belief* (an ability summarized by Peter Elbow's maxim that we are likely to better understand when we methodically "believe when others doubt and doubt when others believe"[2]).

Facet 5. Demonstrates empathy—Is able to . . .

a. Project himself into, feel, and appreciate another's situation, affect, point of view.

b. Operate on the assumption that even an apparently odd or obscure comment, text, person, or set of ideas may contain insights that justify working to understand it.

c. See when incomplete or flawed views are plausible, even insightful, though perhaps somewhat incorrect or outdated.

d. See and explain how an idea or theory can be all too easily misunderstood by others.

e. Watch and listen sensitively and to perceive what others often do not.

Facet 6. Reveals self-knowledge—Is able to . . .

a. Recognize his own prejudices and style and how they color understanding; see and get beyond egocentrism, ethnocentrism, present-centeredness, nostalgia, either/or thinking.

b. Engage in effective metacognition; recognize intellectual style, strengths, and weaknesses.

c. Question his own convictions; like Socrates, sort out mere strong belief and habit from warranted knowledge, be intellectually honest, and admit ignorance.

d. Accurately self-assess and effectively self-regulate.

e. Accept feedback and criticism without defensiveness.

f. Regularly reflect on the meaning of one's learning and experiences.

---

[1]Jean Piaget. (1973). *To Understand Is to Invent: The Future of Education.* New York: Grossman's Publishing Co.
[2]Peter Elbow. (1973). *Writing Without Teachers.* New York: Oxford University Press.

• Mathematics—subtraction. Design a lesson plan, using manipulatives, to teach a new student to our class what "subtraction" is all about.

• Social studies—geography and economics. Create a graphic organizer to show connections between environment, natural resources and economy for two different regions.

• Science—electricity. Develop a trouble-shooting guide for an electric circuit system.

• Foreign language—language structure. Develop a guidebook in which you explain the difference between the various forms of past tense, and when they should and should not be used.

Facet 2: Interpretation

Interpretation requires the student to make sense of stories, art works, data, situations, or claims. Interpretation also involves translating ideas, feelings, or work done in one medium into another.

- History—U.S. history. Select 5–10 songs about the United States written since the Civil War. Use them to explore the questions: Are we the nation we set out to be? How have we seen ourselves as a nation? Which attitudes have changed and which have not?

- Literature—*The Catcher in the Rye* and *Frog and Toad Are Friends.* Answer the question, What's wrong with Holden? Study the words and actions of the main character, and the reaction of other characters to help you make sense of Holden Caulfield. Examine the question, Who is a true friend? Study the words and actions of the main characters, Frog and Toad. Look for patterns to help you answer the question.

- Visual and performing arts—any medium. Represent strong emotions (e.g., fear and hope) through a collage, dance, musical piece, or other medium. How does the medium affect the message?

- Science and mathematics—data patterns. Collect data over time on any complex phenomena (e.g., weather variables). Analyze and display the data in order to find patterns.

Facet 3: Application

Students who understand can use their knowledge and skill in new situations. Place emphasis on application in authentic contexts, with a real or simulated audience, purpose, setting, constraints, and background noise.

- Mathematics—area and perimeter. Design the shape of a fenced-in section of a yard, given a specified amount of fencing material, to maximize the play area for a new puppy.

- Social studies—map skills. Develop a scaled map of your school to help a new student find her way around.

- Health—nutrition. Develop a menu plan for healthful meals and snacks for a family of five for one week, staying within a defined budget.

- Science—environmental studies. Perform a chemical analysis of local stream water to monitor clean water compliance and present your findings to the regional EPA office.

Facet 4: Perspective

Perspective is demonstrated when the student can see things from different points of view, articulate the other side of the case, see the big picture, recognize underlying assumptions, and take a critical stance.

- History—compare and contrast. Review British, French, and Chinese textbook accounts of the U.S. Revolutionary War era. Identify the historical perspective of each, and defend or oppose their use as teaching resources at a simulated school board meeting.

- Arithmetic—different representations. Compare the pros and cons of different views of the same quantity represented in decimals, fractions, and percentages; and in different graphical and symbolic representations.

- English or language arts—literary analysis and writing. Assume you are the editor at a major publishing house. Review a submitted short story for possible plagiarism. (The teacher does not tell students that they are reviewing a story written by one of the authors they have studied this year.) Then write a tactful but firm letter back to the author on the likely source of this manuscript.

- Geometry. Compare the shortest distance between two points in three different spaces: physical corridors in their school building, on the earth's surface, and in Euclidean space.

- Music. Listen to three different recorded versions of the same song and critique each version, as if you are a producer working with your current star to choose an arrangement.

Facet 5: Empathy

Intellectual imagination is essential to understanding, and it manifests itself not only in the arts and literature, but more generally through the ability to appreciate people who think and act differently from us. The goal is not to have students accept the ways of others, but to help them better understand the diversity of thought and feeling in the world; that is, to develop their capacity to walk in someone else's shoes. In this way, students can avoid stereotyping and learn how yesterday's weird idea can be commonplace today.

- History. Using a *Meeting of Minds* format, role-play various characters with other students and discuss or debate an issue (e.g., settlers and Native Americans on Manifest Destiny, Truman deciding to drop the atomic bomb, the reasons for the collapse of the Soviet Union).

- English or language arts—writing. Imagine you are the newly selected poet laureate of the European Union and have been commissioned to write a sonnet about events in the Middle East. It will be published in the *Jerusalem Times* as well as the *Cairo Daily News*. Your goal is to promote empathy for the people suffering on both sides of this struggle.

- Science. Read and discuss premodern or discredited scientific writings to identify plausible or "logical" theories (given the information available at the time), such as Ptolemy's explanation for why the Earth must be at rest, and Lamarck's account of development.

- Literature—Shakespeare. Imagine you are Juliet from *Romeo and Juliet*, and consider your terrible, final act. Write your final diary entry to describe what are you thinking and feeling. *(Note: This prompt was used on a British national exam.)*

Facet 6: Self-Knowledge

It is important to require students to self-assess their past as well as their present work. It is only through self-assessment that we gain the most complete insight into how sophisticated and accurate students' views are of the tasks, criteria, and standards they are to master.

A simple strategy is to make the first and last written assignments for any course *the same question*, and require students to write a self-assessment post-script describing their sense of progress in understanding. Teachers who collected student work samples in portfolios use a related approach by asking students to review their portfolios and respond to reflective questions: How does your work show how you have improved? What task or assignment was the most challenging and why? Which selection are you most proud of and why? In what ways does your work illustrate your strengths and weaknesses as a learner?

Here are some other approaches to self-assessment and metacognition for any subject and level:

• Here I Come! At the end of the school year, write a letter to next year's teacher describing yourself as a learner. Describe your academic strengths, needs, interests, and learning styles. Set specific learning goals based on self-assessment of your performance during the year that is ending. (Ideally, these letters would be systematically collected and sent to the receiving teachers during the summer.)

• What have I learned? Add a postscript to any paper written for a course in which you must dispassionately self-assess the strengths, weaknesses, and gaps in your approach or response. Pose the question, Knowing what I now do, what would I do differently next time?

• How well do I think I did? Middle school, high school, and college students can produce a written or oral self-assessment against the criteria used to evaluate the work (rubrics). The accuracy of the self-assessment is a small part of the grade. *(Note: This practice is used on every major assignment at Alverno College in Milwaukee, Wisconsin.)*

First among equals

We generally need to include the first facet, *explanation,* as part of any task involving the other five facets. We need to know *why* the students performed the way they did, what they think it means, and what justifies their approach, not just that they did it. In performance-based assessment for understanding, in other words, the tasks and performances should require reflection, explicit self-assessment, and self-adjustment, with reasoning or rationale made as evident as possible.

Using essential questions for assessment

If we have done a good job in framing the unit around essential questions, then we have another helpful way to think through and to test the appropriateness of our assessment ideas. The performances should directly or indirectly require the students to address the essential questions.

Look back at our recurring unit on nutrition (Figure 7.10). Note how the Essential Questions provide a helpful framework upon which the right kinds of tasks can be built.

Figure 7.10
Essential Questions Leading to Performance Tasks

Essential Questions	Proposed Performance Tasks
• Why do people have such a difficult time eating right?	• Students collect and analyze survey data to find out where students eat most of their meals
• Must food that is really good for you taste bad and vice versa?	• Students investigate the nutritional value of various foods to compare taste with health benefits
• Why do experts often disagree about dietary guidelines? What agreement exists amidst the disagreement?	• Students compare and evaluate various approaches to good nutrition—USDA, Atkins, Mediterranean—culminating in poster display and oral report

You might start your work by simply assuming that the essential question will be like a blue-book exam question from college—begin your design work by thinking of the questions as final essay prompts. Then, see if you can take the prompt and devise a GRASPS situation in which the same question is being addressed in a more authentic manner.

If a GRASPS scenario seems contrived or you believe that a traditional writing prompt provides the most appropriate assessment, use the essential questions to focus learning and as a part of the final exam. Using the essential questions in this way provides a focus for both teachers and students and renders the assessment process far less mysterious and arbitrary than it needs to be.

Rounding out the evidence

The question we ask when thinking like an assessor is this: What's the evidence we need (given the desired results)? We should have no philosophical axe to grind in answering that question. We should use the best kinds of assessments, including, where appropriate, short-answer prompts and selected-response quizzes. Too often as teachers, we rely on only one or two types of assessment, then compound that error by concentrating on those aspects of the curriculum that are most easily tested and graded by multiple-choice or short-answer items. On the other hand, it is a common misconception that reform is about an exclusive reliance on authentic assessments. This is simply not the case. For evidence of many desired results, especially discrete knowledge and skill, objective quizzes, tests, and observations with checklists often suffice. We can visually depict the relationship of various assessment types to curriculum priorities by considering the chart in Figure 7.11 (p. 170).

Frequently, too, we fail to consider the differences between tests and other forms of assessment that are particularly well suited for gathering evidence of understanding. In fact, in aiming for understanding, we usually err in assuming that formal and summative testing is needed for evidence gathering. The corollary is to assume that everything that is assessed must be graded.

On the contrary, as the phrases "check for understanding" and "feedback" imply, ongoing formative assessments are vital to reveal students' understanding and misunderstanding. A simple device for ongoing assessment of understanding is the "one-minute essay." At the end of each class, students are asked to answer two questions: (1) What is the big point you learned in class today? and (2) What is the main unanswered question you leave class with today? A quick scan of student responses provides the teacher with immediate feedback on the extent of student understanding (or lack thereof). Indeed, professors at Harvard University have called this technique one of the most effective innovations in their teaching (Light, 2001).

In our own teaching, we have required students to bring written questions to class each day. Class begins by having learners discuss their questions in groups of two or three, bringing their most important question to the entire class for consideration. Then, we look for patterns through a web of questions and possible answers. With a few minutes to go at the end of class, we ask one or two students to summarize the conversation and ask everyone to write notes. Perkins (1992) proposes many other strategies, and we suggest other such checks for understanding in Chapter 9.

The need for a variety of assessment evidence in Stage 2 is signaled in the Design Template by one box for key Performance Tasks and another box for all Other Evidence. A balance of types of assessment is good measurement and wise practice in teaching.

In this first look at assessment we have considered designing assessments by working backward from the desired results of Stage 1. We stressed that when understanding is the focus our evidence must be grounded in authentic performance tasks (supplemented as needed by "other evidence") that involve real problems, not

■ MISCONCEPTION ALERT!

When we speak of evidence of understanding, we are referring to evidence gathered through a variety of formal and informal assessments during a unit of study or a course. We are not alluding only to end-of-teaching tests or culminating performance tasks. Rather, the collected evidence we seek may include observations and dialogues, traditional quizzes and tests, performance tasks and projects, as well as students' self-assessments gathered over time.

mere exercises. The facets help us find the right kinds of tasks, and GRASPS helps us further refine each task to ensure its authenticity. And we reminded readers that there is always a need for variety of evidence.

Figure 7.11
Curricular Priorities and Assessment Methods

In effective assessments, we see a match between the type or format of the assessment and the needed evidence of achieving the desired results. If the goal is for students to learn basic facts and skills, then paper-and-pencil tests and quizzes generally provide adequate and efficient measures. However, when the goal is deep understanding, we rely on more complex performances to determine whether our goal has been reached. The graphic below reveals the general relationship between assessment types and the evidence they provide for different curriculum targets.

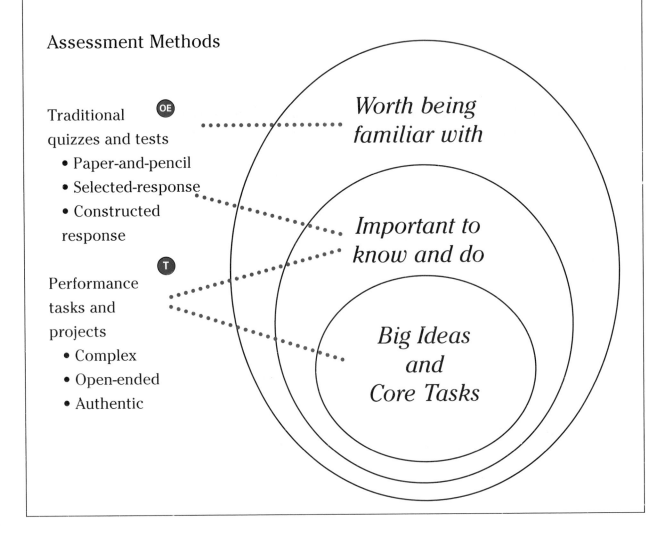

Backward design in action with Bob James

Now I need to think about what would actually serve as evidence of the understandings I'm after. This will be a bit of a stretch for me. Typically in a 3–4 week unit like this one, I give one or two quizzes, have a project, which I grade, and conclude with a unit test (generally multiple choice or matching). Although this approach to assessment makes grading (and justifying the grades) fairly easy, I have come to realize that these assessments don't always provide adequate evidence regarding the most important understandings of the unit. I tend to test what is easy to test instead of assessing what is most important, namely the understandings and attitudes students should take away, above and beyond nutritional facts. In fact, one thing that has always disturbed me is that the kids tend to focus on their grades rather than on their learning. Perhaps the way I've used assessments—more for grading purposes than to document learning—has contributed to their attitude.

Now I need to think about what would actually serve as evidence of the enduring understanding I'm after. After reviewing some examples of performance assessments and discussing ideas with my colleagues, I have decided on the following performance task:

> *Because we have been learning about nutrition, the camp director at the Outdoor Education Center has asked us to propose a nutritionally balanced menu for our three-day trip to the center later this year. Using the USDA food pyramid guidelines and the nutrition facts on food labels, we will design a plan for three days, including three main meals and three snacks (a.m., p.m., and campfire). Our goal is a tasty and nutritionally balanced menu.*

This task also links well with one of our unit projects—to analyze a hypothetical family's diet for a week and propose ways to improve their nutrition. With this task and project in mind, I can now use quizzes to check their prerequisite knowledge (of the food groups and the food pyramid recommendations) and a test for their understanding of how a nutritionally deficient diet contributes to health problems. This is the most complete assessment package I've ever designed for a unit, and I think that the task will motivate students as well as provide evidence of their understanding.

Looking ahead

We need now to consider the second and third questions that lie at the heart of thinking like an assessor: What should we look for when we assess? How can we be confident that our proposed assessments permit valid and reliable inferences back to Stage 1? In the next chapter we will turn to those two questions.

Chapter 8

Criteria and Validity

Assessment and feedback are crucial for helping people learn. Assessment
that is consistent with principles of learning and understanding should:
- Mirror good instruction
- Happen continuously, but not intrusively, as part of instruction
- Provide information about the levels of understanding
  that students are reaching.
—John Bransford, Ann Brown, and Rodney R. Cocking, *How People Learn,* 2000, p. 244

The central problem . . . is that most widely used assessments
of academic achievement are based on highly restrictive beliefs
about learning and competence.
—Committee on the Foundations of Assessment, *Knowing What Students Know:
The Science and Design of Educational Assessment,* 2001, p. 2

In Chapter 7 we focused on the kinds of assessments needed to provide appropriate evidence of our desired results. We noted that there is always a need for a variety of evidence and that assessment plans must be grounded in authentic performance tasks. We also found that the assessment of understanding requires performance assessment: We need to see how well the learner handles performance challenges in context, and what their thought processes were in doing so.

The need for criteria

Because the kinds of open-ended prompts and performance tasks needed to assess for understanding do not have a single, correct answer or solution process, evaluation of student work is based on judgment guided by criteria. Clear and appropriate criteria specify what we should look at to determine the degree of understanding and serve us in making a judgment-based process consistent and fair (Wiggins, 1998, pp. 91–99). How, then, do we come up with appropriate criteria and how do we make them clear to learners?

Appropriate criteria highlight the most revealing and important aspects of the work (given the goals), not just those parts of the work that are merely easy to see or score. For example, when reading a story we want to be engaged, to have our imagination sparked or interest fired. The best stories hook and hold our interest through an effective combination of plot and character. So a key criterion in judging stories is *engagement*. Another might be the author's *craftsmanship* in using effective literary devices and language choices. A third might relate to depth and credibility of the characters—or *character development*. The criteria of a story are not arbitrary. Every book should be engaging, well crafted, and built upon fully developed and credible characters.

Although these three criteria are related, they are also independent. A story might engage us despite cartoonish characters; the story might be engaging but filled with plot gaps or typos. Therefore, when identifying appropriate criteria, we must clarify a set of *independent variables in the performance* that affect our judgment of quality. The criteria would then specify the conditions that any performance must meet to be successful; they define, operationally, the task requirements.

Many teachers make the mistake of relying on criteria that are merely easy to see as opposed to central to the performance and its purpose. So it is common to see research papers that get high scores merely for having numerous footnotes (rather than well-supported research); understanding inferred because the speech was witty (instead of thorough); or exhibits judged as effective because they are colorful and creative (as opposed to supplying accurate information). Just as we need to derive assessments from the goals and understandings, we need to derive criteria from the goals.

From criteria to rubric

A rubric is a criterion-based scoring guide consisting of a fixed measurement scale (4 points, 6 points, or whatever is appropriate) and descriptions of the characteristics for each score point. Rubrics describe degrees of quality, proficiency, or understanding along a continuum. (If the assessment response needs only a yes/no or right/wrong determination, a checklist is used instead of a rubric.) Rubrics answer the questions:

• By what criteria should performance be judged and discriminated?
• Where should we look and what should we look for to judge performance success?
• How should the different levels of quality, proficiency, or understanding be described and distinguished from one another?

Two general types of rubrics—*holistic* and *analytic*—are widely used to judge student products and performances. A holistic rubric provides an overall impression of a student's work. Holistic rubrics yield a *single* score or rating for a product or performance.

Figure 8.1

Top-Level Descriptors from an NWREL Rubric for Writing

Development of Ideas: The paper is clear and focused. It holds the reader's attention. Relevant anecdotes and details enrich the central theme.

Organization: The organization enhances and showcases the central idea or theme. The order, structure, or presentation of information is compelling and moves the reader through the text.

Voice: The writer speaks directly to the reader in a way that is individual, compelling, and engaging. The writer crafts the writing with an awareness of and respect for the audience and the purpose for writing.

Word Choice: The words convey the intended message in a precise, interesting, and natural way. The words are powerful and engaging.

Sentence Fluency: The writing has an easy flow, rhythm, and cadence. Sentences are well built, with strong and varied structure that invites expressive oral reading.

Conventions: The writer shows a good grasp of standard writing conventions . . . and uses conventions effectively to enhance readability. Errors tend to be so few that just minor touch-ups would get this piece ready to publish.

Presentation: The form and presentation of the text enhance the ability of the reader to understand and connect with the message. It is pleasing to the eye.

Source: © NWREL, Portland, OR (2000). Reprinted with permission.
Note: Numerous helpful indicators exist for each level, on a five-point scale. In addition, more learner-friendly versions for younger students have been developed. See Arter & McTighe (2001) for this and other rubrics and a comprehensive look at design and implementation issues for rubrics.

An analytic rubric divides a product or performance into distinct traits or dimensions and judges each separately. Since an analytic rubric rates each of the identified traits independently, a separate score is provided for each. For example, a popular analytic rubric for writing examines six traits: (1) ideas, (2) organization, (3) voice, (4) word choice, (5) sentence fluency, and (6) conventions. A student's writing is rated according to the performance level on each trait. For example, a piece of writing might receive a *3* for *idea development* (trait 1), and a *4* for *use of conventions* (trait 6). The Northwest Regional Educational Laboratory has developed and used a widely implemented set of analytic rubrics involving six criteria (and an optional seventh) called 6 + 1. The traits scored, with the top descriptor for each criterion, are provided in Figure 8.1.

Although a holistic rubric is an appropriate scoring tool when an overall impression is required, we propose that assessors of understanding use analytic rubrics. Why? Because the quality of the feedback to the student is easily compromised in the name of efficiency when we boil down evaluation to a single (holistic) score. For instance, two persuasive essays may be deemed unsatisfactory, but their defects are quite different. One paper is mechanically flawed but filled with wonderful arguments. Another paper is clearly written and grammatically correct, but contains superficial reasoning and an unsupported conclusion. Yet if we are obliged to assign a single score using a holistic rubric, we unwittingly mislead the learner, the parent, and others into thinking that the performances were the same. There are always independent criteria at work in performance, especially when understanding is a target, so we should try to strike a balance between appropriately varied criteria and feasibility.

Rubrics to assess understanding

To bring this general discussion about rubrics and criteria to understanding, recall that understanding is a matter of degree on a continuum. It is not a matter of simple right versus wrong but *more or less* naïve or sophisticated, *more or less* superficial or in-depth. Thus, a rubric for understanding must provide concrete answers to our key assessment questions: What does understanding look like? What differentiates a sophisticated understanding from a naïve understanding, in practice? What does a range of explanations look like, from the most naïve or simplistic to the most complex and sophisticated?

Let's look at two examples of rubrics that describe "understanding." A generic version of a rubric used in the advanced placement exam in U.S. history in the recent past asks readers to attend to the degree to which there is a supported thesis as opposed to a mere description of events:

- *Clear, well-developed thesis that deals in a sophisticated fashion with [key] components . . .*
- *Clear, developed thesis that deals with [key issues] . . .*
- *General thesis responding to all components superficially . . .*
- *Little or no analysis . . . (Educational Testing Service/College Board, 1992, p. 25).*

The rubric explicitly warns judges, first, to assess the degree of student understanding (sophisticated analysis versus mere retelling), and second, to not confuse either the number of factual errors or the quality of the writing with the student's understanding of the time period.

Here is a rubric from a Canadian provincial language arts exam that offers a caution to judges about distinguishing between insight versus the merits of any particular interpretation:

5 Proficient: An insightful understanding of the reading selection(s) is effectively established. The student's opinion, whether directly stated or implied, is perceptive and appropriately supported by specific details. Support is precise and thoughtfully selected.

4 Capable: A well-considered understanding. . . . Opinion is thoughtful. . . . Support is well defined and appropriate.

3 Adequate: A plausible understanding is established and sustained. The student's opinion is conventional but plausibly supported. Support is general but functional.

2 Limited: Some understanding is evidenced, but the understanding is not always defensible or sustained. Opinion may be superficial and support scant and/or vague.

1 Poor: An implausible conjecture. . . . The student's opinion, if present, is inappropriate or incomprehensible. Support is inappropriate or absent.

The evaluation of the answer should be in terms of the amount of evidence that the student has actually read something and thought about it, not a question of whether he/she has thought about it in the way an adult would, or in line with an adult's "correct" answer.

In both cases, the rubrics focus on describing degrees of understanding, the trait being scored. Other traits, such as mechanics, craftsmanship, and organization should be judged separately.

We recommend that assessors consider at least two different traits, regardless of whether the descriptors are formatted as one rubric in a grid or two separate rubrics. We suggest a rubric for "understanding" and a rubric for the qualities of the "performance" (including products and processes, where appropriate) in which that understanding was displayed.

Backward design from criteria and rubrics

It helps when the students themselves identify the characteristics of an exemplary project so that they will have a clearer understanding of the parts of the whole. This means exposing students to many student-generated and professional writing samples, guiding students to identify exactly what makes each a strong (or weak) writing piece, identifying the necessary writing skills, and teaching those skills. Students now have a "map" for each unit, [which] seems to make them much more enthusiastic about the process. With clearly defined units, more purposeful lesson plans, and more enthusiastic students, UbD has made teaching a lot more fun!
—6th grade language arts teacher

Backward design suggests another approach to help us with criteria and rubrics—albeit a counterintuitive one. It turns out that any explicit goal in Stage 1 implies the criteria needed in Stage 2, even *before* a particular task is designed. For example, consider what 6th grade students in Pennsylvania will need to include in their writing to show that they have met the state writing standard:

[Students will] write persuasive pieces with a clearly stated position or opinion and supporting detail, citing sources when needed.

Regardless of whether students compose a persuasive essay, a policy brief, or a letter to the editor, the following criteria (derived directly from the standard) should be employed when judging their writing:

- Clearly stated position or opinion
- Supporting details provided
- Appropriate sources cited (as needed)

The facets and criteria

Since we have argued that understanding is revealed via six facets, these prove useful in identifying criteria and constructing rubrics to assess the degree of understanding. Figure 8.2 provides a partial list of applicable criteria based on the six facets of understanding.

How, then, might we assess for increasing control over the facets of understanding, given these criteria? The rubric shown in Figure 8.3 provides a general framework for making helpful distinctions and sound judgments. The rubric reflects an appropriate continuum—from naïve understanding (at the bottom) to sophisticated understanding (at the top)—for each of the facets.

As the rubric makes clear, understanding may be thought of

■ AN IMPLICATION FOR GIVING GRADES

The regular use of criterion-based rubrics and multiple checks for understanding has implications for grading, especially at the secondary and university level. Many upper-level teachers have two long-standing habits that are counterproductive: They often give grades to each piece of work without making clear the criteria and the appropriate weighting of each criterion, and they typically average those grades over the course of time to come up with a final grade. This latter practice especially makes little sense when assessing against understanding goals and rubrics over time: Averaging a learner's initial versus final level of comprehension of a complex idea will not provide an accurate representation of her understanding. See also Guskey, 2002; Wiggins, 1998; Marzano, 2000.

---

as a continuum—from misconception to insight or from self-conscious awkwardness to autonomic skill proficiency. Moreover, it reflects the reality that individuals can have diverse but valid understandings of the same ideas and experiences. In other words, one person's profile might look very different from another's even as we describe them both, in general, as "sophisticated" (in the same way we give holistic scores to writing performances consisting of different patterns of the analytic traits involved).

Figure 8.2
Facet-Related Criteria

Facet 1 Explanation	Facet 2 Interpretation	Facet 3 Application	Facet 4 Perspective	Facet 5 Empathy	Facet 6 Self-knowledge
• accurate	• meaningful	• effective	• credible	• sensitive	• self-aware
• coherent	• insightful	• efficient	• revealing	• open	• metacognitive
• justified	• significant	• fluent	• insightful	• receptive	• self-adjusting
• systematic	• illustrative	• adaptive	• plausible	• perceptive	• reflective
• predictive	• illuminating	• graceful	• unusual	• tactful	• wise

Figure 8.3
Six-Facet Rubric

Explained	Meaningful	Effective	In Perspective	Empathic	Reflective
Sophisticated and Comprehensive: an unusually thorough, elegant, or inventive account (model, theory, explanation); fully supported, verified, justified; deep and broad; goes well beyond the information given	*Insightful:* a powerful and illuminating interpretation or analysis of the importance, meaning, significance; tells a rich and insightful story; provides a revealing history or context	*Masterful:* Fluent, flexible, efficient, able to use knowledge and skill and adjust understandings well in diverse and difficult contexts—masterful ability to transfer	*Insightful and Coherent:* a thoughtful and circumspect viewpoint; effectively critiques, encompasses other plausible perspectives; takes a long and dispassionate critical view of the issues involved	*Mature:* disciplined; disposed and able to see and feel what others see and feel; unusually open to and willing to seek out the odd, alien, or different; able to make sense of texts, experiences, events that seem weird to others	*Wise:* deeply aware of the boundaries of own and others' understanding; able to recognize own prejudices and projections; has integrity—able and willing to act on understanding
Systematic: an atypical and revealing account, going beyond what is obvious or what was explicitly taught; makes subtle connections; well supported by argument and evidence; novel thinking displayed	*Revealing:* a thoughtful interpretation or analysis of the importance, meaning, significance; tells an insightful story; provides a helpful history or context	*Skilled:* competent in using knowledge and skill and adapting understandings in a variety of appropriate and demanding contexts	*Thorough:* a fully developed and coordinated critical view; makes own view more plausible by a fair consideration of the plausibility of other perspectives; makes apt criticisms, discriminations, and qualifications	*Sensitive:* disposed to see and feel what others see and feel; open to the unfamiliar or different; able to see the value and work that others do not see	*Circumspect:* aware of own ignorance and that of others; aware of own prejudices
In-Depth: an account that reflects some in-depth and personalized ideas; student is making the work his own, going beyond the given; there is supported theory, but insufficient or inadequate evidence and argument	*Perceptive:* a reasonable interpretation or analysis of the importance, meaning, or significance; tells a clear and instructive story; provides a revealing history or context	*Able:* limited but growing ability to be adaptive and innovative in the use of knowledge and skill	*Considered:* a reasonably critical and comprehensive look at major points of view in the context of her own; makes clear that there is plausibility to other points of view	*Aware:* knows and feels that others see and feel differently and is somewhat able to empathize with others	*Thoughtful:* generally aware of what he does and does not understand; aware of how prejudice and projection occur without awareness

Developed: an incomplete account, but with apt and insightful ideas; extends and deepens some of what was learned; some reading between the lines; account has limited support, argument, data, or sweeping generalizations; there is a theory with limited testing and evidence	*Interpreted:* a plausible interpretation or analysis of the importance, meaning, or significance; makes sense with a telling story; provides a telling story or context
Naive: superficial account; more descriptive than analytical or creative; a fragmented or sketchy account of facts, ideas; glib generalizations; a black-and-white account; less theory than an unexamined hunch or borrowed idea	*Literal:* a simplistic or superficial reading; mechanical translation; a decoding with little or no interpretation; no sense of wider importance or significance; a restatement of what was taught or read

Apprentice: relies on a limited repertoire of routines, able to perform well in a few familiar or simple contexts; limited use of judgment and responsiveness to feedback or situation	*Aware:* knows of different points of view and somewhat able to place own view in perspective, but weakness in considering worth of each perspective, especially her own; uncritical about tacit assumptions
Novice: can perform only with coaching or relies on highly scripted, singular "plug-in" (algorithmic and mechanical) skills, procedures, or approaches	*Uncritical:* unaware of differing points of view, prone to overlook or ignore other perspectives; has difficulty imagining other ways of seeing things; prone to ad hominem criticisms

Decentering: has some capacity or self-discipline to walk in others shoes, but is still primarily limited to own reactions and attitudes, puzzled or put off by different feelings or attitudes	*Unreflective:* generally unaware of own specific ignorance; generally unaware of how prejudgments color understanding
Egocentric: has little or no empathy, beyond intellectual awareness of others; see things through own ideas and feelings; ignores or is threatened or puzzled by different feelings, attitudes, views	*Innocent:* completely unaware of the bounds of own understanding and of the role of projections and prejudice in opinions and attempts to understand

Revised and adapted from Wiggins and McTighe (1998). Reprinted with permission. © 1998 Association for Supervision and Curriculum Development.

The criteria, hence rubrics, are piling up! A practical strategy for addressing this complexity is to frame multiple rubrics in light of the fewest key differing aspects of understanding, knowledge, and skill. Here is an example of a set of five criteria in mathematics (edited to just the top score for each of the five rubrics), which can be used to assess the key dimensions of most complex mathematical performance:

■ MISCONCEPTION ALERT!

Where do the most appropriate criteria and indicators come from? How do rubrics move from general to specific descriptors? The answers involve yet another element of backward design: For the descriptors to be appropriate, detailed, and helpful, they must emerge from reviews of many concrete samples of work. The descriptors reflect the distinguishing characteristics of the pile of work at that level. Thus, a rubric is never complete until it has been used to evaluate student work *and* an analysis of different levels of work is used to sharpen the descriptors.

• Mathematical Insight: Shows a sophisticated understanding of the subject matter involved. The concepts, evidence, arguments, qualifications made, questions posed, and methods used are expertly insightful, going well beyond the grasp of the topic typically found at this level of experience. Grasps the essence of the problem and applies the most powerful tools for solving it. The work shows that the student is able to make subtle distinctions and to relate the particular problem to more significant, complex, or comprehensive mathematical principles, formulas, or models.

• Reasoning: Shows a methodical, logical, and thorough plan for solving the problem. The approach and answers are explicitly detailed and reasonable throughout (whether the knowledge used is sophisticated or accurate). The student justifies all claims with thorough argument: Counterarguments, questionable data, and implicit premises are fully explicated.

• Effectiveness of Solution: The solution to the problem is effective and often inventive. All essential details of the problem, and audience, purpose, and other contextual matters, are fully addressed in a graceful and effective way. The solution may be creative in many possible ways: an unorthodox approach, unusually clever juggling of conflicting variables, the bringing in of unobvious mathematics, or imaginative evidence.

• Accuracy of Work: The work is accurate throughout. All calculations are correct, provided to the proper degree of precision and measurement error, and properly labeled.

• Quality of Presentation: The student's performance is persuasive and unusually well presented. The essence of the research and the problems to be solved are summed up in a highly engaging and efficient manner, mindful of the audience and the purpose of the presentation. Craftsmanship in the final product is obvious. Effective use is made of supporting material (e.g., visuals, models, overheads, and videos) and of team members (where appropriate). The audience shows enthusiasm and confidence that the presenter understands what she is talking about and understands the listeners' interests.

If the thought of using so many rubric traits seems overwhelming, start small. Go back to the two basic criteria—quality of the understandings and the quality of the performance. Add a third for process when appropriate, and other rubric traits as time and interest permit. Later, when you have identified multiple traits, use only parts of the set, as appropriate to each assignment. (In the chapter on Macro Design issues, we will argue that sets of such rubrics should be established at the Program level.)

Designing and refining rubrics based on student work

Important criteria for evaluating student understanding and proficiency are initially derived from the desired results of Stage 1. Yet as the Misconception Alert makes clear, the process of building and revising a rubric also relies on an analysis of student performance. The following is a summary of the six-step process that Arter and McTighe (2001, pp. 37–44) propose for analyzing student performance:

Step 1: Gather samples of student performance that illustrate the desired understanding or proficiency. *Choose as large and diverse a set of samples as possible.*

Step 2: Sort student work into different "stacks" and write down the reasons. *For example, place the samples of student work into three piles: strong, middle and weak. As the student work is sorted, write down reasons for placing pieces in the various stacks. If a piece is placed in the "sophisticated" pile, describe its distinguishing features. What cues you that the work reflects sophisticated understanding? What are you saying to yourself as you place a piece of work into a pile? What might you say to a student as you return this work? The qualities or attributes that you identify reveal the important criteria indicators. Keep sorting work until you are not adding anything new to your list of attributes.*

Step 3: Cluster the reasons into traits or important dimensions of performance. *The sorting process used thus far in this exercise is "holistic." Participants in this process end up with a list of comments for high, medium and low performance; any single student product gets only one overall score. Usually, during the listing of comments someone will say something to the effect that, "I had trouble placing this paper into one stack or another because it was strong on one trait but weak on another." This brings up the need for analytical trait scoring systems; i.e., evaluating each student's product or performance on more than one dimension.*

Step 4: Write a definition of each trait. *These definitions should be "value neutral"—they describe what the trait is about, not what good performance looks like. (Descriptions of good performance on the trait are accorded to the "highest" rubric rating.)*

Step 5: Select samples of student performance that illustrate each score point on each trait. *Find samples of student work that illustrate strong, weak and mid range performance on each trait. These examples are sometimes called "anchors" since they provide concrete examples of the levels in a rubric. The anchors can be used to help students come to understand what "good" looks like. (Note: It's important to have more than a single example. If you show students only a single example of what a good performance looks like, they are likely to imitate or copy it.)*

Step 6: Continuously refine. *Criteria and rubrics evolve with use. As you try them out, invariably you will find some parts of the rubric that work fine and some that don't. Add and modify descriptions so that they communicate more precisely, and choose better anchors that illustrate what you mean.*

The challenge of validity

The third question in thinking like an assessor asks us to be careful that we evoke the most appropriate evidence, namely evidence of the desired results of Stage 1. We are not trying to create *merely* interesting and realistic tasks in Stage 2 but to obtain the most appropriate evidence of the desired results framed in Stage 1. This is the challenge of validity.

Validity refers to the meaning we can and cannot properly make of specific evidence, including traditional test-related evidence. We see a student commit a kind act on the playground. What should we infer about that student's propensity to "be kind"? That's the challenge of validity: At what events or data should we look to obtain the most telling evidence of more general abilities?

Consider the challenge currently in any conventional classroom. Mrs. Metrikos, a 6th grade teacher at Carson Middle School, makes up a 20-problem test on fractions. Jose gets 11 right. The teacher infers that Jose's control of the *entire realm of fractions* is very shaky. Valid conclusion? Not necessarily. First, we need to look at the test items and determine if they are representative of all types of problems with fractions. Given that Jose is a recent immigrant, maybe his English is weak but his math strong; does the test factor out the English to let us see only his math ability? Is the test so laden with word problems that the test is really a test of English comprehension? What about the relative difficulty of the problems? Each question counted the same as the others. But what if some are much harder than others?

In scoring the test, Mrs. Metrikos focused solely on the correctness of the answers, ignoring the process each student used to set up and solve each problem. Is correctness indicative of understanding? Not necessarily. The best test papers may simply reflect recall of the formulas involved, without any understanding of why they work. Further, what should we infer when Jose runs up after the papers are handed back to explain his understanding of fractions and why his mistakes were "just" carelessness. Should that affect his grade or our understanding of his understanding? Perhaps as Mrs. Metrikos looks over the results that evening, she sees not only that Jose seemed to have trouble with the English in the word problems, but that Jose has trouble with fractions in which the denominators differ, but had no difficulty in explaining the rule and why you need a common denominator. To say that Jose "doesn't understand" fractions based on the wrong answers is thus an invalid conclusion.

A focus on understanding makes the issue of validity challenging in any assessment. Suppose Jenny got 19 of the 20 problems right, but the one she got wrong asked for an explanation as to why common denominators are needed. Suppose Sara gets all the history facts right on the multiple-choice test part of her history exam, but completely fails the document-based question that calls for analysis of key events during the same time frame? What if Ian does a superb poster on the water cycle, but fails the quiz? These are the challenges that face us all. We have to be sure that the performances we demand are appropriate to the particular understandings sought. Could a student perform well on the test without understanding? Could a student with understanding nonetheless forget or jumble together key facts? Yes and yes—it happens all the time. We want to avoid doubtful inferences when assessing any student work, but especially so when assessing for understanding.

As we noted earlier, understanding is a matter of degree. As the fraction example suggests, we typically pay too much attention to *correctness* (in part because scoring for correctness makes assessment so much easier and seemingly "objective"—machines can do it) and too little attention to the *degree* of understanding (in which someone has to make a valid judgment). So understanding easily falls through the cracks of typical testing and grading.

The issue is made harder still by a common confusion in performance assessment design. Many teacher-designers confuse interesting and engaging learning activities with appropriate evidence from performance. Just because the performance is complex and the task interesting, it doesn't follow that the evidence we gain from student project work is appropriate for the desired results.

We can sum up the challenge in the story about a 5th grade teacher in Virginia. She proposed assessing her students' mastery of standards related to the Civil War by having them construct a diorama. She was developing a unit on the Civil War in a workshop where the goal was twofold: Find creative ways to address the state standards, and honor UbD ideas. She was trying to assess her students' understanding of the causes and effects of the Civil War through the use of an engaging performance task.

She asked if she could use a tried and true project (one that the "kids love") since it involved performance and yielded an assessable product. We said that, in the abstract, there was no reason not to, as long as the project would generate the right kind of evidence. She wasn't sure what we meant, so we asked her to describe the project. Well, she said, the kids must build a diorama of one great battle in the Civil War for a simulated Civil War museum. There have to be maps, explanatory plaques, and relevant artifacts. So we asked for the particulars of the state standard:

■ AN ESSENTIAL QUESTION ABOUT INSIGHT REMAINS

This discussion about validity does not directly address or settle a long-standing controversy among philosophers and psychologists: Whether the act of understanding primarily involves a mental picture separate from the performance. To frame it as a cognitive research essential question, the debate involves asking: Is performance ability necessarily *preceded* by a mental model? Or is understanding more like successful jazz improvisation—something that is *inherently* a performance ability and sensitivity in which prior deliberate thought plays no critical or determining role? Although we don't take sides here, readers interested in the issue might want to read Gilbert Ryle's *The Concept of Mind* (1949), Perkins's chapter in *Teaching for Understanding* (Wiske, 1998), and *The Nature of Insight* (Sternberg & Davidson, 1995).

Civil War and Reconstruction: 1860s to 1877

USI.9   The student will demonstrate knowledge of the causes, major events, and effects of the Civil War by

a. describing the cultural, economic, and constitutional issues that divided the nation;

b. explaining how the issues of states' rights and slavery increased sectional tensions;

c. identifying on a map the states that seceded from the Union and those that remained in the Union;

d. describing the roles of Abraham Lincoln, Jefferson Davis, Ulysses S. Grant, Robert E. Lee, Thomas "Stonewall" Jackson, and Frederick Douglass in events leading to and during the war;

e. using maps to explain critical developments in the war, including major battles;

f. describing the effects of war from the perspectives of Union and Confederate soldiers (including black soldiers), women, and slaves.

We responded by asking her to self-assess the proposed assessment task design against two questions. How likely is it that:

• A student could do well on this performance task, but really not demonstrate the understandings you are after?

• A student could perform poorly on this task, but still have significant understanding of the ideas and show them in other ways?

If the answer to either question is "yes," then the assessment will probably *not* provide valid evidence.

"Oh, of course!" she quickly said. "How could I have been so foolish? It really only gets at a small slice of the standards, and bypasses entirely the issue of cause and effect. How did I miss that?"

Her mistake is a common one—confusing interesting projects or authentic *activities* with valid assessments. In this case, she had taken one small link between her project and the standard (the major military turning points) and tried to draw a conclusion from the evidence that was not warranted. The good news? When asked to self-assess against the two validity questions, she saw the problem immediately. The bad news? Most people don't self-assess their proposed assessments against any design standards, and they often end up with invalid inferences. The aim of Stage 2 is not engaging work; the aim is good evidence for judging achievement against stated goals.

The anecdote also reminds us of the importance of deriving the general criteria from the goals. Given that the content standard focused on *causes and effects* of the Civil War, if the teacher had considered appropriate criteria related to the standard *prior* to designing the specific diorama task, she may have averted the validity problem. In terms of assessing for causal reasoning, any student performance would need to (1) identify multiple causes, (2) identify multiple effects, (3) be historically accurate, and (4) include a clear explanation. Thinking this way also suggests other, more appropriate task possibilities, such as a cause-effect poster showing multiple causes and multiple effects of the war.

The analysis illustrates nicely the paradox of designing local assessments: Left to our own instincts, seeing validity issues is very difficult. With a little disciplined self-assessment against the right standards (not to mention some quick peer review), however, we can solve most of the problems that we encounter.

Backward design to the rescue

Recall the horizontal version of the Template (Figure 7.2, p. 149) and see how it asks us to look at the logical links between Stage 1 and Stage 2. Notice in Figure 8.4 how backward design, using two of the six facets, helps us to better "think like an assessor."

To become more attentive to issues of validity, designers are encouraged to regularly apply the self-test in Figure 8.5 to their current (or past) assessments, which expands on this line of questioning and can be used for any assessment design idea, past or future, to improve validity.

Your answers will likely be less than certain, of course. There are no rules or recipes in validity. Sometimes we just have to make a thoughtful judgment, mindful of our fallibility. But don't underestimate the power of self-assessment in design. It can solve many of your problems and make you more confident and courageous as an assessor—so that you assess what really matters, not merely what is easy to see and score.

> ### ■ MISCONCEPTION ALERT!
>
> *Validity is about inference, not the test itself.* Validity concerns the meaning of evidence: what we ask students to do, and how we assess the resulting work. In other words, validity is about our understanding of the results, not the test itself. We have to be a bit more careful in our talk. Although everyone casually uses the words "valid" and "invalid" as adjectival modifiers of "test," strictly speaking this is inaccurate. Validity is about the *inferences* we try to make from particular test results. And sharpening the power of those inferences is key to becoming a better assessor.

Figure 8.4

Using Backward Design to Think like an Assessor

Stage 1	Stage 2	
If the desired result is for learners to . . .	*Then you need evidence of the student's ability to . . .*	*So the assessments need to include some things like . . .*
Understand that . . . **U** • Statistical analysis and graphic display often reveal patterns in data. • Pattern recognition enables prediction. • Inferences from data patterns can be plausible but invalid (as well as implausible but valid). • Correlation does not ensure causality. **And thoughtfully consider the questions . . .** **Q** • What's the trend? • What will happen next? • In what ways can data and statistics "lie" as well as reveal?	APPLY: What applications would enable us to infer student understanding of what they have learned? What kinds of performances and products, if done well, would provide valid ways of distinguishing between understanding and mere recall? EXPLAIN: What must students be able to explain, justify, support, or answer about their work for us to infer genuine understanding? How can we test their ideas and applications to find out if they really understand what they have said and done?	**T** **OE** • Using past performances in the men's and women's marathon, predict the men's and women's marathon times for 2020. • Chart various scenarios for a savings program (e.g., for college, retirement). Give financial advice. Explain the implausibility of compound interest. • Analyze the past 15 years of AIDS cases to determine the trend. (Note: The data start out looking linear but become exponential.) • Write an article or a letter to the editor about why the marathon analysis is plausible but incorrect. • Develop a brochure to would-be investors on why early saving with small amounts is better than later with large amounts. • Create a graphic display with accompanying written explanation to illustrate the exponential nature of AIDS cases.

Figure 8.5

Self-Test of Assessment Ideas

| Stage 1 | **Desired Results:** |

| Stage 2 | **Proposed Assessment:** |

	very likely	somewhat likely	very unlikely
How likely is it that a student could do well *on the assessment by*			
1. Making clever guesses based on limited understanding?	❑	❑	❑
2. Parroting back or plugging in what was learned, with accurate recall but limited or no understanding?	❑	❑	❑
3. Making a good-faith effort, with lots of hard work and enthusiasm, but with limited understanding?	❑	❑	❑
4. Producing lovely products and performances, but with limited understanding?	❑	❑	❑
5. Applying natural ability to be articulate and intelligent, with limited understanding of the content in question?	❑	❑	❑
How likely is it that a student could do poorly *on the assessment by*			
6. Failing to meet the performance goals despite having a deep understanding of the big ideas? (For example, the task is not relevant to the goals.)	❑	❑	❑
7. Failing to meet the scoring and grading criteria used, despite having a deep understanding of the Big Ideas? (For example, some of the criteria are arbitrary, placing undue or inappropriate emphasis on things that have little to do with the desired results or true excellence at such a task.)	❑	❑	❑

Goal: Make all your answers "very unlikely"

Validity affects rubric design, too. Validity issues arise in rubrics, not just tasks. We have to make sure that we employ the right criteria for judging understanding (or any other target), not just what is easy to count or score. In assessing for understanding we must especially beware of confusing mere correctness or skill in performance (i.e., writing, PowerPoint, graphic representations) with degree of understanding. A common problem in assessment is that many scorers presume greater understanding in the student who knows all the facts or communicates with elegance versus the student who makes mistakes or communicates poorly. But what if the findings of the papers with mistakes are truly insightful and the paper that is well written and based on facts is superficial? Getting clear on what we can and cannot conclude from the evidence—that's always the issue in validity, and it applies to how we score, not just what we score.

In practice, variants of the two questions asked earlier also help us self-assess the validity of criteria and rubrics. Given the criteria you are proposing and the rubrics being drafted from them, consider

- Could the proposed criteria be met but the performer still not demonstrate deep understanding?
- Could the proposed criteria not be met but the performer nonetheless still show understanding?

If your answer to either question is yes, then the proposed criteria and rubric are not yet ready to provide valid inferences.

Reliability: Our confidence in the pattern

A discussion on the appropriateness of the assessment evidence is vital but not sufficient. We need not only a valid inference but a trustworthy one. We need to be confident that a result reflects a pattern. Maybe Jose's 9 errors out of 20 would only end up being 9 out of 50 if he were given another test the next day. The proposed test might be appropriate, but a single result on it unreliable or anomalous. This is the problem of reliability and why we argued in Chapter 7 for having a scrapbook of evidence as opposed to a single snapshot.

Consider your favorite winning sports team to see the reliability problem. Their performance in games is surely an appropriate measure of their achievement. Game results yield valid inferences about achievement in the sport, by definition. But any one game result might not be representative. Consider any night on which the team was upset by a historically weak team. That score is out of the ordinary—unreliable—once we have many results in hand, because the team did quite well over the entire season. Reliable assessments reveal a credible pattern, a clear trend.

Please note that whether various judges agree with one another is a different problem, usually termed "inter-rater reliability." In that case, we want the judgments of multiple judges to form a consistent pattern. But those multiple judges might still only be scoring a single event. In that case, the judges could be reliable, that is, they could all give the same score, but the performance that day may not be "reliable" or typical of the student's pattern of performance.

A second aphorism we like to use in framing the challenge of assessment (in addition to "innocent until proven guilty") is a famous line by Binet, the creator of the IQ test and the founder of modern measurement techniques: "It doesn't matter what tests you use as long as they are *varied* and *many*." That's why in Understanding by Design we ask designers to use a mix of different types of evidence over time.

General guidelines

We can sum up the concerns in Chapters 7 and 8 by offering the following questions and guidelines to consider when constructing a balanced set of local assessments of understanding:

1. The needed evidence is inherently less direct and more complicated than that obtained from objective tests to assess knowledge and skill. We need to look at more than just the percentage of correct answers. Why? Sometimes getting the right answer occurs as a result of rote recall, good test-taking skills, or lucky guessing. In assessing for understanding, we need to ferret out the reasons behind the answers and what meaning the learner makes of the results.

2. Assessment of understanding requires evidence of "application" in performance or products, but that complicates judging results. What do we do when parts of a complex performance are shaky, but we discern clear insight in the content? Or the result is fine, yet we sense that little insight was required to complete the project? How do we design performances that enable us to make precise judgments about the different parts of performance?

3. Since understanding involves the six facets, do some facets take precedence over others? *Which* performances matter most, in *what* situations? What can we infer, for instance, when the "application" and "explanation" of strategy is strong but the "interpretation" of the situation is weak? Or the particular "application" was ineffective, but verbal analysis and self-assessment makes clear that the learner has a solid understanding of the content and process?

4. Try to have parallel versions of the same content across different assessment formats. In other words, counteract the "messiness" of a complex task with a simple quiz in the same content. Or use constructed response questions on the same content to make sure that correct answers cannot hide lack of understanding. Whenever possible, have parallel assessments in diverse formats improve the quality of the evidence of desired results.

5. Try to anticipate key misunderstandings and develop quick preassessments and postassessments to find out if those misunderstandings were overcome—regardless of what other assessment tasks you are using. For example, the following quick assessment task reveals whether students understand the process of isolating variables as part of a science investigation:

Roland wants to decide which of two spot removers is best. First, he tried Spot Remover A on a T-shirt that had fruit stains and chocolate stains. Next, he tried Spot Remover B on jeans that had grass stains and rust stains. Then he compared the results. Is there a problem with Roland's plan that will make it hard for him to know which spot remover is best? Explain.

6. Given that a single application or product may or may not link to larger goals, regularly ask students to "show their work," give reasons for answers, and show connections to larger principles or ideas in the answers.

7. Given that an articulate explanation may be more a function of verbal ability and verbal knowledge with no real understanding, ask the student to "transfer" that explanation to a new or different problem, situation, or issue.

8. Tap into various facets to broaden the evidence: When demanding a hands-on application (Facet 3), also require interpretation (Facet 2), and self-assessment (Facet 6) to make sure that the final product is not overvalued. Require a blend of perspective and empathy whenever possible.

A caveat before closing

Although we've concentrated on more formal and *summative* assessments of understanding in this chapter, daily teacher checks are the vehicles through which we monitor whether students understand. The iterative nature of understanding, the likelihood of confusions or misconceptions, and the need for interactive evidence make it imperative, in fact, that teachers know how to use ongoing assessments to inform their teaching and needed adjustments. Since Stage 2 is about summative assessment, we postpone a further consideration of informal checks for understanding and feedback until Stage 3.

We have postponed for many chapters the work we all typically like to do most: the design of the learning plan. Stage 3 now beckons, where we determine more fully what the learning plan needs to accomplish, given not only the desired understandings and assessment evidence, but who our learners are and what is in their best interest.

Chapter 9

Planning for Learning

> The most fundamental ideas are not usually appropriate as explicit
> content until a fairly advanced stage of understanding has been reached. . . .
> *The place of the representative ideas is not . . . on the lips of the teacher,*
> *but in his mind,* to direct him in the choice of learning experiences
> that will illustrate the ideas he has in mind.
> Thus, in the beginning stages representative ideas are for the guidance of the
> teacher (or the curriculum maker) and not directly for the student. Later they
> may be made explicit for the student and may prove as useful to him in
> advancing and epitomizing his own understanding as they are for the teacher.
> —Phillip Phenix, *Realms of Meaning,* 1964, pp. 327–8, emphasis added

> I hear, I forget.
> I see, I remember.
> I do, I understand.
> —Chinese proverb

We have clarified what we mean by the *desired results,* with a focus on big ideas, and we have discussed appropriate assessments of those results with an emphasis on understanding. We are now ready to consider Stage 3 and plan the appropriate *learning activities* at the heart of everyday classroom life. What does a learning plan for understanding look like? How do we make it more *likely* that everyone might achieve understanding?

The design challenge is reaching a new phase in another sense. We are moving from thinking only about what *we* want to accomplish as the designer to thinking about who the learners—the end-users of our design—are and what *they* will need, individually and collectively, to achieve the desired results of Stage 1 and to perform well at the tasks proposed in Stage 2. Like a software designer, we have to do more than ensure that all the codes and functions are going to work. We must be mindful of who the users are and design so that they are all maximally engaged and productive. Our design must be truly user-friendly, in other words, not just intellectually defensible.

Our treatment of Stage 3 is intended to be suggestive, not exhaustive. We seek to highlight the considerations for design that follow from the logic of backward design and the nature of understanding. In part, we've chosen this approach because the learning plan is familiar to practicing educators and because many useful resources exist to support teaching and learning for understanding. Furthermore, the level of detail needed for a unit plan is less than that required by the daily lesson plans that will follow from this unit design.

Again, we provide an overview of the stage by revisiting the matrix used previously, with a highlight on Stage 3 (see Figure 9.1).

What the teacher-designer must do here above all else is resist the temptation to fall back on comfortable and familiar techniques. The essence of backward design is to be scrupulous in asking this question: Given the desired results and the targeted performances, what kinds of instructional approaches, resources, and experiences are required to achieve these goals? In other words, the essential questions for Stage 3 are these: What do learners need, given the desired results? What is the best use of time spent in and out of the classroom, given the performance goals? Figure 9.2 shows how these questions might be answered for the nutrition unit we've been following throughout the book.

Note that the word *teaching* is not highlighted in either graphic. Instead, we stress that the focus must be on planning the appropriate "learning activities," of which "teaching" (direct instruction) is only one of many, based on the goals and evidence identified in Stages 1 and 2. This is not just a coy semantic move. Rather, it reflects the fundamental shift needed to become a superior educator. As we have said from the beginning, the challenge is to think less about the "teachings" and more about the "learnings" sought. Regardless of our teaching strengths, preferred style, or comfortable habits, the logic of backward design requires that we put to the test *any* proposed learning activity, including "teaching," against the particulars of Stages 1 and 2. (We discuss various kinds of teaching, and their optimal use, at greater length in Chapter 10.)

In Stage 3, designers are especially encouraged to consider, perhaps in new and unfamiliar ways, the ongoing use of assessment as a key to improving learning. Given the likelihood that learners will misunderstand key ideas and make performance errors (not necessarily signs of poor teaching or learning), the design must make sure that teachers as well as learners get the feedback they need to rethink, revise, and refine. As on the field, on stage, or in the studio, building in feedback and the opportunity to use it is a vital aspect of a good learning plan. (One workshop participant noted this "aha!" on the evaluation form: "I'm going to be more of a coach in the classroom, and more of a teacher on the field.")

Figure 9.1
The UbD Matrix: Focus on Stage 3

Key Design Questions	Chapters of the Book	Design Considerations	Filters (Design Criteria)	What the Final Design Accomplishes
Stage 1 • What are worthy and appropriate results? • What are the key desired learnings? • What should students come away understanding, knowing, and able to do? • What big ideas can frame all these objectives?	• Chapter 3—Gaining Clarity on Our Goals • Chapter 4—The Six Facets of Understanding • Chapter 5—Essential Questions: Doorways to Understanding • Chapter 6—Crafting Understandings	• National standards • State standards • Local standards • Regional topic opportunities • Teacher expertise and interest	• Focused on big ideas and core challenges	• Unit framed around enduring understandings and essential questions, in relation to clear goals and standards
Stage 2 • What is evidence of the desired results? • In particular, what is appropriate evidence of the desired understanding?	• Chapter 7—Thinking like an Assessor • Chapter 8—Criteria and Validity	• Six facets of understanding • Continuum of assessment types	• Valid • Reliable • Sufficient	• Unit anchored in credible and useful evidence of the desired results
Stage 3 • What learning activities and teaching promote understanding, knowledge, skill, student interest, and excellence?	• Chapter 9—Planning for Learning • Chapter 10—Teaching for Understanding	• Research-based repertoire of learning and teaching strategies • Appropriate and enabling knowledge and skill	Engaging and effective, using the elements of WHERETO: • Where is it going? • Hook the students • Explore and equip • Rethink and revise • Exhibit and evaluate • Tailor to student needs, interests, and styles • Organize for maximum engagement and effectiveness	• Coherent learning activities and teaching that will evoke and develop the desired understandings, knowledge, and skill; promote interest; and make excellent performance more likely

Figure 9.2
The Logic of Backward Design, Including Stage 3

Stage 1	Stage 2	Stage 3
If the desired result is for learners to . . .	*Then you need evidence of the student's ability to . . .*	*And the learning activities need to . . .*

Stage 1

If the desired result is for learners to . . .

Meet the standards . . . **G**

Standard 6—Students will understand essential concepts about nutrition and diet.
6a—Students will use an understanding of nutrition to plan appropriate diets for themselves and others.
6c—Students will understand their own eating patterns and ways in which those patterns may be improved.

Understand that . . . **U**

- A balanced diet contributes to physical and metal health.
- The USDA food pyramid presents relative guidelines for nutrition.
- Dietary requirements vary for individuals based on age, activity level, weight, and overall health.
- Healthful living requires an individual to act on available information about good nutrition even if it means breaking comfortable habits.

Thoughtfully consider the questions . . . **Q**

- What is healthful eating?
- Are you a healthful eater? How would you know?
- How could a healthy diet for one person be unhealthy for another?
- Why are there so many health problems in the United States caused by poor eating despite all the available information?

Stage 2

Then you need evidence of the student's ability to . . .

- Plan a diet for different kinds of people in different kinds of settings.
- Reveal an understanding that the USDA guidelines are not absolute, but "guides"—and that there are other guides (as well as contextual variables).
- Carefully note and analyze the habits of others as well as oneself, and make supported inferences about why people eat the way they do. **T**

That suggests the need for specific tasks or tests like . . .

- Planning meals for diverse groups.
- Reacting to excessively rigid or loose dietary plans made by others.
- Making a good survey of what people actually eat and why. **OE**

Quizzes: On the food groups and the USDA food pyramid

Prompts: Describe health problems that could arise as a result of poor nutrition and explain how these could be avoided; reflections on one's own eating habits and those of others.

Stage 3

And the learning activities need to . . . **L**

- Hook students into considering the effects of nutrition on their lives and those of others in subtle and interesting ways.
- Help learners understand not only what the food pyramid says, but why it says it, how various interests made it turn out that way, and how there are other possibilities.
- Inform students about how menus and nutritional plans are actually made.
- Teach students, give them practice and feedback in how to make, conduct, and analyze surveys.
- Provide activities that help students come to see through inquiry, analysis, and discussion how eating habits are linked to health and fitness problems.
- Equip learners with all the skills and opportunities needed to develop menus and to critique those of others—on their own.
- Help learners grasp how habits work and can cause all of us to think that our eating habits are better than they really are.

The best designs: Engaging *and* effective

But what exactly do we mean by a good plan for learning, in light of goals? What must any plan be to be a "good" plan? Our simplest answer: It must be engaging and effective.

By *engaging,* we mean a design that the (diverse) learners find truly thought provoking, fascinating, energizing. It pulls them all deeper into the subject and they *have to* engage by the nature of the demands, mystery, or challenge into which they are thrown. The goal is to affect them on many levels; it must not be dry academic content, but interesting and relevant work, intellectually compelling and meaningful. Learners should not merely enjoy the work; it should engage *each* of them in worthy intellectual effort, centered on big ideas and important performance challenges.

By *effective,* we mean that the learning design helps learners become more competent and productive at worthy work. They end up performing to high standards and surpass the usual expectations. They develop greater skill and understanding, greater intellectual power and self-reflection, as they reach identified goals. In other words, the design pays off in substantive, value-added learning. All of them have achieved something of intellectual substance, and they know it.

What are the signs of engagement and effectiveness? How can we "design in" these traits? To make the answers to these questions as understandable and obliging as possible, we developed two constructivist workshop exercises for the teachers we work with in which they draw upon their experience as teachers *and* learners. Both of these exercises can be found in the *Understanding by Design Professional Development Workbook* (McTighe & Wiggins, 2004, pp. 250, 281). In the first exercise, we form two groups (A and B). Then, we ask participants in Group A the following questions: When are students most fully *engaged* in and out of school? What makes them so engaged, and keeps them so engaged, and what are the transferable elements from these exemplary cases? We give members of Group B related questions: When is student learning most *effective?* Under what conditions are learners most productive? Under what conditions is the highest-quality work produced? What makes for the most effective learning, and what are the transferable elements from these exemplary cases? Then, participants in each group share their examples and identify common elements.

Typically, Group A responds that learners are most engaged when the work

- Is hands-on.
- Involves mysteries or problems.
- Provides variety.
- Offers opportunity to adapt, modify, or somehow personalize the challenge.
- Balances cooperation and competition, self and others.
- Is built upon a real-world or meaningful challenge.

• Uses provocative interactive approaches such as case studies, mock trials, and other kinds of simulated challenges.

• Involves real audiences or other forms of "authentic" accountability for the results.

Group B typically finds that student learning is most effective when

• Work is focused on clear and worthy goals.
• Students understand the purpose of, and rationale for, the work.
• Models and exemplars are provided.
• Clear public criteria allow the students to accurately monitor their progress.
• There is limited fear and maximal incentive to try hard, take risks, and learn from mistakes without unfair penalty.
• The ideas are made concrete and real through activities linking students' experiences to the world beyond the classroom.
• There are many opportunities to self-assess and self-adjust based on feedback.

Finally, the two groups unite, compare their respective responses, and fill in the center portion of a Venn diagram to see the overlap. In other words, when is work highly engaging *and* effective? The mixture is revealing. Many of the traits that are at the heart of intellectual engagement (e.g., genuine application to meaningful, real-world problems; hands-on opportunities to "do" the subject; getting helpful feedback along the way) enhance effectiveness, and vice versa.

The second workshop exercise is a variation of the first. We ask people to recall an example of a design in their own experience as learners that was, for them and their classmates, both engaging and effective. After sharing their idiosyncratic stories in small groups, we ask them to generalize: What seems to be common to all the learning experiences, from a design point of view? Next, we facilitate a whole-group sharing of the small-group ideas and record the answers in a PowerPoint document, using the exact language of each group spokesperson. Finally, we show the responses from previous workshops to underscore the objective soundness of the group's answers and the "common" sense of our profession.

The characteristics of the best designs

The answers to the second exercise reveal that our profession has a consistent and clear sense about what constitutes good design for learning. Here is a list of the most commonly cited characteristics:

• Clear performance goals, based on a genuine and explicit challenge
• Hands-on approach throughout; far less front-loaded "teaching" than typical

- Focus on interesting and important ideas, questions, issues, problems
- Obvious real-world application, hence meaning for learners
- Powerful feedback system, with opportunities to learn from trial and error
- Personalized approach, with more than one way to do the major tasks, and room for adapting the process and goal to style, interest, need
- Clear models and modeling
- Time set aside for focused reflection
- Variety in methods, grouping, tasks
- Safe environment for taking risks
- Teacher role resembles that of a facilitator or coach
- More of an immersion experience than a typical classroom experience
- Big picture provided and clear throughout, with a transparent back-and-forth flow between the parts and the whole

These answers are given by educators across the educational spectrum, by kindergarten teachers and college professors, first-year teachers and veteran administrators, instructors in art and mathematics, staff from urban public schools and suburban independent schools. There *is* a "common sense" to draw upon in improving our individual and collective curriculum designs. (Incidentally, the answers become a useful first step in establishing local design criteria and using them in self-assessment and peer review. Because these "standards" are generated by participants, they are more credible and acceptable as a basis for making the traditionally private work of design more appropriately public, standards-based, and subject to scrutiny.)

Understanding by Design thus succeeds to the extent that our recommendations about learning activities and their organization mirror this common sense. That is just what we have set out to do—embody common sense in a set of design rules of thumb and design standards. We succeed as the authors of UbD, then, to the extent that the UbD Template and our strategies reflect what "we already know" in ways that are highly explicit and practical.

How do these general characteristics of good design become more deliberately woven into a design? How does UbD concretely build upon our common sense? That's where our acronym WHERETO comes in.

The WHERETO elements in instructional planning

To better honor what we at some level already know, WHERETO highlights the key considerations:

W—Ensure that students understand WHERE the unit is headed, and WHY.

H—HOOK students in the beginning and HOLD their attention throughout.

E—EQUIP students with necessary experiences, tools, knowledge, and know-how to meet performance goals.

R—Provide students with numerous opportunities to RETHINK big ideas, REFLECT on progress, and REVISE their work.

E—Build in opportunities for students to EVALUATE progress and self-assess.

T—Be TAILORED to reflect individual talents, interests, styles, and needs.

O—Be ORGANIZED to optimize deep understanding as opposed to superficial coverage.

The rest of this chapter explores the specific implications of WHERETO for creating and implementing an effective and engaging plan. We'll explore each element in turn.

W—Where and Why

Where are we headed? Where have we come from? Why are we headed there? What are the student's specific performance obligations? What are the criteria by which student work will be judged for understanding?

In the exercise about best design, the number one characteristic identified by participants over the years is "clear goals" for learners. This requires more than just stating or clarifying our own teaching targets. The designer must make the goals clear to *students*. That means completely demystifying the big ideas, the essential questions, the desired performances, and the evaluative criteria constituting the sought-for achievement. It requires instructors to provide a rationale for the desired learnings—to identify what is most important (and what is not) and *why* it is worth learning.

In addition to clarifying and rationalizing the goals, the *W* reminds teachers to help students become clear about and mindful of the expected performances (and concomitant scoring materials, like samples and rubrics) that will reveal the extent of their understanding. All too rarely do students know where a lesson or unit is headed in terms of their own ultimate performance obligations. Although students don't necessarily need to know much about what the "teaching" will be, it is essential that they understand what the "learning" requires them to eventually do. Knowing the topic, what chapters to read, the directions for each activity, or that a test is coming at the end is not sufficient to focus attention, guide effort,

---

■ MISCONCEPTION ALERT!

We stress here that WHERETO, like the six facets of understanding, serves as an analytic tool for checking the elements of the design rather than a recipe or sequence for how to construct the design. (We discuss this point further in Chapters 11 and 12.) Recall that Bloom's *Taxonomy of Educational Objectives* (1956) represents a way of judging assessment items and tasks for cognitive difficulty, *not* a prescribed sequence for teaching. Similarly, WHERETO represents a way of *testing* lessons and units rather than a formula for building them.

To use an analogy with storytelling, a story needs a plot, characters, and a setting. Those are story elements, just as WHERETO summarizes the design elements. But how should those elements be fashioned into the most engaging and effective whole? There are many possible beginnings, middles, and ends. Just as a storyteller might begin with fragments of dialogue or a description of a character and work toward a plot (or vice versa), design work, too, can emerge over time, following many different paths and sequences. Thus, a teacher might introduce a unit with the final task done in a preliminary form, such as a written draft.

and ensure that goals are understood and met. As soon as possible in the unit or course of study, then, students should know the key questions and the performance specifics (e.g., tasks, tests, assignments, evaluative criteria, and the related performance standards) that they must meet by the end.

This requirement is more stringent than it first appears. It means that the expected work, its purpose, and the final learning obligations must all be transparent to the learner. Students must be able to answer the following questions with specificity as the unit develops, based on activities and materials designed by the teacher:

- What will I have to understand by unit's end, and what does that understanding look like?
- What are my final obligations? What knowledge, skill, tasks, and questions must I master to meet those obligations and demonstrate understanding and proficiency?
- What resources are available to support my learning and performance?
- What is my immediate task? How does it help me meet my overarching obligations?
- How does today's work relate to what we did previously? What is most important about this work?
- How should I allot my time? What aspects of this and future assignments demand the most attention? How should I plan? What should I do next? What has priority in the overall scheme of things?
- How will my final work be judged? Where is my current performance strongest and weakest? What can I do to improve?

Purposeful work

As the above *W* questions suggest, the work must be purposeful from the *student's* point of view in order to properly focus attention and provide direction. Regardless of how abstract the key ideas are, the design must transform those goals into intelligible, practical tasks and criteria that the student can grasp as soon as possible.

Here is an example of how an English teacher provides this information for a unit on the novel *The Catcher in the Rye*. Notice how the teacher begins the unit with a performance challenge and essential question to make clear where the work is headed, how the reading should be approached, and how students' culminating performance will be judged. The teacher says to the class,

> At the end of a close reading of The Catcher in the Rye, *you will act as part of a peer case-review committee at the hospital from which Holden is telling his story. With access to the transcript of Holden's own words, plus selected related materials, you will write a diagnostic report for the hospital and a prescriptive letter to Holden's parents explaining what (if anything) is wrong with Holden. [The rubric for this task is also distributed on the first day.]*

> In addition to this culminating performance task, you will be given three quizzes on the reading and a writing exercise in which you will describe

Holden from the perspective of another character. Following each reading assignment and before the next class, please respond in your Reading-Response Journal to two questions: What is the most important thing you learn about Holden in this section of the novel? What is the most important unanswered question about Holden at this point in the novel? *Your responses to these questions will begin and end daily class discussions.*

At the end of the unit, you will be asked to reflect on your evolving understanding of the novel, as chronicled in your daily journal entries. Final questions for the last days are, What changed in the way you saw Holden as the book went along? *and,* If, as some people claim, "misunderstanding is inevitable" when you encounter new material, what were your misunderstandings at any point during this unit? *Finally, if you were to teach this novel to next year's students,* what would you do to ensure they understand the novel as opposed to just knowing some facts about it?

Consider how this approach to literature differs from the typical opening strategy of passing out copies of a book, reviewing a syllabus of reading assignments, and examining the grading requirements. In this case, the students are given a purpose and a context for their reading, along with a performance challenge (i.e., figuring out *what's wrong with Holden?*). From day one, they know what is expected and how their work will be judged. Note, too, how the different types of assessment provide a "photo album" of evidence for judging student understanding. And the regular journal entries not only provide evidence of comprehension to the teacher, they also engage the students in applying the strategies of effective readers (e.g., summarizing the text and raising questions).

As a practical matter, alerting students from day one to the essential questions of the unit and course is an easy way to signal the priorities to students. Thus, by knowing the essential questions—and that those questions frame the key assessments—students can study, do research, take notes, and ask questions with far greater clarity, focus, and confidence.

"Where to?" *and* "Where from?"

Another dimension of the *W* reminds designers to ask the following questions and to design with the answers in mind. Where are the learners coming from? What prior knowledge, interests, learning styles, and talents do students bring? What misconceptions may exist? These questions highlight the importance of including diagnostic assessments early in the learning plan.

One efficient, effective, and widely used diagnostic technique is known as K-W-L. At the beginning of a new unit or course, the teacher asks students to identify what they already *Know* (or think they know) about the topic. Their responses are listed on a K-W-L chart. The list gives teachers an immediate sense of the prior knowledge of a group of learners, while revealing potential misconceptions that may exist and need to be addressed. Next, the teacher asks students to identify things that they may *Want to* learn about the topic and to raise questions they have about it. These responses are also recorded on the chart and serve as indicators of interest areas that can lead to teachable opportunities. (Sometimes students will actually raise essential questions in "kid language." For example, an elementary school social studies unit featured readings and activities that explored the issue of regions and regional characteristics. One of the student-generated questions, "Are southerners really different from northerners?" captured the interest of the class and led to engaging discussions and investigations about not only regions but stereotypes versus accurate generalizations.) Then, as the unit unfolds, acquired facts and big ideas are recorded on the chart under the *L,* providing a record of key *Learnings.*

A more formal approach, widely used in all performance areas and in special education, is to begin the unit with a nongraded pretest, as part of an explicit pre- and post-assessment strategy. This can yield invaluable evidence about growth in understanding, particularly if the questions target key misconceptions. Indeed, many physics teachers and professors now routinely use the Force Concept Inventory described in Chapter 2 in just that way to gauge their own success in developing a deeper understanding of key ideas in physics. Similarly, a survey about the learner's attitudes and learning style can yield valuable information for later use in teaching.

Regardless of the specific techniques used, information from diagnostic assessments guides teachers in making their learning plan responsive to the needs and knowledge base of their primary "customers." This is not a mere nicety or a tactic to be used by "caring" teachers. In our view, teachers can never achieve excellent results without improving their diagnostic skill and adaptive planning.

An important practical implication is that teachers must leave room in the syllabus for adjustments based on the gathering of useful feedback and the opportunities to use it. Such built-in flexibility is a key aspect of effective instructional design.

■ MISCONCEPTION ALERT!

"Well, what can I possibly do with all that information? It will likely wreck all my plans!" We actually heard this lament from a few college professors attending a workshop. The professors were making the mistake of assuming that one's "plans" should always be impervious to feedback; otherwise they are not really plans. On the contrary, whether it is in homebuilding, sculpture, parenting, fighting wars, financial security, or coaching football, achieving complex performance goals requires *planned adjustment* in light of goals, feedback, and predictable problems.

H—Hook and hold

What are powerful, thought-provoking "hooks" for engaging all students in the big ideas and performance challenges? In what experiences, problems, oddities, issues, and situations can I immerse students to make the big ideas immediately interesting, concrete, and of clear importance? What approaches to this material will generate interest and inquisitiveness into the topic and work at hand? What kinds of opportunities will sustain the interest of learners, especially when the going gets difficult? What are the most off-putting features of typical schooling that minimize risk taking, imagination, and courage to question, and how can those be undone?

Intellectual work leading to sophisticated understanding requires a high degree of self-discipline, self-direction, and delayed gratification in most academic settings. Yet many students come to school somewhat unwilling (and not always expecting) to work hard. And they typically misunderstand that their job is to construct understanding as opposed to merely take in (and give back) information that teachers and texts provide. Historically, schools have acted as if the solution to this problem lies only in extrinsic means, such as the "carrots" of praise, awards, prizes, and privileges; and the "sticks" of low grades, punishment, and public humiliation.

We take a different view. The goal in design is neither to pander to the students' likes nor to cause them to fear bad results. The design challenge is to tap intrinsic motivation more effectively. As Bruner put it long ago, "The best way to create interest in a subject is to render it worth knowing, which means to make the knowledge gained usable in one's thinking beyond the situation in which learning has occurred" (1960, p. 31). As noted in our discussion of the two workshop exercises on good learning situations, some features of design are known as a matter of common sense to be more thought provoking and intellectually engaging than others. The *H* asks us to act on our knowledge about engagement (and disengagement) to achieve our goals as teachers.

Let us put it bluntly. Schoolwork need not be boring or fractured. Indeed, to enable learners to reach higher intellectual standards, we will have to improve our ability to provoke their thought, curiosity, and drive. Schoolwork is often needlessly dull, especially when composed of mind-numbing skill worksheets or excessive passive listening—all of it divorced from interesting problems and from realistic and worthy performance challenges.

Organizing work around provocative questions and challenging problems has already been cited as an effective way to provoke sustained engagement in students. But an issue always comes up when educators begin to craft essential questions. They ask, Should the essential question be framed in "kid language" or framed in terms of how adults discuss, investigate, and argue the question? Our slightly cheeky response: Yes. We should do both, as suggested by the four different meanings of *essential* cited in Chapter 5.

Keep in mind that the point of the UbD Template—and Stage 1, especially—is to guide the adult designer. So getting clear on what questions really matter in the field and on what inquiries will help learners understand the big idea—the first two meanings of *essential*—is critical. Then later, when crafting the materials and activities for students, the designer should edit, modify, and adapt the questions, as needed, to better meet the other two meanings: questions that serve as useful bridges between learners and adult thinking, and questions likely to interest all your students.

Experience suggests caution; just plunking down an essential question at the start of a unit may *not* generate instant interest or lead toward any helpful understanding. The students may not know enough (or care enough) about the issues involved to see the need or value in addressing such a question. It may be essential to a teacher or an expert in the field but not to a learner, as the quote from Phenix at the opening of this chapter points out.

Sometimes, in fact, the best opening questions (or problems) relate more to very particular puzzles, provocations, and tasks such as role-plays and case studies, and essential questions can naturally arise after students have had sufficient experience with the issues. Here are three examples of how this may happen:

• A middle school language arts teacher developed the following essential question to guide students' reading, discussion, and writing: "How does a peer group influence the beliefs and actions of early adolescents?" The question was appropriate for the short stories and novels that made up part of her syllabus. And certainly the question is relevant to the age group. However, the teacher found that the question never resonated with her students, because they viewed it as too "preachy." Using the suggestions of her students, she revised the question to this: "Why do some people act stupid when they are in groups?" It proved to be a winner, instantly engaging student interest and holding it over the long term.

• A high school teacher in New York used this question in a Russian history unit within a Global Studies course: "Was Gorbachev a hero or a traitor to his country?" The question focused learning activities and the culminating debate in which the students role-played various Russian leaders (Gorbachev, Yeltsin, Lenin, Stalin, Marx, Trotsky, and Catherine the Great) in a *Meeting of Minds* format. After using the question with several classes, the teacher realized that it could be punchier, so he changed it to "Who blew it?" Following the role-play debate, students had writing options (a mock newspaper article, an editorial, or an essay) for responding to the original question.

• A 4th grade teacher began her science unit on insects with the question, "What good is a bug?" because she wanted the students to come to recognize the nature and value of various life forms. As she worked with the topic and this question, it became clear to her that the bigger ideas in the state standards had to do with "form and function" and "survival." She then revised her questions and the subsequent unit design: "How do the structure and behavior patterns of insects help them survive?" "If only the strong survive, how strong are insects (compared to other species)?" She retained her original question as a hook to begin the unit.

The introduction of the "official" essential questions can be immediate or delayed, direct or inductive. An essential question can be launched at the opening of a unit or it can be engineered to naturally arise at a later point following focused problem solving, instruction, or other learning activities.

Other kinds of hooks include immersing students in puzzles, challenging them to solve a real-world problem, and engaging them in a role-play to explore relevant issues from different perspectives. Indeed, it is noteworthy that the chapter in which Ted Sizer introduced the idea of the diploma by "exhibition of mastery" in his groundbreaking book *Horace's Compromise* (1984) is entitled "Incentives."

Presenting far-out theories, paradoxes, and incongruities stimulates wonder and inquiry. This was a chief finding of Richard Light (2001) under the heading of the Harvard Assessment Seminar, a multiyear examination of Harvard undergraduate education: The most engaging and effective courses were organized around controversies or opposing arguments. Educator Frank Lyman (1992), who quips that "education should be an itch, not a scratch," favors the use of "weird facts" to provoke initial interest in a topic. He suggests beginning a lesson or unit with an anomaly, such as, "Did you know that according to the laws of aerodynamics the bumblebee should not be able to fly [as a picture of a bee in flight is shown]? How can this be(e)?"

A mystery is always a good starter for thinking, especially when the answers raise essential questions. Here is an example from a problem-based learning lesson for introducing a unit on Westward expansion in the mid-19th century:

> You discover a yellowed copy of the following article from the front page of a very old issue of a New York newspaper stuck in a library book. Only the first paragraph remains, and there is no date or volume number. It reads:
>
> Turning Back the Hands
>
> *At just 9 o'clock, local time, yesterday morning Mr. James Hamblet, general superintendent of the Times Telegraph Company, and manager of the time service of the Western Union Telegraph Company, stopped the pendulum of his standard clock in Room 48 in the Western Union Telegraph Building. The long glistening rod and its heavy cylindrical pendulum ball were at rest for 3 minutes and 58.38 seconds. The delicate machinery of the clock rested for the first time in many months. The clicking of the electric instrument on a shelf at the side of the clock ceased, and with it ceased the corresponding ticks on similar instruments in many jewelry and watch stores throughout the city. When as nearly as it could be ascertained, the time stated above had lapsed, the heavy pendulum was again set in motion and swung backward and forward in its never-varying trips of one second each from one end of its swing to the other. With the starting of the pendulum, the clicking of the little instruments all over the city was resumed. Mr. Hamblet had changed the time of New York City and State.*

Do you know what this article is about? (We provide the answer later in the chapter.) Students are immediately drawn in by this mystery. Once they have figured it out, they use what they have learned to "uncover" other major causes and effects of the American movement westward.

An element of mystery is central to awakening and developing students' powers of inquiry and the understanding that their job is to inquire into what is learned. This approach stands in sharp contrast to how typical content-laden coursework begins and develops (especially when the work is textbook driven). Or we can look at the most popular video games. The *Sims* games are among the most popular computer simulation games in the world, yet they contain none of the violence, explosions, or other clichéd elements of undesirable games—only the drama and puzzle of how to care for people and solve their problems.

Or consider how effective filmmakers raise questions in our mind that remain unanswered as a way of keeping us thinking and wondering. For example, in workshops, we often show the first 10 minutes of Ken Burns's video series, *The Civil War*, to show how this technique of raising questions and bringing in drama works brilliantly as the opener for a documentary. The beginning scenes personalize the devastation wrought by the war. But only tantalizing and limited facts are offered about the people depicted in this dramatic opening, and we are left to wonder with the narrator, How is it that we could kill our brethren in such staggering numbers? Who are these people in the photographs being described in such a sly, incomplete way by narrator John Chancellor (e.g., "the runaway slave" and the "rough man from Illinois"— Frederick Douglass and Abraham Lincoln)?

The best lectures keep us engaged by raising questions and providing interesting insights and anecdotes, too. In fact, with the advent of technology it has become possible to target lectures to emerging student interest and need, in a "just in time" way. Students can do a WebQuest, or go to a Web site for a lecture when certain background information is needed, so that class time can be better spent on teacher-facilitated inquiry and coaching of performance. This is a more subtle form of "hooking" students but an important one. Lecturers often make the mistake of front-loading too much information, in an off-putting way, before an application task or essential question has given rise to the "itch" for the information in the students' minds.

One of us, years ago, watched a very demanding Russian history course whose entire structure was a sequence of biographies. Each student took turns researching the next character, presenting his research, and then joining a press conference, in which four or five other role-players fielded questions from the rest of the class (the press). The biographies were chosen to make the subject interesting and to afford engaging and provocative matches of personality. The *Meeting of Minds* format (based on the old Steve Allen TV show) was the model for the culminating press conferences in which the researchers had to role-play while also replying to questions from the other students, who played the press corps.

Adding to the provocative, sometimes dramatic turns in the course was a devilishly effective trick by the teacher. He set up a reserve library with a few false and disreputable materials about the characters included, so that the students had to be skeptical and cross-check their references. Significantly, this teacher never lectured, although he put dozens of his previous lectures in print and on videotape so they could be checked out of the library (but students had to check them out in pairs and discuss them with another person).

Another example comes from physics. A professor built an entire module around a solar-powered-toy-car competition that required teams of students to work on different aspects of the problem (collecting the energy, transforming the energy into car power, reducing slippage of the tires, steering the car, and so on); a lecture was provided only when one or more teams asked for it.

In sum, as many workshop participants expressed it in the exercise on best design, the most engaging learning designs include fun, mystery, and stimulating challenges. The hook is not extrinsic but intrinsic. The research is quite clear on this point, and teachers must simply stop saying that schooling is inherently not fun. Motivation is increased when the work is of obvious value, has intrinsic interest, and provides transfer. Goodlad's research from *A Place Called School* (1984) is still timely:

> What do students perceive themselves to be learning? We asked [them] to write down the most important thing learned in school subjects. . . . Most commonly students listed a fact or topic . . . noticeably absent were responses implying the realization of having acquired some intellectual power. . . .

> A somewhat different emphasis pervaded the arts, physical education, vocational education and several courses outside the mainstream such as journalism. There was a noticeable shift away from the identification of subjects and topics toward the acquisition of some kind of ability or competence. . . .

> The only subjects getting ratings of "very interesting" from more than a third of junior and senior high school students taking them were the arts, vocational education, physical education and foreign languages. . . . It was especially distressing to see that the kinds of classroom practices found most often in school were liked by small percentages of students. (pp. 233–236)

The comprehensive study of college engagement by the National Survey of Student Engagement (NSSE), involving responses from more than 730 institutions over the last few years, reveals the importance of engaging work:

> Courses that emphasize applying course material, making judgments about value of information and arguments, and synthesizing material into more complex interpretations and relationships are highly related to educational and personal gains. . . . Students' perceptions of the quality of relationships with faculty are strongly correlated with educational and personal gains—as is the frequency with which faculty members give prompt feedback. (2003)[1]

Similarly, Light's research (2001) at Harvard, mentioned above, noted that foreign language gets rave reviews when compared to many other program areas:

> Instructors insist that each student contribute and speak up regularly—even those that are shy. Students are encouraged to work in small groups outside of class. The classes demand regular written assignments . . . and quizzes give students constant feedback, so they can make repeated midcourse corrections. . . . I believe the big message from these findings is that students

are enthusiastic when classes are structured to maximize personal engagement and collegial interaction. (p. 80)

The formal findings simply reinforce what our workshop participants said in large numbers: The most effective and engaging designs involved challenging, meaningful applications of learning.

Beyond entertaining to essential

The challenge, of course, is to point toward what is essential, not merely provide work that is entertaining. The article excerpt "Turning Back the Hands" is not only engaging but also effective in setting up important ideas and issues in U.S. history. Indeed, key questions typically arise from students as the excerpt is deciphered, identified, and discussed. (Have you been wondering what the problem artifact actually is describing? It's an account of the day the United States changed from local time, kept by the rising and setting of the sun, to standard time, which carved the United States into four time zones. The railroads drove this change because of the need for standardized national schedules.)

Many educators who have read this article and role-played a history student in our workshops get noticeably energized, propose dozens of plausible but incorrect theories, and argue excitedly. As a result, they experience first-hand how important questions and researchable issues can be made to emerge *naturally*, and how misconceptions can be elicited and addressed, through a deliberate design.

The following conditions sum up our sense about how to pique intellectual interest:

• *Instant immersion in questions, problems, challenges, situations, or stories that require the student's wits, not just school knowledge.* This way of thinking is central to problem-based learning and the case method. For example, a calculus teacher challenges his classes to determine if the town's water tower, visible from their second floor classroom, actually holds "One million gallons of fresh water," as its painted sign proclaims.

• *Thought provocations.* Anomalies, weird facts, counterintuitive events or ideas, and mysteries appeal to the gut, making the strange familiar and the familiar strange. For example, a mathematics teacher has students read the story *Flatland* to introduce key ideas in geometry.

• *Experiential shocks.* This type of activity can be characterized as an intellectual Outward Bound experience in which students have to confront feelings, obstacles, and problems personally and as a group to accomplish a task. A stock market competition in math or economics, the need to keep a plant or animal alive, or the challenge of immersion situations in world languages are just a few common examples of what we mean.

• *Personal connection.* Students often become more engaged when given opportunities to make a personal connection to the topic or to pursue a matter of interest. For instance, as a preface to studying colonial settlements, elementary students interview their parents and relatives to find out *where we came from* and *why people move.* The reasons they discover help them better understand the universal themes involved in migration and settling in new places.

• *Differing points of view or multiple perspectives on an issue.* A deliberate shift of perspective can nudge students out of their comfort zone to stimulate wonderment and deeper thinking. For example, a middle school history unit might include a reading from another country's textbook to provide a surprisingly different perspective on famous events.

E—Explore and experience, enable and equip

How will students be engaged in exploring the big ideas and essential questions? What learning activities, guided instruction, and coaching will equip students for their final performances? What homework and out-of-class experiences are needed to enable students to develop and deepen their understanding of important ideas?

The core of the learning plan resides here. Students need to experience the big ideas as real, and they need to be equipped for their final performances.

Exploring through experience

The general caution is that teachers, especially at the high school and college level, often fail to adequately consider the deficiencies in the students' prior *experiences*—and then wrongly think that what they need is more *knowledge.* Understanding requires an iterative mix of well-designed experiences, reflections on those experiences, and targeted instruction in light of experiences and goals. The essence of methods as diverse as immersion in another language, Montessori hands-on materials in mathematics, the practicum in education and medicine, and the case method in law and business is that good design involves providing enough real or simulated experience to enable understanding to grow. In other words, a big idea is just another useless abstraction in the absence of a rich experience base in which the idea clarifies the experience.

An example from the teaching of Steven Levy illustrates how experiential activities or simulations can bring abstractions to life (in this case, the facet of empathy):

> *In September 1992, when Levy's students entered their classroom for the first time, they found to their astonishment that the room was empty—no desks, chairs, computers, or bookshelves. Like the Pilgrims, whom they would be studying all year, the students would be shaping their new environment to their needs. Throughout the year, they were given opportunities to experience the concepts specified in the 4th grade curriculum: They built their own desks and chairs; formed a cooperative, acquired shareholders, and gave out dividends*

*to finance their activities; grew and harvested wheat for baking bread; and
dyed and spun wool for weaving mats. (Regional Laboratory for Educational
Improvement of the Northeast & Islands, n.d., p. 1)*[2]

Equipping for performance

The desired understandings identified in Stage 1 and the performances of
understanding specified in Stage 2 inform the nature of the instruction and
learning experiences needed in Stage 3. Thus, backward design suggests the
other meaning of the *E:* it is the teacher's job to *equip* and *enable* the learner
to eventually perform with understanding.

By using the terms *equip* and *enable,* we underscore the vital role that clarity about final transfer tasks, linked to standards or exit outcomes, plays in better design. We are *equipping* students for performance; we are *enabling* them
to perform with understanding, with increasing autonomy. That is very different from *preparing* them for the chapter (or state) test containing 30 discrete
items. Teachers in this phase of the design work must ask themselves, What
kinds of knowledge, skill, and habits of mind are prerequisites for successful
final performance? What kinds of instructional activities will help students
develop and deepen their understanding of key ideas?

When designers look carefully at the logic of backward design to see what
their teaching and coaching obligations entail, they often discover to their surprise that they have not sufficiently planned for the necessary equipping. College professors, for example, routinely complain that students cannot transfer
what they have been taught into new problems, tasks, research, or performance. Yet, when you ask professors to carefully consider all the prerequisites
related to gaining an ability to transfer, they generally make no mention of a
plan for coaching students in learning *how* to transfer knowledge to varied situations. The problem is typically defined as a learner deficit instead of a teaching need.

Similarly, teachers from the primary grades to college express concerns
that students are often quite literal-minded in their reading, struggling with
texts that involve irony, sarcasm, satire, and allegory. Yet, when these teachers self-assess their designs, they often see two flaws: The typical shorter
assignments and assessments do not involve enough *ambiguous* readings,
and little if any instruction has been designed to help students figure out
how to determine—when there are few obvious clues—what kind of reading
requires what kind of response.

In many cases, teachers simply need to provide more concrete experiences of the ideas in question, linked to essential questions, to indicate the
kind of transfer sought. Consider a unit on climate in a high school Earth Science course. For example, by flying kites and forming consulting companies, students will understand the causes and effects of climate. Students will
understand how the unequal heating between the equator and poles, the
earth's rotation, and the distribution of land and ocean generate the global

wind patterns that determine climate. Here is such a unit built upon a variety of engaging experiences:

1. A unit on weather is introduced with reference to the final task: being a consultant to various businesses needing precise weather forecasts during the year. The essential questions: What causes weather? How predictable is weather? (*W*)

2. Students will perform the "Let's Go Fly a Kite" activity. They are challenged to find the best possible kite-flying locale on campus and justify their claim by reference to knowledge about winds and currents. (*H*)

3. Students will evaluate circulation cell diagrams by identifying directions of air movement under specific conditions and explain these movements in terms of differential heating. (*E*)

4. Students will read articles and perform a series of labs that illustrate Newton's First Law and centripetal acceleration and then relate these to the Coriolis effect. (*W, E, R*)

5. Students will analyze maps showing isobars and label the wind directions (and explain why). (*E*)

6. Students will study why the angle of the sun's rays causes differential heating. This will be applied to the different areas of the earth and different seasons in our area. (*H, E, R, T*)

7. Students will analyze an energy budget diagram showing the energy (heat) flow between the Sun, earth's surface, and earth's atmosphere. (*E*)

8. Students will analyze diagrams showing high and low pressure centers and describe air flow around and between these centers. (*E*)

9. Students will study cases (articles supplied by teacher) in which events such as El Niño and volcanoes in one part of the world are thought to affect weather in another part of the world. They will then propose mechanisms by which this is possible. (*W, H, E, T*)

10. Students will complete the "Comparing Climates" proposal, including presentations. (*H, R, E2, T*)

11. Students will take a unit exam based on the understandings for this unit. (*E2*)

12. Students will self-assess their performance and research, using the same rubrics supplied for each. (*E2*)

13. Students return to kite-flying activity and reflect on it now. (*W, H, R, E2*)

Consider also the example in Figure 9.3, in which an explicit organizer, "Adding Up the Facts," is introduced to guide elementary students in coming to an understanding. After introducing and modeling the organizer, the teacher facilitates "adding up the facts" about pioneer life, leading to a big idea. Such a guided approach helps learners construct meaning inductively. The organizer provides students with a cognitive tool that they can apply to a variety of situations in various subject areas, while signaling that seeking such understanding is their key job.

Figure 9.3
Adding Up the Facts

Use the following worksheet to look at a set of facts or data together. What inferences can you make or conclusions can you draw from "adding up the facts"? What's the big idea?

> *Many pioneers, especially children, died from disease.*
>
> *Much hard work was required to settle new land—clearing fields, constructing shelter.*
>
> *The pioneers had to grow, or hunt for, their food. Often, they went hungry.*
>
> **+**   *Settlers faced attacks by Native American tribes on whose lands they traveled or settled.*
>
> **Big Idea:**
>
> > **The pioneers faced many hardships in the settlement of the West.**

Donald Deshler and his colleagues at Kansas State University (Bulgren, Lenz, Deshler, & Schumaker, 2001) have developed an impressive set of such graphic organizers. Initially focused on helping students with special needs, their research has led to a variety of resources for helping *all* students learn how to use organizers. Figure 9.4 is an example of one of their organizers, the Question Exploration Guide, filled in by a student. (The authors call "Critical" what we call "Essential" questions, and "Overall Ideas" what we call "Overarching Ideas.") Of particular note is the fact that the *same* organizer is used *by the teacher* in developing the learning, resulting in the kind of transparency that all designers should seek.

We often talk in education about the need for scaffolding; that's what the best organizers do. They provide tools for the kinds of mental processes that the learner needs to internalize, so that eventually, *when no scaffolding is provided,* the learner has a repertoire of "moves" to employ.

Here is a typical sequence for such scaffolded instruction, in this case applied to a graphic organizer (but applicable to any strategy):

Figure 9.4
Question Exploration Guide

What is the Critical Question?

How does the destruction of the rain forest contribute to the greenhouse effect?

What are the key terms and explanations?

Rain forest	A thick evergreen forest, in a hot, wet area
Greenhouse	A glass house that traps heat for growing plants easily
Greenhouse effect	An event in which CO_2 in the atmosphere absorbs and holds the earth's heat instead of allowing it to leave

---

What are the Supporting Questions and answers?

What is happening to the forests?	They are being burned so that farmers have more land to grow crops.
What does the burning cause?	1. The burning releases more CO_2 into the atmosphere, and 2. The CO_2 that the forest once removed stays in the atmosphere.
What is the effect of the increase in CO_2?	1. Increased CO_2 traps heat in the atmosphere, creating a greenhouse effect, this means that 2. The earth is becoming warmer.

What is the Main Idea?

When rain forests are burned, the resulting increase of CO_2 contributes to the greenhouse effect.

How can we use the Main Idea?

How would cutting rather than burning the rain forests affect the atmosphere?

Is there an Overall Idea? A real-world use?

O.I.: What happens in one part of the world can affect us all.

Use: Any event that happened in one part of the world affecting others . . .

---

1. The teacher shows the students her own completed organizer for the day's lesson.

2. She provides partial examples for students to study.

3. She models how to use the organizer, using a think-aloud process to reveal her thinking.

4. She involves the students in using the organizer, providing guided practice and feedback as they work.

5. Increasingly, students work independently in applying the organizer to diverse and more sophisticated uses.

In *The Question Exploration Routine,* Deshler and his colleagues use the term *routines* to describe this process because the goal is to have the process become routine, through repeated use. Eventually the learner will no longer need the physical organizer as a prompt, because its "routine" will have become internalized.

This ability to perform autonomously, with the scaffolds and cues removed, is the essence of transfer, and we rarely adequately "equip" learners for it. As one teacher put it in a workshop years ago, "You know the trouble with kids? They don't know what to do when they don't know what to do!" That sums up the challenge of teaching for understanding, for the intelligent transfer of knowledge and skill to new situations. Thus, we need to equip (and assess) students for just those situations—in which the conclusion is not obvious, the issues are murky, and the situation is ambiguous in terms of what knowledge and skill are required.[3]

R—Reflect, rethink, revise

How will students be guided to rethink their understanding of important ideas? How might student products and performances be improved through revision based on self-assessment and feedback? How will students be encouraged to reflect on their learning and performance?

When overarching questions and recurring tasks anchor the curriculum, it stands to reason that a linear march through the content is a mistake. How will students master complex ideas and tasks if they encounter them only once? How will the shades of grey and shifts of perspective essential to understanding ever become clear unless we revisit previous understandings? A central premise of Understanding by Design is that the big ideas must constantly be reconsidered and that complex performance is always being refined. Therefore, the flow of the unit and course must be iterative, students must be made fully aware of the *need* to rethink and revise in light of current lessons, and the work must follow the trail back to the original ideas or techniques.

For example, a 1st grade class explores the essential question "What is friendship?" by discussing their experiences with friends and reading various stories about friendship. Students develop a theory of friendship and create a concept web for the topic. The teacher then causes them to rethink their initial conception by raising a second essential question, using an appropriate story of fair-weather friends: "Who is a *true* friend? And how do you know?" The students modify their concept of friendship as they come to understand that a true friend is loyal during hard times, not just a playmate during happy times. Finally, the teacher further challenges students' thinking by presenting them with two proverbs—"The enemy of my enemy is my friend" and "A friend in need is a friend indeed"—and asks them to reexamine their theory of friendship yet again based on these ideas.

Here is another example of engineered rethinking from a middle school unit on ancient civilization. The unit is designed around increasingly demanding induction as students learn to think like archaeologists while examining simulated and genuine artifacts to make inferences about the past. Notice how rethinking of both the process and the product unfolds from the sequence of key experiences.

1. Introduce the unit using these essential questions: What is civilization? How do we know what we know? Have students write a brief definition of civilization. For an additional activity, students can bring in an object they believe symbolizes civilization.

2. In class, students examine the U.S. penny. They make observations and a list of observable facts that will be called *near-facts*. They share facts and near-facts to accumulate as many as possible. They may use magnifying glasses and microscopes to inspect the penny. After each student selects facts and near-facts, they all copy each one onto a small card. Facts are pink and near-facts are blue.

3. Students arrange the layers of facts and near-facts at the bottom of a pyramidal tower. By arranging and rearranging the cards, they combine facts and near-facts to make knowledge claims. The knowledge claims go on yellow cards.

4. After sharing knowledge claims with each other, each student makes a final interpretation of the penny and writes it on a green card. They do this work at home. Some students will make one interpretation for each side of the artifact. They next make a final interpretation on another card of a different color and write a journal entry on the strengths and weaknesses of the interpretation.

5. Students share their interpretations.

6. In partnerships, students accumulate facts and near-facts based on a close observation of the Standard of Ur, an artifact discovered earlier this century. The name of the artifact is not shared with the students because it may influence their interpretation. The same color-coding is used.

7. At home, each student makes knowledge claims and a final interpretation of the artifact. To keep material organized, students should arrange all the facts, near-facts, and knowledge claims based on each side of the artifact in separate sections of the tower.

8. Students present their finished inductive towers to the class. Classmates are encouraged to question the validity of the interpretation.

9. The published interpretation of *The Standard of Ur* by Sir Leonard Woolley is read. At home, students compare and contrast Woolley's interpretation and their own.

10. Students write another definition of civilization with the intention of making a more sophisticated definition based on what they learned in the inductive process.

11. Students write a journal entry on the strengths and weaknesses of the inductive method based on their experiences with the penny, the Standard of Ur, and Woolley's interpretation. A discussion entitled "How Do We Know What We Know?" ends the unit.

A third example shows the generation of rethinking through a deliberate shift in perspective. In this instance, as part of their study of Westward expansion, students are given a graphic organizer representing different perspectives on the settlement of the West, and are asked to consider the views of

- Pioneer parents seeking a better life for their family
- Pioneer children feeling uprooted from friends and familiar surroundings
- Railroad executives seeking to populate the Midwest to generate a greater need for their services
- Native Americans whose lives have been "unsettled" by the settlers

In upper-level science, a common rethinking occurs when we ask students to consider one theoretical approach, followed by new data and analysis that suggest that a different theoretical approach might be more fruitful—for example, exploring the idea of light as a wave and light as a particle, or "nature" followed by "nurture."

As illustrated in these examples, built-in rethinking is a critical and deliberate design element, central to learning for understanding. We must plan to make students constantly reconsider earlier understandings of the big ideas if they are ever to get beyond simplistic thinking and to grasp, more generally, the need for the care and circumspection that lie at the heart of true understanding.

Put differently, the most effective designs for developing in-depth understanding (as well as for signaling to students that something more active than recall is required) highlight the facets of perspective, empathy, and self-understanding. Constant shifts of perspective or required empathy with unfamiliar settings, texts, and characters demand rethinking and reflection—as when considering *The Three Little Pigs* and *The Real Story of the Three Little Pigs* by A. Wolf.

E—Evaluate work and progress

How will students be guided in self-assessment, self-evaluation, and adjustment? How will learners engage in a final self-evaluation to identify remaining questions, set future goals, and point toward new learning? How will students be helped to take stock of what they have learned and what needs further inquiry or refinement?

Here we consider an often overlooked aspect of instructional design—the need to help students self-monitor, self-assess, and self-adjust their work, individually and collectively, as the work progresses. Facet 6 is self-understanding, arguably the most important facet of understanding for lifelong learning. Central to self-understanding is an honest self-assessment, based on increasing clarity about what we do understand and what we don't; what we have accomplished and what remains to be done. The most successful people in life not only have this capacity, they have learned to do so in the most timely and effective ways possible: They self-monitor and self-adjust as needed. They proactively consider what is working, what isn't, and what might be done better as they do it.

The research could not be clearer: In summing up their findings on learning, the authors of *How People Learn* offer three findings. The third involves the vital role of "metacognition" and the importance, as supported by research, of explicitly teaching and requiring such self-monitoring and self-assessment:

> *The teaching of metacognitive skills should be integrated into the curriculum in a variety of subject areas. Because metacognition often takes the form of an internal dialogue, many students may be unaware of its importance unless the processes are explicitly emphasized by teachers. (Bransford, Brown, & Cocking, 2000, pp. 18, 21)*

Here are some simple examples of "designing in" such metacognitive moments:

• Set aside five minutes in the middle and at the end of an inquiry-based lesson (e.g., a Socratic seminar or a problem-based learning episode) to consider these questions: So what have we concluded? What remains unresolved or unanswered?

• Require that a self-assessment be attached to every formal product or performance, with the option of basing a small part of the student's grade on the accuracy of the self-assessment.

• Include a one-minute essay at the end of a lecture, in which students summarize the two or three main points and the questions that still remain for them (and, thus, next time, for the teacher!).

• Require students to attach a postscript to any formal paper or project in which they must be honest about what they do and do not really understand about the subject in question—regardless of how authoritative their work may appear. (Of course, students need to know that they will not be penalized for confessing!)

• Train students to evaluate work in the same way that teachers are trained as advanced placement readers, so that students become more accurate as peer reviewers and self-assessors, and more inclined to "think like assessors" in their work, too.

• Begin class with a survey of the most burning questions on the minds of students, garnered on index cards submitted first by individuals, then ascertained in small groups. (The card could be a homework requirement each night.) Then, as part of closure, save time at the end to judge how well the questions were addressed, which ones remain, and what new ones emerged. (This strategy lends itself to regular journal entries in which the student reflects on a question and its unfolding meaning.)

• Identify a set of beneficial learning strategies tied to desired outcomes (e.g., problem-solving heuristics or reading comprehension strategies) and relevant habits of mind (e.g., persistence or overcoming impulsivity). Have students create visual symbols or cartoon characters depicting each strategy and post these on classroom walls. Regularly point out examples of when a strategy is being employed, and ask students to reflect on their personal use of a posted strategy and its effect.

• Occasionally watch a videotape of deliberately selected instructive moments from your class (e.g., during discussion, problem solving, experimentation, or debate) so that students become more cognizant of effective strategies as well as those that don't work (just as coaches do with game film).

• As is commonly done in courses based on the case method or problem-based learning, leave Part 2 of a unit deliberately "open" to allow students to frame and pursue the inquiry (rather than be directed by the teacher) based on the key questions that remain and clues that emerge at the end of Part 1.

• At the beginning of the year, have students develop a self-profile of their strengths and weaknesses as learners (perhaps based on formal instruments related to learning styles, provided by the teacher). They should consider how they learn best, what strategies work well for them, what type of learning is most difficult, and what they wish to improve upon (in other words, set goals). Then, structure periodic opportunities for journaling, when students can monitor their efforts and reflect on their struggles, and successes, and possible edits to their own profiles.

Teachers who use such explicit strategies to prompt reflection and meta-cognition bear witness to the practical benefits. For instance, a Harvard professor who uses the one-minute essay technique made this observation:

> An unspoken but important side benefit of the one-minute paper is that knowing they will be asked to fill out the paper at the end of class focuses the students' thinking. Students are constantly asking themselves, "What is the big idea here?" and also, "What is unclear to me, and how can I write a few coherent sentences that convey what I don't understand?" They are thinking throughout the class about what they will write. . . . My colleague adds that [the recurring nature of this task] builds continuity over time. It also offers a comfortable way for him to clear up any misunderstandings. (Light, 2001, p. 67)

Alverno College in Milwaukee, Wisconsin, has developed one of the most sophisticated, long-standing, and integrated approaches to self-assessment across the curriculum. At Alverno, self-assessment is an integral part of the curriculum and assessment plan, not just a technique in instruction. For example, all papers must include an attached self-assessment against rubrics, and the accuracy and thoroughness of the self-assessment is graded. In fact, self-assessment is seen as such a key enabling ability that in many early attempts at complex performance the initial grades are given for the student's self-assessment *and* improvement plans, not the product or performance itself. To encourage self-assessment more generally, the college has a developmental rubric system that is used for all courses, campuswide. The components of the rubric are Observing, Interpreting, Judging, and Planning.

Thus, at the heart of the second *E* in WHERETO is the deliberate design of opportunities for constant reflection (e.g., How things are going? What's working? What needs adjustment? So what? Now what?) expected of *all* learners, not just those who are naturally reflective. Such opportunities go hand in hand with the need for clarity about the Where?—a clear and transparent system of performance goals, coupled with a robust feedback system against those performance goals. Otherwise, the reflection will not be focused or helpful.

T—Tailor and personalize the work

How will we differentiate instruction to accommodate the various developmental needs, learning styles, prior knowledge, and interests of students (while remaining true to the desired results)? How will we tailor the learning plan to maximize engagement and effectiveness for all learners?

Throughout the book we have spoken in generalities about what learners need. This design element reminds us that we have to look more closely at who all those different learners really are and adapt our plans accordingly. The best designers tailor their learning plans to accommodate what is *always* a group of diverse learners. Let us consider a few practical methods for differentiating learning in terms of content, process, and product.

Content

In Stage 1 of the UbD Template, the Desired Results should remain consistent—after all, the content standards (as expressed in the Desired Goals) and the Understandings are learning targets for *all* students. However, the Essential Questions (EQs) provide a natural means of accommodating diverse learners because of their open-ended nature. Students with differing levels of prior knowledge and achievement can nonetheless engage in examining provocative questions, such as "How do living things adapt to survive?" or "What makes a great story?" Although some students may respond in greater depth, all learners have the potential to deepen their understanding as a result of tackling the EQs.

The Knowledge and Skill elements of Stage 1 offer another natural venue for tailoring the content to the needs of students. By using diagnostic assessments (part of the *W),* teachers can identify students with gaps in prior knowledge and skills. These needs can be handled through targeted instruction in small groups.

Process

By using a variety of resource materials (such as texts at different reading levels) and addressing various learning modalities (by presenting information orally, visually, and in writing), teachers can address differences in preferred learning styles and achievement levels. Allowing learners some options about *how* they work (for example, alone or in groups) or how they communicate their learning (orally, visually, or in writing) is another appropriate means of tailoring in Stage 3.

Product

Teachers can give students appropriate choices of products and performances for assignments and assessments. For example, an elementary class works on creating a "museum display" to depict the hardships of pioneer life. Students contribute to the display with different products and performances, such as sample diary entries, drawings of daily activities, and role-playing pioneer characters. Such an approach allows all students to participate according to their talents and interests. It is important to note that when students are allowed a choice of products as part of an assessment in Stage 2, the various results should be evaluated using common criteria. In the example of the pioneer museum display, regardless of whether a learner produces a drawing, a diary entry, or an enactment of daily life, we would judge all of the products for *historical accuracy, effective depiction of hardships, revealing empathy,* and *craftsmanship.* In this way, we can allow for appropriate diversity without sacrificing valid assessment or scoring reliability.

Here is an example of selected unit elements from a teacher's plan for tailoring high-level work (studying Shakespeare's *Macbeth*) to students with special needs and limited reading ability:

1. Conduct a brainstorming session in which students say what they know about the Middle Ages; have them create a list on the board as a group project. (Look for chivalry, feudalism, code of honor, kings, knights and warfare, and so forth.) Lead into the fact that the play about to be read is about all these things, as well as about honor and loyalty. (*W, H*)

2. Introduce the essential questions: What is honor? Dishonor? Loyalty? Disloyalty? How can we know whom to trust? How can we avoid losing our integrity? (*W, H, T, E2*)

3. Conduct a class discussion about honor and loyalty and write ideas from group discussion on the board. The result is a list of ideas, thoughts, opinions, and examples that students can refer to when they write their personal essay. Look for a "teachable moment"—when it seems wise to go to the dictionary definitions of these words, based on the conversation. (*W, E*)

4. Ask everyone to help build a wall of appropriate quotes. Put the quotes around the room each day; many quotes—about honor, loyalty, and power, for example—can be brought into discussion where appropriate. Each student adds two over the two weeks. (*H, T*)

5. Discuss case studies of modern and adolescent-related clashes of honor and loyalty, using ideas from group discussion (including references to movies and TV shows). The result—written on the board—is a list of ideas, thoughts,

opinions, and examples that students may use in writing their personal essay on the essential questions. (*H, E, R, T*)

6. Give historical background of the play and a map. Read the first witch scene dramatically; stop and discuss; introduce literary terms such as *paradox* and *setting*. Show how to do a time line of the scenes—an individual project; add to it at regular intervals. (*E*)

7. Act I, Scene ii: Outline characters and events—an advance organizer. Use audio and video of key scenes; permit assistance with reading and writing tasks; have access to abridged and simplified versions of the text. Give students notebooks and help them organize contents for their portfolios. (*W, E, T*)

8. Have students self-assess all work before turning it in and reflect on an essential question in terms of a revealing experience they had with issues of honor and loyalty.

O—Organize for optimal effectiveness

What sequence of learning experiences will best develop and deepen student understanding, while minimizing likely misconceptions? How will we organize and sequence the teaching and learning to maximize engagement and effectiveness?

Up until now, we have thought only about the analytic elements of good design. The *O* requires us to put those elements in the most powerful sequence. What we mean by "most powerful" is the sequence that actually results in the most engaging and effective experience for students.

Sequence is not something many teachers think through sufficiently, especially if they ponder a fairly lengthy unit of study. Yet, as the *H* and *R* of WHERETO signal, the typical sequence of marching through content may rarely be the best choice for engagement or understanding. This is especially important to consider if the sequence is typically dictated by the organization of the textbook, a point to which we return in greater depth in Chapter 10.

At the very least, the sequence should reflect what educators always note in the "best design" exercise: a constant movement back and forth between whole–part–whole and learning–doing–reflecting. And as the *R* implies, we don't just move forward; we must go back to earlier (provisional) facts, ideas, and techniques if we are to get beyond superficial, simplistic, or black-and-white thinking. That's why so many people report that problem-based learning, the case method, or simulations are so intellectually stimulating and memorable—they break with tradition about how learning should be organized.

The implications of the "hook" are clear enough: It is in *our* interest to hook students early and often through *their* interests and by what is inherently intellectually provocative. Thus, the better sequences immerse learners early on in intriguing issues, problems, situations, or other experiences and postpone the teaching of definitions, rules, and theories until they are needed to make sense of experience.

To better appreciate how needlessly dreary and off-putting much typical learning can be when viewed as a flow, consider the following example from a commonly used prealgebra mathematics textbook for middle and high school. The first 80 pages provide nothing but definitions, rules, and drills related to them. On page 36, for example, we find the following as the introduction to the idea of number line:

> *The paired points on a number line . . . are the same distance from the origin but on opposite sides of the origin. The origin is paired with itself. . . .*
>
> *Each number in a pair such as ⁻4 and 4 is called the opposite of the other number. The opposite of* a *is written –a. . . . The numerals –4 (lowered minus sign) and ⁻4 (raised minus sign) name the same number. Thus –4 can mean "negative 4" or "the opposite of 4."*

To simplify notation, lowered minus signs will be used to write negative numbers throughout the rest of this book. Caution: –a, read "the opposite of a" is not necessarily a negative number. For example if a = –2, then –a = –(–2) = 2 (Brown et al., 2000, p. 36).

We wish this were a joke, but, alas, it is not. This is simply unacceptable as pedagogy. It confuses a helpful approach to "getting going" with overly technical hair-splitting, presenting information completely out of context.

We can offer a simple rule of thumb, then: When teaching for understanding, the Why? and So What? questions have to be addressed early and often. To create meaningful and memorable learning, the flow must be back and forth between whole–part–whole and learning–doing–reflecting. Although many teachers think that learning requires that all possible "basic" facts and skills be presented upfront, this is simply not how effective and long-lasting learning works. (We consider this matter further in Chapter 10 on Teaching for Understanding through "uncoverage.")

We offer a final thought on sequence based on an extraordinary learning experience one of us had that encompassed all the WHERETO elements as part of the requirements for becoming certified as a youth-soccer coach. The instructor, a member of the New Jersey MetroStars professional soccer team, laid out a conceptual frame of stimulating activities and problem solving. He first described the importance of scheduling all practices with a clear whole–to–part logic, using the following account of the flow of all good practices in the development of every major skill: discrete skill, game-like, game conditions, game. For example, start with a simple back-and-forth exercise in passing with first one foot then the other in pairs. Then, make it game-like by having all the pairs pass their ball back and forth in the same small space, which requires looking up and timely passing, given all the people and balls. Then, to create game conditions, add to each group a person trying to steal the ball. Then set up more demanding game-like conditions—for example, a scrimmage that requires a maximum of two-touch dribbling before passing. Next, play a game.

Finally, return to earlier small-space passing drill, this time focusing on greater speed and accuracy.

In addition, the instructor argued that every drill should maximize the following elements: fitness, set plays, technical skill, teamwork, and strategic thinking. Not only should a practice maximize these elements, but so should each drill. The instructor then asked the participants to each propose a common soccer drill they knew and to actually lead a run-through of it on the field, using the other participants. The drill was then analyzed using the given elements and always greatly improved as a result of suggestions from the group. In fact, this experience led participants to conclude that some time-tested drills (such as the usual approach to three-on-two) were terribly ineffective.

And talk about heterogeneous groupings! The group of 30 ranged in age from 23 to 61, and in experience from varsity college soccer experience to no soccer experience at all. Every person agreed that it had been one of the most stimulating learning experiences of their lives and had provided a robust framework for transfer—the design of many more drills and practices than were explicitly exhibited or discussed.

Tips on putting the design elements into a powerful whole

Although the elements of WHERETO are helpful for building and testing our design for learning, it is easy to lose sight of the whole—the unit and its purpose. The overriding aim is to ensure that big ideas frame the work and that transfer of learning based on those ideas is accomplished. That's what understanding is. So we have to ensure, in the end, that the learning is coherent and purposeful (as opposed to being a set of isolated "learnings" that, although defensible in isolation, just don't add up to meaningful, enduring knowledge). In other words, if we are not careful, the design could lead to the successful short-term learning of many discrete facts and skills but bypass understandings and transfer tasks.

Backward design from robust performance tasks that require such big-idea-based transfer is a key way to prevent that error, of course. But there are other steps we can take in thinking through Stage 3 that will keep us from straying too far from a focus on understanding. Specifically, we can use the six facets as a reminder of what kinds of understanding-related work must happen in Stage 3 to support performance aims related to use of understanding in Stage 2.

Using the facets in Stage 3

Although the six facets of understanding were originally conceived as indicators of understanding for use in assessment (Stage 2), they have proven to be a useful construct for the design of learning as well. One straightforward approach is to list the six facets and brainstorm possible activities (mindful, of course, of the desired results of Stage 1 and the needed assessment evidence of Stage 2). Here is an example from a middle school unit on the Civil War:

- *Explanation*—Explain the key causes and effects of major events in the Civil War. Compare to other incidents of civil strife.
- *Interpretation*—Interpret the war through the eyes of the main character in *Red Badge of Courage.*
- *Application*—Debate the legacy of the war. (Is it over? Could another Civil War occur in the United States? Has a "cold war" been going on ever since?)
- *Perspective*—Discuss the war from the perspective of the Northern side, the Southern side, a European observer, a Native American, a rich landowner, a poor worker.
- *Empathy*—Role-play to reveal empathy for a Southern family whose home was destroyed by Sherman's army. Find other songs like "The Night They Drove Old Dixie Down."
- *Self-Knowledge*—Reflect: What do you believe is worth fighting for?

Although some facets seem more natural to certain content areas than others, many teachers have reported that they have developed energizing and effective activities by using the facets to "think outside of the box." For example, a physics teacher, after initially rejecting the value of empathy in physics, thought of the following assignment: "Write a journal entry on a day in the life of an electron."

The following general questions have been helpful idea starters for designers:

- *Facet 1: Explanation.* What kind of grist for theorizing and connecting must students encounter if they are to grasp what is not obvious, meet new ideas, test and verify them, and build their own theory or explanation (or fully internalize, through testing, someone else's)? What artifacts, data, behaviors, and events should they have to try to explain to gain practice in generalizing and drawing sound inferences?
- *Facet 2: Interpretation.* How will the work require *students* to make interpretations, derive meaning, explore the importance, or find the significance in material or knowledge? What texts, events, or other resources will be provided "by design" as sufficient grist for significant and revealing interpretive work?
- *Facet 3: Application.* How will the work require and enable students to test their understandings in apt and varying contexts, where authentic situations, purposes, and audiences will require thoughtful transfer of prior learning? How can the work encourage students to propose or even invent new and revealing applications of their learning?
- *Facet 4: Perspective.* How will the materials, assignments, experiences, and discussions be encountered so that students can not only grasp and generate multiple points of view but also critically evaluate them?
- *Facet 5: Empathy.* What kinds of direct or simulated experiences in class might cause students to viscerally connect with the experiences of others?

How might the work help students get beyond empty words and abstractions to find worth or possible value in other people's texts, ideas, or experiences that might initially strike them as dumb, unappealing, or alien? Into what experiences should they be immersed so as to develop possible new insights?

• *Facet 6: Self-Knowledge.* What kinds of experiences will help students self-assess and reflect on what they do or do not know and understand? How will the lessons evoke the habits of mind and biases students bring to the work?

Backward design in action with Bob James

We've seen how teacher Bob James has sketched out his unit on nutrition in previous chapters. He now considers how he might add to or modify his design in light of the criteria and guidelines provided by WHERETO.

Just when I think I've got it nailed, I'm finding that my thinking about the nutrition unit is being stretched by WHERETO. Here are my current ideas:

W—The backward design process has really helped me clarify where I'm going with the unit. Now I need to think about how I can help the students know where they are headed, and why. I think that the essential and entry-point questions will help give direction, especially since I plan to post these questions on the classroom bulletin board. But I probably can make the goals even clearer by introducing the assessment tasks, project, and my evaluation criteria and rubrics early in the unit.

With these performance targets in mind, I'm hoping that the kids will more clearly see the purpose for the particulars they'll be learning—the food groups, the food pyramid, how to read nutrition information on food labels, things like that.

H—I like the suggestion of starting with a hook, something to capture students' interest in the topic. Our social studies textbook has a section on the explorers that will work well, I think. The kids love mysteries, and this is one—the story of the 16th- and 17th-century ocean-going sailors. They developed a mysterious disease, called scurvy, during their long months aboard ship, but their condition improved dramatically once they were back on land.

Once the kids learn that the disease resulted from a lack of vitamin C and that consuming fresh fruits and vegetables was the "medicine," we will be poised to examine the role of nutrition in health.

E—I think that my new lessons will go far to equip my students for the performance tasks and project. And I believe that my teaching will be much more focused now that I've thought through my desired understandings and the assessment evidence I need to collect.

R—The rethinking portion of unit design is probably the greatest stretch for me. Other than when we use revision as a part of the writing process, I have rarely asked my students to formally rethink the ideas we discuss. Yet I'm beginning to realize how important it can be.

Two very interesting questions came up over lunch with the other teachers. If allowed to eat anything they wanted, would children eat a balanced diet? Do animals eat foods that provide for their nutritional needs? One or both should be good midway into the unit to challenge the students to refine their thinking about nutritious eating.

These questions point to another essential question: Does Mother Nature lead living creatures in the direction of nutritious eating? These provocations should stimulate discussion and rethinking, and lead to interesting questions for further research.

E—The performance tasks and culminating camp menu project will give them several opportunities to show me they understand healthy eating—the major goal of the unit. Before evaluating, I'll involve the class in a peer review of the camp menus in cooperative learning groups so that the students will receive feedback. And I'll allow them time for menu revisions before their final menus are due.

Finally, I'll ask each student to complete two self-assessments—one for their camp menu using the rubric, and the second a reflection on if (and how) their personal eating habits have changed because of what they've learned during the unit. These activities should bring the unit to an effective close.

T—Last year I participated in a district inservice program on Differentiated Instruction (DI) and learned ways of tailoring my teaching to reach a variety of learners. I can now see ways to apply some of the DI strategies to this unit. For example, I have six students who will have difficulty reading and comprehending the textbook selection on their own, so I'll have them pair with their language arts "reading buddies." When it comes time for the quizzes, I'll give them orally to those students.

I think that my performance task on the nutrition brochure will accommodate students who are not proficient writers because they can use pictures to illustrate a balanced diet. Our G/T resource teacher gave me a good idea for extending the task for the high achievers by having them design a nutrition brochure for use in a doctor's office rather than for younger children. For the camp menu task, I'll allow the nonwriters to tell me why their menu plan is healthful and tasty rather than requiring them to write an explanatory letter. I'll ask the advanced students to include an alternative menu plan for students with health problems, like diabetes, or specific eating restrictions, like a need for a low-sodium diet.

I think that these adjustments will allow the lower-achieving learners to be more successful, while challenging my advanced students.

O—I am pretty comfortable with the sequence of my unit plan. It begins with a hook, develops needed knowledge through various learning experiences and resources, and then ends with an authentic application of knowledge. I now realize that the UbD process and Template contribute to a well-organized plan, because they've helped me frame the entire unit around important questions and meaningful performance tasks.

I think that the nutrition unit has definitely been enhanced by WHERETO, and I intend to use it when planning other units. I'm eager to see what the results will be with my students.

Next question

These initial considerations lay out in broad brushstrokes what the *unit* needs to do and rules of thumb for how to make it happen more "by design." We now need to ponder the next question: What is the *teacher's* classroom role in helping students understand?

Chapter 10

Teaching for Understanding

> Teachers . . . are particularly beset by the temptation to tell what they know. . . . Yet no amount of information, whether of theory or fact, in itself improves insight and judgment or increases ability to act wisely.
> —Charles Gragg, "Because Wisdom Can't be Told," 1940

> Successful teaching is teaching that brings about effective learning. The decisive question is not what methods or procedures are employed, and whether they are old-fashioned or modern, time-tested or experimental, conventional or progressive. All such considerations may be important but none of them is ultimate, for they have to do with means, not ends. The ultimate criterion for success in teaching is—results!
> —James L. Mursell, *Successful Teaching,* 1946, p. 1

Backward design delays the selection of teaching and other instructional strategies until the last phase of the process. Though such an approach runs counter to the habits of many educators, the delay should make sense in light of what we have said thus far. For until we have specified the desired results, the implied assessment tasks, and the key learning activities required by the goals, a discussion of teaching strategy is premature. The right moves in teaching are made in light of what learning requires. Backward design forces us to move out of comfortable teaching habits to ask, Given the performances of understanding we seek and the learning activities such results require, what should we do as teachers?

To talk at great length about teaching for understanding would obviously take us too far afield, however, in a book about design. Dozens of wonderful books and programs address effective teaching, including several books on teaching for understanding that readers should consult.[1] Instead, the aim of this chapter is to offer some general guidelines about the role of the teacher and the most common instructional resources in light of what we have said about backward design for understanding.

Coverage versus uncoverage

Mursell's epigraph at the beginning of this chapter, although written years ago, is a breath of fresh air, given the endless debates about teaching methods in the field. Teaching should be judged by its results. Which methods should we use in teaching for understanding? Any that work to cause understanding. There is no ideology to it: Do what works in Stage 3 to meet the objectives laid out in Stage 1.

Mursell's words also relate to the Expert Blind Spot we keep bringing up. We are reminded of one of the oldest jokes in education—the one about the boy who claimed he taught his dog to talk. When his friend demands an exhibition and the dog fails to do anything but bark, his friend says: "I thought you said you taught him to talk!" "I did," said the would-be trainer, "I taught him to talk, but I didn't say he learned it."

"I taught it, but they didn't learn it." It is still surprising how often we all say this in good faith at some point in our careers when things don't work out and we get frustrated. We so easily forget: It is not teaching that causes learning. "What do you mean, teaching doesn't cause learning? Are we useless? You must be kidding." No, we're serious about this. Teaching, on its own, never causes learning. Only successful attempts by the learner to learn cause learning. Achievement is the result of the learner successfully making sense of the teaching. That's what we all mean—isn't it?—when we say understanding is a "constructivist" exercise, accomplished by the learner. I can't give you understanding; you must earn it.

To have taught well is not to have used a great set of techniques or given the learner some words to give back, but to have caused understanding through words, activities, tools, guided reflection, the learner's efforts, and feedback. It is a complex interactive achievement, not a one-way set of skills. In other words, we forget, given our blind spot, that the act of teaching—in the sense of direct instruction (talking, professing, informing, telling)—is only one aspect of causing learning (and not the most important aspect, if the arguments in this book are compelling). The design of work for learning is as important as—and perhaps more important than—any articulate sharing of our knowledge. My insights cannot become theirs simply through osmosis. As a causer of learning I have to be empathetic with the novice's more naïve state of mind and "uncover" my ideas through well-designed learning experiences— which will surely include teaching but not be limited to it—to make what I say real and not just words. Only experts (or highly gifted thinkers) can hear a teacher's words and do all the constructivist work in their heads, on their own, without experiences, process guidance and tools (such as graphic organizers), tasks for eliciting responses, and feedback in their attempts to show that their learning has been successful.

So throughout the book we have constantly alluded to the need for uncoverage and the harm of mere coverage. But perhaps until now readers have misunderstood the point: Uncoverage is not a certain *type* of teaching or philosophy of education but the way to make any idea accessible and real, *regardless* of the teaching methods used. Let's therefore clarify what we mean by uncoverage and coverage, and why *every* teacher must uncover and avoid coverage, regardless of their preferred methods of instruction.

Consider the definitions. As a noun, the word *cover* refers to something on the surface, like a bedspread. Applied to teaching, it suggests something superficial. When we "cover" material (as in the history vignette in the book's Introduction), we end up unwittingly focusing on the surface details, without going into depth on any of them. From the learner's perspective, everything appears of equal value—a bunch of facts to be remembered, with no hierarchy, memorable priority, or connected meanings.

"To travel over" is another definition of *cover* (as in, "we covered 600 miles today"). When talking about covering a lot of ground, whether as travelers or teachers, we may have gone far, but that doesn't mean we derived any meaning or memorable insights from our "travels." The movie title *If It's Tuesday, This Must Be Belgium* conjures up an apt image of learning sacrificed to rigid schedule. No matter our good intentions, we end up unable to accomplish in-depth understanding (or even lasting recall) when everything is leveled into a superficial and breathless march through often sketchy and isolated facts, activities, and skills.

Educators typically justify coverage in this sense by saying it's required by external standards, obligated by textbooks, or required by standardized testing. Leaving aside the empirical evidence against these claims (discussed earlier in brief and again in Chapter 13 on relevant research), common sense suggests that "teaching by mentioning" simply cannot yield effective learning culminating in competent performance. We would think it unacceptable for a geometry teacher to argue, for example, that there is no time to inquire into the details of proofs because there are so many theorems to "cover." In other words, this hurried tour is the Expert Blind Spot at work again: If teachers discuss it, learners get it; the more we discuss, the more they get. This is a false logic that confuses our *teaching* with any resultant *learning*—mere *planting* with the *yield,* or *marketing* with *sales.*

An understanding can never be "covered" if it is to be understood. That is the premise of this book, buttressed by research. An understanding sets an end goal, a challenge; it demands the right experiences, discussion, and reflection. No one stated this challenge more baldly than Dewey (1916), when he argued that no genuine idea can be "taught" by direct instruction:

> *No thought, no idea can possibly be conveyed as an idea from one person to another. When it is told, it is, to the one to whom it is told, another given fact, not an idea. . . . Ideas . . . are tested by the operation of acting upon them. They are to guide and organize further observations, recollections, and experiments. (pp. 159–160)*

In a world dominated by coverage of what textbooks say, however, we often end up unwittingly violating this important warning. So let us reflect on the challenge of teaching using textbooks. How can we use resources in support of our aims without unwittingly undercutting the goal of understanding?

To address the question, we need to consider yet another meaning for the term *cover*—an ominous connotation, as in "to cover up" or "to hide from view." A cover-up suggests concealment, a failure to honor an obligation to make something known. To *uncover* something, by contrast, suggests finding something important in what has become hidden—to reveal rather than conceal. When we uncover something, in this sense, we are like investigative reporters, revealing something that would otherwise have remained unknown, to the detriment of our readers. The challenge of working with textbooks is to better understand what they conceal, not just what they reveal.

The textbook and teaching for understanding

In referring to what textbooks "conceal," we are not alluding to nefarious plots. Most "covering up" done by textbooks is unwitting. But the harm is real. By design, textbooks survey and summarize what is known, like an encyclopedia. They simplify expert knowledge to suit the norms of student learning levels, not to mention the needs of teachers in 50 states and competing interest groups. In so doing, the text can easily hide from students (and teachers) the true nature of the subject and the world of scholarship. Like an encyclopedia, few textbooks help students understand the inquiries, arguments, and judgments behind the summaries. The great paradox of educating for understanding is that extensively researched texts can end up providing an impediment to more engaging and thought-provoking learning. As the 1983 Carnegie report on secondary education put it,

> Most textbooks present students with a highly simplified view of reality and practically no insight into the methods by which the information has been gathered and the facts distilled. Moreover, textbooks seldom communicate to students the richness and excitement of original works. (Boyer, 1983, p. 143)

Little has changed in 20 years. The American Association for the Advancement of Science (AAAS) recently reviewed mathematics and science textbooks in middle and high school and found glaring weaknesses:

> Project 2061 rated all popular middle-school science books as "unsatisfactory," and criticized them as "full of disconnected facts that neither educate nor motivate" students. Not one of the 10 widely used high-school biology texts was deemed worthy of a high rating in the rigorous evaluation.

> The in-depth study found that most textbooks cover too many topics and don't develop any of them well. All texts include many classroom activities that either are irrelevant to learning key science ideas or don't help students relate what they are doing to the underlying ideas. (Roseman, Kulm, & Shuttleworth, 2001)

Moreover, its analysis of high school biology texts revealed the following problems:

> • *Research shows that essentially all students—even the best and the brightest—have predictable difficulties grasping many ideas that are covered in the textbooks. Yet most books fail to take these obstacles into account in the activities and questions.*
>
> • *For many biology concepts, the textbooks ignore or obscure the most important ideas by focusing instead on technical terms and superfluous detail—the sorts of material that translate easily into items for multiple-choice tests.*
>
> • *While most of the books are lavishly illustrated, these representations are rarely helpful because they are too abstract, needlessly complicated, or inadequately explained.*
>
> • *Even though several activities are included in every chapter, students are given little guidance in interpreting the results in terms of the scientific concepts to be learned. (Roseman, Kulm, & Shuttleworth, 2001)*

We believe these criticisms of textbooks are sound, and that they apply to the humanities as well as to science and mathematics. Textbooks are unfortunately often bland, overly laden with jargon, and superficial.

Textbook as syllabus: A key misunderstanding

Ultimately, blaming the textbook for poorly designed units is like blaming *Ted Williams on the Science of Hitting* for your poor batting average. The major problem in unit design is not the textbook per se. The problem is if the professor, teacher, or administrator assumes that the textbook *is* the course of study, from which the design of all work must flow. On the contrary: The text is a *resource* that supports the Desired Results specified in Stage 1 of the UbD Template. Even the best textbook will be useful in achieving only some of our desired results, and many goals will require teacher-designers to be proactive and creative in identifying appropriate essential questions, assessments, and experiences to frame the units. Those questions, tasks, and activities may, in fact, routinely require teachers to supplement the text or read selectively in it, as needed. The textbook is neither a map nor an itinerary based on one, but a guidebook in support of a purposeful journey.

Are we implying that textbooks are horribly defective or should not be a key resource? Of course not. We are saying that the text is a tool; it is *not* the syllabus. The big ideas have to be uncovered and made meaningful by intelligent use of many resources and activities. Thus, the teacher's job is not to cover what the textbook offers but to use the text to assist in meeting learning goals. Figure 10.1 helps clarify some differences concerning coverage versus uncoverage when a textbook is used.

Thus, it is our responsibility as designers not merely to choose good textbooks that support our aims but to ensure that we use the textbook for what it does well and compensate for what it does poorly. Textbooks at their best organize information and provide many exercises for reinforcing key knowledge and skill. They typically do a poor job of framing the work around ongoing

Figure 10.1

Uncoverage Versus Coverage in Use of Textbooks

Uncoverage	Coverage
• The text serves as a resource for a course of study designed with specific purposes and learning outcomes.	• The text *is* the syllabus; no explicit purpose exists beyond marching through what the textbook offers.
• The desired results require specific inquiries that culminate in the use of content via performance assessments of understanding.	• Assessment consists exclusively of tests of discrete knowledge and skill from the content of the textbook.
• The text is used to uncover, highlight, and explore essential questions and core performance challenges in the subject.	• The student's job is to know what is in the text; there are no essential questions and performance goals to guide reading, discussion, and preparation.
• Sections of the text are read in a sequence that supports the learning goals framed in the syllabus and the unit desired results.	• The text is read in the order of its pagination.
• The textbook is one resource among many, including primary-source materials—in part because the text generally only summarizes important ideas and glosses over important issues and arguments.	• Primary-source and other secondary-source materials are rarely used; the textbook summaries are taken as givens to be learned, not accounts to be analyzed, explored, tested, and critiqued.

questions and complex assessments based on big ideas, and of offering different perspectives.

So our own unit and course designs must help students see that statements in textbooks, as helpful as they often are in summarizing what is known, may inhibit deeper understanding. How? Because their dry simplification typically hides the questions, the issues, the history of the ideas, and the inquiries that ultimately led to what we now know—the very process needed by the learner to come to an understanding! Textbooks distort how understanding develops, in the expert and the novice, by presenting only the cleaned-up residue. You simply cannot learn to "do" the subject or understand it in depth by studying only a simplified summation of findings; no one becomes a good baseball player by merely reading the box scores of games in the newspaper.

The teacher's crucial role:
Designing the right experiences

> Teaching may best be defined as the organization of learning. It follows,
> therefore, that the problem of successful teaching is to organize learning
> for authentic results. . . . [This] is distinctly preferable as a definition
> to the familiar definitions of teaching either as the direction or guidance
> of learning. It saves us from arguments about whether the teacher
> ought to guide or to direct—arguments that are somewhat futile
> since the truth is he should do both.
> —James L. Mursell, *Successful Teaching,* 1946, pp. 21, 23

Given the unobvious, often counterintuitive, and otherwise abstract nature of big ideas, the understandings have to be "earned" through carefully designed experiences that uncover the possible meanings of core content. Few textbooks are designed around a series of defining experiences, yet well-designed experience is the only way to make ideas real.

This is an old idea in education reform. More than two hundred years ago, Rousseau (1979) championed the idea in *Emile* as he described the education of a mythical child, whereby townspeople were used to engineer appropriate situations for learning about honesty, property, numbers, and astronomy. "Do not give your pupil any verbal lessons; he ought to receive them only from experience" (p. 92). This is a key antidote to the Expert Blind Spot: "We never know how to put ourselves in the place of children; we do not enter into their ideas; we lend them ours and . . . with chains of truths we heap up only follies and errors in their heads" (p. 170). Sharing one's understandings and passions about how the world works is doomed to fail without the right experience:

> *Full of the enthusiasm he feels, the master wants to communicate it to the child. He believes he moves the child by making him attentive to the sensations by which he, the master, is himself moved. Pure stupidity! . . . The child perceives the objects, but he cannot perceive the relations linking them. . . . For that is needed experience he has not acquired. (pp. 168–169)*

Dewey (1933) provides a simple illustration in contrasting what he calls the *fact* of the sphericity of the earth versus the student's meaningful *idea* of it, generated through a well-designed experience. Initially, the spherical nature of the earth is a distant abstraction, a disembodied verbal fact with no intellectual meaning. To make it a working idea requires more than a definition and a globe. It requires helping the student see by constructivist work and coaching the value of the idea for making sense of particular experiences, especially relevant puzzling or inconsistent facts:

> *Ideas, then, are not genuine ideas unless they are tools with which to search for material to solve a problem. . . . He may be shown (or reminded of) a ball or globe, be told that the earth is round like those things; he may then be made to repeat that statement day after day till the shape of the earth and the shape of the ball are welded together in his mind. But he has not thereby*

acquired an idea of the earth's sphericity. . . . To grasp "sphericity" as an idea, the pupil must first have realized certain confusing features in observed facts and have had the idea of spherical shape suggested to him as a possible way of accounting for such phenomena as tops of masts being seen at sea after the hulls have disappeared, the shape of shadows of the earth in an eclipse, etc. Only by use as a method of interpreting data so as to give them fuller meaning does sphericity become a genuine idea. (pp. 133–134)

A concept becomes "real" instead of abstract only if it makes sense of (our) experience and knowledge or provides us with new intellectual powers that open up possibilities.

The work of bringing big ideas to life in this way is made more difficult by our tendency as teachers to use merely verbal approaches:

[Verbal] communication [of an idea] may stimulate the person to realize the question for himself and to think out a like idea, or it may smother his intellectual interest and suppress his dawning effort at thought. But what he directly gets cannot be an idea. Only by wrestling with the conditions of the problem at first hand, seeking and finding his own way out does he think. (Dewey, 1933, pp. 159–160)

We can therefore explain *uncoverage* as bringing a concept to life through experiences. The student needs experience not only with key ideas but also with the phenomena that led to the need for the idea. Whether the idea is "sphericity" or "balance of power" or "place value," the student can understand such ideas only by seeing them for what they really are: not facts but mental models that solve problems or give us greater intellectual power.

The need for such uncoverage is vital, not an option, because all the big ideas are both counterintuitive and abstract. Both intellectual pioneers and naïve students need to know how to get beyond appearances because appearances can deceive. No effective transfer via the big ideas will be possible unless the student is helped to uncover their meaning and interconnection.

Thus, coverage actually makes learning harder. When we "cover" the content, we level everything to verbal "stuff" for recall. This is actually more difficult for the learner than providing a

■ MISCONCEPTION ALERT!

Uncoverage and coverage, depth and breadth: Aren't they the same pairs? No. To "go into depth" on a topic suggests that we need to get "below the surface" of things. In what sense is getting below the surface a key to understanding? A simple analogy reveals it. We may sit in the car, we may know how to drive it, but that doesn't mean we understand (in depth) how it works. For that we need to look under the hood, literally and figuratively. To be an effective mechanic, it is not enough to know how to drive or the theory of the combustion engine. One needs to know how a car works, and how to diagnose trouble and fix things when it doesn't work. You have to understand how cars are the same and how they differ.

Breadth expands one's study of a narrow topic to examine the connections, extensions, and larger implications. Breadth of knowledge (unlike an education based on coverage) is a *good* thing. Indeed, the dictionary notes the power that comes from breadth of knowledge: "freedom from narrowness, as of viewpoint." The mechanic needs broad experience with many different kinds of cars, clients, and diagnostic tools to be successful. Excessive and exclusive depth is no better than excessive coverage; it isn't effective to focus on a single idea, digging the same hole deeper. Any good course of study needs to provide interesting and helpful detail, with bridges to other related topics as well as issues of meaning.

telling experience and a conceptual framework for making sense of the experience. To gain some idea of how abstract and difficult learning can be for students when big ideas are not yet real, imagine, for example, having to learn about "hardware" and "software" without first seeing or using a computer.

Put simply, teaching for understanding always requires something *before* "teaching": thought-through and designed experiences, artfully facilitated, to raise all the right questions and make the ideas, knowledge, and skill seem real and worthwhile. Students need chances to "play" with and "work" with ideas if they are to understand ideas as *useful*. That will also affect how and when we use direct instruction. Teaching after a revealing experience is often more effective than teaching a good amount before any experience.

Uncoverage: Getting inside the subject's processes and arguments

Much of what we call expert knowledge is the result of trial and error, inquiry, and argument. Yet, as noted above, when we teach only from textbooks (without active inquiry into the textbook's claims), students are easily misled into believing that knowledge is somehow just there for the plucking. To truly understand a subject, however, requires uncovering the key problems, issues, questions, and arguments behind the knowledge claims. *The work itself* must gradually inspire a clear need to question, to dig deeper into key claims. In other words, although sometimes the text usefully simplifies and we accept its knowledge happily, when it oversimplifies a big idea, we have to *question* the text. The best teacher-designers know precisely what their students will likely gloss over and misunderstand in the text. They design lessons to deliberately and explicitly require their students to find issues, problems, gaps, perplexing questions, and inconsistencies that were hidden in earlier and present accounts.

Making it needlessly harder to do this is a writing style in which textbook authors suggest that the need for inquiry is over, that the students' job is merely to apprehend What Is Known. Here is a small example of the problem of "coverage" that harmfully and needlessly closes off thought. The following sentence appears, in passing, unexplained, as part of the account of the Revolutionary War in a commonly used U.S. history textbook: "Washington had the daring to put [his patriots] to good use, too, as he broke the rules of war by ordering a surprise attack on the enemy in their winter quarters" (Cayton, Perry, & Winkler, 1998, pp. 111–112).

Nothing further is said about rules of war. But any thoughtful student should be thinking, "Huh? *Rules* of war? How can there be rules for all-out battles to the death? And if surprise attacks were somehow wrong, how did soldiers normally fight, and why?" So we have an essential question for the unit and many others as well: Is all fair in war? How can we be sure that we aren't being hypocritical when we judge such events? What "rules" exist, and by what authority? Have these rules (and crimes) changed over time? What happens (or should happen) when the rules are broken? Is "war crime" a legitimate moral idea or a contradiction in terms—just the vengeance of the victors on the losers?

This example suggests a fruitful uncovering strategy: Scour the text for statements that can be reframed as essential questions for investigation across many other key topics, across units and courses. In fact, the questions about war could not be more frighteningly germane today, as terror and violence against civilians has become seen as an acceptable strategy to some peoples while deeply condemned by others.

Here is a more disturbing example of "covering up" from the same widely used U.S. history textbook:

> *Jefferson, like most members of the Continental Congress, had no intention of surrendering power to people who were not like him. Though he condemned slavery in theory, he was a slaveholder himself, and he could not have imagined a society in which African Americans were treated as his equals. . . .*

> *Jefferson had a passionate commitment to human rights—and yet he owned slaves. Jefferson well knew that slavery was wrong. Few white planters wrote more eloquently about it as a moral evil; and yet he could never bring himself to free more than a few slaves. As a planter, his livelihood depended upon their labor. He would not discard his prejudices and risk losing the personal comfort that slave labor brought him, even for the principles of democratic equality. (Cayton, Perry, & Winkler, 1998, p. 149)*

Leaving aside the needlessly politically correct tone in the passages—is this the best we can say, that Jefferson stood out from among other "white planters"?—more alarming for understanding is the finality of the text. Authorities have spoken; there is no argument; this is what Jefferson believed.

We need only invoke Facets 1 (Explanation), 2 (Interpretation), and 3 (Empathy) to ask, Where is the evidence for this theory? What primary sources justify this view? How do they know what Jefferson felt and thought? The irony in our questions is that such questions are what history is about, yet the text makes it likely that the student will gloss over such issues and thus be discouraged from actually "doing" history (conducting a critical inquiry into the past) to find this out!

It need not be this way. We should seek out textbooks that make clear that important questions are and will always remain alive, that considering ongoing questions is central to a good education. Compare the previous misleading closure to the invitation issued in Joy Hakim's *A History of Us* on the same topic:

> *Just what does "equal" mean? Are we all the same? Look around you. Of course we aren't. Some of us are smarter than others, and others are better athletes . . . but none of that matters, said Jefferson. We are all equal in the eyes of God, and we are all entitled to equal rights. . . .*

> *He said "all men are created equal." He didn't mention women. Did he mean to include women? No one knows. Perhaps not. We do know that in the 18th century the words "men" and "mankind" included men and women. . . . Did Thomas Jefferson mean to include black men when he said "all men"?*

Historians sometimes argue about that. You'll have to decide for yourself. (1993, p. 101)

Though Hakim simplifies the argument for younger students, she doesn't make a simplistic claim. She leaves a debatable historical question open for budding historians to research and argue. (But teachers must supply the needed research materials and directions, again showing how the textbook cannot, by itself, do the job). Teachers need to ensure that all big ideas are similarly treated—made accessible, perhaps, through the textbook, but not made impenetrable or into seemingly intellectual dead-ends unworthy of further thought. Think of the textbook as a platform to jump off of and return to in the course of inquiry into important questions. In fact, such uncovering naturally prompts the consultation of other sources, including other textbooks, to shed further light on the investigation.

The same covering up can be seen in subjects as seemingly staid and unproblematic as geometry. The textbooks say little about the historical controversies surrounding Euclid's key postulates, leading eventually to the revolution unleashed by the development of non-Euclidean geometries. Note, for example, that the following account in a highly regarded geometry text comes a full 600 pages after the idea of postulates was first introduced as a seemingly unproblematic need for starting somewhere with "givens":

You can see that the fifth postulate [Euclid's parallel postulate] is much longer and more complex than the others. This bothered mathematicians, who felt that such a complicated statement should not be assumed true. For 2000 years they tried to prove the fifth postulate from Euclid's other assumptions. . . . The works of these mathematicians greatly influenced all later mathematics. For the first time, postulates were viewed as statements assumed true instead of statements definitely true. (Coxford, Usiskin, & Hirschhorn, 1993, p. 662)

What are we to make of the last sentence, offered as an aside rather than as a prelude to fundamental rethinking: postulates as statements "assumed" true versus "definitely" true? We suspect that no student (and few teachers) appreciate the significance of that remark—a remark that remains unexplained in the text. What's the difference between "assumed true" and "definitely true"? What are the implications of the distinction, for geometers and for students? Any thoughtful learner would want to go further to ask, "Yeah, why *should* these postulates be assumed? Why these and not others? Where do axioms come from anyway? What constitutes an appropriate assumption as opposed to an arbitrary or inadequate assumption? How do I know that Euclid's or anyone else's are not arbitrary? If they aren't arbitrary, why do we assume them? And, anyway, what were those silly mathematicians doing for all those years? What does it mean they were 'trying to prove a postulate true'—you told us they were *assumptions*!"

These questions are glossed over although they are basic to any deep understanding of the big ideas of geometry and the historical revolution whereby mathematics went from being The Truth to an axiomatic system unrestricted to traditional commonsense views of three-dimensional space. In light of the need for rethinking and shifts of perspective, it is easy here to uncover some of the vital inquiries the debate over the postulates spawned: Why *do* we assume what we do? When *should* we change our assumptions and why? *Flatland* (Abbott, 1884/1963), a fictional account of other spatial worlds, is a fascinating and readable introduction to the issues, written more than a century ago to serve just such a purpose.

More to the point (and mindful of all the failures of transfer in geometry cited in earlier chapters), students will never understand the *system* called Euclidean geometry until they see the assumptions as the needed underpinnings of *theorems we wanted to prove*. And then we discover to our surprise that other assumptions led to other geometries with not only intellectual but practical value.

In other words, in an education for *understanding* geometry, a primary goal would be to help the student "rethink" and "see from different perspectives" (to refer back to two of our key ideas) the axioms that earlier were accepted as so many "givens," without question. Then the student can later say, *"Now* I see why we assumed *these* postulates . . ." or "Whoa! When we just assumed those to be true it seemed arbitrary, but now I see it wasn't" or "Huh! Those givens seemed more obvious and less controversial than they do now. Can there be other useful assumptions?"[2] (Yes, there can be, and yes, there are.)

All key assumptions—in mathematics and every other field—are not somehow just brilliantly intuited, nor are systems just found, whole, at our feet. They come from inquiry, over time, based upon a careful search for the logical grounds of insights we have and the proofs we want to make. Euclid knew that to prove that there were 180 degrees in all triangles he *needed* the parallel postulate. This counterintuitive idea is rarely explained or even adequately suggested in textbooks. Is it any wonder, then, that many students are confused about a basic matter—the difference, if any, between axioms and theorems?

Here, then, is another example of what teaching for understanding looks like: Identify the big ideas and revisit them via problems of increasing sophistication as the work unfolds, whether or not the textbook does. Don't "cover" the big ideas (in this case "axiomatic system") but rather "uncover" the real issues lurking below the surface, and keep returning to them, even if the textbook isn't organized to do so.

We realize that the geometry example is a bit esoteric. But the irony is that it *shouldn't* be! Anyone who studies geometry for a year in high school is able to understand the idea that good assumptions also have limits, and that the quest for an all-encompassing theory of everything often turns out to be illusory over time. (This is what Kuhn [1970] meant, after all, when he first coined the term "paradigm" to describe how changes in scientific thinking have happened over time.) The failure to revisit assumptions that at first seemed adequate is an idea with powerful transfer to all walks of life. We "rethink" because although we realize that we had to start somewhere, we learn to understand that every simple beginning point always hides deeper issues, and these issues have to be revisited if we are ever to truly understand the nuances and under-lying dilemmas or compromises at the heart of a subject. That is a lesson a child can learn about friends, an adolescent can learn about values, and a historian must learn about historiography. Indeed, we abet student misunderstandings and encourage students to keep them hidden by making it seem as if all the big ideas are obvious and need only be taken in as presented, apprehended versus comprehended. In other words, another key teacher role is "uncoverer" of stu-dent misunderstandings and persistent performance errors through artful experiences and discussions. Students must learn that these mistakes are not avoidable, or shameful, but key episodes in gaining understanding.

Getting beyond oversimplification: Questioning past and present understandings

At the heart of uncoverage, then, is the designed learning of how to question the material. Although this may sound odd, it points to an important truth about coming to understand. The most important ideas and claims must be tested, not just mentioned, if they are to be understood. This is how we con-struct meaning and overcome simplistic thinking. We might say that content that hasn't been questioned is like courtroom claims that are never examined, leading to a hodgepodge of opinions and beliefs instead of knowledge. This is particularly true in light of how easy it is to misunderstand big ideas.

"Coverage" is not merely unfortunate, then. It exacerbates the forgetful-ness, inertia, and misunderstandings we work to overcome. The danger of textbook-based syllabi is that single simplistic representation goes unchal-lenged. Important ideas do not get revisited or looked at from different points of view. The student "learns" through the coverage approach that there is only one official viewpoint to be taken in for later recall—with no need for proac-tive questioning or any "doing" of the subject:

> One of the most common questions students ask as they embark on a history paper is "Am I on the right track?" or "Is this what you want?" They feel com-pelled to find the one right answer, and the teacher's urging that they think about the difference between an answer and an argument is met with confu-sion. Their problem is deeply rooted in the conventional ways in which text-books have presented history as a succession of facts marching straight to a single, settled outcome or resolution, whose significance one can neatly eval-uate. But once students have learned the fundamental importance of keeping their facts straight, they need to realize that historians may disagree widely on how those facts are to be interpreted. (National Center for History in the Schools, 1996, p. 26)

In sum, all teaching must simplify, but there is a fundamental difference between appropriately simplified accounts and overly simplistic, inquiry-ending coverage. The latter approach, found too often in textbook accounts, hides the underlying uncertainties, arguments, and subtleties that are central to understanding a subject. Overreliance on such accounts implies that further investigation is not really needed except out of interest in the topic. An education for understanding, by contrast, treats the lurking and emergent questions as essential to understanding, not merely a pleasant tangent to be forsaken when time grows short or undertaken as work for gifted students.

More purposeful thinking about how and when to teach

So what should we do in our role as teacher? What requirements for teaching are implied by our discussion of the need to uncover the content to help students achieve understanding? First, let's note all the possible teaching moves we *might* make, given our goals. We have found it helpful to list those moves under the three broad categories of teaching types originally proposed by Mortimer Adler (1984) in *The Paideia Proposal.* The categories are didactic (or direct) instruction, constructivist facilitation, and the coaching of performance (see Figure 10.2).[3] Thus, when we talk about "teaching" a unit, we are referring to *three different possible roles* the person called "teacher" can play in the company of learners; we are not defining "teaching" as direct instruction *only.* This means we can say without contradiction, for example, that "our teacher wisely provided minimal instruction," "the instructor spent most of her time assessing," or "the professor lectured only when needed." (Note that the person called "teacher" plays three additional *noncontact* roles, key to UbD: designer, evaluator of student work, and researcher into one's own effectiveness.)

The question likely to be on most readers' minds is predictable and important. Given these three roles of teaching, what are we recommending as appropriate when teaching for understanding? The question has no possible blanket answer; nor can we prescribe a ratio for the three roles without knowing the desired results and assessments. The question is equivalent to asking, Of the many roles a parent plays, which role should we play most? The answer: It *depends*, on our particular goals, as well as on our style, our children, and the situation. No style-focused or ideologically driven view of teaching is intended—anymore than we had an ideologically driven view about the kinds of assessments to use or not to use when we discussed Stage 2.

To better understand why goal, evidence, and context matter so much, consider two simple examples. If you are lost while driving and you stop to ask someone for directions, you want direct instruction. You don't want Joe Socrates endlessly asking, "And why are you trying to get there as opposed to some other place? What does it mean that you are driving? How do you think you became lost? Have you considered that maybe you are not lost and have found something important?" No, you want Joe to inform you on how to get to Main Street. On the other hand, if your goal is to learn how to cook, you would be profoundly disappointed to be given 30 lectures about every angle on cooking without ever setting foot in a kitchen and "doing" some cooking. Any

Figure 10.2
Types of Teaching

What the teacher uses	What the students need to do
Didactic or direct instruction	**Receive, take in, respond**
• demonstration or modeling	• observe, attempt, practice, refine
• lecture	• listen, watch, take notes, question
• questions (convergent)	• answer, give responses
Facilitative or Constructivist methods	**Construct, examine, and extend meaning**
• concept attainment	• compare, induce, define, generalize
• cooperative learning	• collaborate, support others, teach
• discussion	• listen, question, consider, explain
• experimental inquiry	• hypothesize, gather data, analyze
• graphic representation	• visualize, connect, map relationship
• guided inquiry	• question, research, conclude, support
• problem-based learning	• pose or define problems, solve, evaluate
• questions (open-ended)	• answer and explain, reflect, rethink
• reciprocal teaching	• clarify, question, predict, teach
• simulation (e.g., mock trial)	• examine, consider, challenge, debate
• Socratic seminar	• consider, explain, challenge, justify
• writing process	• brainstorm, organize, draft, revise
Coaching	**Refine skills, deepen understandings**
• feedback and coaching	• listen, consider, practice, retry, refine
• guided practice	• revise, reflect, refine, recycle through

conception about what good teaching is must take into account the goals, the nature of the learners, and the situation.

A return to the nutrition unit

Because context matters, let's consider a specific example—the nutrition unit—from the vantage point of the three types of teaching:

• *Didactic/Direct.* The unit certainly requires direct instruction. Knowledge about fats, protein, carbohydrates, and cholesterol; the food pyramid; the relationship among food consumption, caloric intake, and energy expenditure are most efficiently and effectively learned through explicit teaching and student reading, followed by checks for understanding.

• *Constructivist Facilitation.* The unit also presents numerous opportunities for guided inquiry and facilitated discussions around the essential questions (e.g., what do we mean by "healthy eating?"). In addition, students will need some teacher guidance as they work on the performance tasks and the culminating camp menu project.

• *Coaching.* Coaching occurs when the teacher provides feedback and guidance to students as they work on their tasks and project.

Other units will demand other emphases. Some units may involve only two of the three roles. The ratio of each role against the others will change across units and with teachers teaching the same unit.

Beware of self-deception based on habits and comfort

When choosing instructional approaches, think about what is needed for learning, not just what is comfortable for teaching. How much should we talk and how much should we let learners "do"? How much should we "cover" and how much should we help learners "uncover"? Our sly rule of thumb: The proportions are likely to be a ratio that you are not in the habit of using. Teachers who love to lecture do too much of it; teachers who resist it do too little. Teachers who love ambiguity make discussions needlessly confusing. Teachers who are linear and task-oriented often intervene too much in a seminar and cut off fruitful inquiry. Teachers who love to coach sometimes do too many drills and overlook transfer. Teachers who love the big picture often do a poor job of developing core skills and competence. The upshot? Beware of self-deception! Pedagogical self-understanding—Facet 6—applies to *teachers* as they contemplate each plan for learning and teaching. To teach for understanding requires the routine use of all three types of teaching, in ways that may challenge a teacher's comfortable habits.

Thus, any advice is based on if/then conditional statements. If the unit goal is primarily skill development, then coaching is key. (But remember that facilitating understanding about the big ideas of strategy will become key to using the skill wisely). If the goal is understanding a counterintuitive idea, then lots of facilitated inquiry of well-designed experiences will be needed, even if it makes us feel uneasy about the "loss" of so much time; lectures will often be most useful after experiences, to solidify learning. In short, particular

▓ MISCONCEPTION ALERT!

One of the most common and predictable misconceptions in teaching for understanding concerns direct instruction or lecturing. Many educators believe that we (and others) are suggesting that direct instruction or lecturing is bad and "discovery learning" is good. The myopic corollary is that if lecturing is bad and discovery is good, then more discovery learning is better and giving fewer lectures is less bad. We are neither saying nor implying any such thing. Backward design dictates the answers based on the logic of your aims: what teaching approaches make the most sense given the learning goals, the assessments, and the experiences necessary to make the big ideas real?

All coaches lecture; not even a passionate devotee of the Socratic seminar avoids providing explicit instruction or feedback. When lecturing is *properly* criticized, it is usually because the goals call for more attempts by learners to play with, test, and apply ideas (to "make meaning") than the lectures allow for.

instructional methods, their amount, and their timing are selected based on the specific types of learning needed to achieve the desired performances.

Though the decision to use a particular type of teaching is thus dependent upon the curricular priorities, the needs of students, available time, and other factors, there's not much more we can say here about the specifics of making such choices. Nonetheless, we can offer the following general guidelines:

• *Excess talk correlates with unclear goals. Be explicit with yourself and your students about what the learning is designed to enable the learner to do.* Your decision about how much to tell is greatly influenced by the clarity of performance goals for learners. Think of coaching a sport, teaching someone to play a musical instrument, or teaching someone how to draw. At a certain point, it is foolish to keep on talking instead of letting the learner try the task and get the feedback necessary for learning. If we don't design backward from explicit "doing" by the learner, we tend to overinstruct. Good coaches teach, but in smaller and more timely doses than many classroom teachers, because coaches keep focused on the bottom-line goal of enabling the learner to perform. Conversely, teachers tend to become excessively didactic when there isn't a specific core challenge or performance goal to focus the learning.[4]

• *Distinguish "just in time" from "just in case."* Lessen the front-loading of information. Even when direct instruction is called for, resist front-loading all of the needed information using direct instruction. Memory cannot hold much when key information is presented in large amounts before opportunities for meaningful use. Save lectures for "half-time" and "post-game analysis," after learners have had an opportunity to apply the learning and they are more likely to understand and appreciate your lectures.

• *Build in pre- and post-reflection and metacognitive opportunities.* To paraphrase Dewey, we don't learn by doing unless we reflect on what we have done. Remember the aphorism that flows from the apple vignette in the Introduction: It's the guided reflection on the meaning of the activity, not the activity itself, that causes the learning.

• *Use the textbook as a resource, not the syllabus.* Decisions about when to lecture are made needlessly difficult if the textbook *is* the course, as we noted earlier. Your job is not to explain the textbook. Your job is to use the resources to make it easier for learners to understand important ideas and to use knowledge and skill as indicated by certain performances. You will be more likely to overlecture if you make the textbook the course.

• *Let models do the teaching.* Effective teachers recognize the value of having their students examine both strong and weak models (e.g., in writing or art) as a means of deepening understanding of the qualities of excellent work. Similarly, students learning a skill benefit from viewing proficient performances contrasted with ones that illustrate common problems. Teachers who use models and examples in this way exploit a natural mental process of coming to understand the world. By comparing strong and weak models, the learner develops increasingly refined conceptual and procedural distinctions.

Relating type of teaching to type of content

We should use direct instruction and focused coaching for knowledge and skill that is discrete, unproblematic, and enabling, while reserving constructivist facilitation for those ideas that are subtle, prone to misunderstanding, and in need of personal inquiry, testing, and verification. Consider the chart in Figure 10.3 and its implications for teaching approaches. One way of interpreting the chart is straightforward: When the educational aims in a given unit involve the items in Column A, direct instruction tends to be both efficient and effective. Students can grasp the items in Column A through straightforward apprehension from teacher, activity, or text, in other words. When the aims involve the items in Column B, however, the students will need some form of facilitated experience, guided inquiry, and "constructed understandings" if they are to really understand.

But we can look at the chart from another perspective—as elements in a back-and-forth movement between smaller parts and a more complex whole. For learning to occur in the most effective way possible, students need sufficient knowledge and skill to get going without being bored or overwhelmed, while also confronting the big-picture ideas and challenges that give meaning to the learning. In other words, it does not follow from the two columns that learners should first work in Column A for a long time and then move to Column B. To derive understandings inductively, students need the grist of particular experiences, facts, and teachings; to understand facts and skills, they need to see the problems, questions, and tasks that make content relevant. (Recall that in the "best design" exercise, educators always note that the design moved back and forth repeatedly and transparently between the part and the whole, the facts and the big picture.) So we can then picture the two columns as a kind of double helix, requiring cycles of each type of teaching.

Figure 10.3
Content of Teaching

Column A	Column B
• Facts	• Concepts & principles
• Discrete knowledge	• Systemic connections
• Definitions	• Connotations
• Obvious information	• Subtlety, irony
• Literal information	• Symbolism
• Concrete information	• Abstraction
• Self-evident information	• Counterintuitive information
• Predictable result	• Anomaly
• Discrete skills & techniques	• Strategy (using repertoire & judgment)
• Rules & recipes	• Invention of rules & recipes
• Algorithm	• Heuristic

There is a third perspective on the columns. Column A represents *old* understandings that have been so well internalized they have become facts. Column B represents how *new* ideas and challenges appear, regardless of one's prior level of understanding. The more experienced, advanced, or expert students will likely find that what was once opaque, counterintuitive, and complicated has now *become* obvious, straightforward, and clear. Hard-won "understandings" have become "facts." Advanced students can often apprehend through direct instruction what it takes great constructive labor and coaching for the less experienced or able student to comprehend.

Herein lies the profound danger of the Expert Blind Spot, discussed throughout the book. Teachers are long past being novices. The subject, with its ideas, challenges, and connections, has become "obvious." We lose our empathy, unless we are vigilant, for the likelihood of misunderstanding, confusion, and the need for constructivist learning. We are most prone to covering content inappropriately when we lose our empathy for the objective difficulty of all new ideas and tasks.

Timing is everything

> The secret of success [in teaching] is pace. . . . Get your knowledge
> quickly and then use it. If you can use it you will retain it.
> —Alfred North Whitehead, *The Aims of Education and Other Essays*, 1929, p. 36

In teaching for understanding—as in romance, the stock market, and comedy—timing is everything. Although it is important to decide which role to use and how much, we think there is another important question often overlooked by teacher-designers: When? In cases in which understanding is the goal, when should I engage in direct instruction and when not? When should I facilitate an experience and follow up with reflection? When should I have them try to perform and give them feedback? We can offer a glib generalization: Few teachers get the timing in the use of the three roles just right, even if they have a relatively expansive repertoire. *A major mistake in teaching for understanding is not the overreliance on a single approach but the failure to ponder the timing in using the approach.*

The question, then, is not *should* I lecture? The question is always, Do I know *when* to lecture and *when not to* when understanding is the goal? Do I know when to instruct and when to let learn? Do I know when to lead and when to follow?

Even within each role, these can be hard questions to answer. Take lecturing:

- When should I answer and when should I question?
- When should I advocate and when should I purvey equally plausible alternatives?
- When should I speak my mind and when should I play devil's advocate?

• When should I state the purpose of the lecture and when should I let it be inferred?

• When should I do the research and when should they?

Similarly, in a discussion:

• When should I frame the talk by my questions and when should I ask students to launch the discussion?

• When should I challenge an inappropriate answer and when should I let it go, to let a student challenge it?

• When should I come to the aid of a participant whose views are wrongly being ignored and when should I just wait?

• When should I correct clearly wrong statements of fact and when should I let them go?

• When should I act more like a quiet sideline observer and when should I act like a coparticipant?

We must derive many of our answers to these hard questions not only from what Stages 1 and 3 imply, but what WHERETO suggests. And what the *H, R,* and *O* suggest is that we need to do less direct instruction *upfront* than is typical in U.S. classrooms. To paraphrase the immortal words of Whitehead, written almost a century ago: Get your knowledge and use it quickly.

Fast forward to the present. The following was a key finding of the Third International Mathematics and Science Study (TIMSS): U.S. teachers tend to merely *present* terms, rules, and tactics, whereas teachers from the better-performing nations tend to *develop* key ideas through problems and discussions (see Figure 10.4). Significantly, the problems are typically presented first, followed by the direct instruction. The irony is that less telling can yield more and better learning if our assignments and assessments are well designed and our use of teaching approaches is judicious, well timed, and goal directed. The research on learning as summarized in *How People Learn* and the international studies in math and science (TIMSS) documenting this claim are discussed in detail in Chapter 13.

In many secondary and collegiate classrooms we find too much direct instruction, front-loaded, not too little. The title of the source of the quote at the start of the chapter says it all: "Because Wisdom Can't Be Told." This 50-year-old article lays out the rationale for the use of the case method in Harvard Business School, an approach in which students derive the meaning as they study specific business cases, with Socratic facilitation by the instructor. The same method is now widely used in medical schools, engineering programs, and in problem-based learning units and courses in secondary schools.

Figure 10.4

Average Percentage of Topics with Concepts That Were Developed or Only Stated

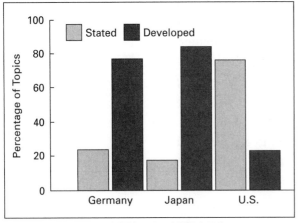

Source: U.S. Department of Education, NCES (1998).

The need for more formative assessment

In designing our teaching and learning experiences, therefore, our job is not only to uncover the big ideas of content. A great shift requires us to be aggressive in assessing as we teach, uncovering the learners' *understandings and misunderstandings* all along the way. Therefore, Understanding by Design emphasizes the regular use of ongoing informal and formal assessments, rather than restricting assessment to end-of-teaching performance tasks, culminating projects, and final exams.

The purpose of such assessment-in-progress is to ferret out the apparent from the genuine understandings, as discussed in earlier chapters. Given both the teacher's propensity to believe correct answers indicate understanding and the students' desire to seem like they get it even if they don't, the teacher needs to be ever vigilant. Remember the maxim based on a judicial analogy: Students should be assumed innocent of understanding until proven guilty. Just because eight students "get it" and there are no further questions doesn't mean the others understand. Just because students answer a simple question on cue doesn't mean they can use that knowledge on their own or know when it is called for when no cue is given.

How, then, might we determine if students "get it" before it's too late? For years, teachers have used a variety of informal techniques to efficiently and effectively check for understanding en route. We offer a number of these in Figure 10.5. Note that although these are assessment techniques, they are *not* used for grading. Instead, they are intended to provide timely feedback on students' current conceptions (or misconceptions) and to inform the instructional adjustments needed to improve their understanding.

Large lecture courses? No problem, given available technology. Consider this example, as reported in the *Boston Globe* (Russell, 2003):

Hoping to make large classes more interactive, a growing number of professors on large campuses are requiring students to buy wireless, handheld transmitters that give teachers instant feedback on whether they understand the lesson—or whether they're even there.

Use of the $36 device has exploded this fall at the University of Massachusetts. . . . Close to 6,000 of the 17,500 undergraduates on the Amherst campus are required to have transmitters in classes this fall. . . .

To connect with students in vast auditoriums, professors sprinkle multiple-choice questions through their lectures. Students point and click their transmitters to answer, pushing blue buttons numbered 1 through 9 on their keypads. A bar graph appears on the professor's laptop, showing the number of right and wrong answers; teachers can slow down or backtrack when there are too many wrong answers. Each device is registered and assigned a number, so professors can check who is present and reach out after class to those who give wrong answers frequently. . . .

Figure 10.5

Techniques to Check for Understanding

1. Index Card Summaries/Questions

Periodically, distribute index cards and ask students to write on both sides, with these instructions:

(Side 1) Based on our study of (unit topic), list a big idea that you understand and word it in the form of a summary statement.

(Side 2) Identify something about (unit topic) that you do not yet fully understand and word it as a statement or a question.

2. Hand Signals

Ask students to display a designated hand signal to indicate their understanding of a specific concept, principle, or process:

- I understand _____ and can explain it. (e.g., thumbs up)

- I do not yet understand _____. (e.g., thumbs down)

- I'm not completely sure about _____. (e.g., wave hand)

3. One-Minute Essay

At the conclusion of a lesson or reading, ask students to write a brief (one-minute) essay summarizing their understanding of the key idea or ideas presented. Collect and review.

4. Question Box or Board

Establish a location (e.g., question box, bulletin board, or e-mail address) where students may leave or post questions about concepts, principles, or processes that they do not understand. (This technique may be helpful to those students who are uncomfortable admitting publicly that they do not understand.)

5. Analogy Prompt

Periodically, present students with an analogy prompt:

(Designated concept, principle, or process) is like _____

because _____.

6. Visual Representation (Web or Concept Map)

Ask students to create a visual representation (e.g., web, concept map, flow chart, or time line) to show the elements or components of a topic or process. This technique effectively reveals whether students understand the relationships among the elements.

Figure 10.5 (continued)

7. Oral Questioning

Use the following questions and follow-up probes regularly to check for understanding:

How is _____ similar to/different from _____?

What are the characteristics/parts of _____?

In what other ways might we show/illustrate _____?

What is the big idea, key concept, moral in _____?

How does _____ relate to _____?

What ideas/details can you add to _____?

Give an example of _____?

What is wrong with _____?

What might you infer from _____?

What conclusions might be drawn from _____?

What question are we trying to answer? What problem are we trying to solve?

What are you assuming about _____?

What might happen if _____?

What criteria would you use to judge/evaluate _____?

What evidence supports _____?

How might we prove/confirm _____?

How might this be viewed from the perspective of _____?

What alternatives should be considered?

What approach/strategy could you use to _____?

8. Follow-Up Probes

- Why?
- How do you know?
- Explain.
- Do you agree?
- What do you mean by _____?
- Could you give an example?

- Tell me more.
- Give your reasons.
- But what about _____?
- Can you find that in the text?
- What data support your position?

9. Misconception Check

Present students with common or predictable misconceptions about a designated concept, principle, or process. Ask them whether they agree or disagree and to explain their response. The misconception check can also be presented in the form of a multiple-choice or true-false quiz.

The technology has spread from the sciences and economics to psychology, statistics, legal studies, and accounting, and an art history class even participated in last year's study.

"It works better than the professor saying 'Raise your hand,' because people don't want to go against the person sitting next to them," [a student] said.

No access to such technology? Use sets of colored index cards, which students can hold up and turn in for each problem, with their names on each card.

These are not just catchy moves. They are as essential to teaching as any reading, lecture, or discussion because they let learner as well as teacher know what is and isn't being understood in time to make any needed adjustments. These approaches signal that teaching is much more than informing; it requires constant attention to the course of the learning, because that's how understanding occurs—through the learner's repeated and increasingly successful attempts to learn, coupled with the teacher's feedback and guidance (in addition to the initial instruction).

Understanding and the use of knowledge and skill

> This discussion rejects the doctrine that students should first learn passively, and then, having learned, should apply knowledge. It is a psychological error. In the process of learning, there should be present, in some sense or other, a subordinate activity of application. In fact, the applications are part of the knowledge. For the very meaning of things known is wrapped up in their relationships beyond themselves. Thus, unapplied knowledge is knowledge shorn of its meaning.
> —Alfred North Whitehead, *The Aims of Education and Other Essays,* 1929, pp. 218–219

In other words, as we have said throughout the book, understanding is about wise performance—transfer and use of big ideas—not mere recall. If you understand, you can *do* important things properly, as common sense and the six facets suggest. Teaching for understanding therefore must be closer to coaching than professing, especially when we look at the flow of learning activities and what they require of the teacher.

An education for application derives its sequence "backward" from specific performance goals that signify success in understanding. Again, Whitehead's maxim of "get your knowledge and use it quickly" always applies. In planning, we aim early for the desired performance, even if the task has to be in simplified or scaffolded form (e.g., T-ball for 6-year-olds, or templates for writers); we build up performance progressively; and we revisit the fundamentals repeatedly as we do so. We eventually take off the intellectual training wheels of cues, prompts, and tools to see if students can perform with understanding on their own. This approach involves a careful task analysis that moves backward from the desired performances, and a whole-part-whole design for learning to perform with understanding.

Unfortunately, many educators, habituated to their own experience as learners and teachers in a textbook-driven world, resist this approach. They argue that "students need to learn all the basics before they can perform" or that "inexperienced students aren't ready to do complex tasks." But this goes against common sense, not just backward design. Consider how *unlikely* eventual mastery of any complex performance in music, drama, athletics, and the professions would be if the training were organized with lots of front-loaded knowledge taught out of context using a linear scope and sequence. If you were going to coach Little League, would you start by spending several days teaching kids all the rules and technical skills of baseball in logical order? Would you delay playing the game for a year or two until the players had mastered all the discrete skills, in logical order? Not if your goal was skilled performance with understanding and your time was limited. Part to whole, whole to part—that's how we come to understand and use our knowledge.

This movement back and forth, from content to performance and back again, from discrete skill to strategy and back again, is familiar to all coaches and performers. In acting, we rehearse a few lines of dialogue, then put them back into Act 2, Scene 4, and rehearse again, as needed. In writing, we fine-tune our story introduction, read the whole story to see if it works, then have the work peer edited. Alas, the introduction confuses the reader, so we work on it again. Similarly, in basketball, we practice shooting and dribbling in isolation, work on drills that combine the two, then have a controlled scrimmage to see if we can put everything together in context. On the basis of the feedback from results in the whole performance, we go back to drill work to overcome misunderstandings, bad habits, or forgotten lessons. We constantly recycle through work on specific elements, chunks of performance, and performance as a whole.

It's the same with the case method now routinely used in law, medicine, and engineering; professors no longer cover all the laws in a field first. By working on authentic cases, the students come to see the importance of the basics in the context of meaningful application. The work is structured as sequences of challenges, models, practice, feedback, practice, performance, and feedback, followed by more such loops as the complexity increases.

The flip side of this iterative logic is also true. With each new group, coaches invariably revisit the basics—how to hold the instrument, how to pass and shoot, and how to sing from the diaphragm and not the throat—no matter how expert a student is. They do not say, "Well, since you learned how to shoot last year, we won't cover it this year." They do not think of this reinforcement as time lost or content sacrificed, because they know they will gain better results by embedding a review of the basics in the context of working toward excellent performance.

Two kinds of learning by doing must keep occurring. Students must practice the new ideas in simplified drill or exercise form, and they must then apply those discrete skills or moves in a more complex and fluid performance—a movement back and forth between part and whole, between scaffolded coaching and trial and error in performance. You may recall that our workshop attendees considered such a movement to be the hallmark of the best-designed learning experiences, regardless of the content. Direct instruction occurs *while* learners play and *after* they play as a way of deriving understanding from the attempts to perform.

In other words, the logic of learning how to do things *with* content is different from the logic of *transmitting* the content—with implications for the kinds of teaching we do *and* the sequence in which we do it. (We consider this issue in greater depth in Chapter 12, in which we discuss the big picture of curriculum design.) Would-be performers don't profit much from lengthy upfront lectures. Rather, they need explicit instruction on a "need to know" basis, so they can begin to see knowledge and skill as tools to accomplish a specific task or a set of tasks within a complex performance.

Don't just take our word for it. Consult the instructional studies accompanying the Third International Mathematics and Science Study (TIMSS) and you'll see that it calls into question the traditional American approach to instruction. This research reveals that math teachers in the top-performing nations, such as Japan, begin with challenging problems in order to develop mathematical understandings inductively (whole–part–whole). (Chapter 13 includes summaries of the TIMSS studies and related research in mathematics and science.)

Now consider history—a subject that is typically conceived as a chronological march through content over time. The typical history course based on a textbook simply lays out information on discrete topics chronologically— "one darn thing after another," in the apocryphal words of a frustrated student. By beginning a history course in a remote and distant past, unmoored from contemporary events, learners' interests, overarching questions, and specific tasks, students are far less likely to be engaged in "doing" history in a way that will allow them to come to understand the "story" of the past and the big ideas that transfer to the present.

Consider this alternative approach to teaching history that would present a more relevant, coherent, and engaging "story" from the student's point of view, *without* sacrificing content. Imagine restructuring a world history course so that it begins and ends with the same essential question (one of, say, four for the year): "Why did the events of September 11, 2001, happen, from a historical point of view? As a historian advising the administration on policy issues (or, alternatively, as a museum curator or a journalist from the Middle East), how will you place these events in historical perspective so that our leaders might better understand why they happened and address the underlying issues?" All readings, discussions, lectures, and research would be focused around answering the question as if the students were journalists, historians, and museum curators, representing different cultural perspectives. The course would culminate in written, oral, and visual products, and interactive performances. The textbook, with its chronological summaries, would serve as a *resource*—to be tapped only as needed. We would move backward and forward in time, uncovering key content and process as needed to equip students to answer the question and perform successfully. The movement would be *logical* though not *chronological*. In short, understanding with the goal of performance requires an iterative curriculum that focuses on overarching questions and explicit tasks, with varied approaches to teaching as dictated by the needs of learners to master such questions and tasks.

These reflections on teaching for understanding only scratch the surface of what is a lifetime undertaking. We trust, though, that we have posed some essential questions and suggested fruitful directions for research into, and reflection about, teaching practice.

Backward design in action with Bob James

The more I ponder all this, the more I realize that sometimes I do too much teaching and not enough coaching; and sometimes I don't do enough teaching, especially when it concerns the skills needed for group work, projects, and presentations.

When do I teach too much? When I just say, in different words, what's in the textbook. When don't I coach enough? When my students are preparing to present. I don't give them enough feedback against the models and rubrics before they present. Likewise, I'm not doing enough checking for understanding, in part because I've used so much class time to teach more stuff or just let them loose on their projects. I think I'll try to use more ungraded quizzes and oral checks for understanding of the big ideas more often. You know, the more I think about it, I often give the slow learners feedback when it's too late—after they have presented. Maybe we can spend more time rehearsing. In fact, maybe I can teach them how to better self-assess their work as they go.

It's funny, I never really thought about the question this way. What's the best use of my time, my expertise in the few minutes we're all together in class? Same for the kids. What's the best use of our time for each of them? When I think about "teaching" in that way I can see that maybe I can be more of an assessor and less of a giver of information, and that it might actually be a better use of our time together. That's certainly what I do in the gym during basketball. I suspect that if I keep asking that question of myself—what's the best use of our limited time together?—then I will get sharper on this essential question, to the benefit of all my teaching.

Looking ahead

Having considered the three stages of design and some thoughts on teaching for understanding, we now consider briefly the process of design. What should designers consider as they try to get underway? What problems and possibilities are they likely to encounter en route? We now turn to these and related questions.

Chapter 11

The Design Process

Architects have the patience to plan. Builders have the savvy
to improvise. Improvisation, however, is not a substitute for planning.
The purpose of planning is to achieve predictable results. The purpose
of improvising is to maintain work progress.
—John McClean, "20 Considerations That Help a Project Run Smoothly," 2003

Americans hold the notion that good teaching comes through artful and
spontaneous interactions with students during lessons. . . . Such views
minimize the importance of planning increasingly effective lessons and lend
credence to the folk belief that good teachers are born, not made.
—James Stigler and James Hiebert, "Understanding and Improving Classroom
Mathematics Instruction," 1997, p. 20

If you have been following our running account of how fictional teacher Bob James is thinking through his design, you may have noticed that he has to rethink elements of his unit as each new idea is presented. For example, his initial understandings were not framed as understandings; they merely summarized the topic. His process illustrates a fundamental idea of UbD—that coming to a deep understanding requires rethinking key ideas, whether we are talking about young students or veteran teacher-designers.

More practically, it underscores a vital lesson about the UbD Template and helps us avoid a common misunderstanding. The template is structured to reflect a completed, organized design, with the elements aligned. It does not follow, however, that the best way to design is to fill in the template in the order that the boxes appear. True, backward design calls for carefully thinking about the goals, logically deriving the assessments from the goals, and finally inferring the appropriate learning activities. But in practice, all design is a non-linear process. Designers—whether they are unit designers, composers, or landscape architects—go back and forth from one aspect of a design to another. Although the final *product* must obey the three-stage logic, the ongoing design *process* unfolds in an unpredictable way, unique to each designer and each design challenge. Yes, you have to end up with a filled-in template, with all elements aligned; however, the pathways for getting there differ.

As an example of how process and product differ in UbD, think of the difference between process and product in cookbooks. Cooks play with ideas, test out possibilities, and eventually produce recipes written up in the familiar step-by-step format. Note, however, that the recipe is not developed in a purely sequential manner. Much trial and error occurs as various combinations of ingredients, temperatures, and timings are tried. A cook may be inspired to start in one of various ways: with a fresh available seasonal ingredient, a specific audience to cook for, or the desire to prepare a Thai meal. Each beginning point suggests its own particular logic. Starting with an idea for a new chicken dish requires a different sequence of activities than beginning with the idea of cooking a Thai dish with whatever ingredients are on hand.

Furthermore, chefs typically try out different proportions of ingredients and cooking times on multiple versions of the dish simultaneously. They write down the final proportions and steps of the recipe late in the process, after they have experimented and tasted many versions. Sometimes an assistant to the chef follows quickly behind, carefully measuring amounts of the various ingredients that the cook only estimated and refined by taste. Cooking from scratch is truly a messy process!

The "mess" is transformed into a recipe through backward design: If someone else, other than the creator, is to replicate the meal, what needs to be done, in what order? Though the process for coming up with the recipe is messy, the final product of the chef's work is presented to the home cook in a uniform and efficient step-by-step recipe format. Similarly, the UbD Template provides a format for self-assessing and sharing the final design "recipe," but not a history of *how* the design work unfolded over time (or how any work "should" proceed).

It may seem surprising for us to suggest that you can start anywhere—even in Stage 3. But this simply recognizes the reality that it is often natural to begin with an existing unit instead of a blank template. Sometimes it makes sense to begin with a key resource (e.g., a text or a science kit) or a planned assessment (e.g., problems to solve in mathematics, a dialogue in a foreign language, a technology project). In an important sense it doesn't matter where you *enter* the design process and how you proceed; it only matters that you *end* with a coherent product.

Although design can be flexible, some paths turn out to be wiser than others. Even when we feel confident in starting with a text that seems worthwhile on its face (such as *Romeo and Juliet* or *Charlotte's Web),* soon the designer must self-consciously justify the choice by linking it to specific purposes and desired results (Stage 1). Why is it being read? What big ideas and links to standards can justify it?

Put in different words, it is more important to test against the backward design logic and standards as you play with ideas rather than to think of design as a step-by-step process in which you don't need to look back. Treating the template as a set of boxes to be filled in one at a time is likely to result in a poor design, because such an approach won't involve the kind of revising and aligning needed to produce a coherent plan.

The quote at the start of the chapter suggests a further consideration. The final learning can be accomplished only with a carefully considered plan. Intelligent improvisation occurs on the foundation of a good blueprint. The best designers in education are thus like good architects and savvy contractors, doing two different tasks: (1) as they work, they creatively play with unit ideas, regardless of where those ideas fit on the template, to eventually produce a solid blueprint; and (2) they test the ideas, before and during their use with students, to make it likely that when all is said and done, the goals are accomplished as concrete learning.

Doorways to design

We have found it useful to identify six common entry points and general approaches to the design process, depending upon such variables as the content, the nature of the learners, available time, and your style as a designer. Some approaches begin with a blank template; others assume you are going to use UbD to revise an existing "traditional" design. Regardless of the approach taken, you should routinely check the emerging design against the UbD Design Standards to ensure that the result is a high-quality design. (See Figure 11.1.)

Begin with content standards

• Look for the key nouns in the standards. (Group related standards together to better see which nouns are key.) Consider the big ideas implied by those nouns.

• Identify the key knowledge and skill called for by the content standards or benchmarks. Infer the related ideas and understandings.

• Ask, What essential questions flow from or point to the standard? What important arguments and inquiries relate to the standard?

• Consider the key verbs; think of them as a blueprint for key performance assessments.

• List the activities that will enable performance and will develop the ability to understand the big ideas.

• Refine the unit to ensure alignment across all three stages.

Begin by considering desired real-world applications

• Clarify the larger purposes and ultimate goals of the content. What does the content enable you to do in the real world if you master it? What are the core challenges and authentic performances in this field?

• Identify specific, complex, real-world tasks that embody those challenges or achievement of those goals.

• Determine the understandings, knowledge, and skill learners will need to achieve mastery of such tasks.

• Sketch a learning plan that will enable practice, feedback, and competent performance.

Figure 11.1
Entry Points for the Design Process

An important topic or content

- What Big Ideas either underlie this topic or emerge from studying it?
- Why is it so important?

Established goals or content standards

- What Big Ideas are embedded in this goal?
- What will students need to understand to really learn this?

An important skill or process

- What will this skill enable students to do?
- What will students need to understand to effectively apply this skill?

Stage 1—Desired Results
Stage 2—Assessment Evidence
Stage 3—Learning Plan

- What will students need to understand to perform well on this test?
- What other evidence of learning is needed?

A significant test

- What Big Ideas will students come to understand as a result of this activity or unit?
- What evidence of understanding is needed?

A favorite activity or familiar unit

- Exactly why are we having students read this text or use this resource?
- What Big Ideas do we want students to understand as a result?

A key text or resource

• Infer the questions performers need to always consider as they try to master the content and the task.

• Identify content standards that explicitly refer to or imply such applications.

• Align the elements of the design, as needed.

Begin with a key resource or favorite activity

• Start with a "winning" activity or a sanctioned resource (e.g., a thought-provoking experience or simulation, or a required novel).

• Consider the "why?" question: Why does this matter? What big ideas would this resource help students to understand?

• Clarify the essential questions that will point students to those ideas as they consider the experience or text.

• Identify the skills, facts, and understandings the resource or activity is meant to yield. Locate relevant content standards. Infer the key concepts and essential questions implied in the larger purposes.

• Revise the assessments and learning activities accordingly.

Begin with an important skill

• Consider the question, What complex and worthy performance does such a skill enable? How does this skill connect to other relevant skills?

• Identify the content standard or standards that refer to such skills directly or indirectly.

• Determine what kind of assessments are implied or explicit in the relevant standard.

• Identify strategies that are helpful in using such skills effectively.

• Identify the big ideas and essential questions that undergird the skill.

• Devise learning activities that will enable learners to use such skill in context and to self-assess and self-adjust.

• Revise for alignment accordingly.

Begin with a key assessment

• Given an assessment (local or state), clarify the goals for which the assessment exists. What kinds of transferability do such tests seek?

• Identify the standards that address such goals.

• Infer the relevant big ideas (understandings, essential questions) required to meet such a standard and pass such a test.

• Develop and refine the performance assessment tasks that parallel the required assessments. Craft and modify the learning activities to ensure effective and purposeful performance.

Begin with an existing unit

• Given traditional lessons and assessments, place the elements in the template and look for alignment across the three stages. Do the goals match the assessments?

• Ask yourself whether the lessons relate to the richest aspect of your goals.

• Focus on clarifying the big ideas and the long-term performance goals related to standards.

• Keep asking, What should students come away understanding?

• Revise the assessments and lessons to do justice to the revised Stage 1 elements.

• Revise the design against the Design Standards, as needed.

Revising existing designs

Understanding by Design provides a framework for improving existing designs as well as creating new ones. Let's look at two designs that were revised using backward design. The first example involves a revision of a social studies unit at the elementary level; the second is for a high school geometry unit.

Figure 11.2 outlines the key activities and assessments of a unit on westward expansion and prairie life that was originally conceived and taught by a team of 3rd grade teachers. With a casual glance, we say, Hmm, looks like an interesting, hands-on, and fun unit for 3rd graders. The teachers have planned a variety of learning experiences to engage various learning styles. They have purposefully integrated literature with the social studies content. The assessments are varied, yet common. Because all teachers use the same assessments, grading is more consistent from classroom to classroom. The culminating activity, Prairie Day, offers an enjoyable and interesting set of hands-on activities for the children and their parents. Finally, the students have an opportunity to reflect on their experiences in the unit.

However, a more careful look reveals several design problems. Note that the framework for the unit is revealing in and of itself: topic, activities, assessments. The activities are literally and figuratively the center of things! There are no explicitly identified content standards or specific learning goals to guide the work; no big ideas or essential questions to focus teaching; and little in the way of valid assessment evidence of important learnings—just a grading scheme.

Perhaps most illuminating are the actual reflections by students who took part in the unit. Consider a few representative samples:

• "I liked the tin punching because you could make your own design or follow other designs. You can see the sunlight through the holes."

• "I liked the station where you wrote a letter. I liked it because you put wax to seal it."

• "It was fun to design an outfit for myself on the computer."

• "I liked the prairie games. My favorite was the sack racing because I like to jump."

Yes, some of the activities are fun and engaging, and the students and parents love Prairie Day. But what are the enduring understandings to be gained

Figure 11.2

Original Version of a Social Studies Unit

Topic
Westward Movement and Pioneer Life Social Studies—3rd Grade

Activities

1. Read textbook section—"Life on the Prairie." Answer the end-of-chapter questions.

2. Read and discuss *Sarah Plain and Tall*. Complete a word-search puzzle of pioneer vocabulary terms from the story.

3. Create a pioneer-life memory box with artifacts that reflect what life might be like for a child traveling west or living on the prairie.

4. Prairie Day activities: Dress in pioneer clothes and complete the learning stations.

    a. Churn butter

    b. Play 19th-century game

    c. Send letter home with sealing wax

    d. Play "dress the pioneer" computer game

    e. Make a corn husk doll

    f. Quilting

    g. Tin punching

Assessments

1. Quiz on pioneer vocabulary terms from *Sarah Plain and Tall*

2. Answers to end-of-chapter questions on pioneer life

3. Show and tell for memory-box contents

4. Completion of seven learning stations during Pioneer Day

5. Student reflections on the unit

by this three-week tour of pioneer life? What transferable skills have the activities yielded? What evidence has been collected to show what important learning, if any, occurred?

Look what happens when we place the original design in the UbD Template—without adding anything new (see Figure 11.3). Already we see the areas needing improvement more clearly.

Now, let's consider the same three-week unit following revision using backward design and the UbD Template (see Figure 11.4). What do we notice when the unit is rethought using backward design? How does the Template help to shape the same content into a more robust design for learning? Here are some observations:

• Appropriate content standards now focus the unit activities and assessments.

• Big ideas clearly frame the work, exemplified in the Essential Questions: *Why do people move?* (migration); *What is a pioneer?* (conceptual definition); *Why did some pioneers survive and prosper while others did not?* (survival, challenges).

• The assessment tasks are now more authentic and require higher-order knowledge and skills.

• The assessment evidence (Stage 2) is varied and better aligned with the desired results (Stage 1)—an indicator of effective backward planning.

• The readings (fiction and nonfiction), computer simulation, and assignments are more purposefully goal-directed.

• The Prairie Day activities remain, but the experience has been honed to better support the goals of the unit.

Framing the unit in the Template had another beneficial effect. It caused the designers to more easily see that their unit was missing a vital perspective (Facet 4), the viewpoint of the displaced Native Americans. So the unit was further revised (see Figure 11.5).

Let's look at another example—this one from a high school geometry unit. Figures 11.6 and 11.7 show the before and after versions, respectively, in the UbD Template. The first example shows the unit taught and assessed exclusively from the textbook. In the revised version, the designer deliberately planned backward from a set of state content standards. By identifying related Understandings and Essential Questions, supplementing the textbook assessments with two Performance Tasks, and including more interesting, real-world explorations, he was able to greatly improve the coherence and authenticity (hence, meaningfulness) of the unit plan.

Again, note how the UbD Template categories compel the designer to worry about a clearer focus on big ideas and greater alignment of the design elements:

• Big ideas now clearly frame the work, exemplified in the Understandings and two Performance Tasks.

Figure 11.3
Social Studies Unit in the UbD Template

Stage 1—Desired Results

Established Goals: (G)

Topic: Westward Movement and Pioneer Life

Understandings: (U) Students will understand that . . .	**Essential Questions:** (Q)

Students will know . . . (K)	*Students will be able to . . .* (S)
• Factual information about prairie life • Pioneer vocabulary terms • The story *Sarah Plain and Tall*	

Stage 2—Assessment Evidence

Performance Tasks: (T)	**Other Evidence:** (OE)
	a. Show and tell for the memory box and its contents: What would you put in it? Why? b. Quiz on pioneer vocabulary from *Sarah Plain and Tall* c. Answers to factual questions on *Sarah Plain and Tall* and from the textbook chapter d. Written unit reflection

Stage 3—Learning Plan

Learning Activities: (L)

a. Read textbook section "Life on the Prairie." Answer the end-of-chapter questions.

b. Read *Sarah Plain and Tall*. Complete word-search on pioneer vocabulary.

c. Create a pioneer-life trunk with artifacts you might take on a journey to a new life.

d. Prairie Day activities:
   1. Churn butter
   2. Play a 19th-century game
   3. Seal a letter with sealing wax
   4. Play "dress the pioneer" computer game
   5. Make a corn husk doll
   6. Quilting
   7. Tin punching

Figure 11.4
Social Studies Unit After Backward Design

Stage 1—Desired Results

Established Goals:

2D—Explain the lure of the West while comparing the illusions of migrants with the reality of the frontier.
5A—Demonstrate understanding of the movements of large groups of people in the United States now and long ago.

Source: National Standards for United States History

Understandings:
Students will understand that . . .

- Many pioneers had naïve ideas about the opportunities and difficulties of moving West.
- People move for a variety of reasons—for new economic opportunities, greater freedoms, or to flee something.
- Successful pioneers rely on courage, ingenuity, and collaboration to overcome hardships and challenges.

Essential Questions:

- Why do people move? Why did the pioneers leave their homes to head west?
- How do geography and topography affect travel and settlement?
- Why did some pioneers survive and prosper while others did not?
- What is a pioneer? What is "pioneer spirit"?

Students will know . . .

- Key facts about the westward movement and pioneer life on the prairie
- Pioneer vocabulary terms
- Basic geography (i.e., the travel routes of pioneers and location of their settlements)

Students will be able to . . .

- Recognize, define, and use pioneer vocabulary in context
- Use research skills (with guidance) to find out about life on the wagon train and prairie
- Express their findings orally and in writing

Stage 2—Assessment Evidence

Performance Tasks:

- Create a museum display, including artifacts, pictures, and diary entries, depicting a week in the life of a family of settlers living on the prairie. (What common misunderstandings do folks today have about prairie life and westward settlement?)
- Write one letter a day (each representing a month of travel) to a friend "back east" describing your life on the wagon train and the prairie. Tell about your hopes and dreams, then explain what life on the frontier was *really* like. (Students may also draw pictures and explain orally.)

Other Evidence:

- Oral or written response to one of the Essential Questions
- Drawings showing hardships of pioneer life
- Test on facts about westward expansion, life on the prairie, and basic geography
- Using pioneer vocabulary in context
- Explanation of the memory box contents

Stage 3—Learning Plan

Learning Activities:

- Use K-W-L to assess students' prior knowledge and identify learning goals for the unit.
- Revise Prairie Day activities (e.g., substitute *Oregon Trail 2* computer simulation for "dress the pioneer" and ask for journal entries while the simulation is played).
- Include other fictional readings linked to the identified content standards or understandings (e.g., *Little House on the Prairie*, *Butter in the Well*).
- Create a time line map of a pioneer family's journey west.
- Add nonfiction sources to accommodate various reading levels, such as *Life on the Oregon Trail*, *Diaries of Pioneer Women* and *Dakota Dugout*. Guide students in using a variety of resources to research the period.
- Review the scoring rubrics for memory box, museum display, letters, and journals before students begin the performance tasks. Include opportunities for students to study examples of these products.

Figure 11.5
Additional Revisions to Social Studies Unit

Stage 1—Desired Results

Established Goals:

2D—Students analyze cultural interactions among diverse groups (consider multiple perspectives).

Source: National Standards for United States History, p. 108

Understandings:
Students will understand that . . .

- The settlement of the West threatened the lifestyle and culture of Native American tribes living on the plains.

Essential Questions:

- Whose "story" is it?
- Who were the winners and who were the losers in the settlement of the West?
- What happens when cultures collide?

Students will know . . .

- Key factual information about Native American tribes living on the plains and their interactions with the settlers

Students will be able to . . .

Stage 2—Assessment Evidence

Performance Tasks:

- Imagine that you are an elderly tribal member who has witnessed the settlement of the plains by the "pioneers." Tell a story to your 8-year-old granddaughter about the impact of the settlers on your life. (This performance task may be done orally or in writing.)

Other Evidence:

- Quiz on facts about Native American tribes living on the plains

Stage 3—Learning Plan

Learning Activities:

- Stage a simulated meeting of a council of elders of a Native American tribe living on the plains as a means to get students to consider a different perspective.

- Discuss: "What should we do when threatened with relocation—fight, flee, or agree to move (to a reservation)? What effect would each course of action have on our lives?"

Figure 11.6
Geometry Unit Before Backward Design

Stage 1—Desired Results

Established Goals: (G)

Topic: Surface Area and Volume (geometry)

Understandings: (U)
Students will understand that ...

Essential Questions: (Q)

Students will know ... (K)

- How to calculate surface area and volume for various 3-dimensional figures
- Cavalieri's Principle
- Other volume and surface-area formulas

Students will be able to ... (S)

- Use Cavalieri's Principle to compare volumes
- Use other volume and surface-area formulas to compare shapes

Stage 2—Assessment Evidence

Performance Tasks: (T)

Other Evidence: (OE)

a. Odd-numbered problems in full Chapter Review, pp. 516–519

b. Progress on self-test, p. 515

c. Homework: each third question in subchapter reviews and all explorations

Stage 3—Learning Plan

Learning Activities: (L)

- Read Chapter 10 in UCSMP Geometry.
- Exploration 22, p. 482: "Containers holding small amounts can be made to appear to hold more than they do by making them long and thin. Give some examples."
- Exploration 25, p. 509: "Unlike a cone or cylinder, it is impossible to make an accurate two-dimensional net for a sphere. For this reason, maps of earth are distorted. The Mercator projection is one way to show the earth. How is this projection made?"

Figure 11.7
Geometry Unit After Backward Design

Stage 1—Desired Results

Established Goals:

IL MATH 7C3b, 4b: Use models and formulas to find surface areas and volumes.
IL MATH 9A: Construct models in 2D/3D; make perspective drawings.

Source: Illinois Mathematics Standards

Understandings:
Students will understand that...

- The adaptation of mathematical models and ideas to human problems requires careful judgment and sensitivity to impact.
- Mapping three dimensions onto two (or two onto three) may introduce distortions.
- Sometimes the best mathematical answer is not the best solution to real-world problems.

Essential Questions:

- How well can pure mathematics model messy, real-world situations?
- When is the best mathematical answer not the best solution to a problem?

Students will know...

- Formulas for calculating surface area and volume
- Cavalieri's Principle

Students will be able to...

- Calculate surface area and volume for various 3-dimensional figures
- Use Cavalieri's Principle to compare volumes

Stage 2—Assessment Evidence

Performance Tasks:

- Packaging problem: What is the ideal container for shipping bulk quantities of M&M's packages cost-effectively to stores? (Note: the "best" mathematical answer—a sphere—is not the best solution to this problem.)
- As a consultant to the United Nations, propose the least controversial 2-dimensional map of the world. Explain your mathematical reasoning.

Other Evidence:

a. Odd-numbered problems in full Chapter Review, pp. 516–519

b. Progress on self-test, p. 515

c. Homework: each third question in subchapter reviews and all explorations

Stage 3—Learning Plan

Learning Activities:

- Investigate the relationship of surface areas and volume of various containers (e.g., tuna fish cans, cereal boxes, Pringles, candy packages).

- Investigate different map projections to determine their mathematical accuracy (i.e., degree of distortion).

a. Read Chapter 10 in UCSMP Geometry

b. Exploration 22, p. 504

c. Exploration 22, p. 482

d. Exploration 25, p. 509

- The Essential Questions promote mathematical reasoning and are transferable to other mathematics units.
- The same knowledge and skill remain as the core content, but they are now embedded in a more meaningful set of issues related to packaging and map-making.
- The textbook serves as a resource, but not the syllabus. The textbook problems remain in the assessment but are properly subordinated to the complex Performance Tasks and the big ideas those tasks embody.

The UbD Template helps us considerably if we use it as a guide for self-assessment of our work. It clarifies and sharpens our purposes, helps us set more meaningful priorities and make them clear to learners. The result is a more powerful and coherent approach with the "same" content.

Standards, not recipes

Some readers and workshop participants become frustrated because we do not present a step-by-step recipe for unit design and redesign that they can follow. Alas, we firmly believe that no such recipe exists. We tried to develop flowcharts for the task, but the charts grew incomprehensible, given all the possible if/then segments! We think that unit design is more like graphic design or sculpture than like following a cookbook recipe. Each design is different and must reflect the interests, talents, style, and resources of the designer.

The authors of a recent book on task analysis in instructional design make the problem clear:

Instructional design is replete with uncertain knowledge and multiple interpretations. So is task analysis. Not every aspect of human thought and behavior can be identified or articulated. How can we reconcile this discrepancy? We cannot, so live with it. That is the nature of the design process. (Jonassen, Tessmer, & Hannum, 1999, p. 5)

Too much reliance on a recipe leads to other problems. It can close off thoughtful responsiveness of the teacher-designer—empathy!—in the false belief that any well-thought-out plan must, of necessity, work, and if it doesn't, it must be the students' fault. Or we run the risk of compromising the very thing we are trying to design: "If we attempted to eliminate all ambiguity in task analysis, we would have to over-proceduralize a complex set of decisions—to develop a cookbook . . . the design process is largely dependent upon the reasoning ability of the designer. (Jonassen, Tessmer, & Hannum, 1999, p. 5)

For that matter, real cooking involves moving beyond recipes, too:

Recipes, which began as such useful things, have become tyrants, leaving even the most well-meaning cook unsure of his own instincts. A slavish devotion to recipes robs people of the kind of experiential knowledge that seeps into the brain. . . . Most chefs are not fettered by formula; they've cooked enough to trust their taste. Today that is the most valuable lesson a chef can teach a cook. (O'Neill, 1996, p. 52)

Rather, what designers need to become accustomed to is the back-and-forth rhythm between the creative brainstorming and trying out of ideas, and the careful and critical testing of the emerging design against the design standards. As the description of the various entry points earlier in the chapter suggests, it doesn't matter too much where you start; it matters more that you end up with a design that meets the standards. That goal makes seeking feedback (early and often) about your emerging design against the standards of design a key part of the process. Another reason this is a useful experience for the teacher-designer is that it concretely illustrates why ongoing assessment is vital to performance success.

The unavoidable dilemmas in design

The before-and-after examples from the 3rd grade social studies unit and the high school geometry unit help to show what the process entails. But, like weight-loss commercials that feature such comparisons, the examples may, ironically, serve only to bring gnawing worries to the surface. How do we design or redesign to focus on big ideas without losing sight of content? How feasible are such units, given the time we have available for the topic, given all our other obligations? How do we determine whether the blueprint is a good one, capable of being turned into effective learning, or whether it is an unrealistic dream? How easy is it to reconcile the architect's vision with the reality of available resources, the skill of the students who do the "construction," and the "building code" of state standards?

Such concerns are reasonable. In fact, it's worth emphasizing that the tensions within designs are inherent and inevitable, whether in home building or unit design. We think it imperative that teachers be helped to express and explore such worries because of the *unavoidable dilemmas* involved in instructional planning and curriculum design. The work is not merely demanding, but also inherently problematic. It always has been! How can we be sure that the understandings sought will be accessible to all students? How much time and energy can we afford to give to complex performance tasks or difficult ideas? How can we accommodate the various achievement levels, interests, and learning styles of the students we teach? *Every* design requires compromise; we always have to weigh pros and cons.

We use the word *dilemma* deliberately, therefore. Not only must we think through all the elements of design in a thoughtful way; we also have to deal with inherent tensions within any design if we are to accomplish our goals. Many design challenges involve competing—even conflicting—elements; for example, a big idea but limited time in which to address it, or the desire for a complex application as the basis for valid assessment but the lack of reliability of a single performance. You don't "solve" these problems; you carefully negotiate them. It is the rare design that leaves the designer completely satisfied, because compromises are inevitable.

The following is a catalog of key dilemmas facing all designers of learning for understanding, with some final thoughts on how to weigh the options.

- *Big ideas and transfer versus specific knowledge and skills.* How do we balance the goals of "understanding" with "facts" and "skill"? How do we focus the work on big ideas without making the work too philosophical or abstract, leaving students without essential knowledge and know-how? On the other hand, how do we avoid the all-too-frequent focus on discrete information and isolated skills that leaves students with little meaningful learning and limited ability to apply what they have learned?

- *Complex, realistic, and messy performance versus efficient and sound tests.* When should we strive for contextual realism in assessment and when should we strive for the obvious efficiency of traditional (indirect) testing? Authentic application is clearly a good thing, but it is difficult and time-consuming to implement easily and to evaluate precisely. However, traditional tests of knowledge and skill, although easy to design and grade, often yield invalid results and unhelpful feedback about what learners actually understand. How, then, do we make assessment rich and educative while also feasible and efficient?

- *Teacher control versus learner control of the work.* When is it the expert's job to frame the issues and guide the learning? When is it wise, by contrast, to enable students to pursue *their* questions, interests, and approaches? When should our understandings drive the design and the instruction? When should we strive to help students come to their own understandings?

- *Direct versus constructivist approaches.* When does direct instruction help learning and when does it impede it? When does efficiency demand explicit teaching, and when should we teach more inductively? (Similarly, in training teachers, when should new teachers be creative as designers, and when is it wiser to have teachers work from expert designs to avoid reinventing the wheel?) More generally, when *must* the work involve constructivist uncoverage and the inevitably messy and personalized "construction of meaning" required if understanding is to occur, and when is direct instruction just more efficient?

- *Depth versus breadth of knowledge.* How do we balance the desire to provide an in-depth and thorough understanding against the reality of what is feasible, given all the demands and constraints teachers face? When are we obligated to provide a broad survey of material, exposing students to a wide array of information and ideas? When do we perform a greater service by limiting breadth, delving more deeply into fewer subjects, in the service of real understanding? Similarly, when is it wise pedagogy to design interdisciplinary work around a few big ideas, and when does such work unwittingly result in superficial learning by trying to do too much in too little time?

- *Comfort and a feeling of competence versus a real challenge.* How do we strike the right balance between an important "stretch" for students and the need for a comfortable learning environment? When should we provide a low-stress context for learners to feel that they can take risks and still be successful, and when do we appropriately challenge students (and even cause them stress) in the service of powerful new learning? How, for example, should we construct learning around essential questions, knowing that they may provoke student irritation and confusion? When and how should we use complex performance tasks even though they may frustrate less able or easily defeated learners?

• *Uniform versus personalized work and expectations.* We typically teach classes with students who differ in prior knowledge, achievement levels, work habits, interests, and learning styles. How should we manage the competing demands? How should we design for and instruct a large group efficiently and effectively, without losing learners along the way? How do we simultaneously hold appropriately different expectations of understanding without lowering standards or treating some students as second-class citizens? How can we personalize the work without driving ourselves crazy and losing focus? How do we know when differentiation is appropriate in teaching for understanding and when it is counterproductive?

• *Effective versus merely engaging.* The work we provide by design should be interesting and engaging, but those criteria are not sufficient. The design must address the goals and standards efficiently and effectively. How do we hook learners but also hold them to perform to standard? How do we make the work minds-on, not merely hands-on? How can we keep sight of our responsibilities as teacher and assessor without failing in our role as provider of interesting work—and vice versa? How do we avoid aimless (yet fun) activities without going to the other extreme of making the work boring and ineffective?

• *Simplified versus simplistic.* How do we make big ideas accessible to all learners without dumbing down those ideas? How do we get at the richness and complexity of genuine intellectual questions and issues without losing students or focus? How do we simplify a complex subject without being so simplistic we cut off future inquiry and discussion? How do we ensure developmental appropriateness without rendering the work vapid?

• *A well-crafted plan versus appropriate flexibility and open-endedness.* Achieving goals requires a carefully thought-out design, but we can usually achieve our goals only by deviating from the plan, in response to the considerable feedback and teachable moments that will occur in class. How do we avoid being too rigid and thus ultimately ineffective? On the other hand, how do we avoid losing sight of our goals in response to every student reaction or question? How do we balance our design goals with the serendipity of opportunities for learning?

• *A great individual unit versus larger goals and other designs.* How can each unit have a natural flow, standing on its own as an elegant and logical work of design, while honoring all local program goals and content standards that frame our obligations? How do we use textbooks and work in all required content without subverting the principles of good design? How do we deal with pressures to raise test scores while teaching for understanding? How do we develop a logical learning plan, while mindful of all the differing, and perhaps competing, demands we face?

Humble advice on grappling with these dilemmas

We offer no rule or set of prescriptions on how to address each particular dilemma. As we said earlier, you don't "solve" a dilemma; you balance the competing elements in each design as best you can. But we can offer a general piece of advice for learning how these dilemmas work and how they can be better negotiated. The advice is this: Aggressively seek feedback as you work. As we also noted earlier, the key to excellent design is to try something, see how it works, and make adjustments—namely, get feedback against your desired results (as well as feedback against design standards).

In any field, the value of regular feedback is recognized as a key to continuous improvement. In education, the benefit of the "design, try, get feedback, adjust" approach was formally recognized in a major study of college teaching:

> *We asked faculty members and students what single change would most improve their current teaching and learning. Two ideas from faculty and students swamped all others. One is the importance of enhancing students' awareness of "the big picture," the "point of it all," and not just the details of a particular topic. The second is the importance of helpful and regular feedback from students so a professor can make mid-course corrections. (Light, 1990, p. 66)*

Notice how both ideas are central to UbD: a focus on big ideas, and the need for *everyone* (learner, teacher, curriculum designer) to rethink in response to feedback.

We needn't make the process of getting feedback too formal or demanding, and we must not confuse it with official course evaluations. The goal is frequent, timely, helpful, and nonintrusive feedback as to how the design is working from the learner's perspective. Consider the following two questions for gathering ongoing feedback:

- What worked for you this week? Say why, briefly.
- What didn't work? Say why, briefly.

A former colleague of one of us asked this pair of questions to students in all of his classes every Friday, handing out index cards for the students' responses (he saved the results all year). Note the questions: They concern *what works* as opposed to what the students did or did not like. The answers are typically much more helpful to the teacher-designer because they make clear that there is "nothing personal" in the anonymous feedback (which will make some students less fearful and more honest in their responses).

A more thorough inquiry could be done using survey questions linked specifically to the dilemmas. Such an inquiry could be implemented not only by individuals but also by a study group of teachers, by grade-level teams, by departments, or schoolwide, with survey results shared at faculty meetings and in electronic or written communication. Figure 11.8 provides an example of a format that can be used for this type of inquiry.

Figure 11.8
Weekly Feedback Form

What Worked? What Didn't?

1. What was the most interesting thing we did in class this week? What made it so interesting?

2. What was the most boring thing we did in class this week? What made it so boring?

3. What worked the best for you this week in this class? In other words, what specific activity, lesson, technique, or tool helped you learn the most? Why?

4. What didn't work for you this week? What activity, assignment, or lesson was the most confusing or unhelpful? Why?

5. Please answer Yes or No to the statements below. Please explain any No response.

	Yes	No
The work was focused on big ideas, not just unconnected little facts and skills. We were learning important things.		
I found the work thought-provoking and interesting.		
I was very clear on what the goals of the unit were. We were shown what was important, what was high-quality work, what our job was, and what the purpose of the unit was.		
We were given enough choice or freedom in how to go about achieving the goals.		
The assessments were just right. What we were asked to do was a "fair test" of our learning.		

Feedback improves *everyone's* performance. Yet we have noted with some sadness that few teachers voluntarily solicit ongoing feedback, whether from students, peers, supervisors, parents, or outside experts. We empathize with the fear. However, the fear is counterproductive to becoming more effective. The good news is that many educators tell us that being enticed into peer review and self-assessment against the UbD Design Standards has been one of the most rewarding and energizing experiences of their careers. How could it not be, really? For once, you can talk about your struggles in the face of real dilemmas and get helpful feedback and advice from fellow professionals. Any healthy and effective learning organization will make such collegial collaboration on design, with feedback against design standards, a regular part of the job, with training and time allocated to it. Figure 11.9 illustrates how ongoing cycles of feedback fit into the drafting and implementing aspects of Understanding by Design.

■ MISCONCEPTION ALERT!

"All this planning and design work will reduce my spontaneity and ability to respond to the teachable moment," you may say. Not so, we think. In fact, we believe the opposite is true. Keeping clear goals and core performances sharply in focus heightens our attentiveness to purposeful, teachable moments.

Even the best teachers sometimes get so wrapped up in their excellent plan that they do not hear, or give short shrift to, comments that threaten the flow. But then they have lost sight of their true goal—*causing learning* as opposed to *teaching*. On the other hand, many teachers rationalize their propensity to wing it by arguing that "going with the flow" is more student centered and obviates the need for thorough planning. Yet in such cases we risk being a passive victim of whatever students do or do not bring up. That's "understanding by good fortune," not by design.

Figure 11.9
Unit Design Cycles

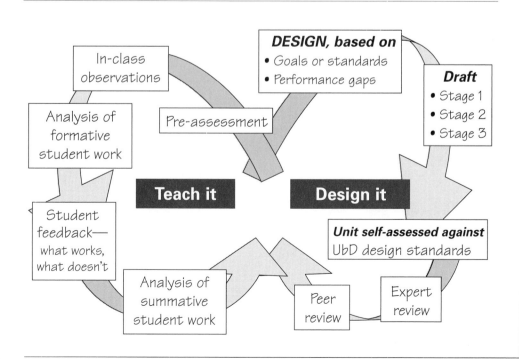

Making adjustments

As Figure 11.9 suggests, there is more to design than dreaming up units while on our own, away from the class and our colleagues. We need feedback at various phases of research and development—from self-assessment, from peers, from expert reviewers, from students, from our own observations about what is and isn't working. Furthermore, we aren't finished with our design until we factor in the particular students whom we will be teaching. A diagnostic pre-assessment of their needs, abilities, and interests is a crucial part of the most successful work. We cannot truly honor the *T* in WHERETO (Tailor the work; i.e., personalize and perhaps differentiate the work) unless we make last-minute adjustments to our units, based on who the learners are and our recent history with them. In addition, we will need to adjust the design in light of misunderstandings, unanticipated rough spots, and serendipitous opportunities that arise, so that we can better meet our goals. Figure 11.10 suggests the steps in an adjustment process, based on diagnostic and formative feedback.

In sum, Pasteur's famous aphorism applies here: Fortune favors the prepared mind. The truly appropriate teachable moment is more visible and comes more frequently to the teacher-designer who has carefully thought through her goals and how to achieve them. And the constant solicitation of feedback, given the inherent dilemmas, can only improve a design and the results that provide its purpose.

Having considered the design process and its inherent dilemmas, we can now apply what we have considered thus far to the larger design questions. Given that units are only the building blocks, what should the whole edifice look like? How should unit design be informed by the overarching ideas, tasks, and standards that must inevitably influence unit design work? We now turn to those questions.

Figure 11.10
Design and Feedback Chart

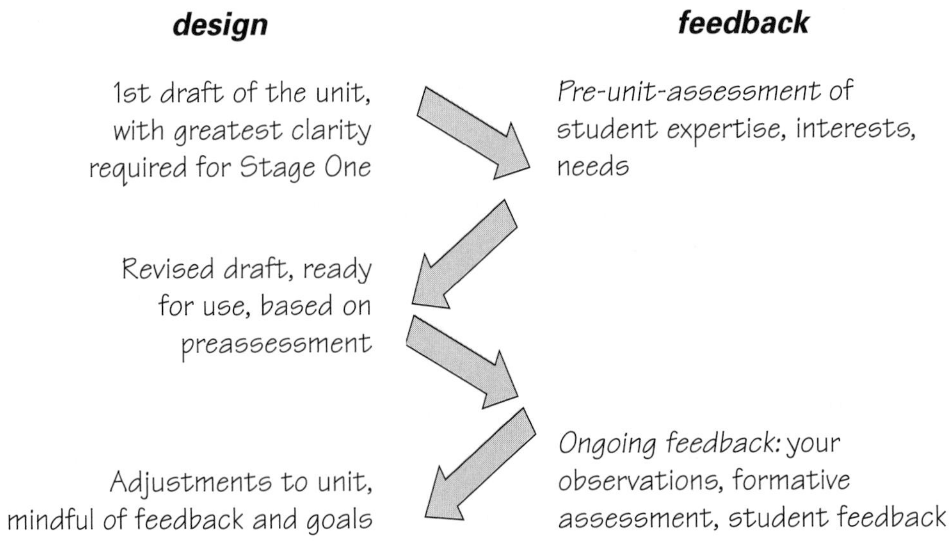

design

1st draft of the unit, with greatest clarity required for Stage One

Revised draft, ready for use, based on preassessment

Adjustments to unit, mindful of feedback and goals

feedback

Pre-unit-assessment of student expertise, interests, needs

Ongoing feedback: your observations, formative assessment, student feedback

Chapter 12

The Big Picture:
UbD as Curriculum Framework

We might ask, as a criterion for any subject taught . . . whether, when fully
developed, it is worth an adult's knowing, and whether having known it as a
child makes a person a better adult. If the answer to both questions is
negative or ambiguous, then the material is cluttering the curriculum.
—Jerome Bruner, *The Process of Education,* 1960, p. 52

Unless a given experience leads out into a field previously unfamiliar, no
problems arise, while problems are the stimulus to thinking. . . . The new facts
and new ideas thus obtained become the ground for further experiences in
which new problems are presented. The process is a continuous spiral.
—John Dewey, *Experience and Education,* 1938, pp. 82, 87

Until now, we have concentrated the UbD process on unit design. This was
sensible for a variety of reasons. The unit is a comfortable design focus for
teachers—not so small that it leads to isolated lessons and overly discrete
learnings, yet not so large that it seems overwhelming and too broad to guide
day-to-day teaching.

However, many of you have probably found our approach illogical (maybe
even truly backward!) given that any unit has to fit into an earlier course of
study or yearlong grade-level curriculum, and an even larger program framework. How, then, should the big picture, the "macro" curriculum, be conceived
and implemented to fully reflect backward planning with an emphasis on
understanding?

A full account of the design of a systemic, multiyear curriculum is beyond
the scope of this book. We focus instead on the question that arises from individual teacher units: What design work at the macro level will render unit
design more efficient, coherent, and effective? Our predictable answer: the
design of *course* syllabi and *program* frameworks using backward design and
the same key elements found on the UbD unit template. Specifically, we advocate that programs and courses be conceived and framed in terms of *essential
questions, enduring understandings,* key *performance tasks,* and *rubrics.* These

overarching elements thus serve as a blueprint for all units and the connections between them.

How big is big?

You may have been understandably frustrated a bit by the fact that in earlier chapters we never specified the ideal scope of questions and understandings, or how to more sharply distinguish overarching from topical elements. We will now say that the question "How 'big' should a 'big idea' be?" cannot be answered in isolation from course and program goals. Some ideas *are* clearly "bigger" than others—that is, conceptually more general, with greater transferability and impact. Ideas with that great a reach should anchor coursework and entire programs. No single unit could possibly do justice to the most complex ideas.

So agreeing on the core ideas and assessment tasks—whether this is done by district curriculum teams or school departmental and grade-level teams—significantly lightens the unit-designer's load. We also thereby rid the curriculum of the incoherence that would result from allowing units to be designed in isolation. Figure 12.1 illustrates our UbD macro view.

Figure 12.2 provides an illustration of one district's work to frame its year-long U.S. history syllabus around big ideas and essential questions. Individual units were then constructed under this comprehensive umbrella.

Essential questions as course and program foundations

> The most significant [impact] is probably the district's model for course outlines and curriculum maps. . . . We are mapping all curricula with the enduring understandings and essential questions as a key component.
>
> —Dorothy Katauskas, Assistant to the Superintendent,
> New Hope-Solebury, Pennsylvania

The overarching and recursive nature of essential questions makes them ideally suited to framing the macro curriculum of programs and courses. By their nature, essential questions focus on big ideas that are typically not unit-specific. They can be properly addressed only across many units and, in some cases, years of study. Practically speaking, that means essential questions can be used to provide the backbone of courses and programs into which individual units fit. The following examples illustrate how the use of essential questions to frame the entire curriculum makes the work of unit design easier and more coherent for students.

Consider the following set of essential questions, posed by two history scholars (Burns & Morris, 1986) as a way of understanding the U.S. Constitution.

Figure 12.1
A UbD Curriculum Framework: Macro and Micro

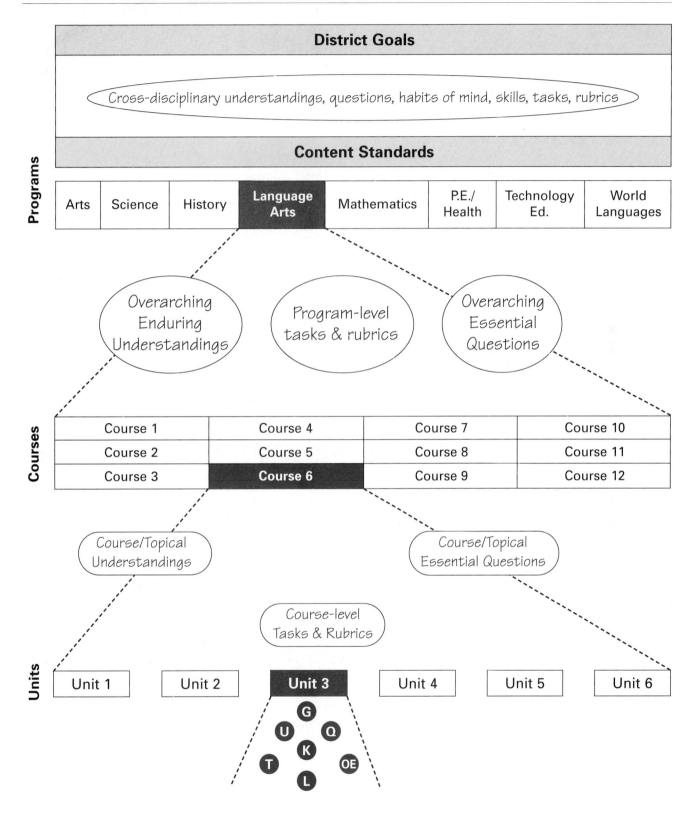

Figure 12.2
A Sample UbD Curriculum Plan: Stage 1

7th Grade United States History

Course Understandings	Course Essential Questions	Course Skills
Students will understand that . . .	1. Are we becoming the nation we set out to be?	The student will develop skills for historical and geographical analysis, including the ability to

Course Understandings

Students will understand that . . .

- The preambles to the Declaration of Independence and the Constitution establish the ideal for why we need government—and principles that should guide the government's decision making—providing a framework by which we can evaluate our nation's progress and suggest means for improvement.

- Progress often comes at a price—the extent of which allows history to judge its success.

- Specific individuals, even outside of elected leaders, can have a profound impact on history.

- America abandoned its isolationist policy as economic and geopolitical interests began to change, becoming the dominant world power, with new challenges and responsibilities.

- To promote the general welfare, the government has attempted to balance the need to let the market operate freely with the need to regulate in order to safeguard public interests.

- Geography continues to influence the economic, political, and social development of our nation.

- Throughout American history, wartime fears and perceived threats to security have led to the denial of certain civil liberties.

- American culture reflects the events of the day and shapes how Americans perceive themselves.

- Ratification of the Constitution did not end the debate on governmental power; rather, economic, regional, social, and ideological tensions that emerged and continue to emerge further debates over the meaning of the Constitution and the proper balance between federal and state power.

- The government and public commitment to civil and equal rights has advanced.

Course Essential Questions

1. Are we becoming the nation we set out to be?

- What price progress?
- How do individuals make a difference?
- How did the United States become the world power?
- What issues determine our involvement in foreign affairs?
- Why did the United States abandon its traditional isolationist foreign policy?
- Should commitment to the ideals in the Constitution extend beyond our borders?
- What is the government's responsibility to promote the general welfare?
- Should the government be more hands-on or hands-off with regard to the economy?
- How does geography influence history?
- Historically, why is there a struggle between security and liberty?
- How has the cultural identity of America changed over time?
- How has the struggle between states' rights and federal power played out over time?
- How has the government's commitment to "establish justice" changed over time?
- How has the definition of "justice" changed historically to become more inclusive?

Course Skills

The student will develop skills for historical and geographical analysis, including the ability to

- Identify, examine, and interpret primary and secondary source documents to increase understanding of events and life in U.S. history;
- Make connections between the past and the present;
- Sequence significant events in United States history from Constitutional times to present;
- Interpret ideas and events from different historical perspectives;
- Evaluate and discuss issues orally and in writing;
- Create and explain maps, diagrams, tables, charts, and graphs;
- Analyze and interpret maps to explain relationships among landforms, water features, climatic characteristics, and historical events.
- Analyze political cartoons, political advertisements, pictures, and other graphic media;
- Distinguish between relevant and irrelevant information;
- Review information for accuracy, separating fact from opinion;
- Identify a problem and recommend solutions;
- Select and defend positions in writing, discussion, and debate.

Mark Wise and the Middle School Social Studies Team, West Windsor–Plainsboro, New Jersey

Think of how any course in U.S. history could address these questions through the specifics of each unit:

Too much—or too little—national power? *Are the limits placed on the federal government's powers by the Constitution realistic and enforceable?*

Does federalism work? *Is the Constitution maintaining an efficient and realistic balance between national and state power?*

Is the judicial branch too powerful? *Are the courts exercising their powers appropriately as interpreters of the Constitution and shapers of public policy?*

Can liberty and security be balanced? *How can republican government provide for the national security without endangering civil liberties?*

What do we mean by "All men created equal"? *What kinds of equality are and should be protected by the Constitution and by what means?*

Are the rights of women and minorities adequately safeguarded?

Does the President possess adequate—or too much—power over war-making and foreign policy?

Are there too many Constitutional checks and balances? *Does the separation of powers between the three branches of government create a deadlock in governance?*

Here are excerpts from two syllabi for college courses, the first on business law and the second on U.S. history, revised to reflect UbD thinking:

Students will focus on four questions during this class:

1. Why does the government regulate certain activities? Should it?

2. Who are the actors involved in governmental policymaking and what power base are they operating from?

3. How is governmental regulation enforced?

4. To what extent do laws and judicial opinions interpreting laws reflect the policy underlying governmental regulation?

Everything we do in this course addresses one or more of the following questions:

1. What is the story of U.S. history?

2. How do historians construct and evaluate the stories they tell?

3. Why study history?

Any course and program of study may be similarly organized. Here is a set of overarching questions for use in framing a program in art:

• In what ways do artists influence society? In what ways does society influence artists?

• What makes art "great"? What is beauty? What is taste? Are they related? Do they matter?

• How do different conceptions of beauty influence the work?

• How do artists from different eras present similar themes? How does art change era by era? How and why do artists choose tools, techniques, and materials to express their ideas?

- What motivates artists? How and where do artists get their ideas? Is the artistic process primarily intuitive? Are artists made or born? Does an artist know, or need to know? Does the answer matter?

- How can we "read" a work of art? Can art be meaningfully explained? Critiqued? Does art need to be explained and critiqued, or is it ruined by trying?

- Do artists have a responsibility to their audiences or to society?

- Do the arts have rules? Who should make them?

- Should we ever censure or restrict artistic expression?

And here is a set of overarching questions for use in framing a mathematics program:

- What kind of problem is it? What should we do when we're stuck? How do you know if you're done? What do the best problem solvers do? How might we show . . . ? In what other ways (how else)? How do we best represent the part/whole relationship? The pattern? The sequence?

- What is a number? Can everything be quantified? What couldn't we do if we didn't have or couldn't use numbers? Why do we have negative numbers? Irrational numbers? Imaginary numbers?

- What is the pattern here? How confident are we? How do we find patterns? What can patterns reveal? How can they mislead?

- What are the strengths and limits of mathematical modeling? In what ways does a model illuminate and in what ways does it distort? How can numbers (data) lie or mislead? When might a correct answer not be the best solution to the problem?

- How does what we measure influence how we measure? How does how we measure influence what we conclude? When is estimation better than counting and when is it not? When is simplification helpful? Harmful? When should we sample? When shouldn't we? How much or how many (of a sample) is enough?

- How sure are you? What's the likely margin of error? How accurate (precise) is it? How accurate (precise) does this need to be? What is proof? Do I have one?

Typical curriculum frameworks emphasize lists of discrete content knowledge and skills. This has the effect of subtly encouraging teachers to "cover" things in a mechanistic and overly didactic way that we know is less engaging, coherent, and effective. Framing curriculum around essential questions, as opposed to content, makes connective, thought-provoking, and recurring inquiries more appropriately central to the learning experience. As Mark Wise, the social studies supervisor who led the development of the history framework presented in Figure 12.2, puts it, "UbD is a philosophy for teaching and learning. Once you 'get it,' it is very difficult to go back to creating disconnected activities or covering facts without a broader context."

Cross-disciplinary questions

As many workshop participants have noted, essential questions often jump curricular boundaries, even when cross-disciplinary design is not the aim. Take two of the questions from the previous lists: What's the pattern? Is the process primarily intuitive? The questions relate to both mathematical problem solving *and* artistic expression. This is one of the great virtues of framing curriculum around questions as opposed to content. Good questions make it more likely that the work will yield interesting and fruitful connections and meanings.

Consider essential questions, then, at an even higher level of generality. Central Park East Secondary School in New York, founded by MacArthur Fellow Deborah Meier, builds its entire curriculum around a set of essential questions cast as key "habits of mind" for students to internalize:

In every class and every subject, students will learn to ask and to answer these questions:

- *From whose viewpoint are we seeing or reading or hearing? From what angle or perspective?*
- *How do we know when we know? What's the evidence, and how reliable is it?*
- *How are things, events or people connected to each other? What is the cause and what is the effect? How do they fit together?*
- *What's new and what's old? Have we run across this idea before?*
- *So what? Why does it matter? What does it all mean?*

In *The Basic School,* Ernest Boyer, former president of the Carnegie Institute for the Advancement of Teaching, proposed an education built upon a foundation of cross-disciplinary "core commonalities" and companion essential questions. Here is one example with a set of accompanying questions, meant to be explored across all the elementary and middle school grades:

Everyone holds membership in a variety of groups.

- *Which groups did I join at birth?*
- *Which groups do I belong to?*
- *Why do people join groups?*
- *Can I leave a group? (1995, p. 90)*

Yet another example comes from the International Baccalaureate Primary Years Program (PYP). Every unit in any IB PYP program must address one or more of the following essential questions:

- What is it like?
- How does it work?
- Why is it the way it is?
- How is it changing?

- How is it connected to other things?
- What are the points of view?
- What is our responsibility?
- How do we know?

Frameworks built around big ideas and essential questions need not be restricted to the humanities or other content-focused subjects. Figure 12.3 is an example of an entire physical education curriculum framed around UbD elements.

Framing curriculum by performance tasks

As we have stressed, robust evidence of student achievement requires more than a single snapshot such as that provided by a once-a-year state test. And understanding requires complex tasks providing evidence of the ability to transfer. Thus, the local assessment plan has to involve more high-quality, application-focused performance tasks constructed around the six facets. Yet most curriculum frameworks ignore or give short shrift to assessments, even though specificity about the curriculum requires clarity about the performance targets that embody its goals—the assessments and rubrics.

A different way to frame the macro curriculum, then, is to frame it via—the assessments! What are the key performance types or genres that a student should have to master? Figure 12.4 provides an example from Greece, New York, where the secondary English/language arts teachers have agreed on a districtwide set of quarterly writing assessments judged by common rubrics. Each student completes two writing tasks for each genre shown in the figure. A districtwide prompt is used for one task for each genre at each grade. This coordinated focus on common assessments has brought greater coherence to the *instructional* program for writing, resulting in improved student performance.

Alverno College has designed its entire curriculum this way for more than 25 years. Goals are framed for subject areas and across disciplines in eight areas of general competence. Professors serve dual roles. In addition to designing and teaching courses in their subject, they serve on committees to design assessments for the eight areas of competence. This has two powerful benefits. Each professor learns to think in bigger terms about her role in relation to the overall mission, and the competencies are not allowed to fall through the cracks of typical subject-focused course design.

A benefit of framing curricula around essential questions is that the questions naturally suggest the right kinds of higher-order assessment tasks to anchor local curriculum. A practical strategy for drafting the most appropriate performance assessments is to imagine that the essential questions provide the general "specs" for any particular assessment. Then, as we saw in the two college examples from business law and U.S. history, we can say upfront and throughout, to students of any age, "By the end of this course, we will have considered these questions from various points of view, and you will address

Figure 12.3
A Physical Education Curriculum Framed Around UbD

Big Ideas	Enduring Understanding	Essential Questions	Standards
Leadership	One person can make a difference.	Who has the power and how do they keep it?	4b, 4c, 4d, 4e, 5c, 5d, 6b
Communication	Words are powerful. Speak gently about yourself.	When should you open your mouth?	4b, 4d, 4e, 5c, 6a, 6b
Teamwork	Not everyone thinks or plays like you.	When is there an "I" in TEAM? When do we win the battle and lose the war?	4b, 4c, 4d, 5c, 5d, 6a, 6b
Exploration	Risk taking has unexpected consequences.	What are the potential pitfalls? Can you handle them?	1d, 5a, 6c, 6d
Strategy	Where you are going is more important than how you get there.	What's the plan? How is it going for you?	2b, 2c, 2d
Rules	Rules are restrictions and opportunities.	How do rules change the way you play?	1b, 1c, 2a, 4a
Fitness	Fitness is a process, not a product.	What does a fit person look like?	3a–f
Wellness	You must prepare to prevent.	Are you failing your body? Is your body failing you?	Health: Injury and Disease Prevention Physical Education: 3d, 3e
Sportsmanship	It's not what you do, but HOW you do it.	What makes a game worth playing?	4a, 4b, 4d, 4e, 5c, 5d, 6b
Competition	Every match can make you stronger.	How does competition motivate you? When does it cross the line?	1a, 4b, 4e, 5b, 5d, 6c
Technique	Deliberately first. Naturally second.	When will you get it? What do you do until then?	1 a–d, 2 a–d

them in various kinds of projects and performance—so keep them constantly in mind."

If essential questions seem a bit too conceptual or philosophical for courses focused primarily on skills, simply identify questions or problems related to key performance challenges that require the intelligent use of those skills. In mathematics, two questions—"So what's the pattern?" and "How should this be modeled?"—can frame an entire curriculum *if* we also provide students with a carefully designed set of problems that suit the questions and require the desired skills. For example, the mathematics equivalent to the English/language

Figure 12.4
A Districtwide Assessment Plan for Writing

Grade	Expository	Persuasive	Literary Analysis	Creative/Expressive
6	Research report	Position paper	Literary essay on setting or conflict	Original myth
7	Autobiography	Policy evaluation	Literary essay on character	Personal writing
8	Research report	Problem/solution essay	Literary essay on symbolism	Narrative fiction
9	Cause/effect essay	Editorial	Analysis of multiple literary elements	Poetry
10	Research report	Social issue essay	Critical lens essay	Historical persona
11	Definition essay	Argumentative essay	Comparative genre essay	Parody/satire
12	Research paper	Position paper	Response to literary criticism	Irony

Adapted from Department of Curriculum and Instruction, Greece Central School District, Greece, NY

arts genres shown in Figure 12.4 would involve presenting students with the same or similar problems, based on the same *messy* data set, each year. Or the same basic problem could require (and support) answers across various levels of math sophistication, as suggested, for example, by a question such as "What's the ideal package for shipping M&M's in bulk?" Such challenges also enable us to differentiate among students much more than is now possible using assessment items based on discrete facts and skills.

Framing courses through strategy-flexible assessment tasks can be especially helpful when dealing with content-packed courses such as history. Here is an example designed to meet New York state standards in World History:

1. Design a tour of the world's most holy sites, including accurate maps; a guidebook with descriptions of local norms, customs, and etiquette for visiting pilgrims; an analysis of the most cost-effective routes and means of transportation; a short history of the major sites, made interesting to your peers; and an annotated bibliography (recommended readings for other students).

2. Write a Bill of Rights for use in Afghanistan, Iraq, and emerging democracies. Refer to past attempts (e.g., U.S. Bill of Rights, UN resolutions, World Court) and their strengths and weaknesses, and obtain signatures from a diverse group of peers and adults to simulate the need for consensus.

3. Prepare a report on Latin America for the Secretary of State. Choose a Latin American country and provide policy analysis and a background report. What should be our current policy, and how effective has recent policy with that country been?

4. Collect and analyze media reports from the Internet on other countries' views of U.S. policies in the Middle East. Put together a "briefing book" of photo-copied press clips for the President, with your commentary on the accuracy and impact of those reports. Produce a QuickTime video of various newscasts summarizing world reaction to a recent U.S. policy decision related to the Middle East.

5. Produce an oral history, with PowerPoint graphics, to highlight the immigrant nature of the United States, the reasons why people from all over the world move here, and the reasons why people now seek to limit or restrict immigration. Interview recent U.S. immigrants and record their reasons for leaving their home country and coming here. Interview people in favor of restricting immigration and ask them about how their families came to America. What do they think is the same and what is different now?

6. Design a trade show exhibit demonstrating the connections between a European country's geography and economy, and the impact of its membership in the new European Economic Union.

7. Write and deliver on videotape a speech by a visiting head of an African country about the history of U.S.-Africa relations and a response by the U.S. Secretary of State.

8. Take part in a formal debate on a controversial issue of global significance, such as UN aid to Iraq, the U.S. role in the Middle East, or global warming.

9. Organize a model UN by forming groups of two to three students, each representing a country, and try to pass a Security Council resolution on terrorism.

10. Provide the Foreign Relations Committee with a briefing on the current state of Russia, the last century of U.S.-Russia relations, and future worries and possibilities. Is Russia a friend or foe?

11. Prepare a report on India and outsourcing. To what extent is the global economy a good thing for the United States? For India? For India's neighbors?

From tasks to rubrics

The development of core performance tasks naturally leads to the selection or design of companion scoring rubrics. Imagine the power of a system built around 30 rubrics that are used consistently throughout a district or school by teachers *and* students. For example, suppose *systemwide* scoring rubrics existed for the following performance criteria.

Effective	Purposeful	Accurate
Clear	Efficient	Precise
Elegant	Persistent	Supported
Graceful	(Self-) Critical	Verified
Well crafted	Thoughtful	Focused
Well presented	Careful	Insightful
Organized	Responsive	Fluent
Thorough	Methodical	Proficient
Coherent	Polished	Skilled

This set could be amended, as needed, with bullets or other indicators for particular tasks, while the more general framework remains intact so that students get a consistent message about the nature of quality work. Here is an example of a rubric for the criteria "clear," with bulleted items showing how the general expectations might be interpreted for a 3rd grade task involving a poster:

Clear

6 The communication is unusually clear. Language is sophisticated and precise. Sentence structure is varied and complex. Usage is correct. Minor errors in mechanics and spelling, if they occur, do not interfere with the fluency of the paper. The work is thoroughly and logically developed, and the meaning is unambiguous. The intention of the work is achieved through an unusual control over form and content.

   • *Wow! Really clear. We know just what you meant to tell us. You call our attention to your Big Idea cleverly by the way you organize, color, write things, and the words you used.*

   • *No mess or confusion on the poster. Excellent penmanship, artwork, and use of space.*

   • *No spelling or grammar mistakes at all.*

5 The communication is clear. Language is apt and precise. Sentence structure is varied. Usage is correct. Minor errors in mechanics and spelling, if they do occur, do not interfere with the fluency of the paper. The work is logically developed, and the meaning intended is unambiguous. The work reveals a well thought-through message or meaning and good control over how to convey it best.

   • *A clear poster. We get your message with no difficulty. Neat and well organized to make clear what your Big Idea is.*

   • *No spelling or grammar mistakes at all.*

4 The communication is mostly clear. Language is apt but not always sufficiently precise. Sentence structure is varied. Minimal errors in usage, mechanics, or spelling do not interfere with the fluency of the paper. There are some instances of ambiguity, vagueness, or otherwise hard-to-discern language (especially concerning the more subtle or complex ideas). The work suggests, however, a thought-through meaning.

   • *A pretty clear poster. We get your message, but there may be some things that distract us a bit.*

   • *Overall, a nice design to support your point, but there might be places where we aren't sure what is most important.*

   • *One or two minor spelling or grammar mistakes that don't confuse or distract us.*

3 The communication is somewhat clear. Language may be inadequate, not always well suited or up to the demands of the task. Sentence structure is mostly correct. Errors in usage, mechanics, or spelling may have a minor effect on the fluency of the paper. There are major instances of ambiguity, vagueness, or otherwise hard-to-discern meanings. Key ideas are insufficiently developed or explained. The work is insufficient to communicate the meaning effectively and/or the work suggests an insufficiently worked through meaning.

- *Somewhat unclear poster. Figuring out the message is not as easy as it should be, because the layout, words, or pictures are confusing or messy. We may have trouble figuring out your message: "What's the point?" may be a common response. May be too much of a list.*
- *A few spelling or grammar mistakes that distract us from your point.*

2 The communication is unclear. There may be major errors in sentence structure, usage, mechanics, or spelling that interfere with the fluency of the paper. There are many places where intended meanings cannot be discerned. Language may be too imprecise, inappropriate, or immature to convey the intended message and/or the work suggests an insufficiently thought-through meaning. Key ideas are neither connected nor developed.

- *Unclear poster. Figuring out the message is hard, because of messiness or an incomplete job.*
- *We have a hard time figuring out the words, due to penmanship, spelling, or grammar mistakes.*

1 The communication is difficult, if not impossible to decipher, or there is no evidence in the work of an intended or deliberate meaning.

- *We just can't figure out your message. Not enough stuff here OR it's just a big jumble and/or there are too many confusing words, pictures, and spelling and grammar mistakes.*

As with all rubrics, students will need to see examples of work for each score point if the rubric is to be useful for self-assessment, self-adjustment, and understanding of the teacher's final judgment.

Longitudinal rubrics are helpful for charting progress over time. Great Britain uses a set of such rubrics for the various subjects as part of its standards-based national curriculum. Here is the rubric that describes increasing levels of understanding in science for students from ages 5 through 16 (School Curriculum and Assessment Authority, 1995):[1]

Attainment target 1: Scientific inquiry

Level 1 Pupils describe or respond appropriately to simple features of objects, living things, and events they observe, communicating their findings in simple ways *for example, talking about their work, through drawings, simple charts.*

Level 2 Pupils respond to suggestions about how to find things out and, with help, make their own suggestions about how to collect data to answer questions. They use simple texts, with help, to find information. They use simple equipment provided and make observations related to their task. They observe and compare objects, living things, and events. They describe their observations using scientific vocabulary and record them, using simple tables when appropriate. They say whether what happened was what they expected.

Level 3 Pupils respond to suggestions and put forward their own ideas about how to find the answer to a question. They recognize why it is important to collect data to answer questions. They use simple texts to find information. They make relevant observations and measure quantities, such as length or mass, using a range of simple equipment. Where appropriate, they carry out a fair test with some help, recognizing and explaining why it is fair. They record their observations in a variety of ways. They provide explanations for observations and for simple patterns in recorded measurements. They communicate in a scientific way what they have found out and suggest improvements in their work.

Level 4 Pupils recognize that scientific ideas are based on evidence. In their own investigative work, they decide on an appropriate approach *for example, using a fair test* to answer a question. Where appropriate, they describe, or show in the way they perform their task, how to vary one factor while keeping others the same. Where appropriate, they make predictions. They select information from sources provided for them. They select suitable equipment and make a series of observations and measurements that are adequate for the task. They record their observations, comparisons, and measurements using tables and bar charts. They begin to plot points to form simple graphs, and use these graphs to point out and interpret patterns in their data. They begin to relate their conclusions to these patterns and to scientific knowledge and understanding, and to communicate them with appropriate scientific language. They suggest improvements in their work, giving reasons.

Level 5 Pupils describe how experimental evidence and creative thinking have been combined to provide a scientific explanation *for example, Jenner's work on vaccination at key stage 2, Lavoisier's work on burning at key stage 3*. When they try to answer a scientific question, they identify an appropriate approach. They select from a range of sources of information. When the investigation involves a fair test, they identify key factors to be considered. Where appropriate, they make predictions based on their scientific knowledge and understanding. They select apparatus for a range of tasks and plan to use it effectively. They make a series of observations, comparisons, or measurements with precision appropriate to the task. They begin to repeat observations and measurements and to offer simple explanations for any differences they encounter. They record observations and measurements systematically and, where appropriate, present data as line graphs. They draw conclusions that are consistent with the evidence and begin to relate these to scientific knowledge and understanding. They make practical suggestions about how their working methods could be improved. They use appropriate scientific language and conventions to communicate quantitative and qualitative data.

Level 6 Pupils describe evidence for some accepted scientific ideas and explain how the interpretation of evidence by scientists leads to the development and acceptance of new ideas. In their own investigative work, they use scientific knowledge and understanding to identify an appropriate approach. They select and use sources of information effectively. They make enough measurements, comparisons, and observations for the task. They measure a variety of quantities with precision, using instruments with fine-scale divisions. They choose scales for graphs and diagrams that enable them to show data and features effectively. They identify measurements and observations that do not fit the main pattern shown. They draw conclusions that are consistent with the evidence and use scientific knowledge and understanding to explain them. They make reasoned suggestions about how their working methods could be improved. They select and use appropriate methods for communicating qualitative and quantitative data using scientific language and conventions.

Level 7 Pupils describe some predictions based on scientific theories and give examples of the evidence collected to test these predictions. In their own work, they use scientific knowledge and understanding to decide on appropriate approaches to questions. They identify the key factors in complex contexts and in contexts in which variables cannot readily be controlled, and plan appropriate procedures. They synthesize information from a range of sources, and identify possible limitations in secondary data. They make systematic observations and measurements with precision, using a wide range of apparatus. They identify when they need to repeat measurements, comparisons, and observations in order to obtain reliable data. Where appropriate, they represent data in graphs, using lines of best fit. They draw conclusions that are consistent with the evidence and explain these using scientific knowledge and understanding. They begin to consider whether the data they have collected are sufficient for the conclusions they have drawn. They communicate what they have done using a wide range of scientific and technical language and conventions, including symbols and flow diagrams.

Level 8 Pupils give examples of scientific explanations or models that have had to be changed in the light of additional scientific evidence. They evaluate and synthesize data from a range of sources. They recognize that investigating different kinds of scientific questions requires different strategies, and use scientific knowledge and understanding to select an appropriate strategy in their own work. They decide which observations are relevant in qualitative work and include suitable detail in their records. They decide the level of precision needed in comparisons or measurements, and collect data enabling them to test relationships between variables. They identify and begin to explain anomalous observations and measurements and allow for these when they draw graphs. They use scientific knowledge and understanding to draw conclusions from their evidence. They consider graphs and tables of results critically. They communicate findings and arguments using appropriate scientific language and conventions, showing awareness of a range of views.

Exceptional performance   Pupils give examples of scientific explanations and models that have been challenged by subsequent experiments and explain the significance of the evidence in modifying scientific theories. They evaluate and synthesize data from a range of sources. They recognize that investigating different kinds of scientific questions requires different strategies, and use scientific knowledge and understanding to select an appropriate strategy in their own work. They make records of relevant observations and comparisons, clearly identifying points of particular significance. They decide the level of precision needed in measurements and collect data that satisfy these requirements. They use their data to test relationships between variables. They identify and explain anomalous observations and measurements, allowing for these when they draw graphs. They use scientific knowledge and understanding to interpret trends and patterns and to draw conclusions from their evidence. They consider graphs and tables of results critically and give reasoned accounts of how they could collect additional evidence. They communicate findings and arguments using appropriate scientific language and conventions, showing their awareness of the degree of uncertainty and a range of alternative views.

The UbD rubric for the six facets of understanding (see Figure 8.3) can serve as a framework for building other developmental rubrics. Similar developmental rubrics already exist in foreign language. The American Council on the Teaching of Foreign Languages (ACTFL), for example, has developed proficiency guidelines for speaking and writing (ACTFL, 1999). Various rubric systems also chart literacy development. For instance, the omnibus system codeveloped by early childhood researcher Samuel Meisels indicates literacy development by grade level, noting that kindergartners predict the next events in a story, 1st graders may skip new words, and 2nd graders may use a picture to make meaning from unfamiliar words. The omnibus system focuses on development from kindergarten through 5th grade (Jablon et al., 1994).

Applying "scope and sequence" to a curriculum for understanding

Children rarely [are provided work in] redefining what has been encountered, reshaping it, reordering it. The cultivation of reflectiveness is one of the great problems one faces *in devising curricula:* how to lead children to discover the powers and pleasures that await the exercise of retrospection.
—Jerome Bruner, *Beyond the Information Given,* 1957, p. 449 (emphasis added)

An overarching framework of big ideas, core tasks, and developmental rubrics—isn't that all we need, then, to build a powerful curriculum? The answer is no, as suggested by Bruner's quote, the arguments about WHERETO, the discussion about "uncoverage," and a focus on big ideas and core performance. If understanding requires rethinking and constant (re-)application in a *unit,* then what follows for an entire *curriculum?* Issues of scope and sequence assume great importance in a macro framework—far greater than many educators may realize.

Questions about the ideal "sequence" in scope and sequence sound abstract, but the impact of one flow versus another is real and immediate, as we noted in discussing the organization of units in Chapter 10. An apprentice mechanic would think it odd and unhelpful, for example, if a senior mechanic took apart an entire car engine, laid out the parts on the garage floor, and gave thorough lectures, with great audio-visuals, on each engine part and its relationship to the others as a response to the question "What's wrong with this carburetor?" Yet the expert could argue that the lectures presented a logical and thorough treatment of all the relevant information about automobile engines.

In other words, both content and instructional methods could be of the highest quality, but the course could utterly fail to yield effective learning. Sequencing the learning, mindful of performances and big ideas that recur, is as important as the quality of the curricular elements—perhaps more so, if learner engagement, understanding, and productivity are the criteria for judging the sequence. We believe that the aim of learner understanding is at risk in course and curriculum sequences that involve one tour of each topic, in a flow dictated by the separate content elements as opposed to learner performance goals related to understanding.

Here's a simple way to sum up what scope and sequence needs to become, given our arguments about big ideas and core performance tasks: The flow of learning work in a classroom should be the same as it is on the athletic field or in the art studio. The goal in all cases is to be able to *do* the subject with understanding—to acquire knowledge and skill not for their own sake but as the means for handling key tasks in the field. Whether we are talking about physics or field hockey, then, if the goal is wise performance, the overall logic for learning must be the same: (1) backward design from explicit performance goals, with work adjusted constantly in response to feedback from learners and performance results (i.e., evidence of understanding); (2) a constant and frequent movement between an element of performance (learning and using discrete knowledge and skill) and the whole complex task that prioritizes and justifies the learning; (3) a regular movement back and forth between being instructed and trying to apply the learning; and (4) a sequence that enables learning from results, without penalty, before moving on and becoming ready to formally perform.

The logic applies to all curricula in all fields, we believe, even though many of you might instinctively object that performance-based programs are inherently different from the core content areas. But recall that when workshop participants were asked to describe the flow of work in the "best design" exercise mentioned earlier, irrespective of content they said that the best learning involves a movement back and forth between whole performance and discrete elements of knowledge and skill, and a constant application of the content based on clear performance goals. *Whatever* the subject, we learn best by going through many part–whole–part learning cycles—trying it out, reflecting, adjusting. We learn just enough content to be able to use it, and we make progress by tackling increasingly complicated ideas and aspects of performance.

Yet most academic courses have historically been organized like the expert mechanic's course in auto repair: a march through content, from the basics to the advanced material, with a long—sometimes endless—delay in application, to the detriment of engagement and effectiveness. Somehow in the liberal arts it does not seem as silly as it would be in the garage, at the computer, in the band room, or on the playing field. But this is how long years of habit blind us. Science, mathematics, and history, as they are actually practiced, involve considerably more than just ticking off recalled facts. We use the word *discipline* for a reason. A subject area is ultimately about the *doing* of a subject—using the content in a *disciplined* way.

Furthermore, there is an irony in the time-honored logic of typical courses. No matter how modern their *content,* their *flow* is typically based on a premodern view of learning. A march through What Is Known, organized by the logic of the *content,* is a medieval tradition, used before there were printing presses, before there were deep and public intellectual disagreements about truth, and before education aimed to serve the learner's interests as a user. In the premodern view, *understanding* required only receptivity and contemplation of truths, organized logically into words—which deliberately distinguished a liberal education from any practical learning.

We propose, then, that the structure of much curriculum is woefully inadequate, and that merely improving the way content is framed and delivered is insufficient to make learning understanding-focused. In fact, the more content we put in and pursue "logically," in the name of rigor and timeliness, the harder it will be for learners to grasp the big ideas and core tasks within the traditional approach to sequence. We propose that the curriculum sequence found in the more "modern" performance areas (whether we consider engineering, Spanish, business, jazz band, or cooking) is truer to what we know about how and why people learn and should be applied to all traditional academic areas if learner understanding (and even recall) are to improve.

The logic of content versus the logic of coming to understand content

Let's clarify how the logic of learning to *perform* with content is quite different from the logic of the *content itself.* To use a simple example, consider the flow of learning required to master software. The aim is to be able to use the software productively as quickly as possible. Many manufacturers even provide a little booklet called *Getting Started,* designed for people who don't wish to read manuals or get too bogged down in facts! Further, the software makers typically supply at least two different manuals: one for working with the software in typical day-to-day situations and a thicker manual including all features and troubleshooting procedures to be consulted as needed. More complex software also provides hands-on tutorials for becoming familiar and comfortable with key features of the program. The thicker manual is most like a traditional textbook and is organized differently than the print tutorial materials. In the thicker reference manual, all the features are explained one by one; in the tutorial, the flow is dictated by the logic of learning to use the content in increasingly complicated applications.

It is thus no accident, we think, that even children master complex software use, whereas college students struggle to learn history or biology. When self-sufficient and productive use is the goal, the approach to both content and sequence changes dramatically in terms of information delivery. This is precisely what is needed in all academic learning. The thing we call a "subject" from the point of view of learning is not the "stuff" any more than the "stuff" of software from the user's perspective is the underlying code and a list of all the features. We have thus far failed in academia to see what the wider world has learned in training. The point is maximal transferability—the effective *use* of stuff, not merely the *learning* of stuff. Performance needs and priorities dictate the timing and approaches used in learning the content. The sequence of learning is framed by the key performance tasks, not the table of contents of the reference materials used in training.

Again, this idea is nothing new. Whitehead (1929) said it in a vivid way almost a century ago:

> Let the main ideas which are introduced into a child's education be few and important, and let them be thrown into every combination possible. The child should make them his own, and should understand their application here and now. . . . Pedants sneer at an education which is useful. But if an education is not useful, what is it? Is it a talent to be hidden away in a napkin? . . . Of course education should be useful. . . . It is useful because understanding is useful. (p. 2)

Alas, look at any mathematics, science, or history textbook. Irrespective of the inclusion of activities, exercises, and graphics, the textbook is like the software reference manual. The presentation basically goes through the topics in order, divorced from any meaningful use or overarching important questions. Instead of being treated as a resource serving specific goals related to use, the textbook has unhelpfully become a sealed-off syllabus, inappropriately viewed as both form and content in the eyes of authors and users.

This way of thinking should help us see more clearly a dysfunctional characteristic of conventional curricula. Because they are content-driven, it is not an overstatement to claim that they reveal no genuine priorities. Every topic appears to be equal to every other topic, and the flow is impervious to performance need or learner misunderstanding. Genuine priorities, by contrast, are made tangible as recurring questions related to key performance goals.

Learning priorities have to be set apart from the textbook, in other words, as when a soccer or acting coach frames goals for performance separate and apart from any resource materials that might be used. Understanding, competence, and even accurate and timely recall are at risk, regardless of how time-honored the approach, when we merely cover topics.

One might call the typical approach a brick-by-brick view of learning. If the bricklayers merely do what they are told, brick by brick, the house of understanding will follow. This is simply not how learning works. We have to have the big picture, the blueprint, as workers; we have to play with, try out, and use what we are given to see its value and meaning. Learning is more like solving difficult crossword puzzles or sculpting with an idea in mind than it is like laying bricks. Whole–part–whole activity is crucial, as is the movement back and forth between the mastery of elements and the questions about their importance, and the inevitable rethinking along the way.

To better see the unwitting harm of a piece-by-piece approach to sequence in learning, think of an entire curriculum as collapsed into one course, supported by one book. In other words, think of what we now do as equivalent to organizing all learning around both the form and content of the encyclopedia. Organized summaries like that are useful only when we have specific questions, curiosities, or performance needs (as the software manual writers know). When we have a question in mind, the organization and content of the encyclopedia is most useful, enabling us to find enough of what we need. But when we do not yet know the subject, when no high-priority questions or problems guide inquiry, an endless march is confusing, devoid of meaning, and off-putting, as if we just read one encyclopedia entry after another and were tested on our knowledge.

As a result, in far too many courses, from kindergarten through undergraduate college years, the most basic learner questions about purpose—Why this? Why now? So what?—are unendingly postponed or ignored *by the work itself* (regardless of any verbal rationale supplied by the teacher). At what cost to understanding or even engagement? Should it surprise us, then, that the only students who persevere are those who are most able to delay gratification or to trust adults? Could it be that we have it upside down? Perhaps our best and brightest are those students who persist *in spite* of the lack of meaning provided by so much of the work, who can find value in schoolwork on their own.

Rethinking scope and sequence

There is an ironic history here. The phrase *scope and sequence* is well known to educators as the label for the logic of the curriculum. But most educators have lost sight of its original meaning. Hollis Caswell, a Deweyan progressive who made the phrase popular, was trying to capture many of the ideas we have discussed thus far in a useful framework for educators. In its original meaning, the *scope* referred to "the major functions of social life," and the *sequence* referred to the "centers of interest" in students' lives at a particular point in time. The proper sequencing of topics—the "logic" of the syllabus—was thus meant to derive from the unfolding of work that would seem most natural and interesting to the learner.[2]

Dewey, Caswell's mentor, had seen this issue more clearly than anyone, one hundred years ago. He repeatedly argued in his writings, without success, that relying on the logic of the content to guide both sequence and pedagogy was a major cause of the disappointing results we see in education:

> *There is a strong temptation to assume that presenting subject matter in its perfected form provides a royal road to learning. What is more natural than to suppose that the immature can be saved time and energy, and be protected from needless error by commencing where competent inquirers have left off? The outcome is written large in the history of education. Pupils begin their study . . . with texts in which the subject is organized into topics according to the order of the specialist. Technical concepts and their definitions are introduced at the outset. Laws are introduced at an early stage, with at best a few indications of the way in which they were arrived at. . . . The pupil learns symbols without the key to their meaning. He acquires a technical body of information without ability to trace its connections [to what] is familiar—often he acquires simply a vocabulary. (1916, p. 220)*

In other words, from the learner's point of view, the "logic" of the content is illogical for learning what is important about the content—namely, what it can help you see and do for the better (e.g., help you solve a problem or tackle a challenge). Again, Dewey's insight is valuable:

> *Every subject in the curriculum has passed through—or remains in—what may be called the phase of "anatomical" method: the stage in which understanding the subject is thought to consist of multiplying distinctions . . . and attaching some name to each distinguished element. In normal growth, specific properties are emphasized and so individualized only when they serve to clear up a present difficulty. (1933, p. 127)*

Hook and rethinking, rethought

Thus, a look at the first few weeks of any course of study is highly revealing. "Well, you start with the basic facts and elements and move logically forward. You start with the axioms in math or way back in the past in history or with the basic laws in science—where else *would* you begin and how else could the course possibly unfold?" But how does this honor the *W* or *H* in WHERETO? How does a syllabus signal the priorities and immediately arouse learner interest in them? Textbooks are no help here. Almost all of them, based as they are on the logic of content, start with an often confusing and ultimately dreary march through definitions, rules, and algorithms, or the most distant events in time—totally removed from the context of any problem, question, or performance.

As we noted in talking about the WHERETO elements for units, the point of Where and Hook questions, issues, experiences, and problems suggests a way to completely rethink sequence. A first order of business in a course or program must be to establish the questions and issues that make the content seem interesting, meaningful, and valuable. Consider this proposal for upper-level science made years ago by author Lewis Thomas (1983):

> I suggest that the introductory courses in science at all levels be radically revised. Leave the fundamentals, the so-called basics, aside for awhile, and concentrate the attention of students on the things that are not known. . . . Let it be known, early on, that there are deep mysteries and profound paradoxes. . . . Let it be known that these can be approached more closely and puzzled over once the language of mathematics has been sufficiently mastered. Teach at the outset, before any of the fundamentals, the still imponderable puzzles of cosmology. (pp. 151–152)

Or consider this advice from mathematics professor and educator Morris Kline (1973):

> The traditional approaches treat mathematics as a cumulative logical development. . . . The new approach would present what is interesting, enlightening, and culturally significant . . . every topic must be motivated. The students' question "Why do I have to learn this material?" is thoroughly justified. (pp. 178–179)

Kline's suggestion lets us more clearly grasp a prevalent misunderstanding in mathematics education. Many math teachers have said to us over the years, "Math is sequential; the textbook merely reflects that things logically build. Since math follows a logical sequence, it has to be taught that way." This is simply not true. Mathematical *elements* are organized in logical sequence in textbooks, just as the dictionary is alphabetized or baseball rulebooks are constructed. Math teachers who argue this way are confusing the logic of the summary with the logic of learning. If they were right, we would teach the English language via the dictionary and flash cards or baseball by studying the rules in order. It does *not* follow that one should learn words or rules in the order in which they appear in the reference book, even though the texts are "logically organized." Similarly, just because mathematical elements and theorems are most easily organized into their logical hierarchy, it doesn't follow that the textbook summary of each is the best way to learn the key ideas and the *meaning and value of their relationships.*

The spiral curriculum

You might think that these ideas about sequence are fanciful at best, foolish at worst. Yet reformers have long challenged the logic of piece-by-piece coverage, as the earlier Whitehead remarks suggest. A well-known alternative approach to scope and sequence is the spiral curriculum. The idea of the spiral as a metaphor for learning and rethinking what was learned was first articulated fully by Dewey and later championed by Bruner, but is rooted in a long philo-sophical and pedagogical tradition running back through Piaget, G. Stanley Hall, and the recapitulationists, and further back to the philosophers Kant, Rousseau, and Hegel. But although many praise the idea, few curriculums have been built to embody it. We are perhaps now at the time when learning theory, disappointing achievement results, and common sense can combine to point toward a more learning-friendly approach to the flow of learning.

A spiral approach develops curriculum around recurring, ever-deepening inquiries into big ideas and important tasks, helping students come to under-stand in a way that is both effective and developmentally wise. An example of this spiral approach appears in the unfolding of the archaeology unit dis-cussed in Chapter 9. The same ideas and materials are revisited in more and more complex ways to arrive at sophisticated judgments and products. Simi-larly, when students confront the poetry of e. e. cummings and the stories of James Joyce on the heels of more familiar forms, they gain a deeper under-standing of earlier lessons in form, mechanics, and impact.

Bruner (1960) popularized the ideal of the spiral curriculum with his stark and provocative postulate that "any subject can be taught effectively in some intellectually honest form to any child at any stage of development" (p. 33). It is, as he said, a "bold" hypothesis, but central to a coherent education for rethinking and eventual understanding:

> The foundations of any subject may be taught to anybody of any age in some form. Though the proposition may be startling at first, its intent is to under-score an essential point often overlooked in the planning of curricula. It is that the basic ideas at the heart of all science and mathematics and the basic themes that give form to life and literature are as simple as they are power-ful. To be in command of these basic ideas, to use them effectively requires a continual deepening of one's understanding of them that comes from learn-ing to use them in progressively more complex forms. It is only when such basic ideas are put in formalized terms as equations or elaborated verbal concepts that they are out of reach of the young child, if he has first not understood them intuitively and had a chance to try them out. (pp. 12–13 [emphasis in original])

Dewey (1938) first used the analogy of the spiral to describe how subject matter should be organized to move from problem to problem, causing knowl-edge to increase in depth and breadth. In this way, coursework could develop student thinking and interest in a purposeful and systematic way, pointing toward the full fruits of each discipline. The task is to move back and forth between the known and the problematic; otherwise, "no problems arise, while problems are the stimulus to thinking" (p. 79). The teacher's task is to design related challenges so that learning results in "the production of new ideas," as it does for the scholar. The new facts and ideas "become the ground for further experiences in which new problems are presented. *The process is a continual spiral*" (p. 79, emphasis in original).

Ralph Tyler, Dewey's student and the dean of modern student assessment, underscored in his seminal book on design, *Basic Principles of Curriculum and Instruction* (1949), the need to think about curricular matters from the perspective of desired outcomes and the learner's needs. Indeed, more than anyone, Tyler laid out the basic principles of backward design. He proposed three criteria for effective organization—continuity, sequence, and integration—to show how the logic of curriculum should suit the learner's, not the experts', sense of order:

> *In identifying important organizing principles, it is necessary to note that the criteria, continuity, sequence, and integration apply to the* experiences of the learner and not to the way in which these matters may be viewed by someone already in command of the elements to be learned. *Thus, continuity involves the recurring emphasis in the learner's experience upon these particular elements; sequence refers to the increasing breadth and depth of the learner's development; and integration refers to the learner's increased unity of behavior in relating to the elements involved. (p. 96 [emphasis added])*

Apropos our earlier discussion, Tyler explicitly warns that the typical sequential approach of marching through content chronologically in history does *not* pass the test of intelligent continuity.

Why has this overuse of piecemeal learning based on the logic of content persisted? A root factor is an overreliance on the textbook or other instructional resources, which tend to be organized around the content. Why does overreliance on the textbook as syllabus persist? Here is one answer:

> *There are a number of reasons why this procedure has persisted so long. The dominant one, perhaps, is that the procedure is logical and may be easily applied. It simplifies and objectifies the task of the curriculum worker, the teacher, and the administrator. The least capable teacher can assign pages in a textbook and hear pupils recite the facts involved. He can give evidence that he has done his part by covering a given number of pages. Thus he has an alibi for failure because he can place the blame for low achievement on his pupils. From the administrator's point of view, it is easy to divide the work of the school, to tell precisely where every child should be in his work, and to have a systematic organization that appears to operate smoothly. Even though educational theory has been challenging, with increasing emphasis, the basic assumptions of the procedure for three decades, it is probably still the dominant means of determining the scope of work in American schools. (Caswell & Campbell, 1935, p. 142)*

Plus ça change. This remark was made in 1935! If anything, the situation is worse now than it was in the 1930s. For example, in most kindergarten through college-level science courses in the United States, the textbook is the syllabus. Yet consider again some of the criticisms made by AAAS through George Nelson, former director of Project 2061, in an article in the online version of the magazine *Prism:*

One of the major problems reflected in the textbooks, says Nelson, is that "the education community's understanding of science is that it's a heap of facts and vocabulary words." Glencoe Life Science, for example, lists "Science Words" in the margin at the start of each chapter, and many are terms that even a well-educated scientist in another field would probably not know, nor need to know. Saprophyte, Punnett Square, auxism, Islets of Langerhans, commensalism, and taiga are but a few of the terms seventh-grade biology students are asked to master. Macmillan/McGraw-Hill Life Sciences offers up, in its unit on plants, phloem cells, cortex cells, xylem cells, apical meristem, palisade cells, and cambium. The exercises included in each chapter frequently amount to nothing more than regurgitation of these words and definitions. . . .

The incoherence in the texts occurs at a far deeper level, however, and this goes to the heart of the criticism from the AAAS and other experts. [A commonly used textbook] is one of the least cluttered books, but it, like all of the standard texts, throws a welter of concepts and terms at students in confusing order. It brings in atoms on the first few pages with the didactic and, to most students, probably incomprehensible assertion that "matter consists of atoms of various weights that interact in accordance with specific principles." (Budiansky, 2001)

This call for better sequence in curriculum, derived independently from the content and pagination of textbooks, is simply the idea of backward design pushed to a new level. We must redesign scope and sequence *itself,* based on standards related to learning goals.

Of course, centuries of tradition die hard. But change is afoot in those areas that now define themselves in terms of performance rather than content. A hundred years ago, "writing" was taught primarily through learning grammar, syntax, parsing, sentence diagramming, and reading good writing. One supposedly learned to write by first learning the "logical" elements of writing. (It was actually still possible 20 years ago to test for "writing" ability on a standardized test without asking students to write.) Even sports once relied on this abstract, analytic, piece-by-piece approach. Veteran skiers will recall the Stem Christie and other piece-by-piece approaches. Now, novice skiers are immediately introduced to the holistic process of parallel skiing, beginning on short skis and gentle slopes. And today, the writing process is more faithful to the goal of good writing because it gets students going right from the start, even if they haven't yet mastered all the mechanics.

Many graduate schools have also experienced a revolution. Now, it is not just law and business that are taught by the case method; in a surprisingly short time, medicine, engineering, design, and other programs have revamped their entire approach to curriculum design to make it more transfer-focused.

If we think of a subject area as the "discipline" of performing with expertise rather than the "stuff" with which the expert performs, then we can easily apply the lessons learned in skiing, software development, writing, medicine, and engineering to the core academic areas. All we need to do is agree on the core performance tasks in each field, and design programs and syllabi backward from them, just as we do in youth soccer when little kids get to play the real game in a scaffolded way, rather than first learning a lot of simplistic "stuff" out of context, in a sequence dictated by the "stuff."

Why isn't there more experimentation about sequence in the core academic areas or in textbooks themselves? Old habits again. It took more than 30 years for the elective system to take root in higher education. Creatively organized textbooks have often found no market. Perhaps a more prosaic answer is that many teachers have never thought of other possibilities nor experienced other sequences.

Toward a better syllabus

We offer a practical solution, mindful of the fact that much research is needed to find more effective approaches to long-term curricular sequencing. We suggest that sequence first be thought through more carefully at a manageable level: the course (or, in elementary school, the year of work in each subject in each grade level). We propose that *course syllabi be required of all teachers* K–12, just as is true of college professors. And, as is the case in college, we propose that *the syllabus be a public document, available to students, parents, and colleagues.*

What would differ from current practice in many places is that there would also be public standards for the syllabus, parallel to the standards for units, supported by examples. Format might vary, but whether a template, a narrative, or a calendar, the document would have to specify at least the following elements:

- The essential questions and core problems at the heart of the subject
- The core performances and challenges that frame all work and imply all learning
- The rubrics and scoring systems used
- A summary and justification of the assessment and grading policies, in reference to institutional goals and state standards
- A summary of the *major* "learning goals" (as opposed to a list of topics) in a brief week-by-week calendar
- Built-in flexibility to ensure the syllabus can adapt to feedback based on student performance and understanding

Until we grasp that a course of study must be organized backward from big ideas and performance goals related to their use (with content as the means), educational results will continue to be disappointing and understanding will fall through the cracks of instruction.

In sum, sequence would thus begin to look more like the logic in a syllabus for learning to ski rather than the logic of textbook physics; more like the chronology in learning to write than the logic of grammar by itself; more like learning how to improve in building a spreadsheet than learning the times tables in order; more like designing increasingly complex tiled courtyards than marching through Euclidean theorems.

"Just in time" teaching would be the mantra, as opposed to "just in case" surveys of content out of context. A curriculum that constantly postpones the *meaning* of content cannot yield understanding, maximal recall, or a passion for learning except in those few students who are willing and able to learn on their own. (The Expert Blind Spot also causes many educators to falsely believe that what worked for them will likely work for most others.)

We must check our bad habit of building frameworks around the logic of content instead of the logic of learning. To put the matter in blunt terms, most frameworks and courses merely reflect the organization of content in textbooks, not the needs of learners trying to understand. Any reform of curriculum depends upon putting textbooks in their proper place—as resources—and framing syllabi and programs around the optimal flow of inherently iterative, nonlinear learning to use big ideas effectively, with understanding, in performance.[3]

■ MISCONCEPTION ALERT!

That we cannot predict the actual future performance needs of each learner is beside the point. It is unlikely that most of our students will become professional artists, musicians, or soccer players. Nonetheless, we organize the sequence around performance mastery because that is how people learn most effectively.

Chapter 13

"Yes, but . . ."

> The work is difficult and requires constant revision. It is particularly difficult for teachers who have to "unlearn" their prior practice.
> —Mark Wise, Social Studies Supervisor, West Windsor-Plainsboro, NJ

> Now consider what their release and healing from bonds and folly might be like. . . . Take a man who is released and suddenly compelled to stand up, to turn his neck round and look toward the light . . . who, moreover, in doing all this is in pain, and because he is dazzled, is unable to make out the shadows he knew before. . . . And if he were compelled to look at the light itself, would his eyes hurt and he would flee . . . and if someone dragged him by force along the rough ascent, wouldn't he be distressed and annoyed? He would.
> —Plato, *The Republic,* c. 360 B.C.E.

In this book, we have set forth a vision of and pathway toward meaningful curricular, assessment, and instructional reform, all carefully designed around planning for understanding. We understand that our reform vision is neither highly original nor very radical. It parallels the vision of many educators, researchers, and reformers in the past decades.

Nonetheless, whenever reform ideas are proffered, it is common to hear a chorus of "Yes, but . . ." from well-intentioned teachers and administrators. The proposed reforms are damned with faint praise and undercut by the rejoinder that these fine ideas cannot work in today's world of state standards and high-stakes testing. Some reformers remain adamant that good pedagogy and state standards and testing are inherently incompatible; many educators worry that there might not be a research base to support our arguments, no matter how commonsensical.[1]

We empathize with these laments and the concerns they are based on, given the accountability pressures facing educators. Yet many of the recurring arguments are based on misunderstandings about learning, assessment, standardized testing, teaching for understanding of big ideas, and the relationship between local pedagogy and state standards. In this chapter, we provide the arguments and research in support of our views while examining three key misconceptions that often hold back or interfere with comprehensive reform. We explain why each *is* a misconception by "unpacking" the implicit and questionable assumptions underlying the "yes, but . . ." concerns, and offer a friendly but firm rebuttal.

The misconceptions we address:

"Yes, but . . . we have to teach to the state and national tests."

"Yes, but . . . we have too much content to cover."

"Yes, but . . . the needed curriculum and assessment work is hard and I simply don't have the time to do it well."

Misconception 1: "Yes, but . . . we have to teach to the test."

State, provincial, or national content standards and concomitant testing programs have emerged worldwide with the intention of focusing local curriculum and instruction on boosting student achievement by holding schools accountable for results. Ironically, the key lever in this standards-based reform strategy—the use of high-stakes external tests—has unwittingly provided teachers with a rationalization for avoiding or minimizing the need to *teach well*, that is, to teach for in-depth understanding.

For many educators, instruction and assessing for understanding are viewed as incompatible with state mandates and standardized tests. Though research is rarely offered to support this oft-heard claim, the speaker clearly implies that school faculties are stuck teaching to the test—against their will. They *would* teach for understanding, if they could. The implicit assumption is key: The only way to safeguard or raise test scores is to "cover" those things that are tested and "practice" the test format (typically selected-response or brief constructed-response) by having local assessment mimic state assessment. By implication, there is no time for in-depth and engaging instruction that focuses on developing and deepening students' understanding of big ideas; nor is there time for performance assessment.

This opinion is so widely held that many readers may be thinking that *we* are the ones harboring the misunderstanding (or myopia or naïveté) about the real world of education. Isn't it a fact that we have to teach to the test and leave aside more higher-order, big-idea-focused, and performance-based approaches? Many certainly think, say, and act accordingly. Although we are obligated to teach to content standards, it does not follow that the best way to meet those standards is to mimic the format of the state test in all local testing and haphazardly cover all prescribed content through superficial and scattered teaching.

To more clearly show why the common complaint and reluctant solution are based on a misunderstanding, consider a rephrasing of the reason given for focusing on test items at the expense of depth. The speaker asks us to believe that the only way to *raise* test scores is to teach *worse*. That is not how the speaker usually puts it, of course, but that is what the argument amounts to. "I would love to teach for understanding, but I just can't; it won't pay. I'm better off teaching discrete facts and skills, just the way they are tested" is what the first "yes, but . . ." response really means.

Just putting it this way should cause a raised eyebrow or two. Is it *really* either/or? Must we avoid effective and engaging forms of instruction to *raise* test scores? Is more passive, fragmented, and superficial teaching *more* likely to maximize student interest and performance? We think this theory is incorrect, based on a misunderstanding about how testing works.

The parallel with the doctor's physical

To begin to uncover the flaw in this reasoning, consider an analogy. Once a year, we go to the doctor for a physical exam. No one particularly relishes the thought of such an exam, but we go with the understanding that it is in our long-term interest to get an objective (yet superficial) measure of our health. In fact, it is more like an audit because the nurse and lab technicians perform a few tests in a short span of time (such as blood pressure, pulse, temperature, blood work for cholesterol). The physical is a small sample of tests, yielding a few useful health status indicators. Its validity and value stem from the fact that the results *suggest* our state of health, not because the physical *defines* healthfulness. We experience a relatively quick and unintrusive physical exam so that various indicators can be examined for signs of trouble demanding further scrutiny.

Now suppose we are terribly concerned about the final numbers (e.g., weight or blood pressure) and that the numbers ultimately link to our personal health insurance costs. What we might do, in our panicky state prior to each annual physical, would be to "practice" for the test—focus all our energy on the physical exam (as opposed to what its indicators suggest). If our doctors knew of our actions, their response would surely be something like this "Whoa! You have it backward. The best way to 'pass' your physical is to live a healthful life on a regular basis—exercising, watching weight, lowering intake of fats, eating more fiber, getting sufficient sleep, and avoiding tobacco. You're fixating on the indicator instead of on the causes of good results."

Why? None of the elements of true healthfulness—your diet, your fitness regimen—are tested directly in the physical; doctors audit your health *indirectly* through factors including blood pressure, weight, skin tone, and color. Thus, "normal blood pressure" and "normal weight" are only indicators of overall wellness and fitness, not to be confused with overall health. The physical exam involves assessing a few quick, usually accurate indicators. So to confuse the indicator with the thing itself is poor policy. The more that you concentrate only on your weight, for example, to the exclusion of everything else in your daily regimen, the less likely it is that you will be healthy in the long run.

Like the doctor, state education agencies give schools a "checkup" once a year by viewing indirect evidence—state tests—of student intellectual health. A test, like the physical exam, is an audit related to the state standards. Like the physical, the state test provides indirect indicators about our health. Test items indirectly assess the quality of our "daily regimen" in the same way that a look at blood pressure and weight are proxies for the daily "tests" of real fitness and wellness.

We *can* get some good information about the rigor of our regimen from quick-and-dirty indicators. Any good test—whether in the school or the exam room—need not involve the core performance we should be engaged in daily. For schools, it only matters that the indicators yield valid inferences to the standards. That is the nature of test validity, as we saw in previous chapters—establishing a link between one set of easy-to-obtain indicators with a related set of complex and desired results.[2]

It would be thought silly to practice for the physical exam as a way to be healthy. But this error is precisely what we see in too many schools all over North America. Local educators, fearful of results, are focusing on the indicators and not the causes of happy results.

Please understand that this explanation does not constitute an endorsement of any specific test question or current state practice in which we rely heavily on one-shot external testing, often done in secret with tests improperly vetted. In fact, we feel strongly that state agencies and policy makers bear a responsibility for allowing the confusion about the relationship between local practice and state tests to persist by not making local assessments part of a comprehensive state accountability system, and by not making more of an effort to design more transparent accountability (such as through release of all tests and results once the test has been administered, for the sake of both feedback and fairness).

What matters for local reform is that we take to heart the point of the analogy: *We* are responsible for wellness, not the state. The state's job is to audit—just as the physical exam does—not to provide the daily regimen we should engage in at home. Indeed, the state could not possibly assess everything of value in an authentic way, even if we all wanted it, because of excessive costs and the desire to limit the intrusions of external testing. Doctors have a similar problem—requiring every patient to come in for a multiday comprehensive fitness program and workup at a medical lab would be excessively time-consuming and costly (never mind the unlikelihood of getting our insurers to foot the bill). So, in the absence of data to show that the indicators yield invalid inferences, the task is to focus on local rigor, not test prep.

The misunderstanding about what is cause and what is effect in performance gains may well be related to misunderstandings about the "face validity" of tests, as test-makers term it. Educators might look at both test format and content and conclude that the test neither rewards teaching for understanding nor performance-based local assessment. That view, while understandable, is mistaken. Validity is about the empirical link between test results, the objectives tested, and local practice. That is why tests that appear inauthentic can yield valid inferences (e.g., vocabulary tests are often good predictors of academic success) if designed properly, and why some performance-based projects yield poor results (since the projects often end up unrelated to state standards, as in the diorama example discussed in Chapter 9). Making matters worse, many teachers then erroneously infer that instructional practice is somehow dictated by test format, so they teach a *random and superficial survey of content*—making it far less likely that student learning will be engaging and effective.

To invoke a different analogy to explain the error in logic, state standards are like building codes; local instructional design is our architecture. The goal of architectural design is not to meet building and zoning codes in a slavish fashion. The goal is to design something that is practical, pleasing, and stylish—while meeting building and zoning codes.

In fact, the situation regarding education is far better than many assume. Most state standards stress the importance of in-depth understanding and mastery of key complex performances and genres in which knowledge, skill, and understanding are revealed. Understanding by Design (and other programs and reform approaches) provides a way in which a focus on big ideas, robust assessment, and a focused and coherent learning plan makes it likely that state standards are addressed and met.

Research base

The best news is there is an empirical basis to this logical argument. In the mid-1990s, Newmann (1996) and others conducted a study of restructured schools at the elementary, middle, and high school levels. This ambitious study measured how well 24 restructured schools implemented authentic pedagogy and authentic academic performance approaches in mathematics and social studies, and whether schools with high levels of authentic pedagogy and academic performance significantly increased achievement over those that measured at low levels. Authentic pedagogy and performance were measured by a set of standards that included higher-order thinking, deep-knowledge approaches, and connections to the world beyond the classroom. Selected classes were observed four times during the school year in each school. The researchers observed 504 lessons and analyzed 234 assessment tasks. They also analyzed student work.

Students in classrooms with high and low levels of authentic pedagogy and performance were compared, and the results were striking. Students in classrooms with high levels of authentic pedagogy and performance were helped substantially whether they were high- or low-achieving students. Another significant finding was that the inequalities between high- and low-performing students were greatly decreased when normally low-performing students used authentic pedagogy and performance strategies and assessments.

The study provides strong evidence that authentic pedagogy and assessments pay off in improved academic achievement for all students, but especially for low-performing students. This research supports the Understanding by Design approach, which emphasizes the use of authentic performance assessments and pedagogy that promotes a focus on deep knowledge and understanding, and active and reflective teaching and learning.

Two recent studies of factors influencing student achievement were conducted in Chicago public schools through the Consortium on Chicago School Research. In the first study, Smith, Lee, and Newmann (2001) focused on the link between different forms of instruction and learning in elementary schools. Test scores from more than 100,000 students in grades 2–8 and surveys from more than 5,000 teachers in 384 Chicago elementary schools were examined. The results provide strong empirical support that the nature of the instructional approach teachers use influences how much students learn in reading and mathematics. More specifically, the study found clear and consistent evidence that interactive teaching methods were associated with more learning in both subjects.

For the purposes of the study, Smith, Lee, and Newmann characterized interactive instruction as follows:

The teacher's role is primarily one of guide or coach. Teachers using this form of instruction create situations in which students . . . ask questions, develop strategies for solving problems, and communicate with one another. . . . Students are often expected to explain their answers and discuss how they arrived at their conclusions. These teachers usually assess students' mastery of knowledge through discussions, projects, or tests that demand explanation and extended writing. Besides content mastery, the process of developing the answer is also viewed as important in assessing the quality of the students' work.

In classrooms that emphasize interactive instruction, students discuss ideas and answers by talking, and sometimes arguing, with each other and with the teacher. Students work on applications or interpretations of the material to develop new or deeper understandings of a given topic. Such assignments may take several days to complete. Students in interactive classrooms are often encouraged to choose the questions or topics they wish to study within an instructional unit designed by the teacher. Different students may be working on different tasks during the same class period. (p. 12)

The type of instruction found to enhance student achievement parallels methods advocated by Understanding by Design for developing and assessing student understanding. Smith, Lee, and Newmann (2001) summarize their results as follows:

The positive effects of interactive teaching should allay fears that it is detrimental to student achievement of basic skills in reading and mathematics. Conversely, the findings call into serious question the assumption that low-achieving, economically disadvantaged students are best served by emphasizing didactic methods and review. Our results suggest precisely the opposite: to elevate mastery of basic skills, interactive instruction should be increased and the use of didactic instruction and review moderated. (p. 33)

A related study (Newmann, Bryk, & Nagaoka, 2001) examined the relationship of the nature of classroom assignments to standardized test performance. Researchers systematically collected and analyzed classroom writing and mathematics assignments in grades 3, 6, and 8 from randomly selected and control schools over the course of three years. In addition, they evaluated student work generated by the various assignments. Finally, the researchers examined correlations among the nature of classroom assignments, the quality of student work, and scores on standardized tests. Assignments were rated according to the degree to which they required "authentic" intellectual work, which the researchers described as follows:

Authentic intellectual work involves original application of knowledge and skills, rather than just routine use of facts and procedures. It also entails disciplined inquiry into the details of a particular problem and results in a product or presentation that has meaning or value beyond success in school. We summarize these distinctive characteristics of authentic intellectual work as construction of knowledge, through the use of disciplined inquiry, to produce discourse, products, or performances that have value beyond school. (pp. 14–15)

This study concluded that

Students who received assignments requiring more challenging intellectual work also achieved greater than average gains on the Iowa Tests of Basic Skills in reading and mathematics, and demonstrated higher performance in reading, mathematics, and writing on the Illinois Goals Assessment Program. Contrary to some expectations, we found high-quality assignments in some very disadvantaged Chicago classrooms and [found] that all students in these classes benefited from exposure to such instruction. We conclude, therefore, [that] assignments calling for more authentic intellectual work actually improve student scores on conventional tests. (p. 29)[3]

Readers will immediately recognize the parallels with UbD. The instructional methods that were found to enhance student achievement are basic elements of the pedagogy in the 3-stage planning model. As in the researchers' conception of authentic intellectual work, UbD instructional approaches call for the student to construct meaning through disciplined inquiry. Assessments of understanding call for students to apply their learning in authentic contexts and explain or justify their work.

We have been asked, "Are you then saying that a more concerted effort to 'teach to the test' *lowers* scores?" No, we are not. Teaching to the test clearly has *some* effect, particularly if prior to such practice there was little attention to common standards and a focus on results. Scores do increase in the short run when a school or district focuses more carefully on a common goal. No surprise here: Greater attention to an outcome will improve performance on *any* measure. But once the test particulars are figured out and students have become familiar with the test format and test-taking skills, there is rarely long-term progress. More ominously, the scores typically drop when the test is altered or re-normed.[4]

Finally, consider common sense evidence for our claim. Do we see more "teaching and assessing for understanding" in the *worse* performing schools? Do we see students more involved in slavish practicing of state and national tests in the most *high-achieving* schools? On the contrary, during the past 15 years of work with hundreds of schools and districts throughout the United States and Canada (including some of the best public and private schools in the country), we have observed more in-depth teaching and demanding assessment in the higher-performing schools. In contrast, within the lower-performing schools we found drill and practice orientations ostensibly designed to raise standardized test scores—often at the expense of more meaningful learning and lasting performance gains.

The bottom line is that we should be teaching to standards and developing the kinds of complex assessments reflected in the language of the standards, not the audit.

Misconception 2: "Yes, but . . . we have too much content to cover."

Teachers of students from kindergarten to graduate school wrestle with the reality described in the familiar phrases "information age" and "knowledge explosion." They face the challenge daily—there is simply too much information, and it is expanding too rapidly, to ever hope to "cover" it all.

In theory, the standards movement promised a solution to the problem of information overload by identifying curricular priorities. Content standards were intended to specify what is most important for students to know and be able to do, thus providing a much-needed focus and prioritization for curriculum, instruction, and assessment. In practice, content standards committees at the national, state, and district level often worked in isolation to produce overly ambitious lists of essentials for their disciplines. Rather than streamlining the curriculum, the plethora of standards in many states contributed to the overload problem.

The stress is needlessly heightened by the propensity of many teachers to treat textbooks as their teaching obligation. Those teachers have a basic misunderstanding and we can correct it: They need to use the textbook as a resource, not the syllabus. A course has certain priorities, framed as performance goals and understandings. It makes no sense to assume that everything in the textbook should be taught in class or learned by all students. U.S. textbook publishers try to cover the waterfront in order to appease 50 state textbook adoption committees, national subject-area organizations, and various special-interest groups. The result is invariably superficial treatment of the entire array of expert knowledge.

Seeing overloaded textbooks and long lists of content standards frequently leads to a fundamental misconception on the part of many teachers that their job is to cover lots of content. The perceived need to "cover" is typically based upon two implicit assumptions that we think are quite unfounded: (1) if I "teach" it (e.g., talk about it and assign some work on it), it will be adequately learned for tests; and (2) if I don't address it in a didactic way, it won't be learned.

As we have noted throughout the book, the Expert Blind Spot is hard at work here. "Teaching by mentioning" is unlikely to ensure that novices recall, much less understand, the key ideas and core processes of the subject. A superficial and disconnected teaching of information simply cannot yield optimal results on any test. We are once again confusing the teaching with the learning.

Interestingly, when teachers maintain that they are *required* to march through texts and syllabi (irrespective of the degree of student understanding or the learning results), they often cite reports of external pressures from supervisors. We have never been able to trace such reports to the administrative source nor have we found a supervisor who claimed to have issued such an edict. Our inquiries into these claims revealed that teachers were often interpreting a principal's or supervisor's focus on test scores as an *implied* request to stick closely to textbooks and test preparation as the sole strategy.

The obligation to state content standards raises an important question regarding the fit between state standards and a nationally marketed textbook or commercial resource. Ask teachers to review their textbook against state or district content standards to determine the degree of correlation. Ask them to choose the illustration in Figure 13.1 that best represents the relationship between their standards and the textbook.

In the absence of a perfect correlation between the textbook and the syllabus, the textbook should at best serve as only one of many resources, *not* the syllabus. The illustrations labeled 2 and 3 suggest that a portion of the textbook's content does not contribute to learning the standards (will not need to be learned), but that other resources will be needed.

A more disturbing exercise is to seek and find the few independent reviews of textbooks. The most thorough reviews are from Project 2061 of the American Association for the Advancement of Science (AAAS) and relate to texts for high school biology, middle school science, and algebra. The results are alarming.

> Today's high-school biology textbooks fail to make important biology ideas comprehensible. . . . [The president of the National Academy of Sciences notes that] "sadly, it appears that our textbooks continue to be distorted by a commercial textbook market that requires that they cover the entire range of facts . . . thereby sacrificing the opportunity to treat the central concepts in enough depth to give our students a chance to truly understand them."[5]
>
> Not one of the widely used science textbooks for middle school was rated satisfactory. . . . "Our students are lugging home heavy texts full of disconnected

Figure 13.1
Correlation Between Textbooks and Standards

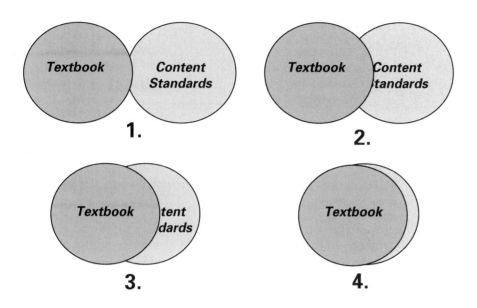

facts that neither educate nor motivate them," said Dr. George Nelson, Director of Project 2061. . . . *"This study confirms our worst fears about the materials used to educate our children in the critical middle grades."*[6]

Even if good textbooks are available, it is simply a misunderstanding to claim that a teacher's job is to teach the text. The job of design, instruction, and assessment is to shape a syllabus in light of content standards, intellectual priorities, and student needs and interests to achieve explicit goals. Thus, the textbook should serve as one resource among many in the service of meeting the standards. The textbook is a reference book. Its purpose is to summarize knowledge—not unlike the encyclopedia. Treating the textbook as the syllabus ensures a lack of purpose and coherence to the overall design. Treating the textbook as the course of study is akin to marching through the encyclopedia from *A* to *Z*. Logical and efficient, yes; purposeful and effective, no.

Why isn't this misconception seen more clearly? Perhaps because school systems fail to adequately address the essential question, "What *is* my job?" when hiring, supervising, and evaluating staff. Few systems have performance-based job descriptions. Most curricula in middle and high schools assume the textbook is the syllabus. School staff members are typically hired on the basis of credentials to fill an available slot (U.S. history, 3rd grade). So, without further clarification, it is easy to fall into thinking that the textbook is the job. It is fair to say, though, that even with this lack of clarity, we've *never* seen a district contract that specifies that a teacher's job is to get through the maximum number of textbook pages. We *do* know that 49 of 50 states have established state content standards and that teachers in those states are expected to teach to them.[7]

What we learn from the international studies

The Third International Mathematics and Science Study (TIMSS), conducted in 1995, supports this view. Researchers tested mathematics and science achievement of students in 42 countries at three grade levels (4, 8, and 12). TIMSS was the largest, most comprehensive and rigorous assessment ever undertaken. Although the outcomes of TIMSS are well known—U.S. students were outperformed by students in most other industrialized countries (Martin, Mullis, Gregory, Hoyle, & Shen, 2000)—the results of the less-publicized companion TIMSS teaching study offer intriguing explanatory insights concerning the issue of content coverage in textbooks. In short, in-depth teaching for understanding using a problem-based approach supported by small texts provides far better results than the typical overloaded-textbook-focused U.S. approach.

Following an exhaustive analysis of classroom teaching in the United States, Japan, and Germany, researchers present striking evidence of the benefits of teaching for understanding in optimizing performance. For example, data from the TIMSS tests and instructional studies clearly show that, although Japanese teachers teach fewer topics in mathematics, their students achieve better results. Rather than randomly covering many discrete skills, teachers in Japan state that their primary aim is to develop conceptual understanding in their students. They emphasize depth versus superficial coverage. Although teachers in Japan cover less ground in terms of discrete topics or pages in a textbook, they emphasize problem-based learning in which rules and theorems are derived and explained by the students, thus leading to deeper understanding (Stigler & Hiebert, 1999).

Despite the fact that mathematics teachers in Japan cover fewer topics, their students achieve better results on tests. Rather than saying that their aim is the development of many discrete skills, these teachers report that their aim is conceptual understanding, and their teaching practices reflect these aims, which contrasts sharply with the views U.S. teachers have of their job. In Japan, the goal of a lesson is for students to develop mathematical thinking, whereas in other countries the goal is to acquire a specific mathematical procedure. Researchers summarized the differences between typical 8th grade mathematics lessons in Japan, Germany, and the United States:

The emphasis on understanding is evident in the steps typical of Japanese eighth-grade mathematics lessons:

> *Teacher poses a complex, thought-provoking problem.*
> *Students struggle with the problem.*
> *Various students present ideas or solutions to the class.*
> *The teacher summarizes the class' conclusions.*
> *Students practice similar problems.*

In contrast, the emphasis on skill acquisition is evident in the steps common to most U.S. and German mathematics lessons:

Teacher instructs students in a concept or skill.

Teacher solves example problems with the class.

Students practice on their own while the teacher assists individual students. (U.S. Department of Education, 1999).

Teachers in Japan emphasize problem-based learning in which rules and theorems are often derived, not merely stated and reinforced through drill. Forty-two percent of their 8th grade math classes involved student presentation of possible alternative solutions to problems as opposed to only 8 percent in U.S. classrooms. Students in Japan spend 44 percent of class time trying to induce the idea to be learned from problems; students in U.S. classrooms spend less than 1 percent on that skill. In contrast, 95 percent of the time in U.S. classrooms is spent practicing a procedure to be learned, something that happens only 40 percent of the time in a Japanese classroom.

In a related finding, the researchers noted that U.S. teachers address far more topics in mathematics and science than do their international colleagues. They also make far fewer connections to other lessons—96 percent of middle school teachers in Japan made such links as compared with only 40 percent of teachers in the United States:

One way to measure coherence is to look for threats to coherence, features of lessons that make it difficult to design "design" and sustain a smoothly developing story. Threats include things like switching topics frequently, or being interrupted by outside intrusions. We found that U.S. lessons contained significantly more topics than Japanese lessons, and significantly more switches from topic to topic than did both German and Japanese lessons. (Stigler & Hiebert, 1999, p. 61)

Japanese teachers go into far greater depth than U.S. teachers:

We defined "developed" quite generously to include cases in which the concept was explained or illustrated, even with a few sentences or brief example. We found that one-fifth of the topics in U.S. lessons contained developed concepts, while four-fifths contained only stated concepts. . . . This distribution was nearly reversed in . . . Japan. (p. 60)

One of the reasons we dubbed American teaching "learning terms and practicing procedures" is that lessons in United States seemed to place greater emphasis on definitions of terms and less emphasis on underlying rationale. When we counted the number of definitions presented in all lessons, we found that there were about twice as many in the United States as in Germany or Japan. (p. 58)

Teaching versus learning

As the discussion of definitions implies, an assumption often hidden under the "need to cover" lies in thinking that everything that we want learned must be taught and that teaching the key facts is what causing learning is. This is simply not true, as a moment's reflection on assignments that are grounded in student research, discussion, and actual performance—using facts to *do* the subject—indicate. Much of what we aim for students to learn is gained from well-designed work and as they make the effort to understand (perhaps by watching the artist, athlete, and computer scientist). Many critics of E. D. Hirsch's work misunderstand—nowhere does he advocate the direct teaching of all those core facts, only that the student learns them if he is to be equipped for the cultural literacy needed for high-level intellectual performance. (*Understanding by Design* has been successfully used in Core Literacy schools based on Hirsch's work as well as alternative project-based schools at the opposite end of the political spectrum.) Hirsch (1988) did not say that the famous list of facts is all that matters or that it must be taught didactically:

> *The extensive curriculum can be taught in a highly formal traditional school or in an informal progressive school. Any sort of school can find ways of incorporating these minimal contents in its courses. . . . The intensive curriculum, though different, is equally essential. Intensive study encourages a fully developed understanding of a subject, making one's knowledge of it integrated and coherent. . . . To understand how isolated facts fit together in some coherent way, we must always acquire mental models of how they cohere, and these schemata can only come from detailed, intensive study and experience. (pp. 128–129)*

As we noted in discussing understandings, teaching big ideas as information to be recalled must fail. Big ideas—justice, irrational numbers, irony—are inherently abstract or even counterintuitive to the naïve learner. They need uncoverage—intensive study. In fact, overly didactic teaching is a major cause, we believe, of the student misunderstanding described in earlier chapters.[8]

Then, it surely is not too controversial to say that the job of teaching is to optimize student learning of what is worthy—not to "cover" a book, nor to "teach, test and hope for the best," irrespective of results. We think that backward design, from content and performance standards (and the assessments they imply), not textbook layout, is the best way to honor that obligation.

Our own informal research findings are germane here. Recall the most common answers given by educators when they are asked to reflect on the qualities of the best instructional designs:

- Clear performance goals, based on a genuine and explicit challenge
- Hands-on approach throughout; far less front-loaded teaching than typical
- Focus on interesting and important ideas, questions, issues, problems
- Obvious real-world application, hence meaning for learners
- Powerful feedback system, with opportunities to learn from trial and error
- Personalized approach, with more than one way to do the major tasks, and room for adapting the process and goal to style, interest, need
- Clear models and modeling
- Time set aside for focused reflection

- Variety in methods, grouping, tasks
- Safe environment for taking risks
- Teacher role resembles that of a facilitator or coach
- More of an immersion experience than a typical classroom experience
- Big picture provided and clear throughout, with a transparent back-and-forth flow between the parts and the whole

The formal research on learning lends further support to the common sense of educators. In the most exhaustive summary of learning conducted in recent years, the authors of *How People Learn* make clear that more coverage does not equal more learning. Three findings form the basis of that book:

1. Students come to the classroom with preconceptions. If their initial understanding is not engaged, they may fail to grasp the new concepts and information.

2. To develop competence in an area of inquiry, students must (a) have a deep foundation of factual knowledge, (b) understand facts and ideas in the context of a conceptual framework, and (c) organize knowledge in ways that facilitate retrieval and application.

3. A metacognitive approach to instruction can help students learn to take control of their learning by defining learning goals and monitoring their progress in achieving them.

In short, "evidence from research indicates that when these three principles are incorporated into teaching, student achievement improves" (Bransford, Brown, & Cocking, 2000, p. 21).

What are some of the key implications for design and instruction? Here we'll highlight a few of the most relevant proposed by the authors, on transfer and understanding:

A major goal of schooling is to prepare students for flexible adaptation to new problems and settings. Students' ability to transfer what they have learned to new situations provides an important index of adaptive, flexible, learning. (p. 235)

Knowledge of a large set of disconnected facts is not sufficient. To develop competence in an area of inquiry, students must have opportunities to learn with understanding. Deep understanding of subject matter transforms factual information into usable knowledge. . . . A key finding in the . . . literature is that organizing information into a conceptual framework allows for greater "transfer." (pp. 16, 17)

Learning with understanding is more likely to promote transfer than simply memorizing information. . . . Many classroom activities . . . focus on facts or details rather than larger themes of causes and consequences.

Students develop flexible understanding of when, where, why, and how to use their knowledge to solve new problems if they learn how to extract underlying themes and principles from their learning experiences. *Understanding how and when to put knowledge to use . . . is an important characteristic of expertise. Learning in multiple contexts most likely affects this aspect of transfer. (p. 236 [emphasis added])*

Superficial coverage of all topics must be replaced with in-depth coverage of fewer topics that allows for key concepts in that discipline to be understood. (p. 20)

Despite the typical U.S. educational mantra and fears about having to teach to the test, coverage—with equal attention to each little fact or subskill (as opposed to a focus on ideas and performance challenges that give meaning to the facts and subskills)—simply does not work to maximize test scores.

Misconception 3: "Yes, but . . . this work is too hard and I just don't have the time."

Even if we are able to convince educators that the first and second "Yes, but . . ." statements are based on misunderstandings and sustained mostly by habit, a third argument invariably arises: The time needed to do all of this work is not currently available. We agree, in part. On the surface this statement is not a misconception. Yes, aligning curriculum with state standards, identifying "big ideas," creating essential questions, designing more authentic assessments, developing plans to teach for understanding in engaging ways, analyzing the resulting student work, and conducting action research to validate interventions is very challenging work, and time must be given to it. And no, individual teachers do not have all the time needed for this difficult work (if it is to be done well). But we need to work smarter, not merely harder or more.

To work smarter we have to realize that a few other misunderstandings lurk as somewhat unconscious assumptions: (1) that *each* teacher, *each* school or *each* district must climb this mountain alone; (2) that the time required must come directly from teaching time, which (we agree) is already in short supply; (3) each standard and benchmark must be addressed separately, in dozens of units designed from scratch; and (4) that "hard and time-consuming" is a *bad* thing.

Building ongoing collaborative research and development into the job

As the exercise on best design suggests, deeper teacher understandings can often be best developed through local study groups and action research. We must apply what the list says and what the book proposes to teacher understanding: An *in-depth* investigation of big ideas in learning is what matters, and school must make that learning more central to professional development and the job description. At the heart of so many of these problems is a variant of the teacher blind spot: "I taught it, so they must have learned it; if I teach more stuff, they will learn more." No. Left to ourselves, the habit of coverage is always likely to seem more defensible than it is. We have to better *understand* learning. We must develop "perspective" and learn to better "apply" sound theoretical "explanations" and "interpretations" of educational research to our work.

Teachers, teams, departments, and entire faculties must ask themselves *each* year: What approaches to curriculum design, teaching, and assessing actually yield the greatest student learning, regardless of our habits and attitudes? We learn from the answers to those questions that we must practice in professional development what Understanding by Design says about understanding: We must uncover, not cover the big ideas, through ongoing inquiry and discussion.

But mindful of both real issues of time and the need for intensive study, let the local research be small in scope but deep—focused on a single unit a year. One unit, designed in collaboration with others, tried out and adjusted a few times per year, with intensive analysis of the student work—surely such a process is possible within existing time allotted for in-service days and team meetings. Consider an analogy to see both the feasibility and value of proceeding this way: How many busy educators prepare gourmet meals *every evening* during the school year? We chuckle at the thought. Even the avid cooks among us don't have the time or energy. But a few times per year, maybe more, we do engage in more elaborate home dining (e.g., a family holiday dinner) that requires more extensive planning, preparation time, and attention to presentation than do typical daily meals. Let it be a job requirement of teaching, backed by supervision, that one "gourmet" unit per year must be developed, collected, reviewed and shared. (Imagine, then, the resulting school or district curriculum "cookbook" ten years hence!)

Such an incremental approach, grounded in the development of design exemplars from which we can all learn, was the central recommendation in *The Teaching Gap.* In addition to the instructional differences between teachers in Japan and the United States, the researchers noted another important difference in the ongoing teacher education in the two countries. In Japan, teacher education seeks depth, not breadth, uncoverage not coverage, learning on the job, not "teaching" of new techniques. For decades, teachers in Japan have used a process known as lesson study, whereby they regularly work in small teams to develop, teach, and refine one research lesson per year. They share the results of their action research and concomitant lesson designs not only with their colleagues in staff meetings, but in regional lesson fairs so that other teachers will benefit from their insights.

We stress that reforming professional development for teachers is the only guaranteed way to improve standard practice and professionalism among all teachers:

> *Another important benefit of the collaborative nature of lesson study is that it provides a benchmarking process that teachers can use to gauge their own skills. . . . At the same time, the collaborative nature of lesson study balances the self-critiquing . . . with the idea that improved teaching is a joint*

process. . . . Problems that emerge are generally attributed to the lesson as designed by the group. . . . It thus becomes possible for teachers to be critical. (Stigler & Hiebert, 1999, p. 125)[9]

This process of collaborative unit and lesson design, refinement, and regional sharing is reflected in the UbD peer-review process. Specific information, directions, and samples are in the *Understanding by Design Professional Development Workbook* (McTighe & Wiggins, 2004).

What is odd about the lack-of-time complaint is that it is only partly true. Every school system devotes at least 12 hours a year to professional development days and approximately 16 hours to staff, grade-level, and departmental meetings. Just imagine what could be accomplished by rethinking those hours and devoting half of them to some form of required lesson study as a job requirement, embedded in grade-level and departmental meeting schedules, as well as the in-service days. Over time, action research would become part of the obligation of all teams and departments, with annual reports issued as to achievement targets tackled, research and development undertaken, results found, and new inquiry proposed for the future.

Consider the following example of how this approach works. Imagine that teachers in your school or district had the opportunity once every three years to take part in a regional summer curriculum design workshop. They would be invited to bring the best (e.g., most engaging and effective) unit that they teach (connected, of course, to state or district content standards). They would join with one or two other teachers of the same subject and level who have identified a similar unit topic, and work with the guidance of a content expert to prepare a "gourmet" unit. Their work in progress would be reviewed against a set of curriculum design standards (such as those in *Understanding by Design*), and they would make adjustments based on the feedback received from peers and experts. They would then enter their best ideas on a computer in an agreed-upon format such as the UbD 3-stage backward design template, and as happens with the UbD Exchange (http://ubdexchange.org).

During the following school year, they would field-test their enhanced unit and collect student work as evidence of the results. They would meet during the year (perhaps during a scheduled in-service day) to collectively evaluate the student work, and make needed adjustments to their unit design. Their completed design would be eligible for regional review by content experts (based on the design standards and the results from student work). Those units that were deemed exemplary would be made available to other educators through the electronic database. We have helped many school faculties develop such a system over the past five years.[10]

A misconception in the way of more such collaboration (fostered in part by local culture, where teachers are dysfunctionally isolated from one another) is that we often presume that content standards and benchmarks need to be addressed discretely, one at a time through narrow targeted lessons, by each teacher, isolated in a classroom. That understandably breeds the feeling that the work is too much for any one of us to handle, but the premise is flawed. This confusion relates back to the first "Yes, but . . ." argument and the problem of the face validity of the state tests. Standardized tests typically sample the standards one at a time through decontexualized (aptly named) "items." Thus, the look and feel of the tests and the lists of standards often misleadingly suggest that we should teach to the standards one bit at a time, as if each standard, benchmark, and indicator is of equal importance.

On the contrary, we are back to the beginning of Understanding by Design: the 3-circle graphic whereby we set priorities around big ideas and core tasks, derived from the standards. Then, when units involve rich and in-depth work, culminating in complex performance, dozens of standards are addressed simultaneously, in appropriate hierarchical order—and with more coherence from the learner's perspective. The challenge at the local level is not to design a lesson per indicator, but to design rich units that ultimately address all standards and clearly signal to students the priorities. This is a problem that is solvable by better unpacking of standards, curriculum writing, mapping, and data collection.

We contend that all such action research will yield four distinct benefits:

1. Walking the Talk. By applying standards to *our own* professional work, the quality of curriculum and assessment designs is enhanced. Instead of assuming that our designs are sound because we worked hard or included activities that students enjoy, the designs must be validated against design standards. Curriculum designs that meet the standards and result in student learning are designated as exemplars, and thus, establish high standards for future curriculum work.

2. Mental Templating. The logic of backward design calls for clarity about desired results and needed assessment evidence *before* identifying learning activities or selecting resources. When teachers use a backward design template to design curriculum units, they develop a productive mental model for planning that helps to avoid the twin problems of activity-oriented and coverage-oriented curricula. Such a design process is particularly valuable for new teachers who have not yet developed a file cabinet of favorite activities or been fully seduced by reliance on textbooks.

3. Working Smarter Using Technology. Most educators are obligated to teach to their state content standards, so why shouldn't statewide sharing be the norm? Because state standards in the various disciplines are more similar than different, couldn't this sharing be extended to a national level? We believe so. Rather than each teacher, school, and district unnecessarily reinventing the same wheels, this approach provides a mechanism for working smarter using a searchable database of validated units. We need not feel guilty that we do not prepare gourmet meals every day. Focusing regularly on exemplars (be they recipes or curriculum designs) is good for everyone. We can thus devote our energies to developing one or two high-quality units, and develop increasingly

higher standards and more refined design skills as we work. And, as with cookbooks, it is far smarter to share our designs so that everyone can benefit from proven recipes.

4. Enhancing Professional Conversations. In addition to higher-quality curriculum products, the *process* of shared design work provides rich professional development. Responses from teachers working in cross-district design teams (as part of regional and state consortia) have confirmed the value of the experience. Unlike one-size-fits-all staff development sessions on generic topics, this design work concentrates on the unique aspects of teaching and assessing specific content topics and results in tangible products of immediate value to teachers. Conversations focus on matters at the heart of the profession: What are the big ideas that we want students to understand? How will we know that they really learned this? What does it mean to meet these standards? What teaching and learning experiences are most engaging and effective? What does student work reveal about the strengths and needs of our curriculum and instruction? Given the limited available time for professional development, it is imperative that it be results-oriented in such a manner—as opposed to coverage of educational trends by outside speakers.

Time-consuming hard work is not a bad thing. It is a good and vital thing, as the quote from Plato's *Republic* at the opening of the chapter suggests. Learning, true learning, is always difficult. It *always* upends old learning, leading to disequilibrium and resistance. We have found that many educators have a paradoxical resistance to learning—especially teachers used to working alone and thinking that smooth control of all that happens in their space, based on their habits, is what matters most. Perhaps the best reason to redesign schools around ongoing collaborative research is that this is the only way to overcome teacher resistance to changing habits, a timidity about experimentation, and a fear of criticism and failure. There is greater courage—and helpful peer pressure to *learn*—when a group of teachers works together to do research into their individual and collective practice.

The six facets are involved here. Teachers need work that will develop greater empathy and self-understanding if they are to truly understand how to cause learning. The blind spot hides from us the pain of all learning, not just the likelihood of student misconception or the individual differences and needs of learners. We are not teachers; we are causes of and students of learning. The job should therefore require that we get and remain "inside" how learning works, to constantly remind ourselves of how difficult it really is. School should require teachers to do action research so that they constantly *feel* what it is like to learn, to be reminded that real learning is always frightening, frustrating, and able to cause self-doubt, regardless of age or talent. If the job and schedule make us think of ourselves as only teachers instead of also as model learners, we miss vital opportunities to make education more honest, invigorating, and self-correcting for everyone, adult and child. The time needed for this work should not be construed as extra but as essential.

Conclusion

We have considered a few widely held views about the obstacles to designing, teaching, and assessing for understanding in a world of external accountability, and we have attempted to reveal their underlying misconceptions. We have suggested that ideas from Understanding by Design are central to improving performance on external measures while preserving intellectual engagement for staff and students: (1) teach and assess for understanding of big ideas and mastery of core subject-area tasks; (2) apply design standards to review and refine local curriculum and assessment, as part of on-going local research and development embedded in the job.

We do not ask or expect you to take us at our word. We know from experience that habits and misunderstandings are rarely overcome by argument—by our covering them! No, the claims in this chapter and in the book as a whole need to be locally uncovered and discussed, tested, argued, and explored by you in your own setting if they are to be accepted (or rejected) on rational grounds. This, too, was, a key conclusion about U.S. school reform drawn by the authors of *The Teaching Gap*:

> *Because teaching is complex, improvements in teaching will be most successful if they are developed in the classrooms where teachers teach and students learn. . . . What works in one classroom might or might not work in another classroom. Ideas for improvement that come from afar—including, for example, what we've learned from Japanese lessons—will need to be tested and adapted to our own local classrooms. (Stigler, & Hiebert, 1999, p. 134)*

We challenge you to investigate what understanding is and isn't, how to best teach for it, and how to best assess for it—all this, in your world of particular standards, tests, and students. All the research in the world means little if you cannot see it at work in *your* classes, with *your* students. Understanding this book means doing the work of trying out the ideas in the book. That's what lesson study sets in motion.

It is our hope that by uncovering some of these often-heard pessimistic claims, we may encourage a more proactive stance by school faculties and district leaders toward what you *can* do to improve learning, regardless of the setting in which you find yourself and the hard work required. The research findings are heartening. Regardless of all the things about students, schools, and society that we cannot control, the things that are in our control—design, instruction, giving feedback—can still significantly affect achievement.

Afterword: Getting Started

> Having teachers stop and think, and sifting and sorting through their repertoire of activities and lessons was quite a paradigm shift in and of itself. Teachers were thinking about what they were teaching. They were evaluating each and every assignment and assessment to ensure validity. Teachers were letting go of time-honored and favorite lessons and activities that were not aligned to the desired results. This was BIG, really BIG!
>
> —Angela Ryan, Instructional Facilitator, Hershey, Pennsylvania

> Just do it!
>
> —Nike Corporation advertising slogan

After elucidating the rationale, the research base, and the key ideas of Understanding by Design, we conclude on a practical note by providing some proven ideas for getting started effectively with UbD.

Creating a design is the natural beginning point. For most teachers, we recommend starting with a curriculum unit. Typically, teachers select a familiar one for restructuring around the UbD elements. Alternatively, teachers planning for a new topic often find it beneficial to design the new unit from the ground up using backward design and the UbD Template. Keep in mind that a companion volume, *Understanding by Design Professional Development Workbook* (McTighe & Wiggins, 2004), with more than 250 pages of worksheets, exercises, examples, and design tips, is available to support the design work.

For administrators, we suggest two options for applying the ideas of UbD: (1) work with a teacher to codesign a curriculum around identified content standards, or (2) use backward design and the UbD Template to plan a professional development workshop or course for adult learners. Many educators have commented that they did not fully understand or appreciate UbD until they had applied it to an actual curriculum design and received feedback from colleagues. As with any big idea, it is easier to fully grasp the nuances and subtleties of this framework after application and reflection.

Regardless of the design topic, in addition to using the *Understanding by Design Professional Development Workbook*, we recommend that you investigate the Understanding by Design Web site (http://ubdexchange.org), which offers the following features:

• *An online curriculum design environment featuring electronic design templates based on the three stages of backward design.* The common format provides consistency for local curriculum designs and ease of sharing among staff. Hot links to many supporting Web sites are tied to the various template fields. For example, Stage 2 provides immediate access to a variety of sites on performance assessment and rubrics.

• *A searchable database of curriculum designs in a common format.* The interrelated database contains units, performance tasks, and scoring rubrics. It contains more than 5,000 designs, with new ones added regularly. Multiple search variables allow users to locate designs by program, subject, course title, key word, grade level, district, school, designer's name, unit title, and any combination of these. A "My Favorites" book-marking feature is included.

• *An online peer review protocol based on the UbD Design Standards.* This process encourages designers to self-assess their work against the Design Standards and interact with other users to give or receive feedback. The Design Standards establish a quality control procedure while promoting a continuous improvement philosophy of curriculum design. Designers may request an expert review by a team of UBD and content-area specialists who provide detailed feedback online.

• *Online guidance, tutorials, and interactive self-assessments to support users.* Technical assistance and an "Ask the Authors" forum is available online.

• *A variety of specialized administrative functions.* These are included to assist school or district administrators in managing their subscriptions.

Enhancing efforts through collaboration

In conjunction with the creation of a curriculum unit (ideally on the UbD Exchange Web site), we strongly encourage the regular use of the UbD Design Standards for self-assessment and peer review. The standards articulate the qualities of effective UbD design, and encourage teacher reflection and revision.

The value of the Understanding by Design framework escalates when it is adopted and applied in a coordinated manner by teams, schools, or entire districts. Here are some practical actions that grade-level or department teams, school faculties, or entire district staff can take to get started, and move forward, with UbD:

• Form a study group to read and discuss selected sections of *Understanding by Design, Expanded 2nd Ed.*

• View and discuss the ASCD videos *What Is Understanding?* and *Using Backward Design.*

• Send a representative team of teachers and administrators to local, regional, or national introductory UbD workshops or conferences.

• Sponsor an introductory UbD workshop in your district or school (e.g., on a scheduled in-service day).

• Explore UbD-related Essential Questions in faculty and team meetings (e.g., How can we teach to all these content standards in engaging and effective ways? What content is worth understanding? How do we know that students really understand what we teach? How do we raise achievement without fixating on "practice" tests?).

• Send a scout team to visit a school or district in the region using UbD, and report back on potential benefits for your school or district.

• Identify a cadre of teachers and administrators to spearhead UbD efforts in the school or district.

• Send cadre members to a three- to five-day regional or national UbD Institute.

• Provide time (and other incentives) for cadre members to design and share UbD units.

• Conduct peer reviews of locally designed units using the UbD Design Standards.

• Purchase membership in the ubdexchange.org Web site for cadre members and have them search and share UbD "blue ribbon" units on topics taught, review existing units on the Web site using the UbD Design Standards, and design a unit online and request expert review.

• Work in grade-level or departmental groups to unpack content standards (i.e., identify understandings and essential questions).

• Work in grade-level or departmental groups to prioritize content standards and textbook content using the three-ovals worksheet (Figure 3.3 in Chapter 3).

• Create a school or district curriculum map based on UbD (i.e., containing understandings, essential questions, and core performance tasks).

• Post essential questions in classrooms. Share examples during faculty meetings.

• Develop core performance tasks (based on the six facets of understanding) and common scoring rubrics.

• Work in grade-level or departmental groups to review and evaluate student work on core performance tasks. Select schoolwide or districtwide "anchors" for the rubrics.

• Analyze external achievement test data and student work to identify areas of student misunderstanding and develop intervention plans.

• Establish and implement Action Research and Lesson Study teams around achievement problem areas.

• Develop and implement an induction program to introduce new teachers to UbD.

- Apply backward design to planning various school and district initiatives.
- Seek state, federal, and foundation grants to support UbD implementation.

Walking the talk

No single pathway will lead an individual or team to develop understanding of, and proficiency with, UbD. However, we do recommend that educators "walk the talk" and use backward design in planning for how they will use Understanding by Design.

Appendix: Sample 6-Page Template

Use the following completed six-page template as a guide as you design your own UbD units.

Unit Cover Page

Unit Title: You Are What You Eat   Grade Levels: 5th

Subject/Topic Areas: Health and Nutrition

Key Words: nutrition, health, wellness, balanced diet, food pyramid

Designed by: Bob James   Time Frame: 3 weeks

School District: Montgomery Knolls P.S.   School: Cheshire Cat Elem.

Brief Summary of Unit (including curricular context and unit goals):

    In this introductory unit of the health education course, students will learn about human nutritional needs, the food groups, the nutritional benefits of various foods, the USDA food pyramid guidelines, and health problems associated with poor nutrition. They will design an illustrated nutrition brochure to teach younger children about the importance of good nutrition for healthy living, work in cooperative groups to analyze a hypothetical family's diet and recommend ways to improve their nutritional value, and conduct research on health problems resulting from poor eating habits.

    In the culminating performance task, students develop and present a proposed menu for an upcoming three-day outdoor education program. Their menu for meals and snacks should meet the USDA food pyramid recommendations. The unit concludes with students evaluating their personal eating habits and the extent to which they eat healthily.

Unit design status: ☑ Completed template pages—Stages 1, 2, and 3

☑ Completed blueprint for each performance task   ☐ Completed rubrics

☐ Directions to students *and* teachers   ☐ Materials and resources listed

☐ Suggested accommodations   ☐ Suggested extensions

Status: ◯ Initial draft (date ___3/12___)   ☑ Revised draft (date ___7/14___)

☑ Peer reviewed   ☑ Content reviewed   ☑ Field tested   ◯ Validated   ◯ Anchored

Stage 1—Identify Desired Results

Established Goals:

> Standard 6—Students will understand essential concepts about nutrition and diet.
> 6a—Students will use an understanding of nutrition to plan appropriate diets for themselves and others.
> 6c—Students will understand their own individual eating patterns and ways in which those patterns may be improved.

What essential questions will be considered?

> • What is healthful eating?
> • Are you a heathful eater? How would you know?
> • How could a healthy diet for one person be unhealthy for another?
> • Why are there so many health problems in the United States caused by poor nutrition despite all the available information?

What understandings are desired?

> *Students will understand that . . .*
>
> • A balanced diet contributes to physical and mental health.
> • The USDA food pyramid presents *relative* guidelines for nutrition.
> • Dietary requirements vary for individuals based on age, activity level, weight, and overall health.
> • Healthful living requires an individual to act on available information about good nutrition even if it means breaking comfortable habits.

What key knowledge and skills will students acquire as a result of this unit?

> *Students will know . . .*
>
> • Key terms—protein, fat, calorie, carbohydrate, cholesterol.
> • Types of foods in each food group and their nutritional values.
> • The USDA food pyramid guidelines.
> • Variables influencing nutritional needs.
> • General health problems caused by poor nutrition.

> *Students will be able to . . .*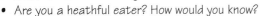
>
> • Read and interpret nutrition information on food labels.
> • Analyze diets for nutritional value.
> • Plan balanced diets for themselves and others.

Stage 2—Determine Acceptable Evidence

What evidence will show that students understand?

Performance Tasks:

You Are What You Eat—Students create an illustrated brochure to teach younger children about the importance of good nutrition for healthful living. Offer younger students ideas for breaking bad eating habits.

Chow Down—Students develop a three-day menu for meals and snacks for an upcoming Outdoor Education camp experience. They write a letter to the camp director to explain why their menu should be selected (by showing that it meets the USDA food pyramid recommendations, yet it is tasty enough for the students). Include at least one modification for a specific dietary condition (diabetic or vegetarian) or religious consideration.

What other evidence needs to be collected in light of Stage 1 Desired Results?

Other Evidence:
(e.g., tests, quizzes, prompts, work samples, observations)

Quiz—The food groups and the USDA food pyramid

Prompt—Describe two health problems that could arise as a result of poor nutrition and explain how these could be avoided.

Skill Check—Interpret nutritional information on food labels.

Student Self-Assessment and Reflection:

1. Self-assess the brochure, *You Are What You Eat.*
2. Self-assess the camp menu, *Chow Down.*
3. Reflect on the extent to which you eat healthfully at the end of unit (compared with the beginning).

Stage 2—Determine Acceptable Evidence   (continued)

Assessment Task Blueprint

What understandings or goals will be assessed through this task?

> Students will plan appropriate diets for themselves and others.

What criteria are implied in the standards and understandings regardless of the task specifics? What qualities must student work demonstrate to signify that standards were met?

> - Nutritionally sound
> - Comparison of taste vs. nutrition
> - Feasible

Through what authentic performance task will students demonstrate understanding?

> **Task Overview:**
>
> Since we have been learning about nutrition, the camp director at the Outdoor Ed Center has asked us to propose a nutritionally balanced menu for our three-day trip to the center later this year. Using the USDA food pyramid guidelines and the nutrition facts on food labels, design a plan for three days, including the three main meals and three snacks (a.m., p.m., and campfire). Your goal is a tasty and nutritionally balanced menu. In addition to your menu, prepare a letter to the camp director explaining how your menu meets the USDA nutritional guidelines. Include a chart showing a breakdown of the fat, protein, carbohydrates, vitamins, minerals, and calories.

What student products and performances will provide evidence of desired understandings?

> Menu with chart of nutritional values

> Letter to camp director

By what criteria will student products and performances be evaluated?

> - Menu meets USDA guidelines
> - Nutritional values chart is accurate and complete
> - Menu addresses the audience and the situation

> - Effective explanation of nutritional value and taste appeal of proposed menu
> - Proper letter form
> - Correct spelling and conventions

Stage 3—Plan Learning Experiences

WHERETO

What sequence of teaching and learning experiences will equip students to engage with, develop, and demonstrate the desired understandings? Use the following sheet to list the key teaching and learning activities in sequence. Code each entry with the appropriate initials of the WHERETO elements.

1. Begin with an entry question (Can the foods you eat cause zits?) to hook students into considering the effects of nutrition on their lives.   **H**

2. Introduce the Essential Questions and discuss the culminating unit performance tasks (Chow Down and Eating Action Plan).   **W**

3. Note: Key vocabulary terms are introduced as needed by the various learning activities and performance tasks. Students read and discuss relevant selections from the Health textbook to support the learning activities and tasks. As an ongoing activity, students keep a chart of their daily eating and drinking for later review and evaluation.   **E**

4. Present concept attainment lesson on the food groups. Then have students practice categorizing pictures of foods accordingly.   **E**

5. Introduce the food pyramid and identify foods in each group. Students work in groups to develop a poster of the food pyramid containing cut-out pictures of foods in each group. Display the posters in the classroom or hallway.   **E**

6. Give quiz on the food groups and food pyramid (matching format).   **E**

7. Review and discuss the nutrition brochure from the USDA. Discussion question: Must everyone follow the same diet to be healthy?   **R**

8. Working in cooperative groups, students analyze a hypothetical family's diet (deliberately unbalanced) and make recommendations for improved nutrition. Teacher observes and coaches students as they work.   **E-2**

9. Have groups share their diet analyses and discuss as a class.   **E, E-2**
(Note: Teacher collects and reviews the diet analyses to look for misunderstandings needing instructional attention.)

10. Each student designs an illustrated nutrition brochure to teach younger children about the importance of good nutrition for healthy living and the problems associated with poor eating. This activity is completed outside of class.   **E, T**

11. Students exchange brochures with members of their group for a peer assessment based on a criteria list. Allow students to make revisions based on feedback.   **R, E-2**

12. Show and discuss the video "Nutrition and You." Discuss the health problems linked to poor eating.   **E**

13. Students listen to, and question, a guest speaker (nutritionist from the local hospital) about health problems caused by poor nutrition.   **E**

14. Students respond to written prompt: Describe two health problems that could arise as a result of poor nutrition and explain what changes in eating could help to avoid them. (These are collected and graded by teacher.)   **E-2**

15. Teacher models how to read and interpret food label information on nutritional values. Then students practice using donated boxes, cans, and bottles (empty!).   **E**

16. Students work independently to develop the three-day camp menu. Evaluate and give feedback on the camp menu project. Students self- and peer-assess their projects using rubrics.   **E-2, T**

17. At the conclusion of the unit, students review their completed daily eating chart and self-assess the healthfulness of their eating. Have they noticed changes? Improvements? Do they notice changes in how they feel and their appearance?   **E-2**

18. Students develop a personal "eating action plan" for healthful eating. These are saved and presented at upcoming student-involved parent conferences.   **E-2, T**

19. Conclude the unit with student self-evaluation regarding their personal eating habits. Have each student develop a personal action plan for a "healthful eating" goal.   **E-2, T**

Stage 3—Plan Learning Experiences (continued)

Consider the WHERETO elements.

Monday	Tuesday	Wednesday	Thursday	Friday
1 (HW) 1. Hook students with a discussion of eating habits and "zits." 2. Introduce essential questions and key vocabulary. 3. Have students begin a food diary to record their daily eating patterns.	**2** (E) 4. Present concept attainment lesson on food groups, then categorize foods. 5. Have students read and discuss the nutrition brochure from the USDA.	**3** (ET) 6. Present lesson on the food pyramid and identify foods in each group. 7. Read and discuss relevant selections from the Health textbook. Provide illustrated pamphlet for lower-level readers.	**4** (ET) 8. Present and discuss the video "Nutrition and You." 9. Have students design an illustrated nutrition brochure to teach younger children about the importance of good nutrition for healthy living.	**5** (ET) 10. Assess and give feedback on the brochures. Allow students to self- and peer-assess the brochures using a list of criteria.
6 (E) 11. Working in cooperative groups, have students analyze a diet for a hypothetical family and make recommendations for improved nutrition.	**7** (R) 12. Conduct a group review and give feedback regarding the diet analyses. Allow revisions.	**8** (E) 13. Have students listen to and question guest speaker (nutritionist from local hospital) about health problems caused by poor nutrition.	**9** (ET) 14. Have students conduct research on health problems resulting from poor eating. Provide students with options for how they share their findings.	**10** (E) 15. Model how to interpret food label information for nutritional values. Have students practice interpreting food labels.
11 (E) 16. Review the camp menu rubric so that students understand the criteria. Have them work independently to develop a three-day camp menu.	**12** (E) 17. Observe and coach students as they work on their menus.	**13** (E) 18. Evaluate and give feedback on the camp menu project. Have students self- and peer-assess their projects using the rubric.	**14** (ET) 19. Have students review their food diaries to look for changing patterns in their eating. Have each student set a personal goal for improved nutrition.	**15** (ET) 20. Conclude the unit with student self-evaluation regarding their personal eating habits. Have each student develop a personal action plan for a healthful eating goal.

L

Endnotes

Chapter 1

1. For additional information and examples of cognitive tools, see McTighe & Lyman (1988).

Chapter 2

1. This is a fake song in which French words are used to make up a familiar rhyme about numbers—in accented English. Hint: the book is called *Mots d'Heures: Gousses, Rames.* (*Mots d'Heures: Gousses Rames,* by Luis d'Antin Van Rooten [Penguin Books, 1980; first published by Grossman Publishers, 1967]).

2. Information on the Science Education Project is available from the Harvard-Smithsonian Center for Astrophysics, 60 Garden Street, Cambridge, MA 02138, http://cfa-www.harvard.edu/.

Chapter 3

1. We highly recommend this text from long ago. It presents one of the most clear and helpful analyses of the problem of framing curriculum ever presented, especially since one of the authors was a key figure in progressive education, with practical experience in trying to honor almost all the ideas presented in *Understanding by Design*. The book can be found in various locations on the Internet, for example, the online library www.questia.com.

2. For additional sources, see Erickson (1998), Tomlinson et al. (2001), the *Dictionary of the History of Ideas*, a multivolume reference set built upon key concepts, and Adler (1999).

Chapter 4

1. Compare Schank (1990) and Egan (1986) on the importance of narrative for cognition and learning.

Chapter 5

1. This is not a blanket call for a discovery approach to instruction. Rather, we merely note that understanding a big idea typically requires the kind of active inquiry, discussion, and applications we describe here. See Chapter 9 for a more comprehensive look at the problem in our discussion of sequence of instruction.

2. See Chapter 1 of Erickson (1998) for a thorough discussion of the limits of various national standards documents and the need to be clearer about the questions and understandings sought.

Chapter 6

1. Note that Lynn Erickson stresses what she calls "conceptual" generalizations, thereby making what we call topical understandings more like facts. We prefer our distinction between topical and overarching understandings as opposed to facts because both kinds of understandings require inference from facts.

2. See the supplementary materials in Science (Michigan: http://www.miclimb.net) and History/Social Studies (New York: http://www.emsc.nysed.gov/ciai/socst/ssrg.html; Virginia: http://vastudies.pwnet.org/sol/c_framework.htm; Texas: http://www.tea.state.tx.us/resources/ssced/toolkits/html/toc_ubd.htm).

3. See Piaget (1973, 1973/1977).

4. This is true even when we think of the target as requiring the student to "understand how to . . ." Even though we may focus on key processes or performances, we still expect students to grasp specific insights in order to enhance their performance. See Erickson (1998), p. 83. Compare with Erickson (2001), Chapter 2 on "Concept-based Curriculum."

Chapter 9

1. From the 2003 Annual Report of the National Survey of Student Engagement (NSSE), available at http://www.iub.edu/~nsse/html/report-2003.shtml. Other studies from NSSE are available at http://www.iub.edu/~nsse/. See also Kuh (2003).

2. See also Levy (1996) for his own account of his teaching.

3. Readers are encouraged to review "Ten Tools for Transfer" for a helpful list of the kinds of experiences most likely to develop transfer of learning. See Fogarty, Perkins, & Barell (1992).

Chapter 10

1. See, for example, Blythe & Associates (1998), Bottoms & Sharpe (1996), White & Gunstone (1992), Saphier & Gower (1997), Marzano & Pickering (1997).

2. Readers familiar with educational history will hear an echo of the idea that learning should be designed to "recapitulate" the history of knowledge in this and other examples. Though we do not subscribe to the idea of recapitulation as a sound educational theory, the idea that students should experience authentic inquiry and sometimes re-create or simulate how knowledge was developed is part of what we mean by uncoverage. See Egan (1997), Gould (1977), and Wiggins (1987), for more on recapitulation.

3. Readers are referred to Adler (1984) and follow-up volumes for further insight into the rationale for the three columns and how to decide what kind of teaching best suits what kind of objective.

4. See Finkel (2000).

Chapter 12

1. See http://www.ncaction.org.uk/ for all the rubrics, including samples of tasks and student work for each score point, and other helpful assessment-related information.

2. See Kliebard (1987), pp. 223–224. Kliebard wryly notes, however, that even here the idea of making curricula interest-centered had been corrupted somewhat from the more radical approach intended by the "activity curriculum" proponents such as Kilpatrick. To Kliebard it appears "open to question" whether the proposed sequence of topics "actually represented interests of children" or a more benign but still arbitrary adult conception of how to order topics.

3. For background reading on a logic of inquiry, see Collingwood (1939), Gadamer (1994), and Bateman (1990).

Chapter 13

1. See, for example, Kohn (2000).

2. Although it may surprise many readers for us to argue this way, given our long-standing documented opposition to overreliance on indirect tests, the issue here is more

narrowly focused on test validity. Numerous arguments can be made on behalf of more performance assessment in educational testing, but the issue here is the reverse: Indirect—"inauthentic"—tests can yield valid inferences, just as "authentic" tasks can yield invalid inferences.

3. The complete research reports are available at http://www.consortium-chicago.org/publications/p0001.html.

4. Furthermore, recent studies have cast doubt on the extravagant claims made by SAT-prep companies about the gains in scores that they cause.

5. From http://www.project2061.org/about/press/pr000627.htm. Project 2061 of the American Association for the Advancement of Science (http://www.aaas.org) has conducted evaluations of mathematics and science textbooks in the United States. See http://www.project2061.org/publications/articles/textbook/default.htm.

6. From http://www.project2061.org/about/press/pr990928.htm.

7. Iowa, the one state that has not promulgated standards from the state level, requires school districts to develop local standards and assessments; in addition to these local efforts, many districts also use the Iowa Test of Basic Skills.

8. See Gardner (1991), Chapter 8; and Bransford, Brown, & Cocking (2000), p. 10ff.

9. Additional information about this research may be found on the TIMSS Web site (http://nces.ed.gov/timss/). For more on lesson study, see Lewis (2002).

10. Our Understanding by Design Exchange (http://ubdexchange.org) has been operating since 2001 in partnership with the Association for Supervision and Curriculum Development (ASCD). It contains more than 1,000 units designed in an electronic version of the UbD Template. The Exchange offers a robust forum for the creation, sharing, and peer review of units for all subscribers. It affords teachers the opportunity to share lesson and assessment ideas with colleagues who teach the same topics. And it offers a host of resources for school and district administrators, including sophisticated search capabilities, curriculum mapping, and expert reviews of local designs.

Glossary

academic prompt   A form of assessment between an authentic performance task and a short-answer test or quiz. Academic prompts are open-ended written performance tests.

As the word *academic* suggests, they are tests that occur only in school or exam situations. The tester prompts a response to a particular quote, idea, or request for performance. Such prompts are not authentic (even though they prompt performance) because typical school constraints are placed on the task, the access to resources, time allotted, and opportunity to talk to others. *Contrast* **authentic assessment** and **quiz**.

achievement target   A synonym for *desired result, learning outcome,* and similar terms related to the educational end sought. *See also* **desired result**.

analytic-trait scoring   A type of scoring that uses several distinct criteria to evaluate student products and performances. In effect, a performance is assessed several times, using the lens of separate criteria each time. For example, in the analytic scoring of essays, we might evaluate five traits—organization, use of detail, attention to audience, persuasiveness, and conventions. Analytic-trait scoring contrasts with **holistic scoring**, whereby a judge forms a single, overall impression about a performance. *See also* **rubric**.

anchors   Samples of work or performance used to set the specific performance standard for each level of a **rubric**. For example, attached to the paragraph describing a level-six performance in writing would be two or three samples of writing that illustrate what a level-six performance is. (The anchor for the top score is often called the "exemplar.")

Anchors contribute significantly to scoring reliability. A rubric without such anchors is typically far too ambiguous to set a clear standard for judges and performers alike. Such phrases as "sophisticated and persuasive" or "insightful mathematical solution" have little meaning unless teachers have examples of work that provide concrete and stable definitions.

Anchors also support students by providing tangible models of quality work.

application   One of the six **facets** of understanding and a time-honored indicator of understanding. The ability to apply knowledge and skill in diverse situations provides important evidence of the learner's understanding.

The idea is not new or specific to UbD. Bloom and his colleagues (1956) saw application as central to understanding and quite different from the kind of plugging-in and fill-in-the-blanks activity found in so many classrooms: "Teachers frequently say: If a student really comprehends something, he can apply it. . . . Application is different in two ways from knowledge and simple comprehension: the student is not prompted to give specific knowledge, nor is the problem old-hat" (p. 120). *See also* **empathy**; **explanation**; **interpretation**; **perspective**; **self-knowledge**.

assess   To thoroughly and methodically analyze student accomplishment against specific goals and criteria. The word comes from the Latin *assidere,* meaning "to sit beside." *See also* **performance task**.

assessment   Techniques used to analyze student accomplishment against specific goals and criteria. A test is one type of assessment. Others include clinical interviews (as in Piaget's work), observations, self-assessments, and surveys. Good assessment requires a balance of techniques because each technique is limited and prone to error.

To refer to "assessments" instead of just "tests" is also a distinction of manner and attitude, as implied by the Latin origin of the word *assess;* to assess is to "sit with" the student. The implication is that in an assessment the teacher makes thoughtful observations and disinterested judgments, and offers clear and helpful feedback.

Assessment is sometimes viewed as synonymous with evaluation, though common usage differs. A teacher can assess a student's strengths and weaknesses without placing a value or a grade on the performance. *See also* **performance task; standardized**.

audit test   Our term for the state or national standardized test. Like the business audit or doctor's physical exam, it is a brief test that assesses something important and complex using simpler indicators. The test questions are proxies for more important goals and standards, in the same way that a blood pressure reading gives a quick snapshot of overall health. We think it important to make this point to remind readers that the goal and look of the standardized test is very different from the goal and look of more direct assessment of the goals and standards, so it makes little sense to attend solely to the audit. Rather, the audit will go well to the extent that "health" is attended to locally. *Contrast* **direct test**.

authentic assessment, authentic task   An assessment composed of **performance tasks** and activities designed to simulate or replicate important real-world challenges. The heart of authentic assessment is realistic performance-based testing—asking the student to use knowledge in real-world ways, with genuine purposes, audiences, and situational variables.

Thus, the context of the assessment, not just the task itself and whether it is performance-based or hands-on, is what makes the work authentic (e.g. the "messiness" of the problem, ability to seek feedback and revise, access to appropriate resources). Authentic assessments are meant to do more than "test": they should teach students (and teachers) what the "doing" of a subject looks like and what kinds of performance challenges are actually considered most important in a field or profession. The tasks are chosen because they are representative of essential questions or challenges facing practitioners in the field.

An authentic test directly measures students on the valued performances. By contrast, multiple-choice tests are indirect measures of performance. (Compare, for example, the road test versus the written test for getting a driver's license.) In the field of measurement, authentic tests are called "direct" tests. *Contrast* **academic prompt** and **quiz**.

backward design   An approach to designing a curriculum or unit that begins with the end in mind and designs toward that end. Although such an approach seems logical, it is viewed as backward because many teachers begin their unit design with the means—textbooks, favored lessons, and time-honored activities—rather than deriving those from the end—the targeted results, such as content standards or understandings. We advocate the reverse of habit: starting with the end (the desired results) and then identifying the evidence necessary to determine that the results have been achieved (assessments). With the results and assessments clearly specified, the designer determines the necessary (enabling) knowledge and skill, and only then, the teaching needed to equip students to perform.

This view is not new. Ralph Tyler (1949) described the logic of backward design clearly and succinctly more than 50 years ago:

> *Educational objectives become the criteria by which materials are selected, content is outlined, instructional procedures are developed and tests and examinations are prepared. . . . The purpose of a statement of objectives is to indicate the kinds of changes in the student to be brought about so that instructional activities can be planned and developed in a way likely to attain these objectives. (pp. 1, 45)*

benchmark   In an assessment system, a developmentally appropriate standard; sometimes called a "milepost" standard. For example, many districtwide systems set benchmarks for grades 4, 8, 10, and 12. In many state content standards, benchmarks provide further concrete indicators for the standards—they serve as substandards. In athletics and industry, the term is often used to describe the highest level of performance—the exemplars. Used as a verb, *benchmark* means to search for a best performance or achievement specification for a particular objective. The resulting benchmark (noun) sets the highest possible standard of performance, a goal to aim toward. Thus, a benchmark in this sense is used when teachers want their assessment to be anchored by the best possible samples of work (versus being anchored by samples of work from an average school district).

An assessment anchored by benchmarks, in either sense of the word, should not be expected to yield a predictable curve of results. Standards differ from reasonable expectations. (*See also* **standard**.) It is possible that very few products or performances—or even none at all—will match the benchmark performance.

big idea   In Understanding by Design, the core concepts, principles, theories, and processes that should serve as the focal point of curricula, instruction, and assessment. By definition, big ideas are important and enduring. Big ideas are transferable beyond the scope of a particular unit (e.g., adaptation, allegory, the American Dream, significant figures). Big ideas are the building material of understandings. They can be thought of as the meaningful patterns that enable one to connect the dots of otherwise fragmented knowledge.

Such ideas go beyond discrete facts or skills to focus on larger concepts, principles, or processes. These are applicable to new situations within or beyond the subject. For example, students study the enactment of the Magna Carta as a specific historical event *because* of its significance to a larger idea, the rule of law, whereby written laws specify the limits of a government's power and the rights of individuals, such as due process. This big idea transcends its roots in 13th-century England and is a cornerstone of modern democratic societies.

A big idea can also be described as a "linchpin" idea. The linchpin is the pin that keeps the wheel in place on an axle. Thus, a linchpin idea is one that is essential for understanding, without which the student cannot go anywhere. For instance, without grasping the distinction between the letter and the spirit of the law, students cannot understand the American constitutional and legal system—even if they are highly knowledgeable and articulate about facts of history. Without a focus on linchpin ideas with lasting value, students may be left with easily forgotten fragments of knowledge.

Bloom's Taxonomy   The common name of a system that classifies and clarifies the range of possible intellectual objectives, from the cognitively easy to the difficult; in effect, a classification of degrees of understanding. More than 40 years ago, Benjamin Bloom and his colleagues in testing and measurement developed this schema for distinguishing the simplest forms of recall from the most sophisticated uses of knowledge in designing student assessments. Their work was summarized in the now ubiquitous text titled *Taxonomy of Educational Objectives: Cognitive Domain.*

As the authors often note, the writing of this book was driven by persistent problems in testing. Educators needed to know how educational objectives or teacher goals should be measured, given the absence of clear agreement about the meaning of objectives such as "critical grasp of" and "thorough knowledge of"—phrases that test developers typically use.

In the introduction to the *Taxonomy,* Bloom and his colleagues (1956) refer to "understanding" as a commonly sought but ill-defined objective:

For example, some teachers believe their students should "really understand," others desire their students to "internalize knowledge," still others want their students to "grasp the core or essence." Do they all mean the same thing? Specifically, what does a student do who "really understands" which he does not do when he does not understand? Through reference to the Taxonomy . . . teachers should be able to define such nebulous terms. (p. 1)

They identified six cognitive levels: Knowledge, Comprehension, Application, Analysis, Synthesis, and Evaluation, with the last three commonly referred to as "higher order." Note that in this scheme, higher-order thinking does not include *application* as they defined it. This seems odd, given the seemingly complex demands of application and the concern expressed by many advocates of authentic assessment about getting the student to more effectively apply knowledge. But this is not what Bloom and his colleagues meant by *apply.* They were speaking of those narrower cases in which a student must use discrete knowledge or skill in an exam setting, as when constructing a sentence or solving a math word problem; they were not referring to the more sophisticated act of drawing upon a repertoire to solve a complex, multifaceted, contextualized problem. The authors' description of *synthesis* thus better fits the meaning of *application* used in *Understanding by Design* in particular and the performance assessment movement in general, because they stress that such an aim requires the "students' unique production."

concept   A mental construct or category represented by a word or phrase. Concepts include both tangible objects (e.g., chair, rabbit) and abstract ideas (e.g., democracy, bravery). Overarching understandings are derived from concepts.

content standards   *See* **standard**.

coverage   A teaching approach that superficially teaches and tests content knowledge irrespective of student understanding or engagement. The term generally has a negative connotation: It implies that the goal is to march through a body of material (often a textbook) within a specified time frame. (Ironically, one meaning of the term *to cover* is "to obscure.") Teachers often couple the term with an excuse linked to demands of curriculum frameworks ("I would have liked to go into greater depth, but we *have* to cover the content") or external testing ("but the students will be tested on . . . and the results are published in the paper"). *Contrast* **uncoverage**.

criteria   The qualities that must be met for work to measure up to a standard. To ask, "What are the criteria?" is the same as asking, "What should we look for when examining students' products or performances to know if they were successful? How will we determine acceptable work?"

Criteria should be considered *before* the design of specific performance tasks (though this seems odd to novice designers). Designing a task that measures critical thinking requires knowing beforehand what the indicators of such thinking are, and then designing the task so that students must demonstrate those traits through performance.

An assessment must also determine how much weight each criterion should receive relative to other criteria. Thus, if teachers agree that spelling, organization, and the development of ideas are all important in judging writing, they must then ask, "Are they of equal importance? If not, what percentage should we assign to each?"

The criteria used in judging performance, like a test itself, can be valid or invalid, and authentic or inauthentic. For example, a teacher can assign students to do some original historical research (an authentic task) but grade the work only on whether four sources were used and whether the report is exactly five pages long. Such criteria would be invalid because a piece of historical work could easily not meet those two criteria but still be excellent research. Criteria should correspond to the qualities of masterful performance.

Many performance assessments undervalue so-called impact criteria. (See Chapters 5 and 6 in Wiggins [1998] for more on these types of criteria.)

curriculum   Literally, "the course to be run." In *Understanding by Design,* the term refers to the explicit and comprehensive plan developed to honor a framework based on content and performance standards.

design   To plan the form and structure of something or the pattern or motif of a work of art. In education, teachers are designers in both senses, aiming to develop purposeful, coherent, effective, and engaging lessons, units, and courses of study and accompanying assessments to achieve identified results.

To say that something happens by design is to say that it occurs through thoughtful planning as opposed to by accident or by "winging it." At the heart of Understanding by Design is the idea that what happens *before* the teacher gets in the classroom may be as or more important than the teaching that goes on inside the classroom.

design standards   The specific standards used to evaluate the quality of unit designs. Rather than treating design as merely a function of good intentions and hard work, standards and a peer review process provide a way for teacher work to be assessed in the same way that student work is assessed against rubrics and anchors. The design standards have a dual purpose: (1) to guide self-assessment and peer reviews to identify design strengths and needed improvements; and (2) to provide a mechanism for quality control, a means of validating curricular designs.

desired result   A specific educational goal or achievement target. In Understanding by Design, Stage 1 sums up all desired results. Common synonyms include *target, goal, objective,* and *intended outcome.* Desired results in education are generally of five kinds: (1) factual or rule-based declarative knowledge (e.g., a noun is the name of a person, place, or thing); (2) skills and processes (e.g., rendering a perspective drawing, researching a topic); (3) understandings, insights derived from inferences into ideas, people, situations, and processes (e.g., visible light represents a very small band within the electromagnetic spectrum); (4) habits of mind (e.g., persistence, tolerance for ambiguity); and (5) attitudes (e.g., appreciation of reading as a valuable leisure-time pursuit).

Though they involve complex learnings, the desired results must be cast in measurable terms. Any valid assessment, in other words, is designed to measure the degree to which the learner's work hit the target. *See also* **achievement target**.

direct test   A test that measures the achievement of a targeted performance in the context in which the performance is expected to occur (e.g., the parallel-parking portion of a driving test). In comparison, an **indirect test** uses often deliberately simplified ways of measuring the same performance out of context (e.g., written portion of a driver's test). A direct test is more authentic than an indirect test, by definition. *Contrast* **audit test**.

empathy   One of the six **facets** of understanding. Empathy, the ability to "walk in another's shoes," to escape one's own emotional reactions to grasp another's, is central to the most common colloquial use of the term *understanding.* When we "try to understand" another person, people, or culture, we strive for empathy. It is thus not simply affective response; it is not sympathy. It is a *learned* ability to grasp the world (or text) from someone else's point of view. It is the discipline of using one's imagination to see and feel as others see and feel, to imagine that something different might be possible, even desirable.

Empathy is not the same as **perspective**. Seeing something in perspective involves seeing from a critical distance; detaching oneself to see more objectively. Empathy involves seeing from inside another person's worldview;

embracing the insights, experience, and feelings that are found in the subjective or aesthetic realm.

The term was coined by a German scholar, Theodor Lipps, at the turn of the 20th century to describe what the audience must do to understand a work or performance of art. Empathy is thus the deliberate act of finding what is plausible, sensible, or meaningful in the ideas and actions of others, even if they appear puzzling or off-putting. *See also* **application**; **explanation**; **interpretation**; **perspective**; **self-knowledge**.

enduring understandings   The specific inferences, based on **big ideas**, that have lasting value beyond the classroom. In UbD, designers are encouraged to write them as full-sentence statements, describing what, specifically, students should understand about the topic. The stem "Students will understand *that . . .*" provides a practical tool for identifying understandings.

In thinking about the enduring understandings for a unit or course, teachers are encouraged to ask, "What do we want students to understand and be able to use several years from now, after they have forgotten the details?"

Enduring understandings are central to a discipline and are transferable to new situations. For example, in learning about the rule of law, students come to understand that "written laws specify the limits of a government's power and articulate the rights of individuals, such as due process." This inference from facts, based on big ideas such as "rights" and "due process," provides a conceptual unifying lens through which to recognize the significance of the Magna Carta as well as to examine emerging democracies in the developing world.

Because such understandings are generally abstract in nature and often not obvious, they require **uncoverage** through sustained inquiry rather than one-shot **coverage**. The student must come to understand or be helped to grasp the idea, as a result of work. If teachers treat an understanding like a fact, the student is unlikely to get it.

entry question   A simple, thought-provoking question that opens a lesson or unit. It often introduces a key idea or understanding in an accessible way. Effective entry questions spark discussion about a common experience, provocative issue, or perplexing problem, as a lead-in to the unit and essential questions.

Entry questions should be framed for maximal simplicity, be worded in student-friendly language, have provocation value, and point toward the larger unit and essential questions. The design challenge is to enable essential and unit questions to arise naturally from the entry questions, problems, and activities.

essential question   A question that lies at the heart of a subject or a curriculum (as opposed to being either trivial or leading), and promotes inquiry and **uncoverage** of a subject. Essential questions thus do not yield a single straightforward answer (as a leading question does) but produce different plausible responses, about which thoughtful and knowledgeable people may disagree.

An essential question can be either overarching or topical (unit-specific) in scope. (Note that this represents a change in language use from earlier UbD material. In the first edition of *Understanding by Design,* essential questions were overarching only.)

explanation   One of the six **facets** of understanding. Understanding involves more than just knowing information. A person with understanding is able to explain *why* it is so, not just state the facts. Such understanding emerges as a well-developed and supported theory, an account that makes sense of data, phenomena, ideas, or feelings. Understanding is revealed through performances and products that clearly, thoroughly, and instructively explain *how* things work, *what* they imply, *where* they connect, and *why* they happened.

Understandings in this sense thus go beyond merely giving back "right" answers to providing *warranted* opinions (to justify how the student got there and why it's right). Such verbs as *justify, generalize, support, verify, prove,* and *substantiate* get at what is needed. Regardless of content or the student's age or sophistication, understanding in this sense reveals itself in the ability to "show your work," to explain *why* the answer is correct, to subsume current work under more general and powerful principles, to give valid evidence and argument for a view, and to defend that view. *See also* **application**; **empathy**; **interpretation**; **perspective**; **self-knowledge**.

facet, facet of understanding   A way in which a person's understanding manifests itself. Understanding by Design identifies six kinds of understanding: **application**, **empathy**, **explanation**, **interpretation**, **perspective**, and **self-knowledge**. True understanding thus is revealed by a person's ability to

- Explain: provide thorough, supported, and justifiable accounts of phenomena, facts, and data.
- Interpret: tell meaningful stories; offer apt translations; provide a revealing historical or personal dimension to ideas and events; make something personal or accessible through images, anecdotes, analogies, or models.
- Apply: effectively use and adapt knowledge in diverse contexts.
- Have perspective: see points of view, with critical eyes and ears; see the big picture.
- Empathize: get inside, find value in what others might find odd, alien, or implausible; perceive sensitively, based on prior direct experience.
- Have self-knowledge: perceive the personal style, prejudices, projections, and habits of mind that both shape and impede understanding; be aware of what is not understood and why it is so hard to understand.

Speaking of facets of understanding implies that understanding (or lack of it) reveals itself in different mutually reinforcing ways. In other words, the more a student can explain, apply, and offer multiple points of view on the same idea, the more likely it is that the student understands that idea.

A facet is thus more like a criterion in performance assessment than a learning style. It refers more to how teachers judge whether understanding is present than their need to appeal to a learner's abilities or preferences. In the same way that an essay, to be effective, has to be persuasive and logical (whether or not a person has those traits or values them), so, too, do the facets suggest what teachers need to see if they are to conclude a student has understanding.

This is *not* meant to imply that all six facets are *always* involved in any particular matter of understanding. For example, self-knowledge and empathy would not often be at stake in looking for evidence of student understanding of many mathematical concepts. The facets do not present a quota but a framework or set of criteria for designing lessons and assessments that better develop and measure understanding.

genre of performance   A type or category of intellectual performance or product. For example, people commonly speak of genres of writing (narrative, essay, letter) or speaking (seminar discussion, formal speech, giving directions). A genre is thus a subset of the three main modes of intellectual performance: oral, written, displayed.

holistic scoring   A representation of an overall impression of the quality of a performance or product. Holistic scoring is distinguished from **analytic-trait scoring**, in which separate rubrics are used for each separate criterion that makes up an aspect of performance. However, multiple holistic scores are possible for a multifaceted performance task involving several standards. For example, separate holistic scores might apply to an oral presentation and a written report that are part of the same task, without breaking down those scores into the analytic components of each mode (e.g., the organization and clarity of the oral performance).

ill-structured   A term used to describe a question, problem, or task that lacks a recipe or obvious formula to answer or solve it. Ill-structured tasks or problems do not suggest or imply a specific strategy or approach guaranteed to yield success. Often the problem is fuzzy and needs to be further defined or clarified before a solution is offered. Such questions or problems thus demand more than knowledge; they demand good judgment and imagination. All good essay questions, science problems, or design challenges are ill structured: Even when the goal is understood or the expectations clear, a procedure must be developed along the way. Invariably, ill-structured tasks require constant self-assessment and revision, not just a simple application of knowledge transfer.

Most real problems in life are ill structured; most test items are not. Test questions are well structured in that they have a single, unambiguous right answer, or an obvious solution procedure. Such items are fine for validly assessing elements of knowledge but not appropriate for judging the student's ability to use knowledge wisely—namely, how to judge which knowledge and skill to use when. (A basketball analogy clarifies the distinction. The "test" of each drill in basketball differs from the "test" of playing the game well in performance: The drill is predictable and structured; the game is unpredictable and not scriptable.)

indirect test   A test that measures performance out of its normal context. Thus, any multiple-choice test of any complex performance (reading, writing, problem solving) is, by definition, indirect. The ACT and SAT are indirect ways of assessing likely success in college, because their results correlate with freshman grade-point averages.

An indirect test is less authentic than a direct test, by definition. However, an indirect test of performance can be valid; if results on the indirect test correlate with results on direct tests, then the test is valid by definition.

intelligent tool   A tool that puts abstract ideas and processes in a tangible form. An intelligent tool enhances performance on cognitive tasks, such as the design of learning units. For example, an effective graphic organizer like a story map helps students internalize the elements of a story in ways that enhance their reading and writing of stories. Likewise, routinely using intelligent tools like the unit planning template and the Understanding by Design tools should help users develop a mental template of the key ideas of UbD. *See also* **template**.

interpretation   One of the six **facets** of understanding. To interpret is to find meaning, significance, sense, or value in human experience, data, and texts. It is to tell a good story, provide a powerful metaphor, or sharpen ideas through an editorial.

Interpretation is thus fraught with more inherent subjectivity and tentativeness than the theorizing or analyzing involved in **explanation**. Even if one knows the relevant facts and theoretical principles it is necessary to ask, What does it all mean? What is its importance? (In fact, one definition in the dictionary for the verb *understand* is "know the import of.") A jury trying to understand child abuse seeks significance and intent, not accurate generalizations from theoretical science. The theorist builds objective knowledge about the phenomenon called abuse, but the novelist may offer as much or more insight through inquiry into the psychic life of a unique person.

This narrative building is the true meaning of constructivism. When teachers say that students must "make their own meaning," they mean that handing students prepackaged interpretations or notions of significance, without having the students work it through and come to see some explanations and interpretations as more valid than others, leads to sham understanding. A purely didactic teaching of *the* interpretation is likely to lead to superficial and quickly forgotten knowledge, and it misleads students about the inherently arguable nature of all interpretation. *See also* **application**; **empathy**; **explanation**; **perspective**; **self-knowledge**.

iterative   Requiring continual revisiting of earlier work. An iterative approach is thus the opposite of linear or step-by-step processes. Synonyms for iterative are *recursive, circular,* and *spiral-like.* The curricular design process is always iterative; designers keep revisiting their initial ideas about what they are after, how to assess it, and how they should teach to it as they keep working on each element of the design. They rethink earlier units and lessons in light of later designs and results—the learning that does (or does not) occur.

leading question   A question used to teach, clarify, or assess for knowledge. Unlike **essential questions**, leading questions have correct and straightforward answers. To call a question "leading" is not to damn it; leading questions have a useful role in teaching and checking for understanding. But their purpose is quite different, therefore, from the purpose of essential questions.

longitudinal assessment   Assessment of the same performances over numerous times, using a fixed scoring continuum, to track progress (or lack thereof) toward a standard; also called "developmental assessment." For example, the National Assessment of Educational Progress (NAEP) uses a fixed scale for measuring gains in mathematics performance over the 4th, 8th, and 12th grade. Similarly, the American Council on the Teaching of Foreign Languages (ACTFL) uses a novice-expert continuum for charting the progress of all language students over time. Most school testing, whether done locally or statewide, is not longitudinal because the tests are one-time events with one-time scoring systems. Understanding by Design proposes an assessment system that uses scoring scales and tasks that can be used across many grade levels to provide longitudinal assessment.

open-ended question   A term used to describe tasks or questions that do not lead to a single right answer. This does not imply that all answers are of equal value, however. Rather, it implies that many different acceptable answers are possible. Such answers are thus "justified" or "plausible" or "well-defended" as opposed to "correct." Essay test questions, for example, are open-ended, whereas multiple-choice tests are not (by design).

outcome   In education, shorthand for "intended outcomes of instruction." An intended outcome is a **desired result**, a specific goal to which educators commit. Understanding by Design uses the terms *achievement target* and *goal* to describe such intents. To determine if outcomes have been attained requires agreement on specific measures—the assessment tasks, criteria, and standards.

Despite the controversies in past years about Outcomes-Based Education, the word *outcome* is neutral, implying no particular kind of target or educational philosophy. It refers to the priorities of a curriculum or an educational program. An outcome-based approach focuses on desired outputs, not the inputs (content and methods). The key question is results-oriented (What will students know and be able to do as a result of instruction?) rather than input-based (What instructional methods and materials shall we use?).

perform   To act upon and bring to completion. *See also* **performance task**.

performance   *See* **performance task**.

performance task   Also called "performance." A task that uses one's knowledge to effectively act or bring to fruition a complex product that reveals one's knowledge and expertise. Music recitals, oral presentations, art displays, and auto mechanic competitions are performances in both senses.

Many educators mistakenly use the phrase "performance assessment" when they really mean "performance test" (*see* **assess**, **assessment**). A performance assessment involves more than a single test of performance and might use other modes of assessment as well (such as surveys, interviews of the performer, observations, and quizzes).

Tests of performance, whether authentic or not, differ from multiple-choice or short-answer tests. In a test of performance, the student must put it all together in the context of ill-structured, nonroutine, or unpredictable problems or challenges. By contrast, most conventional short-answer or multiple-choice tests are more like the drills in sports than the test of performance. Real performers (athletes, debaters, dancers, scientists, or actors) must learn to innovate and use their judgment as well as their knowledge. By contrast, multiple-choice test items merely ask the student to recall, recognize, or "plug in" isolated, discrete bits of knowledge or skill, one at a time.

Because many types of performance are ephemeral actions, a fair and technically sound assessment typically involves the creation of products. This ensures adequate documentation and the possibility of appropriate review and oversight in scoring the performance. *See also* **perform**.

perspective   One of the six **facets** of understanding. The ability to see other plausible points of view. It also implies that understanding enables a distance from what one knows, an avoidance of getting caught up in the views and passions of the moment. *See also* **application**; **empathy**; **explanation**; **interpretation**; **self-knowledge**.

portfolio   A representative collection of one's work. As the word's roots suggest (and as is still the case in the arts), the sample of work is fashioned for a particular objective and carried from place to place for inspection or exhibition.

   In academic subject areas, a portfolio often serves two distinct purposes: providing a documentation of the student's work, and serving as the basis for evaluation of work in progress or work over time. The documentation typically serves three functions: revealing the student's control over all the major areas, techniques, genres, and topics of the course or program; allowing students to reflect on and show off their best work (by letting them select which works will be put in the portfolio); and providing evidence of how works evolved and were refined.

prerequisite knowledge and skill   The knowledge and skill required to successfully perform a culminating performance task or achieve a targeted understanding. Typically prerequisites identify the more discrete knowledge and know-how required to put everything together in a meaningful final performance. For example, knowledge of the USDA food pyramid guidelines would be considered a prerequisite to the task of planning a healthy, balanced diet for a week. *Contrast* **resultant knowledge and skill**.

process   In the context of assessment, the intermediate steps the student takes in reaching the final performance or end-product specified by the assessment. Process thus includes all strategies, decisions, subskills, rough drafts, and rehearsals used in completing the given task.

   When asked to evaluate the process leading to the final performance or product, the assessor is sometimes asked to explicitly judge the student's intermediate steps, independent of what can be inferred about those processes from the end result. For example, one might rate a student's ability to work within a group or prepare an outline as a prewriting component of a research project, independent of the ultimate product the group or individual writer produces. However, evaluating process skills separately requires caution. The emphasis should be on whether the final product or performance met the standards set—irrespective of how the student got there.

product   The tangible and stable result of a performance and the processes that led to it. The product is valid for assessing the student's knowledge to the extent that success or failure in producing the product (1) reflects the knowledge taught and being assessed, and (2) is an appropriate sample from the whole curriculum of the relative importance of the material in the course.

project   A complex set of intellectual challenges, typically occurring over lengthy periods of time. Projects typically involve extensive student inquiry, culminating in student products and performances. A unit might be composed of a single project but include other forms of assessment evidence (quizzes, tests, observations) along the way.

prompt   *See* **academic prompt**.

proposition   A statement that describes a relationship between or among concepts. Understanding by Design suggests that targeted understandings be framed as specific propositions to be understood, not just phrases that refer to the topic or content standard. Propositions include principles, generalizations, axioms, and laws.

question   *See* **entry question**; **essential question**; **leading question**; **open-ended question**.

quiz   Any selected-response or short-answer test (be it oral or written) whose sole purpose is to assess for discrete knowledge and skill. *Contrast* **academic prompt** and **authentic assessment**.

reliability   In measurement and testing, the accuracy of the score. Is it sufficiently free of error? What is the likelihood that the score or grade would be constant if the test were retaken or the same performance were rescored by someone else? Error is unavoidable; all tests, including the best multiple-choice tests, lack 100 percent reliability. The aim is to minimize error to tolerable levels.

In performance assessment the reliability problem typically occurs in two forms: (1) To what extent can we generalize from the single or small number of performances to the student's likely performance in general? and (2) What is the likelihood that different judges will see the same performance in the same way? The second question involves what is typically termed "inter-rater reliability."

Score error is not necessarily a defect in the test-maker's methods, but a statistical fact related to (1) how extraneous factors inevitably influence test-takers or judges, or (2) the limits of using a small sample of questions or tasks in a single sitting.

It is possible to obtain adequate reliability by ensuring that there are multiple tasks for the same outcome; better reliability is obtained when the student has many tasks, not just one. Also, scoring reliability is greatly improved when evaluation is performed by well-trained and supervised judges, working from clear rubrics and specific anchor papers or performances. (These procedures have long been used in large-scale writing assessments and in the advanced placement program.)

result, desired   *See* **desired result**.

resultant knowledge and skill   Knowledge and skill that are meant to result from a unit of study. In addition to the targeted understanding, teachers identify other desired outcomes (for example "skill in listening").

Resultant knowledge and skill differs from **prerequisite knowledge and skill**. Resultant knowledge is the goal of the unit. Prerequisite knowledge is what is needed to accomplish the goals of the unit. For example, in a unit that culminates in a historical role-play, the prerequisite knowledge involves the biographical facts of the people being portrayed and the prerequisite skill is the ability to role-play. Designers using UbD identify the resultant knowledge and skill in Stage 1, and they weave the prerequisite knowledge into Stage 3, the learning plan.

rubric   A criterion-based scoring guide that enables judges to make reliable judgments about student work and enables students to self-assess. A rubric assesses one or more traits of performance. The rubric answers the question, What does understanding or proficiency for an identified result look like? *See also* **analytic-trait scoring**.

sampling   All unit and test design involves the act of sampling from a vast domain of possible knowledge, skills, and tasks. Like the Gallup polls, sampling enables the assessor to draw valid inferences from a limited inquiry if the sample of work or answers is appropriate and justified.

Unit and test design uses two different kinds of sampling: sampling from the wider domain of all possible curricular questions, topics, and tasks; and sampling that involves assessing only a subset of the entire student population instead of testing everyone. These two kinds of sampling get combined in large-scale testing systems to form matrix sampling, whereby one can test many or all students using different tests to cover as much of the domain of knowledge as possible.

Teachers attempting to sample the domain of subject matter in a unit through a specific task must ask, What feasible and efficient sample of tasks or questions will enable us to make valid inferences about the student's overall performance (because we cannot possibly test the student on everything that was taught and learned)? When teachers try to use a subset of the population to construct a more efficient and cost-effective approach to testing, they are asking the question the pollsters ask: What must be the composition of any small sample of students so that we can validly infer conclusions about the systemwide performance of all students using the results from our sample?

scoring scale   An equally divided continuum (number line) used in evaluating performance. The scale identifies how many different scores will be used. Performance assessments typically use a much smaller scale for scoring than standardized tests. Rather than a scale of 100 or more, most performance-based assessment uses a 4- or 6-point scale.

Two interrelated reasons explain this use of a small number of score points. Each place on the scale is not arbitrary (as it is in norm-referenced scoring); it is meant to correspond to a specific criterion or quality of work. The second reason is practical: To use a scale of so many discrete numbers reduces scoring reliability.

scoring guide   *See* **rubric**.

secure   A term used to describe a test with questions that are not accessible to teachers or students for purposes of preparation. Most multiple-choice tests *must* be secure or their validity is compromised, because they rely on a small number of uncomplicated questions. Many valid performance assessments are not secure, however. Examples include a baseball game or the road test for getting a driver's license. The student to be assessed often knows the musical piece, debate topic, oral exam questions, or term paper subject in advance, *and* the teacher appropriately "teaches to the test" of performance.

self-knowledge   One of the six **facets** of understanding. As discussed in the context of the facets theory, self-knowledge refers to accuracy of self-assessment and awareness of the biases in one's understanding because of favored styles of inquiry, habitual ways of thinking, and unexamined beliefs. Accuracy of self-assessment in this case means that the learner understands what he does not understand with clarity and specificity. (Socrates referred to this capacity as "wisdom.")

Self-knowledge also involves the degree of awareness of biases and how these influence thinking, perceptions, and beliefs about how the subject is to be understood. One does not just receive understanding (like images through eyes), in other words; ways of thinking and categorizing are projected onto situations in ways that inevitably shape understanding. *See also* **application**; **empathy**; **explanation**; **interpretation**; **and perspective**.

standard   To ask, "What is the standard?" is to question *how well* the student must perform, at *what kinds* of tasks, based on *what content*, to be considered proficient or effective. Thus, there are three kinds of standards, each addressing a different question. *Content standards* answer the question, "What should students know and be able to do?" *Performance standards* answer the question, "How well must students do their work?" *Design standards* answer the question, "What worthy work should students encounter?" Most state documents identify only content standards. Some also identify performance standards—a specific result or level of achievement that is deemed exemplary or appropriate (typically measured by a standardized test). Understanding by Design also identifies and emphasizes **design standards** related to the quality of the task itself; these are the standards and criteria by which educators distinguish sound from unsound units.

Confusions abound because of these various kinds of standards. Worse, the word *standard* is sometimes used as a synonym for *high expectations.* At other times, it is used as a synonym for *benchmark*—the best performance or product that can be accomplished by anyone. And in large-scale testing, *standard* has often implicitly meant *minimal standard;* that is, the lowest passing score. One also often hears standards discussed as if they were general guidelines or principles. Finally, *standard* is routinely confused with the *criteria* for judging performance. (Many people falsely believe that a rubric is sufficient for evaluation. But an articulated performance standard, often made real by anchors or exemplars, is also necessary.)

When talking about standards-based education, educators should consider a number of points. First, in a general sense, they must be careful not to confuse standards with expectations. A performance standard is not necessarily meant to be reachable by all who try and are well trained; that's better thought of as an expectation. A standard remains worthy whether or not few people or *any* people can meet it. That is very different from an expectation that happens to be high or a "reach"—something that a good number of students not only can but *ought to* meet, if they persist and get good teaching from teachers (who have high expectations).

Second, a performance standard in assessment is typically set by an "exemplary" **anchor** performance or some specification or cut-off score. Consider wider-world benchmarks: the four-minute mile, the Malcolm Baldrige Award–winning companies, Hemingway's writing, Peter Jennings's oral presentation. Few student performers, if any, will meet such standards, but they are still worthy targets for framing a program and an assessment. School tests rarely set performance standards using such professional benchmarks (though such exemplars serve as instructional models and as sources of **criteria** for **rubrics**). A school standard is typically set through the selection of peer-based anchors or exemplars of performance—what might be called "milepost" or "age-appropriate" standards. The choice of such exemplary work samples sets the de facto standard.

A key assessment question thus becomes, Where should the samples of student work come from? What would be a valid choice of anchors? And how do teachers link school standards to wider-world and adult standards? What teachers typically do is select the best work available from the overall student population being tested. (Proponents of UbD believe, however, that students need to be more routinely provided with anchors that come from slightly more advanced and experienced students, to serve as a helpful longer-range target and to guide ongoing feedback.)

Third, a standard differs from the criteria used to judge performance. The criteria for the high jump or the persuasive essay are more or less fixed no matter the age or ability of the student. All high jumps, to be successful, must meet the same criterion: The bar must stay on. In writing, all persuasive essays must use appropriate evidence and effective reasoning. But how high should the bar be? How sophisticated and rigorous should the arguments be? Those are questions about standards. (The descriptors for the different levels in a rubric typically contain both criteria and standards.)

Standards are not norms, however, even if norms are used to determine age-appropriate standards. Traditionally, performance standards have been put into operation by fixing a minimally acceptable performance level through so-called cutoff, or cut, scores. Typically, in both classroom grading and on state tests, a score of 60 is considered a minimal standard of performance. But test designers are rarely asked to establish a defensible cut score. Stating at the outset that 60 is passing and 59 is failing is arbitrary; few tests are designed so that a significant, qualitative difference distinguishes a 59 and a 61. It is thus all too easy, when thinking of a standard as a cutoff point, to turn what should be a criterion-referenced scoring system into a norm-referenced scoring system.

Thus, improving content standards will not necessarily raise performance standards. Content refers to input and performance to output. Content standards state the particular knowledge the student should master. Many current reforms assume improving the inputs will necessarily improve the output. But this is clearly false. One can still receive poor-quality work from students in a demanding course of study. In fact, it is reasonable in the short term to expect to obtain worse performance by raising content standards only; establishing higher standards only in the difficulty of what is taught will likely lead to greater failure by students, if all other factors (teaching and time spent on work) remain constant.

The key question to ask in setting valid and useful performance standards must always be, At what level of performance would the student be "appropriately qualified or certified"? An effective solution to putting standards into operation is thus to equate internal teacher and school standards to some equivalent, worthy level of achievement in the outside world—a wider-world benchmark—thus lending substance, stability, and credibility to the scoring. This is a common feature of vocational, musical, athletic, and other performance-based forms of learning.

standardized A term used to describe a test or assessment in which the administrative conditions and protocol are uniform for all students. In other words, if all students face similar logistical, time, material, and feedback guidelines and constraints, then the test is standardized.

Standardized tests prompt three common misconceptions:

• "Multiple-choice test" and "standardized test" are synonymous. A performance task, administered uniformly as a test, is also a standardized test, as seen, for example, in the road test for a driver's license or a qualifying meet for the Olympics.

• Standardized tests are always objectively (that is, machine) scored. The advanced placement exam essays and all state writing tests are scored by judges yet are standard in their administration.

• Only national norm-referenced or criterion-referenced tests (such as the SAT) can be standardized. A departmental exam in a high school is also a standardized test.

An important implication, then, is that all formal tests are standardized. This is not true of an assessment, however. In an assessment, the administrator is free to vary the questions, the tasks, the order of the tasks, and the time allotted in order to be satisfied that the results are fair, valid, and reliable. This was the argument made by Piaget for his "clinical method" as opposed to the "test method" of Binet. *See also* **assessment**.

target, achievement *See* **achievement target**.

template A guide or framework for designers. In everyday usage, the term refers to a form, constructed of paper, wood, or sheet metal, whose edge provides a guide for cutting a particular shape. In *Understanding by Design*, the unit planning template provides a conceptual guide to applying the various elements of **backward design** in the development or refinement of a unit of study. Each page of the template contains key questions, prompting the user to consider particular elements of backward design, and a graphic organizer containing frames for recording design ideas. *See also* **intelligent tool**.

transferability The ability to use knowledge appropriately and fruitfully in a new or different context from that in which it was initially learned. For example, a student who understands the concept of "balanced diet" (based on the USDA food pyramid guidelines) transfers that understanding by evaluating hypothetical diets for their nutritional values and by creating nutritional menus that meet the food pyramid recommendations.

uncoverage A teaching approach that is required for all matters of understanding. To "uncover" a subject is to do the opposite of "covering" it, namely to go into depth. Three types of content typically demand such uncoverage. The content may be *principles, laws, theories,* or *concepts* that are likely to have meaning for a student only if they are seen as sensible and plausible; that is, the student can verify, induce, or justify the content through inquiry and construction. The content may be counterintuitive, nuanced, subtle, or otherwise easily misunderstood ideas, such as gravity, evolution, imaginary numbers, irony, texts, formulas, theories, or concepts. The content may be the conceptual or strategic element of any skill (e.g., persuasion in writing or "creating space" in soccer). Such uncoverage involves clarifying effective and efficient means, given the ends of skill, leading to greater purposefulness and less mindless use of techniques. *Contrast* **coverage**.

understanding   An insight into ideas, people, situations, and processes manifested in various appropriate performances. To understand is to make sense of what one knows, to be able to know why it's so, and to have the ability to use it in various situations and contexts.

unit   Short for a "unit of study." Units represent a coherent chunk of work in courses or strands, across days or weeks. An example is a unit on natural habitats and adaptation that falls under the yearlong strand of living things (the course), under 3rd grade science (the subject), and under science (the program).

Though no hard and fast criteria signify what a unit is, educators generally think of a unit as a body of subject matter that is somewhere in length between a lesson and an entire course of study; that focuses on a major topic (e.g., Revolutionary War) or process (e.g., research process); and that lasts between a few days and a few weeks

validity   The inferences one can confidently draw about student learning based on the results of an assessment. Does the test measure what it purports to measure? Do the test results correlate with other performance results educators consider valid? Does the sample of questions or tasks accurately correlate with what students would do if tested on everything that was taught? Do the results have predictive value; that is, do they correlate with likely future success in the subject in question? If some or all of these questions must have a "yes" answer, a test is valid.

Because most tests provide a sample of student performance, the scope and nature of the samples influence the extent to which valid conclusions may be drawn. Is it possible to accurately and reliably predict from the performance on a specific task that the student has control over the entire domain? Does one type of task enable an inference to other types of tasks (say, one genre of writing to all others)? No. Thus, the typically few tasks used in performance assessment often provide an inadequate basis for generalizing. One solution is to use a wide variety of student work of a similar type or genre, collected over the year, as part of the summative assessment.

To be precise, it is not the test itself that is valid, but the inferences that educators claim to be able to make from the test results. Thus, the purpose of the test must be considered when assessing validity. Multiple-choice reading tests may well be valid if they are used to test the student's comprehension ability or to monitor grade-level reading ability of a district's population as compared to other large populations. They may not be valid as measures of a pupil's repertoire of reading strategies and the ability to construct apt and insightful responses to texts.

The format of the test can be misleading; an inauthentic test can still be technically valid. It may aptly sample from the subject domain and predict future performance accurately but nonetheless be based on inauthentic, even trivial, tasks. The SAT college admissions test and tests such as the Otis-Lennon School Ability Test are said by their makers to be valid in this more limited sense: they are efficient proxies that serve as useful predictors. Conversely, an authentic task may not be valid.

The scoring system can raise other questions about validity. To ask if a performance task is valid is to ask, within the limits of feasibility, if the scoring targets the most important aspects of performance as opposed to that which is most easily scored. Have the most apt criteria been identified, and is the rubric built upon the most apt differences in quality? Or has scoring focused merely on what is easy to count and score? Has validity been sacrificed for reliability, in other words?

WHERETO An acronym for **W**here is it going?; **H**ook the students; **E**xplore and equip; **R**ethink and revise; **E**xhibit and evaluate; **T**ailor to student needs, interests, and styles; **O**rganize for maximum engagement and effectiveness. Considered in greater detail, WHERETO consists of the following components:

- **W**here is the work headed? Why is it headed there? What are the student's final performance obligations, the anchoring performance assessments? What are the criteria by which student work will be judged for understanding? (These are questions asked by students. Help the student see the answers to these questions upfront.)
- **H**ook the student through engaging and provocative entry points: thought-provoking and focusing experiences, issues, oddities, problems, and challenges that point toward essential questions, core ideas, and final performance tasks.
- **E**xplore and equip. Engage students in learning experiences that allow them to explore the big ideas and essential questions; that cause them to pursue leads or hunches, research and test ideas, try things out. Equip students for the final performances through guided instruction and coaching on needed skill and knowledge. Have them experience the ideas to make them real.
- **R**ethink and revise. Dig deeper into ideas at issue (through the facets of understanding). Revise, rehearse, and refine, as needed. Guide students in self-assessment and self-adjustment, based on feedback from inquiry, results, and discussion.
- **E**valuate understanding. Reveal what has been understood through final performances and products. Involve students in a final self-assessment to identify remaining questions, set future goals, and point toward new units and lessons.
- **T**ailor (personalize) the work to ensure maximum interest and achievement. Differentiate the approaches used and provide sufficient options and variety (without compromising goals) to make it most likely that all students will be engaged and effective.
- **O**rganize and sequence the learning for maximal engagement and effectiveness, given the desired results.

Bibliography

Abbott, E. (1884/1963). *Flatland: A romance of many dimensions.* New York: Barnes & Noble Books. (Original work published 1884)

Adler, M. (1982). *The Paideia proposal: An educational manifesto.* New York: Macmillan.

Adler, M. (1984). *The Paideia program: An educational syllabus.* New York: Macmillan.

Adler, M. (1999). *The great ideas: A lexicon of Western thought.* New York: Scribner Classics.

Adler, M., & Van Doren, C. (1940). *How to read a book.* New York: Simon & Schuster.

Alverno College Faculty. (1979). *Assessment at Alverno College.* Milwaukee, WI: Alverno College.

American Association for the Advancement of Science. (1993). *Benchmarks for science literacy.* New York: Oxford University Press.

American Association for the Advancement of Science. (1995). *Assessment of authentic performance in school mathematics.* Washington, DC: Author.

American Association for the Advancement of Science. (2001). *Atlas of science literacy.* New York: Oxford University Press.

American Council on the Teaching of Foreign Languages. (1999). *ACTFL proficiency guidelines—speaking.* (Report). Alexandria, VA: Author. Available: http://www.actfl.org.

American Council on the Teaching of Foreign Languages. (2001). *ACTFL proficiency guidelines—writing.* (Report). Alexandria, VA: Author. Available: http://www.actfl.org.

Anderson, L. W., & Krathwohl, D. R. (Eds.). (2001). *A taxonomy for learning, teaching, and assessing: A revision of Bloom's taxonomy of educational objectives.* New York: Longman.

Andre, T. (1979). Does answering higher-level questions while reading facilitate productive learning? *Review of Educational Research, 49,* 280–318.

Arendt, H. (1963). *Eichmann in Jerusalem: A report on the banality of evil.* New York: Viking Press.

Arendt, H. (1977). *The life of the mind.* New York: Harcourt, Brace, Jovanovich.

Arter, J., & McTighe, J. (2001). *Scoring rubrics in the classroom: Using performance criteria for assessing and improving student performance.* Thousand Oaks, CA: Corwin Press.

Ashlock, R. B. (1998). *Error patterns in computation* (7th ed.). Upper Saddle River, NJ: Merrill.

Association for Supervision and Curriculum Development. (1997). *Planning integrated units: A concept-based approach* [video]. Alexandria, VA: Producer.

Bacon, F. (1620/1960). In F. Anderson (Ed.), *The new organon (Book I).* New York: Bobbs-Merrill. (Original work published 1620)

Barell, J. (1995). *Teaching for thoughtfulness.* White Plains, NY: Longman.

Barnes, L., Christensen, C. R., & Hansen, A. (1977). *Teaching and the case method.* Cambridge, MA: Harvard Business School Press.

Baron, J. (1993, November). *Assessments as an opportunity to learn: The Connecticut Common Core of Learning alternative assessments of secondary school science and mathematics*. (Report No. SPA-8954692). Hartford: Connecticut Department of Education, Division of Teaching and Learning.

Baron, J., & Sternberg, R. (1987). *Teaching thinking skills: Theory and practice.* New York: W. W. Freeman & Co.

Barrows, H., & Tamblyn, R. (1980). *Problem-based learning: An approach to medical education.* New York: Springer.

Bateman, W. (1990). *Open to question: The art of teaching and learning by inquiry.* San Francisco: Jossey-Bass.

Beane, J. (Ed.). (1995). *Toward a coherent curriculum: The 1995 ASCD yearbook.* Alexandria, VA: Association for Supervision and Curriculum Development.

Berenbaum, R. L. (1988). *The cake bible.* New York: William Morrow Co.

Bernstein, R. (1983). *Beyond objectivism and relativism: Science, hermeneutics, and praxis.* Philadelphia: University of Pennsylvania Press.

Bloom, B. S. (Ed.). (1956). *Taxonomy of educational objectives: Classification of educational goals. Handbook 1: Cognitive domain.* New York: Longman, Green & Co.

Bloom, B., Madaus, G., & Hastings, J. T. (1981). *Evaluation to improve learning.* New York: McGraw-Hill.

Blythe, T., & Associates. (1998). *The teaching for understanding guide.* San Francisco: Jossey-Bass.

Bottoms, G., & Sharpe, D. (1996). *Teaching for understanding through integration of academic and technical education.* Atlanta, GA: Southern Regional Education Board.

Boyer, E. (1983). *High school: A report on secondary education in America by the Carnegie Foundation for the Advancement of Teaching.* New York: Harper & Row.

Boyer, E. L. (1995). *The basic school: A community for learning.* New York: Carnegie Foundation for the Advancement of Teaching.

Bransford, J., Brown, A., & Cocking, R. (Eds.). (2000). *How people learn: Brain, mind, experience, and school.* Washington, DC: National Research Council.

Brooks, J., & Brooks, M. (1993). *In search of understanding: The case for constructivist classrooms.* Alexandria, VA: Association for Supervision and Curriculum Development.

Brown, R., Dolcani, M., Sorgenfrey, R., & Cole, W. (2000). *Algebra: Structure and method book I.* Evanston, IL: McDougal Littell.

Brown, S., & Walter, M. (1983). *The art of problem posing.* Philadelphia: Franklin Institute Press.

Bruner, J. (1957/1973a). *Beyond the information given: Studies in the psychology of knowing.* J. Anglin (Ed.). New York: W. W. Norton. (Original work published 1957)

Bruner, J. (1960). *The process of education.* Cambridge, MA: Harvard University Press.

Bruner, J. (1965). Growth of mind. *American Psychologist, 20*(17), 1007–1017.

Bruner, J. (1966). *Toward a theory of instruction.* Cambridge, MA: Harvard University Press.

Bruner, J. (1973b). *The relevance of education.* Cambridge, MA: Harvard University Press.

Bruner, J. (1990). *Acts of meaning.* Cambridge, MA: Harvard University Press.

Bruner, J. (1996). *The culture of education.* Cambridge, MA: Harvard University Press.

Budiansky, S. (2001, February). The trouble with textbooks. *Prism Online.* Available: http://www.asee.org/prism/feb01/html/textbooks.cfm.

Bulgren, J. A., Lenz, B. K., Deshler, D. D., & Schumaker, J. B. (2001). *The question exploration routine.* Lawrence, KS: Edge Enterprises.

Burns, J. M., & Morris, R. (1986). The Constitution: Thirteen crucial questions. In Morris & Sgroi (Eds.), *This Constitution.* New York: Franklin Watts.

Carroll, J. M. (1989). *The Copernican plan: Restructuring the American high school.* Andover, MA: Regional Laboratory for Educational Improvement of the Northeast Islands.

Caswell, H. L., & Campbell, D. S. (1935). *Curriculum development.* New York: American Book Company.

Cayton, A., Perry, E., & Winkler, A. (1998). *America: Pathways to the present.* Needham, MA: Prentice-Hall.

Chapman, A. (Ed.). (1993). *Making sense: Teaching critical reading across the curriculum.* New York: College Entrance Examination Board.

Coalition for Evidence-Based Policy. (1992, November). *Bringing evidence-driven progress to education: A recommended strategy for the U.S. Department of Education.* Washington, DC: Author.

College of William and Mary, Center for Gifted Education. (1997). *The Chesapeake Bay: A problem-based unit.* Dubuque, IA: Kendall Hunt.

Collingwood, R. G. (1939). *An autobiography.* Oxford, UK: Oxford-Clarendon Press.

Committee on the Foundations of Assessment. Pellegrino, J. W., Chudowsky, N., & Glaser, R. (Eds.). (2001). *Knowing what students know: The science and design of educational assessment.* Washington, DC: National Academy Press.

Content Enhancement Series. Lawrence, KS: Edge Enterprises.

Costa, A. (Ed.). (1991). *Developing minds: A resource book for teaching thinking.* Vol. 1 (Rev. ed.). Alexandria, VA: Association for Supervision and Curriculum Development.

Covey, S. R. (1989). *The seven habits of highly effective people: Powerful lessons in personal change.* New York: Free Press.

Coxford, A., Usiskin, Z., & Hirschhorn, D. (1993). *Geometry: The University of Chicago school mathematics project.* Glenview, IL: Scott Foresman.

Darling-Hammond, L., Ancess, J., & Falk, B. (1995). *Authentic assessment in action: Studies of schools and students at work.* New York: National Center for Restructuring Education, Schools and Teaching (NCREST), Teachers College, Columbia University.

Darling-Hammond, L., et al. (1993). *Authentic assessment in practice: A collection of portfolios, performance tasks, exhibitions, and documentation.* New York: National Center for Restructuring Education, Schools and Teaching (NCREST), Teachers College, Columbia University.

Darwin, C. (1958). *The autobiography of Charles Darwin.* New York: W. W. Norton.

Delisle, R. (1997). *How to use problem-based learning in the classroom.* Alexandria, VA: Association for Supervision and Curriculum Development.

Desberg, P., & Taylor, J. H. (1986). *Essentials of task analysis.* Lanham, MD: University Press of America.

Descartes, R. (1628/1961). Rules for the direction of the mind. In L. LaFleur (Ed. and Trans.), *Philosophical essays.* Indianapolis, IN: Bobbs-Merrill. (Original work published 1628)

Detterman, D. K., & Sternberg, R. J. (Eds.). (1993). *Transfer on trial: Intelligence, cognition, and instruction.* Norwood, NJ: Ablex Publishing Corporation.

Dewey, J. (1916). *Democracy and education: An introduction to the philosophy of education.* New York: Macmillan.

Dewey, J. (1933). *How we think: A restatement of the relation of reflective thinking to the educative process.* Boston: Henry Holt.

Dewey, J. (1938). *Experience and education.* New York: Macmillan/Collier.

Diamond, J. (1997). *Guns, germs, and steel: The fates of human societies.* New York and London: W.W. Norton.

Dillon, J. T. (1988). *Questioning and teaching: A manual of practice.* New York: Teachers College Press.

Dillon, J. T. (1990). *The practice of questioning.* New York: Routledge.

Drucker, P. F. (1985). *Innovation and entrepreneurship.* New York: Harper & Row.

Duckworth, E. (1987). *"The having of wonderful ideas" and other essays on teaching and learning.* New York: Teachers College Press.

Educational Testing Service/College Board. (1992). *Advanced placement United States history free-response scoring guide and sample student answers.* Princeton, NJ: Author.

Educators in Connecticut's Pomperaug Regional School District 15. (1996). *A teacher's guide to performance-based learning and assessment.* Alexandria, VA: Association for Supervision and Curriculum Development.

Egan, K. (1986). *Teaching as story-telling: An alternative approach to teaching and curriculum in the elementary school.* Chicago: University of Chicago Press.

Egan, K. (1997). *The educated mind: How cognitive tools shape our understanding.* Chicago: University of Chicago Press.

Einstein, A. (1954, 1982). *Ideas and Opinions.* New York: Three Rivers Press. (Original work published 1954)

Elbow, P. (1973). *Writing without teachers.* New York: Oxford University Press.

Elbow, P. (1986). *Embracing contraries: Explorations in learning and teaching.* New York: Oxford University Press.

Erickson, L. (1998). *Concept-based curriculum and instruction: Teaching beyond the facts.* Thousand Oaks, CA: Corwin Press.

Erickson, L. (2001). *Stirring the head, heart, and soul: Redefining curriculum and instruction* (2nd ed.). Thousand Oaks, CA: Corwin Press.

Fink, L. D. (2003). *Creating significant learning experiences: An integrated approach to designing college courses.* San Francisco: Jossey-Bass.

Finkel, D. L. (2000). *Teaching with your mouth shut.* Portsmouth, NH: Heinemann.

Fogarty, R., Perkins, D., & Barell, J. (1992). *How to teach for transfer.* Palatine, IL: Skylight Publishing.

Fosnot, C. T., & Dolk, M. (2001a). *Young mathematicians at work: Constructing multiplication and division.* Portsmouth, NH: Heinemann.

Fosnot, C. T., & Dolk, M. (2001b). *Young mathematicians at work: Constructing number sense, addition, and subtraction.* Portsmouth, NH: Heinemann.

Freedman, R. L. H. (1994). *Open-ended questioning: A handbook for educators.* Menlo Park, CA: Addison-Wesley.

Frome, P. (2001). *High schools that work: Findings from the 1996 and 1998 assessments.* Triangle Park, NC: Research Triangle Institute.

Gadamer, H. (1994). *Truth and method.* New York: Continuum.

Gagnon, P. (Ed.). (1989). *Historical literacy: The case for history in American education.* Boston: Houghton-Mifflin.

Gall, M. (1984). Synthesis of research on teacher questioning. *Educational Leadership, 42*(3), 40–46.

Gardner, H. (1991). *The unschooled mind: How children think and how schools should teach.* New York: Basic Books.

Goodlad, J. (1984). *A place called school.* New York: McGraw-Hill.

Gould, S. J. (1977). *Ontogeny and phylogeny.* Cambridge, MA: Harvard University Press.

Gould, S. J. (1980). Wide hats and narrow minds. In S. J. Gould (Ed.), *The panda's thumb.* New York: W. W. Norton.

Gragg, C. (1940, October 19). Because wisdom can't be told. *Harvard Alumni Bulletin.*

Grant, G., et al. (1979). *On competence: A critical analysis of competence-based reforms in higher education.* San Francisco: Jossey-Bass.

Greece Central School District. (n.d.). www.greece.k12.ny.us/instruction/ela/6-12/writing.

Greenberg, M. J. (1972). Euclidean and non-Euclidean geometries: Development and history. San Francisco: W. H. Freeman Co.

Griffin, P., Smith, P., & Burrill, L. (1995). *The American literacy profile scales: A framework for authentic assessment.* Portsmouth, NH: Heinemann.

Gruber, H., & Voneche, J. (1977). *The essential Piaget: An interpretive reference and guide.* New York: Basic Books.

Guillen, M. (1995). *Five equations that changed the world: The power and poetry of mathematics.* New York: MJF Books.

Guskey, T. (2002). *How's my kid doing? A parent's guide to grades, marks, and report cards.* San Francisco: Jossey-Bass.

Hagerott, S. (1997). Physics for first graders. *Phi Delta Kappan, 78*(9), 717–719.

Hakim, J. (1993). *A history of us: From colonies to country.* New York: Oxford University Press.

Halloun, I., & Hestenes, D. (1985). The initial knowledge state of college physics students, *American Journal of Physics, 53,* 1043–1055.

Halpern, D. F. (1998). Teaching critical thinking across domains: Dispositions, skills, structure training, and metacognitive monitoring. *American Psychologist, 53*(4), 449–455.

Hammerman, E., & Musial, D. (1995). *Classroom 2061: Activity-based assessments in science, integrated with mathematics and language arts.* Palatine, IL: IRI/Skylight.

Haroutunian-Gordon, S. (1991). *Turning the soul: Teaching through conversation in the high school.* Chicago: University of Chicago Press.

Harvard-Smithsonian Center for Astrophysics. (1997). *Minds of our own* (videotape). Available through learner.org, Annenberg CPB.

Hattie, J. (1992). Measuring the effects of schooling. *Australian Journal of Education, 36*(2), 99–136.

Heath, E. (1956). *The thirteen books of Euclid's elements* (Vols. 1–3). New York: Dover.

Heath, T. (1963). *Greek mathematics.* New York: Dover.

Hegel, G. W. F. (1977). *Phenomenology of spirit* (A. V. Miller, Trans.). London: Oxford University Press.

Heidegger, M. (1968). *What is called thinking?* (J. Gray, Trans.). New York: Harper.

Hestenes, D., & Halloun, I. (1995). Interpreting the FCI. 1992. *The Physics Teacher, 33,* 502–506.

Hestenes, D., Wells, M., & Swackhamer, G. (1992, March). Force Concept Inventory, *The Physics Teacher, 30,* 141–158. The revised Force Concept Inventory can be found at: http://modeling.asu.edu/R&E/Research.html.

Hirsch, E. D., Jr. (1988). *Cultural literacy: What every American needs to know.* New York: Vintage Books.

Hunter, M. (1982). *Mastery teaching.* Thousand Oaks, CA: Corwin Press.

Jablon, J. R., et al. (1994). *Omnibus guidelines, kindergarten through fifth grade* (3rd ed.). Ann Arbor, MI: The Work Sampling System.

Jacobs, H. H. (Ed.). (1989). *Interdisciplinary curriculum: Design and implementation.* Alexandria, VA: Association for Supervision and Curriculum Development.

Jacobs, H. H. (1997). Mapping the big picture: Integrating curriculum and assessment K–12. Alexandria, VA: Association for Supervision and Curriculum Development.

James, W. (1899/1958). *Talks to teachers on psychology and to students on some of life's ideals. New York*: W. W. Norton. (Original work published 1899)

Johnson, A. H. (Ed.). (1949). *The wit and wisdom of John Dewey.* Boston: Beacon Press.

Jonassen, D., Tessmer, M., & Hannum, W. (1999). *Task analysis methods for instructional design.* Mahwah, NJ: Lawrence Erlbaum.

Kant, I. (1787/1929). *The critique of pure reason* (N. Kemp Smith, Trans.). New York: Macmillan. (Original work published 1787)

Kasulis, T. (1986). Questioning. In M. M. Gilette (Ed.), *The art and craft of teaching.* Cambridge, MA: Harvard University Press.

Kliebard, H. (1987). *The struggle for the American curriculum, 1893–1958.* New York: Routledge & Kegan Paul.

Kline, M. (1953). *Mathematics in Western culture.* Oxford: Oxford University Press.

Kline, M. (1970, March). Logic vs. pedagogy. *American Mathematical Monthly, 77*(3), 264–282.

Kline, M. (1972). *Mathematical thought from ancient to modern times.* New York: Oxford University Press.

Kline, M. (1973). *Why Johnny can't add: The failure of the new math.* New York: Vintage Press.

Kline, M. (1980). *Mathematics: The loss of certainty.* Oxford, UK: Oxford University Press.

Kline, M. (1985). *Mathematics and the search for knowledge.* New York: Oxford University Press.

Kobrin, D. (1996). *Beyond the textbook: Teaching history using documents and primary sources.* Portsmouth, NH: Heinemann.

Koestler, A. (1964). *The act of creation: A study of the conscious and unconscious in science and art.* New York: Macmillan.

Kohn, A. (2000). *The case against standardized testing: Raising the scores, ruining our schools.* Portsmouth, NH: Heinemann.

Krause, E. (1975). *Taxicab geometry: An adventure in non-Euclidean geometry.* New York: Dover Publications.

Kuh, G. (2003, March 1). What we're learning about student engagement from NSSE. *Change 35*(2), 24–32.

Kuhn, T. (1970). *The structure of scientific revolutions* (2nd ed.). Chicago: University of Chicago Press.

Levy, S. (1996). *Starting from scratch: One classroom builds its own curriculum.* Portsmouth, NH: Heinemann.

Lewis, C. (2002). *Lesson study: A handbook of teacher-led instructional change.* Philadelphia: Research for Better Schools.

Lewis, N. (1981). *Hans Christian Andersen's fairy tales.* Middlesex, UK: Puffin Books.

Light, R. (1990). *The Harvard assessment seminar: Explorations with students and faculty about teaching, learning, and student life (Vol. 1).* Cambridge, MA: Harvard University Press.

Light, R. J. (2001). *Making the most of college: Students speak their minds.* Cambridge, MA and London: Harvard University Press.

Liping, M. A. (1999). *Knowing and teaching elementary mathematics: Teachers' understanding of fundamental mathematics in China and the United States.* Mahway, NJ: Lawrence Erlbaum.

Lodge, D. (1992). *The art of fiction.* New York: Viking.

Lyman, F. (1992). Think-pair-share, thinktrix, and weird facts. In N. Davidson & T. Worsham (Eds.), *Enhancing thinking through cooperative learning.* New York: Teachers College Press.

MacFarquhar, N. (1996, September 27). For Jews, a split over peace effort widens. *New York Times*, p. A1.

Mansilla, V. B., & Gardner, H. (1997). Of kinds of disciplines and kinds of understanding. *Phi Delta Kappan, 78*(5), 381–386.

Martin, M., Mullis, I., Gregory, K., Hoyle, C., & Shen, C. (2000). *Effective schools in science and mathematics: IEA's Third International Mathematics and Science Study.* Boston: International Study Center, Lynch School of Education, Boston College.

Marzano, R. J. (2000). Analyzing two assumptions underlying the scoring of classroom assessments. Aurora, CO: Mid-continent Research for Educational Learning.

Marzano, R. J. (2003). *What works in schools: Translating research into action.* Alexandria, VA: Association for Supervision and Curriculum Development.

Marzano, R., & Kendall, J. (1996). *A comprehensive guide to designing standards-based districts, schools, and classrooms.* Alexandria, VA: Association for Supervision and Curriculum Development.

Marzano, R., & Pickering, D. (1997). Dimensions of learning teacher's manual (2nd ed.). Alexandria, VA: Association for Supervision and Curriculum Development.

Marzano, R., Pickering, D., & McTighe, J. (1993). *Assessing student outcomes: Performance assessment using the dimensions of learning model.* Alexandria, VA: Association for Supervision and Curriculum Development.

Marzano, R., Pickering, D., & Pollock, J. (2001). *Classroom instruction that works: Research-based strategies for increasing student achievement.* Alexandria, VA: Association for Supervision and Curriculum Development.

Massachusetts Department of Education. (1997a). *English language arts curriculum framework.* Boston: Author.

Massachusetts Department of Education. (1997b*). History curriculum framework.* Boston: Author.

McCarthy, B. (1981). *The 4-Mat system.* Barrington, IL: Excel.

McClean, J. (2003, Spring/Summer). 20 considerations that help a project run smoothly. *Fine Homebuilding: Annual Issue on Houses,* 24–28.

McCloskey, M., Carramaza, A., & Green, B. (1981). Naive beliefs in "sophisticated" subjects: Misconceptions about trajectories of objects. *Cognition, 9*(1), 117–123.

McGuire, J. M. (1997, March). Taking a storypath into history. *Educational Leadership, 54*(6), 70–72.

McKeough, A., Lupart J., & Marini, Q. (Eds.). (1995). *Teaching for transfer: Fostering generalizations in learning.* Mahwah, NJ: Lawrence Erlbaum.

McMillan, J. H. (1997). *Classroom assessment: Principles and practice for effective instruction.* Boston: Allyn & Bacon.

McTighe, J. (1996, December–1997, January). What happens between assessments? *Educational Leadership, 54*(4), 6–12.

McTighe, J., & Lyman, F. (1988). Cueing thinking in the classroom: The promise of theory-embedded tools. *Educational Leadership, 45*(7), 18–24.

McTighe, J., & Wiggins, G. (2004). *Understanding by design professional development workbook.* Alexandria, VA: Association for Supervision and Curriculum Development.

Meichenbaum, D., & Biemiller, A. (1998). *Nurturing independent learners: Helping students take charge of their learning.* Cambridge, MA: Brookline Books.

Milgram, S. (1974). *Obedience to authority.* New York: Harper.

Milne, A. A. (1926). *Winnie the Pooh.* New York: E. P. Dutton.

Mursell, J. L. (1946). *Successful teaching: Its psychological principles.* New York: McGraw-Hill.

Nagel, N. G. (1996). *Learning through real-world problem solving: The power of integrative teaching.* Thousand Oaks, CA: Corwin Press.

National Assessment of Educational Progress. (1988). *The mathematics report card: Are we measuring up? Trends and achievement based on the 1986 national assessment.* Washington, DC: U.S. Department of Education.

National Center for History in the Schools, University of California. (1994). *History for grades K–4: Expanding children's world in time and space.* Los Angeles: Author.

National Center for History in the Schools, University of California. (1996). *National standards for United States history: Exploring the American experience, Grades 5–12* (Expanded Version). Los Angeles: Author.

National Center for Research in Vocational Education. (2000). *High schools that work and whole school reform: Raising academic achievement of vocational completers through the reform of school practice.* Berkeley, CA: University of California at Berkeley.

National Center on Education and the Economy. (1997). *Performance standards: English language arts, mathematics, science, applied learning.* Pittsburgh, PA: University of Pittsburgh.

National Survey of Student Engagement. (2001). *Improving the college experience: Using effective educational practices.* Bloomington, IN: Indiana University Center for Postsecondary Research.

National Survey of Student Engagement. (2002). *From promise to progress: How colleges and universities are using engagement results to improve collegiate quality.* Bloomington, IN: Indiana University Center for Postsecondary Research.

National Survey of Student Engagement. (2003). *Converting data into action: Expanding the boundaries of institutional improvement.* Bloomington, IN: Indiana University Center for Postsecondary Research. Available: http://www.iub.edu/~nsse/html/report-2003.shtml.

Newmann, F. N., & Associates. (1996). *Authentic achievement: Restructuring schools for intellectual quality.* San Francisco: Jossey-Bass.

Newmann, F., Bryk, A., & Nagaoka, J. (2001). *Authentic intellectual work and standardized tests: Conflict or coexistence?* Chicago: Consortium on Chicago School Research. Available: http://www.consortium-chicago.org/publications/p0001.html.

Newmann, F., Marks, H., & Gamoran, A. (1995, Spring). Authentic pedagogy: Standards that boost student performance. Issue Report No. 8. Madison, WI: Center on Organization and Restructuring of Schools.

Newmann, F. N., Secada, W., & Wehlage, G. (1995). *A guide to authentic instruction and assessment: Vision, standards and scoring.* Madison: Wisconsin Center for Education Research.

New York State Department of Education. (1996). *Learning standards for the arts.* Albany, NY: Author.

New York Times (2003, November 11). Science Times. p. D1.

Ngeow, K. Y. (1998). Motivation and transfer in language learning. ERIC Digest ED427318 98.

Nickerson, R. (1985, February). Understanding understanding. *American Journal of Education 93*(2), 201–239.

Nickerson, R., Perkins, D., & Smith, E. (1985). *The teaching of thinking.* Hillsdale, NJ: Lawrence Erlbaum.

O'Neill, M. (1996, September 1). *New York Times Sunday Magazine.* p. 52.

Osborne, R., & Freyberg, P. (1985). *Learning in science: The implications of children's science.* Aukland, NZ: Heinemann.

Parkes, J. (2001). The role of transfer in the variability of performance. *Educational Assessment, 7*(2).

Passmore, J. (1982). *The philosophy of teaching.* Cambridge, MA: Harvard University Press.

Peak, L., et al. (1996). *Pursuing excellence: A study of U.S. eighth grade mathematics and science teaching, learning, curriculum, and achievement in international context* (NCES 97-198). Washington, DC: U.S. Department of Education, National Center for Education Statistics.

Perkins, D. (1991, October). Educating for insight. *Educational Leadership, 49*(2), 4–8.

Perkins, D. (1992). *Smart schools: From training memories to educating minds.* New York: Free Press.

Perkins, D. N., & Grotzer, T. A. (1997). Teaching intelligence. *American Psychologist, 52*(10), 1125–1133.

Perry, W. (1970). *Forms of intellectual development in the college years: A scheme.* New York: Holt, Rinehart & Winston.

Peters, R. S. (1967). *The concept of education.* London: Routledge & Kegan Paul.

Phenix, P. (1964). *Realms of meaning.* New York: McGraw-Hill.

Piaget, J. (1965). *The moral judgment of the child.* New York: Humanities Press.

Piaget, J. (1973). *To understand is to invent: The future of education.* New York: Grossman's Publishing Co.

Piaget, J. (1973/1977). Comments on mathematical education. In H. Gruber and J. Voneche (Eds.), *The essential Piaget.* New York: Basic Books. (Original work published 1973)

Poincaré, H. (1913/1982). Science and method. In *The foundations of science* (G. B. Halstead, Trans.). Washington, DC: University Press of America. (Original work published 1913)

Polya, G. (1945). *How to solve it: A new aspect of mathematical method.* Princeton, NJ: Princeton University Press.

Popper, K. (1968). *Conjectures and refutations.* New York: Basic Books.

Pressley, M., (1984). Synthesis of research on teacher questioning. *Educational Leadership, 42*(3), 40–46.

Pressley, M., et. al. (1992). Encouraging mindful use of prior knowledge: Attempting to construct explanatory answers facilitates learning. *Educational Psychologist, 27*(1), 91–109.

Redfield, D. L., & Rousseau, E. W. (1981). A meta-analysis of experimental research on teacher questioning behavior. *Review of Educational Research, 51,* 237–245.

Regional Laboratory for Educational Improvement of the Northeast & Islands. (undated). *The voyage of pilgrim '92: A conversation about constructivist learning* [newsletter].

Roseman, J. E., Kulm, G., & Shuttleworth, S. (2001). Putting textbooks to the test. *ENC Focus, 8*(3), 56–59. Available: http://www.project2061.org/publications/articles/articles/enc.htm.

Rothstein, E. (2003, August 2) Shelf life: A bioethicist's take on Genesis. *New York Times,* p. B7.

Rousseau, J. (1979). *Emile, or education.* (A. Bloom, Trans.). New York: Basic Books.

Ruiz-Primo, M. A., et al. (2001). On the validity of cognitive interpretations of scores from alternative concept-mapping techniques. *Educational Assessment, 7*(2).

Russell, J. (2003, September 13). On campuses, handhelds replacing raised hands. *Boston Globe.*

Ryle, G. (1949). *The concept of mind.* London: Hutchinson House.

Salinger, J. D. (1951). *The catcher in the rye.* Boston: Little Brown.

Sanders, N. (1966), *Classroom questions: What kinds?* New York: Harper & Row.

Saphier, J., & Gower, R. (1997). *The skillful teacher: Building your teaching skills* (5th ed.). Carlisle, MA: Research for Better Teaching.

Schank, R. (1990). *Tell me a story: Narrative and intelligence.* Evanston, IL: Northwestern University Press.

Schmoker, M. (1996). *Results: The key to continuous school improvement.* Alexandria, VA: Association for Supervision and Curriculum Development.

Schneps, M. (1994). *"A private universe" teacher's guide.* Washington, DC: The Corporation for Public Broadcasting.

Schoenfeld, A. (1988). Problem solving in context(s). In R. Charles & E. Silver (Eds.), *The teaching and assessing of mathematical problem solving.* Reston, VA: National Council on Teachers of Mathematics/Erlbaum.

Schön, D. A. (1989). *Educating the reflective practitioner: Toward a new design for teaching and learning.* San Francisco: Jossey-Bass.

School Curriculum and Assessment Authority. (1995). *Consistency in teacher assessment: Exemplifications of standards (science).* London: Author.

School Curriculum and Assessment Authority. (1997). *English tests mark scheme for paper two (Key stage 3, Levels 4–7).* London: Author.

Schwab, J. (1971). The practical: Arts of eclectic. *School Review, 79,* 493–542.

Schwab, J. (1978). The practical: Arts of eclectic. In *Science, curriculum, and liberal education: Selected essays.* Chicago: University of Chicago Press.

Senk, S., & Thompson, D. (2003). *Standards-based school mathematics curricula: What are they? What do students learn?* Mahwah, NJ: Lawrence Erlbaum.

Serra, M. (1989). *Discovering geometry: An inductive approach.* Berkeley, CA: Key Curriculum Press.

Shattuck, R. (1996). *Forbidden knowledge: From Prometheus to pornography.* New York: St. Martin's Press.

Shulman, J. (1992). *Case methods in teacher education.* New York: Teachers College Press.

Shulman, L. (1999 July/August). Taking learning seriously, *Change, 31*(4), 10–17.

Singh, S. (1997). *Fermat's enigma: The epic quest to solve the world's greatest mathematical problem.* New York: Walker & Co.

Sizer, T. (1984). *Horace's compromise: The dilemma of the American high school.* Boston: Houghton Mifflin.

Skemp, R. R. (1987). *The psychology of learning mathematics: Expanded American edition.* Hillsdale, NJ: Lawrence Erlbaum.

Smith, J., Lee, V., & Newmann, F. (2001). *Instruction and achievement in Chicago elementary schools*. Chicago: Consortium on Chicago School Research. Available: http://www.consortium-chicago.org/publications/p0001.html.

Smith, R. J. (1997, January 5). The soul man of suburbia. *New York Times Sunday Magazine,* sec. 6, p. 22.

Southern Regional Education Board. (1992). *Making high schools work*. Atlanta, GA: Author.

Spiro, R., et al. (1988). *Cognitive flexibility theory: Advanced knowledge acquisition in ill-structured domains.* Hillsdale, NJ: Lawrence Erlbaum.

Stavy, R., & Tirosh, D. (2000). *How students (mis-)understand science and mathematics: Intuitive rules*. New York: Teachers College Press.

Steinberg, A. (1998). *Real learning, real work: School-to-work as high school reform.* New York: Routledge.

Steinberg, A., Cushman, K., & Riordan, R. (1999). *Schooling for the real world: The essential guide to rigorous and relevant learning.* San Francisco: Jossey-Bass.

Stepien, W., & Gallagher, S. (1993, April). Problem-based learning: As authentic as it gets. *Educational Leadership, 50*(7), 23–28.

Stepien, W., & Gallagher, S. (1997). *Problem-based learning across the curriculum: An ASCD professional inquiry kit.* Alexandria, VA: Association for Supervision and Curriculum Development.

Stepien, W., & Pyke, S. (1997). Designing problem-based learning units. *Journal for the Education of the Gifted, 20*(4), 380–400.

Stepien, W., Gallagher, S., & Workman, D. (1993). Problem-based learning for traditional and interdisciplinary classrooms. *Journal for the Education of the Gifted, 16*(4), 338–357.

Sternberg, R., & Davidson, J. (Eds.). (1995). *The nature of insight.* Cambridge, MA: MIT Press.

Stiggins, R. J. (1997). *Student-centered classroom assessment.* Upper Saddle River, NJ: Prentice-Hall.

Stigler, J. W., & Hiebert, J. (1997, September). Understanding and improving classroom mathematics instruction: An overview of the TIMSS video study. *Phi Delta Kappan, 79*(1), 14–21.

Stigler, J. W., & Hiebert, J. (1999). *The teaching gap: Best ideas from the world's teachers for improving education in the classroom.* New York: Free Press.

Stone, C. L. (1983). A meta-analysis of advance organizer studies. *Journal of Experimental Education, 54,* 194–199.

Strong, M. (1996). *The habit of thought: From Socratic seminars to Socratic practice.* Chapel Hill, NC: New View.

Sullivan, K. (1997, December 22). Japanese director commits suicide. *Washington Post,* p. C1.

Sulloway, F. (1996). *Born to rebel: Birth order, family dynamics, and creative lives.* New York: Pantheon Press.

Tagg, J. (2003). *The learning paradigm in college.* Bolton, MA: Anker Publishing Company.

Tannen, D. (1990). *You just don't understand: Women and men in conversation.* New York: Ballantine Books.

Tharp, R. G., & Gallimore, Ronald (1988) *Rousing minds to life: Teaching, learning, and schooling in social context.* Cambridge, UK: Cambridge University Press.

Thier, H. D., with Daviss, B. (2001). *Developing inquiry-based science materials: Guide for educators.* New York and London: Teachers College Press.

Thomas, L. (1983) *Late night thoughts on listening to Mahler's Ninth Symphony.* New York: Viking Press.

Tishman, S., & Perkins, D. (1997). The language of thinking. *Phi Delta Kappan, 78*(5), 368.

Tomlinson, C. A., Kaplan, S. N., Renzulli, J. S., Purcell, J., Leppien, J., & Burns, D. (2001). *The parallel curriculum: A design to develop high potential and challenge high-ability learners.* Thousand Oaks, CA: Corwin Press.

Trible, P. (2003, October 19) Of man's first disobedience, and so on. *New York Times,* sec. 7, p. 28.

Tyler, Ralph W. (1949) *Basic principles of curriculum and instruction.* Chicago: University of Chicago Press.

U.S. Department of Education, National Center for Education Statistics (NCES). (1998). *Third international math and science study* [Online]. Available: http://nces.ed.gov/timss/.

U.S. Department of Education, National Center for Education Statistics (NCES). (1999, February). The TIMSS videotape classroom study: Methods and findings from an exploratory research project on eighth-grade mathematics instruction in Germany, Japan, and the United States, NCES 99-074, by James W. Stigler, Patrick Gonzales, Takako Kawanaka, Steffen Knoll, and Ana Serrano. Washington, DC: U.S. Government Printing Office. Available: http://nces.ed.gov/timss/.

U.S. Department of Health, Education, and Welfare. (1976). *The American Revolution: Selections from secondary school history books of other nations* (HEW Publication No. OE 76-19124). Washington, DC: U.S. Government Printing Office.

Vaishnav, A. (2003, August 3). MCAS's most onerous questions revealed. *Boston Globe.*

Van de Walle, J. A. (1998). *Elementary and middle school mathematics: Teaching developmentally.* New York: Longman.

Vanderstoep, S. W., & Seifert, C. M. (1993). Learning "how" versus learning "when": Improving transfer of problem-solving principles. *Journal of the Learning Sciences, 3*(1), 93–11.

Van Manen, M. (1991). *The tact of teaching: The meaning of pedagogical thoughtfulness.* Albany: State University of New York Press.

Von Hippel, E. (1988). *The sources of innovation.* New York: Oxford University Press.

Weil, M. L., & Murphy, J. (1982). Instructional processes. In H. E. Mitzel (Ed.), *Encyclopedia of educational research.* NY: Free Press.

Wenglinsky, H. (1998). *Does it compute? The relationship between educational technology and student achievement in mathematics.* New Jersey: Educational Testing Service.

White, R., & Gunstone, R. (1992). *Probing understanding.* London: Falmer Press.

Whitehead, A. N. (1929). *The aims of education and other essays.* New York: Free Press.

Wiggins, G. (1987, Winter). Creating a thought-provoking curriculum. *American Educator, 11*(4), 10–17.

Wiggins, G. (1987). *Thoughtfulness as an educational aim* (unpublished dissertation: Harvard University Graduate School of Education).

Wiggins, G. (1989, November). The futility of teaching everything of importance. *Educational Leadership, 47*(3), 44–59.

Wiggins, G. (1993). *Assessing student performance: Exploring the purpose and limits of testing.* San Francisco: Jossey-Bass.

Wiggins, G. (1996, January). Practicing what we preach in designing authentic assessments. *Educational Leadership, 54*(4), 18–25.

Wiggins, G. (1997, September). Work standards: Why we need standards for instructional and assessment design. *NASSP Bulletin, 81*(590), 56–64.

Wiggins, G. (1998). *Educative assessment: Designing assessments to inform and improve performance.* San Francisco: Jossey-Bass.

Wiggins, G., & McTighe, J. (1998). *Understanding by design* (1st ed.). Alexandria, VA: Association for Supervision and Curriculum Development.

Wilson, J. (1963). *Thinking with concepts.* London: Cambridge University Press.

Wiske, M. S. (1998). *Teaching for understanding: Linking research with practice.* San Francisco: Jossey-Bass.

Wittgenstein, L. (1953). *Philosophical investigations.* New York: Macmillan.

Wolf, D. (1987, Winter). The art of questioning. *Academic connections.*

Woolf, V. (1929). *A room of one's own.* New York: Harcourt Brace & World.

Wynn, C. M., & Wiggins, A. W. (1997). *The five biggest ideas in science.* New York: John Wiley & Sons.

Index

Note: A page number followed by the letter *f* indicates reference to a figure.

About the Authors

Grant Wiggins is president of Authentic Education in Monmouth Junction, New Jersey. He consults with schools, districts, and state education departments on a variety of reform matters; organizes conferences and workshops; and develops print materials and Web resources on curricular change, based on Understanding by Design. Wiggins's work has been supported by the Pew Charitable Trusts, the Geraldine R. Dodge Foundation, the National Science Foundation, and the Education Commission of the States, among other organizations.

Over the past 15 years, Wiggins has worked on some of the most influential reform initiatives in the country, including Vermont's portfolio system and the Coalition of Essential Schools. He has established a statewide Consortium devoted to assessment reform and designed a performance-based and teacher-run portfolio assessment prototype for the states of North Carolina and New Jersey.

Wiggins is the author of *Educative Assessment* and *Assessing Student Performance*. His many articles have appeared in such journals as *Educational Leadership* and *Phi Delta Kappan*.

His work is grounded in 14 years of secondary school teaching and coaching. Wiggins taught English and electives in philosophy, coached varsity soccer, cross country, junior varsity baseball, and track and field. Recently he has coached his two sons and daughter in soccer and baseball. In 2002, Wiggins was a Scholar in Residence at the College of New Jersey. He earned his doctorate in education from Harvard University and his bachelor of arts degree from St. John's College in Annapolis. Wiggins also plays guitar and sings in the Hazbins, a rock band.

Wiggins can be reached at Authentic Education, 4095 US Route 1, Box 104, Monmouth Junction, NJ 08852. Phone: (732) 329-0641. E-mail: grant@authentic education.org.

Jay McTighe brings a wealth of experience developed during a rich and varied career in education. He served as director of the Maryland Assessment Consortium, a state collaboration of school districts working together to develop and share formative performance assessments. Prior to this position, McTighe was involved with school improvement projects at the Maryland State Department of Education. He is known for work with thinking skills, having coordinated statewide efforts to develop instructional strategies, curriculum models, and assessment procedures for improving the quality of student thinking. McTighe also directed the development of the Instructional Framework, a multimedia database on teaching. In addition to his work at the state level, McTighe has experience at the district level in Prince George's County, Maryland, as a classroom teacher, resource specialist, and program coordinator. He also served as director of the Maryland Summer Center for Gifted and Talented Students, a statewide residential enrichment program held at St. Mary's College.

McTighe has published articles in leading journals and books, including *Educational Leadership* (ASCD), *Developing Minds* (ASCD), *Thinking Skills: Concepts and Techniques* (National Education Association), and *The Developer* (National Staff Development Council). He coauthored three books on assessment, *Assessing Learning in the Classroom* (NEA), *Assessing Student Outcomes: Performance Assessment Using the Dimensions of Learning Model* (ASCD), and *Evaluation Tools to Improve as Well as Evaluate Student Performance* (Corwin Press). He is coauthor, with Grant Wiggins, of *Understanding by Design Professional Development Workbook* (ASCD), *Understanding by Design Handbook* (ASCD), and other essential Understanding by Design titles with ASCD.

McTighe has an extensive background in staff development and is a regular speaker at national, state, and district conferences and workshops. He is also a featured presenter and consultant for videotape programs including *Performance Assessment in the Classroom* (Video Journal of Education), *Developing Performance Assessments* (ASCD), and *Understanding by Design* video series (tapes 1–3) (ASCD).

McTighe received his undergraduate degree from The College of William and Mary, earned a master's degree from The University of Maryland and has completed postgraduate studies at The Johns Hopkins University. He was selected to participate in The Educational Policy Fellowship Program through the Institute for Educational Leadership in Washington, D.C. McTighe served as a member of the National Assessment Forum, a coalition of education and civil rights organizations advocating reforms in national, state, and local assessment policies and practices. He also completed a three-year term on the ASCD Publications Committee, serving as committee chair during 1994–95.

McTighe can be reached at 6581 River Run, Columbia, MD 21044-6066. Phone: (410) 531-1610. E-mail: jmctigh@aol.com. Web site: jaymctighe.com.

Related ASCD Resources: Understanding by Design

At the time of publication, the following ASCD resources were available; for the most up-to-date information about ASCD resources, go to www.ascd.org. ASCD stock numbers are noted in parentheses.

Audiotapes

Applying Understanding by Design to School Improvement Planning by Jay McTighe and Ronald S. Thomas (#202143)

Structures That Support Understanding by Design by Fran Prolman and Grant Wiggins (#299321)

Understanding by Design: Structures and Strategies for Designing School Reform by Jay McTighe and Grant Wiggins: (#202189)

Walking the Talk: Applying Standards to Our Own Work by Jay McTighe and Grant Wiggins (#200334)

What Does Understanding by Design Have to Do with Professional Development by Harolyn Katherman and others (#202137)

Working Smarter in Curriculum Design by Jay McTighe and Grant Wiggins (#20114)

Networks

Visit the ASCD Web site (www.ascd.org) and click on About ASCD. Under the header of Your Partnership with ASCD, click on Networks for information about professional educators who have formed groups around topics, including "Arts in Education," "Authentic Assessment," and "Brain-Based Compatible Learning." Look in the Network Directory for current facilitators' addresses and phone numbers.

Online Courses

Understanding by Design: An Introduction (register for these online or by calling ASCD)
Understanding by Design: Six Facets of Understanding
Understanding by Design: The Backward Design Process

Print Products

The Understanding by Design Handbook by Jay McTighe and Grant Wiggins (#199030)

Understanding by Design Professional Development Workbook by Jay McTighe and Grant Wiggins (#103056)

Understanding by Design Study Guide (#100246)

Understanding by Design Bundle for Study Groups, includes 10 copies of Understanding by Design and 1 copy of the Study Guide (#100245)

Training

The ASCD Understanding by Design Faculty: ASCD will arrange for a UBD expert to deliver onsite training tailored to the needs of your school, district, or regional service agency. Call (703) 578-9600, ext. 5677.

Videotapes

The Understanding by Design Video Series, three tapes (#400241)

Web Products

Professional Development Online, at http://pdonline.ascd.org, features several UbD-related online study courses.

The UbD Exchange, at http://www.ubdexchange.org/, features a database of units designed using the Understanding by Design framework. It contains short tutorials and self-checks to guide designers through the electronic unit template as they build units and assessments to store in the database. Users of the Exchange can interact with others by giving and receiving feedback on curriculum units using the design standards.

Exemplars of essential questions, enduring understandings, performance tasks, rubrics, and learning activities are highlighted with blue ribbons and trophies awarded by the authors and other expert UbD trainers.

For additional resources, visit us on the World Wide Web (http://www.ascd.org), send an e-mail message to member@ascd.org, call the ASCD Service Center (1-800-933-ASCD or 703-578-9600, then press 2), send a fax to 703-575-5400, or write to Information Services, ASCD, 1703 N. Beauregard St., Alexandria, VA 22311-1714 USA.